NOTES FROM UNDERGROUND

D1232833

SUNY Series in
The Sociology of Culture

Charles R. Simpson, editor

NOTES FROM UNDERGROUND

Rock Music Counterculture in Russia

Thomas Cushman

State University of New York Press

Published by
State University of New York Press, Albany

For information, address State University of New York Press,
State University Plaza, Albany, N.Y., 12246

Production by Marilyn P. Semerad
Marketing by Theresa Abad Swierzowski

Library of Congress Cataloging-in-Publication Data

Cushman, Thomas, 1959-
    Notes from underground : Rock music counterculture in Russia /
Thomas Cushman.
        p.   cm. — (SUNY series in the sociology of culture)
    Includes bibliographical references (p.   ) and index.
    ISBN 0-7914-2543-6. — ISBN 0-7914-2544-4 (pbk.)
    1. Rock music—Russia (Federation)—History and criticism.
2. Music and society. I. Series.
ML3534.C88 1995
306.4′84—dc20   95-1541
                                                                          CIP
                                                                          MN

10 9 8 7 6 5 4 3 2 1

For Sophie and Eliza

The literature of the poor, the feelings of the child, the philosophy of the street, the meaning of household life, are the topics of the time. It is a great stride. It is a sign—is it not?—of a new vigor, when the extremities are made active, when currents of warm life run into the hands and the feet. I ask not for the great, the remote, the romantic . . . I embrace the common, I explore and sit at the feet of the familiar, the low. Give me insight into to-day and you may have the antique and future worlds.

—Ralph Waldo Emerson

What we regard as freedom is often in fact only a change in obligations; as a new obligation replaces one that we have borne hitherto, we sense above all that the old burden has been removed. Because we are free from it, we seem at first to be completely free—until the new duty, which we initially bear, as it were, with hitherto untaxed and therefore particularly strong sets of muscles, makes its weight felt as these muscles, too, gradually tire. The process of liberation now starts again with this new duty, just as it had ended at this very point.

—Georg Simmel, *The Philosophy of Money*

Liberation has left everyone in an undefined state (it is always the same, once you are liberated, you are forced to ask who you are). . . .

—Jean Baudrillard, *America*

Contents

Preface

This book is a sociological case study of a community of rock musicians in St. Petersburg, Russia. It traces the experiences of members of this community from the time when rock music made its first entrance into Soviet society in the 1960s, through the period of cultural renaissance brought on by *glasnost* and *perestroika* in the late 1980s, and into the present period of rapid capitalist reformation of post-Soviet society. It is a study of a Russian musical *counterculture*, a community united by a common way of life and a common commitment to the production and dissemination of rock music as a means of cultural opposition and as a means for claiming autonomous space and identity in Russian society. I present a sociological account of rock counterculture in St. Petersburg as a poignant case study which dramatizes the struggle of human expressivity and agency in the face of the changing social circumstances, each of which posed a different set of constraints on cultural expression. During the socialist period, this constraint occurred by conscious design, the product of the calculated efforts of political elites and state culture managers to plan and control all aspects of social and cultural life in the Soviet Union. In the present, however, constraint manifests itself in new and unanticipated ways through the operation of market forces which have been borne into post-communist Russia as a result of Western capitalist "shock therapy."

From the time it made its first entrance into Soviet society in the 1960s through the Brezhnev era, rock music was a cultural practice which was rigidly circumscribed by a bureaucratic state apparatus specifically designed to regulate the production and dissemination of such autonomous forms of modern culture. Yet, only a short time after the ascension of Mikhail Gorbachev to the post of General Secretary of the Communist Party, rock music emerged as a freely expressible modern art form. By 1989, rock musicians—at least in major urban centers of the country such as St. Petersburg—were allowed to make and play music freely without the harassment and interference of the state which were the hallmarks of earlier years. During the glasnost period, even the most oppositional rock musicians who had been hounded continually by state cultural bureaucrats throughout the 1970s and early 1980s were, in some cases, actively enabled in their musical practice by those same bureaucrats and by new organizations for cultural production. Some rock musicians found themselves used by reformers as evidence of the authenticity of glasnost. In the official exhibits of Soviet culture that appeared across the globe, one could increasingly find rock videos proudly displayed by the "curators" of such exhibits as evidence that glasnost was "for real." Other rock musicians found their previously banned culture products readily available for sale at kiosks around the city. In St. Petersburg, the individual who clandestinely produced and recorded much of the most popular underground rock music in the 1970s and early 1980s—an act that was considered criminal according to the Soviet law of that period—was elected president of the division of the Leningrad branch of the state-owned recording industry, Melodiya. In this new role, the individual "repackaged" previously "subversive" culture products for general distribution, and they began to appear in stores across the country. On state-controlled television stations that had previously served as the major conduits of conservative cultural criticism, former heroes of the rock underground appeared in concerts and interviews which were filled with commentary and debate on the important role of forms of culture such as rock music in the life of Soviet society.

These ironic turnarounds in Russian cultural history raised a number of interesting sociological questions: How, in such a short time, did a renegade cultural criminal become the president of the most important recording studio in what was arguably the most important cultural center in the entire USSR? How did Soviet officials come to actively support and promote a form of culture that only a few short years before was considered by the state to be deviant and even criminal? How did rock musicians and their "profane" culture become an acceptable part of modern Soviet cultural landscape, a landscape notorious for both its persecution of and elitist disdain for rock music? And finally, what effects would such drastic changes in state-culture relations have on rock music and rock culture in the context of late socialist society?

A desire to provide answers to these basic questions was the original impetus for this book. Spurred by the euphoria of cultural ferment and change, I traveled to Leningrad (now St. Petersburg) in 1990 to explore the dimensions of this cultural renaissance and some of the ironies and paradoxes which it had created. I secured an apartment, gained entrance into the city's rock community, and lived and worked for three months within that community as a participant-observer of its way of life. The central questions of this study can be organized into three broad categories.

The first category deals generally with the nature of Russian rock culture, a phenomenon which was virtually unexplored by Western historians and political scientists and which had never been explored by Western sociologists. How did people come to be rock musicians in an environment where such a choice was rigidly circumscribed by a state infrastructure of cultural repression? What were the dynamics of Russian rock counterculture? What kinds of alternative identities had members of this counterculture crafted for themselves under conditions of Soviet industrial modernity?

A second category of questions deals more specifically with the ways in which musical culture was produced and distributed in a socialist industrial society and the function of music generally in Russian society. What was the role, meaning, and function of rock music in Russian society? Why was rock music such a central cultural force in the formation of alternative communities with their own values, attitudes, beliefs, and practices which stood counter to those of the dominant society? How was rock music produced and distributed in a setting where its production and distribution were formally circumscribed by a strong authoritarian state?

Finally, a third category of questions aims at understanding the fate and future of rock musicians and their culture under conditions of rapid social, political, and economic reform. What happens when the critical messages encoded in art forms such as rock music begin to appear in the speeches of popular culture's "enemies," powerful men like Mikhail Gorbachev or Boris Yeltsin who, just a few short years ago, were the guardians of a social order that was the very wellspring of the restless and angry Russian rock temperament? What happens when the utopian hopes and aspirations embodied in rock music begin to be realized in a society which, just a short time before, treated such hopes and aspirations as, at best, hopelessly naïve or, at worst, criminal? What happens to musicians whose very roles and identities were fundamentally dependent on the existence of authoritarian social structures when the latter begin to evaporate? What happens when musicians are forced, because of the changing vicissitudes of history, to turn from a relaxed bohemian lifestyle of "hanging out" and making music, to the more arduous task of making a living from their music? What happens to dissent when it ceases to be dissentious, to opposition when it ceases to be oppositional, to resistance when it ceases to have anything to resist? What happens when musicians are obligated to join the ranks of what

Marx called "productive laborers," and when the culture products of their labors become just another commodity in a new universe of goods and services? What happens, in short, to forms of oppositional underground culture when they come up from underground?

My original intention in traveling to Leningrad was to provide a sociological account of the unique paradoxes and ironies facing rock culture during the transition to a market economy. My training in sociological theory and in the sociology of culture, combined with the emergence of unprecedented opportunities for independent research in Russia in the late 1980s, made it possible to attempt the first Western sociological interpretation of rock musical culture from the "inside," that is, from the point of view of those who actually made that culture and used it as the basis for the formation of alternative lifestyles and identities. Western sociologists and anthropologists have long been fascinated with the study of subcultures, countercultures, and alternative communities in capitalist society. Yet, for a variety of reasons, Western sociologists had never studied these phenomena in the Soviet Union. Nor had scholars in Soviet studies—a field which included very few sociologists and still fewer interpretive sociologists—ever offered accounts of Soviet subcultures or countercultures which drew specifically on sociological methods and theoretical frameworks.

After three months in Leningrad, I returned home with mountains of taped interviews with rock musicians, managers, producers, distributors, and journalists—in short, the whole range of people who constituted the city's rock community. While analyzing this data, though, history caught up with and surpassed me: at the end of 1991, the Soviet Union dissolved and with it the particular social conditions that I had been studying. While euphoric about the democratic possibilities inherent in the dissolution of the Soviet Union, I feared that my study had been rendered superfluous and obsolete, or, at best, historically uninteresting in the face of such drastic social changes. This curious mix of euphoria and dread will be readily recognized by any scholar who was working on any aspect of contemporary Russian or Soviet affairs. For in the wake of the earth-shattering events of 1991, scholars in what is now called "post-Soviet studies" were all asking themselves the same question: "What am I going to do now that the Soviet Union is dead?" After a period of initial shock and some considerable intellectual reconnaissance, I returned to Russia in the spring of 1992 to continue my study of musical culture in what was now called St. Petersburg. That is when this book began to take its present form.

Instead of corroborating my fears about the obsolescence of my previous research, what I found was that new social conditions in Russia presented a unique opportunity for research in the sociology of culture. The dissolution of the Soviet Union had accelerated the process of capitalist development in Russian society which had begun during the era of glasnost and perestroika. Upon returning to St. Petersburg, I found that the more moderate market reforms which had begun in the mid-1980s had given way to more radical and earth-shattering economic reforms. The latter are often referred to as "shock therapy." The basic principles behind shock therapy were simple: old forms of state control over production, distribution, private property, and prices had to be dissolved quickly and replaced with a market economy, the privatization of property, the abolition of price controls, and the privatization of the process of production and distribution. As a result of shock therapy, the command control of the economy began to be replaced by a form of "anarchic capitalism" (Burawoy and Krotov 1992). When I returned to Russia in 1992, the transition of post-Soviet society to a market economy was beginning to affect all areas of Russian society and culture. The Russian rock music counterculture in St. Petersburg was no exception.

Instead of abandoning the study or recasting it as an exercise in historical sociology, I was presented with a new challenge: to explore the enticing sociological question of the fate of a vibrant form of culture under conditions of rapid anarchic, capitalist development. The forces of historical change presented an opportunity to explore a most interesting and ironic sociological problem: What happens to cultural communities whose existence and social significance are fundamentally related to the structural conditions characteristic of a state socialist society when they encounter new forms of social and economic organization characteristic of capitalist society? This general question is perhaps the most central for all those interested in any aspect of post-Soviet Russian culture. Indeed, I would even argue that *the* central problem for a sociology of contemporary Russian culture (and for the more general sociology of the culture of post-communist societies) ought to be the study of the adaptation and transformation of culture under new patterns of political, economic, and social organization (Verdery 1991, p. 434).

Russian rock culture is unique in relation to that of the West in that it emerged and operated in a social context characterized by the complete lack of a market system for the production and distribution of culture. While the Soviet state co-opted some rock musicians in the 1970s and early 1980s and invented a tradition of state-sponsored rock, a large number of rock musicians remained resistant to "internal colonization" by the process of economic rationalization simply because this process was not present within this social space. Petersburg rock musicians represent a particularly "pristine" or "organic" community which had little experience with the economic forces which are so central to rock culture in Western capitalist countries. Precisely because of their lack of experience with forms of capitalist economic rationality, their encounters with new forms of capitalist economic rationality offer us a tremendous opportunity to explore *in situ* the effects of economic rationalization on Russian culture. As such, the case presented here is directly relevant to a more general issue in the sociology of culture: the relationship between forms of aesthetic culture and capitalism.

The distinctive task of what C. Wright Mills (1959) called the "sociological imagination" is to capture the complex, dialectical intersection between human subjectivity and social and historical forces. This intersection is best understood through the application of methodological and theoretical approaches which are generally "untried" in the Soviet or post-Soviet context. Chapter 1 offers an overview of the theoretical logic and methodological orientations of this book. The theoretical logic of this study allows us to view the origins and the meanings of rock practice in relation to changing historical circumstances in Russia. In both communist and post-communist contexts, rock music is a cultural practice which is a product of the dialectical interaction between human agency and objective historical conditions. What is more important, rock music in Russia takes on its meanings in relation to the conditions in which it is produced. The dialectical view of culture and social structure presented in this chapter serves as an important framework for the interpretation of the particular case of the St. Petersburg musical counterculture. Yet I hope that the theoretical perspective put forth in this chapter can be used as a more general theoretical grounding for the analysis of historical and emergent forms of culture in communist and post-communist societies.

In contrast to a view which stresses Russia's uniqueness (a view shared by most historians of Russia), I conceive of Soviet history as a particular type of industrial modernity. Lying behind the infrastructure of socialist industrial modernity was a hyperrational cultural logic of bureaucratic, instrumental rationality. While totalistic and even "totalitarian," the severity of socialist industrial modernity provided the existential conditions which fostered the emergence of a variety of unique cultural communities and forms of individual and collective identity in the Russian urban environment. These communities emerged dialectically in relation to a world stripped of meaning by the intensity and pace of Soviet industrialization. They offered individuals, to use Christopher Lasch's metaphor, "havens in a heartless world" and served as a means for the re-enchantment of a world which was made disenchanting by the hyperrational cultural logic of the socialist industrial state. Running through these communities was the germ of a passionate, radical, oppositional, and democratic sentiment and a strong sense of community, fraternity, and solidarity. In the philosophical terms of Arthur Schopenhauer, it might be said that such communities represented a remarkable and indefatigable "will to life" which existed within and drew its very sustenance from the infrastructure of Soviet modernity, an infrastructure which is one of the most poignant manifestations of the relentless "will to power" in the twentieth century. In chapter 2, chapter 3, and chapter 4, I portray this remarkable will to life as it expressed itself in different historical periods, and as I uncovered it through the use of techniques of qualitative sociological research.

The dissolution of the Soviet Union signified the end of the Soviet project of modernity. Yet this project is now being replaced by the project of Western capitalist modernity. The rapid transition to a market economy has brought on new quandaries for Russians who have just recently shed the mantle of one form of domination only to find themselves facing another. Unlike most Western analysts of contemporary Russian society, I do not conceive of the current situation in Russia unproblematically as a situation of "liberation" or "freedom." Rather, I see it as the substitution of one form of domination for another. The eminent sociologist Philip Rieff once quipped that "freedom is a change of masters." However depressing such a view might be, I believe Rieff's insight is an invaluable starting point for the sociology of Russian culture which I launch in the following pages. Granted, the new capitalist masters may be more to the liking of the Russian people, although the new system does seem to many Russians to be more than they bargained for. Granted, what Max Weber might have termed "capitalist domination" might be infinitely preferable to "communist domination" from a number of moral and ethical standpoints. Yet, I view "the transition" (as the current maelstrom of social change is referred to in the current literature on post-communist societies) as a transition to a new form of domination. The analysis of the effects of this new form of domination on one cultural community in one Russian city is a central task of this book.

During the Brezhnev era, before the cultural reforms of glasnost, the crisis of rock music—indeed, of all forms of independent cultural expression in Russia—revolved around the intrusion of the centralized, bureaucratic state apparatus into the expressive activities of those who had chosen the path of independent and autonomous cultural expression. Under the influence of social reforms, the formal structures of authority responsible for the limitation of independent musical expression began to disappear. With the dissolution of the Soviet Union, such structures disappeared completely. They were replaced, however, by new practices which represent new sources of constraint upon post-Soviet Russian musicians. When I embarked on this research in 1990, I expected to hear from musicians glorious stories of cultural renaissance and cultural freedom. I did hear such stories, but such optimism was almost always hedged by a rhetoric of crisis. Musicians spoke constantly of a new "crisis" caused by the infusion of the "spirit of capitalism" into their cultural sphere. If the "enemy" for musicians in the pre-glasnost era was the state and its bureaucratic logic of domination, then the new enemy which emerged in the late 1980s and gained strength in the early 1990s was the logic of the marketplace where everything, including human affect, can be converted into a commodity. The introduction of the cultural logic of capitalism into the sphere of cultural production has brought on a new and distinct set of quandaries for Russian musicians. These quandaries and their effects on the production and meaning of rock musical culture in Russia are explored in detail in chapter 5 and chapter 6.

Many people in the West—academics, politicians, and the public at large—often assume without question that capitalist economic development is *the* major force which will drive the process of democratization in Russia. There is little doubt that there is a strong relationship between capitalism, cultural freedom, and democratization. In its best capacities, capitalism fuels innovation, variety, and freedom of cultural expression. Freedom of cultural expression is a fundamental condition of a democratic society. Capitalism and culture have evolved in tandem in the West: Western producers of aesthetic culture and the capitalist infrastructures in which they work have evolved together. The result is that Western artists, even if the market intrudes on their autonomy, have learned how to "play the market." Yet capitalism is a "foreign" element in Russian society, and this is how it has been experienced by many musicians and other producers of culture in this society. In the process of the movement from command to market control of culture, many members of the Petersburg musical community have found themselves in a paradoxical position of having escaped more overt political constraints on their freedom of expression only to find themselves subject to the forces of economic constraints which their pasts leave them ill-equipped to face.

In addition to theorizing culture, a central concern of this book is to explore the issue of individual and cultural freedom in relation to the present social-structural changes in Russian society. Like most interpretive social scientists, I am concerned with gathering empirical facts to weave a story about the meaning of cultural forms in their social contexts. Yet the attempt to answer questions about the meaning of cultural forms and about the development of individual and collective identities under conditions of modernity inevitably led me to explore more philosophical questions about the nature of freedom or the problems and prospects of constructing a democratic Russian future. Therefore, I conclude this book with a sociological discussion of the complex relation between capitalism, cultural freedom, and democracy in contemporary Russian society. There are two reasons for this. The first is that questions about cultural autonomy and freedom were constantly raised by the people whose lives serve as the basis for this book. The second reason has to do with the calling of sociology as I define it. Presumptuously, perhaps, I have modeled my own work on that of some of the great thinkers in the sociological tradition. Various insights of Weber, Durkheim, Simmel, Cooley, and Marx frame and illuminate the empirical content of the book. All of these thinkers, to varying degrees, were interested in the problematic relation between the individual and society and, by way of that, in the issue of freedom.

Long before the Soviet government fell, and long before the Western theoreticians of democracy and the architects of economic shock therapy descended on the post-Soviet social morass, Petersburg musicians were living in a kind of prototypical civil society of their own creation. Like many other individuals in the communist world, many Petersburg musicians lived, in the words of Polish philosopher Adam Michnik, as if the external world did not exist. Sometimes that external world marched into their worlds, very often altering and thwarting their expressive activity. Yet this is precisely why they were so adamant in creating autonomous forms of culture and using the latter to claim their own space within the infrastructure of socialist domination. One of the most important theoretical insights which guides my interpretation of rock culture in the following chapters comes from the great German sociologist Georg Simmel who noted, "Even in the most oppressive and cruel cases of subordination, there is still a considerable measure of personal freedom" (1971, p. 97). Simmel's view has inspired me to rethink the notion of freedom as a sociological concept and to re-examine Soviet history in order to discover the myriad ways in which actors in this context, to paraphrase Jean-Paul Sartre, made something out of what was made of them.

The discourse of Soviet studies has generally tended to stress the inhibitory effects of Soviet social structure on human expressivity. While a humanist of any stripe is obligated to recognize the repressive dimensions of the Soviet system, a purely negative view fails to realize that the very nature and essence of cultural expression in Russia during the Soviet era was intimately tied to and, indeed, dependent on the specific structural arrangement of Soviet society. In this book, I stress an affirmative view of human expressivity which focuses on the ways in which Russian music-makers exerted their agency through the creation and deployment of autonomous forms of culture within their social environment. The story which emerges in the first part of the book ought to be read as a case history of a particular type of freedom. The second part of the book explores the fate of that freedom within an emergent infrastructure of capitalist domination.

Using the word *freedom* in connection with a discussion of culture in a so-called totalitarian society is likely to puzzle readers who have been conditioned to think that life in such a society is, by definition, not free. Yet there are many senses of the idea of freedom. The most obvious ones are the ones we think of as the cornerstones of American democracy: freedom of speech, freedom of religion, freedom of assembly. Such freedoms were clearly denied to citizens of Soviet-type societies. Yet this does not mean that people who lived in these societies did not craft for themselves alternative experiences of freedom. Indeed, in contrast to citizens of Western countries who often take their freedom for granted, Soviet citizens found individual freedom within themselves through a process of "internal immigration" into their own subjective lifeworlds and through the communication of the experiences which they found within themselves. Analyses of these more existential and subjective senses of freedom are not present in Western studies of Russian culture because most Western scholars have simply not considered the various senses and meanings of conceptions of freedom as they appear across a broad range of social thought and disciplines. The experiences of musicians in St. Petersburg offer us a different sense of what it meant to be "free" within the context of socialist industrial society and accentuate the limitations of using the word *freedom* to describe the post-Soviet Russian social context.

This book is meant to be a contribution to the tradition of critical-interpretive sociology. In its interpretive dimensions, it stresses the local meanings of rock music and the meaning of countercultural existence as these meanings can be educed from those who have lived their lives as counterculturalists. In its critical dimensions, it focuses on the ways in which local meanings and the alternative identities which these meanings give rise to are affected by both long-standing socialist and emergent capitalist forms of domination in Russian society. One of the aims of critical social science is to invest knowledge back into the world in service to the people who provide us with our understandings of social phenomena. The practical dimension of this study is most evident in the last chapter, in which I examine the prospects for the development of individual and cultural freedom and democracy in a society increasingly infused with the spirit of capitalism. It might seem rather strange to move from the analysis of mundane and even "profane" realities of a form of culture such as rock music to lofty notions such as freedom and democracy. However, as Paul Willis (1979, p. 1) notes, it is through the understanding of such forms of "profane creativity" that we can understand better the prospects for radical and democratic social and cultural change.

Is Russian culture "free" now? What exactly do sociologists mean by cultural freedom? And if culture is not free, in what ways is it not? What does the actual fate of cultural freedom in the post-Soviet context tell us about the presumed relation between the free market and democracy which is so often made by political and economic elites, both from Russia and from the West? These are difficult but important questions, and they are meant to serve as the very basis of a critical sociology of contemporary Russian culture.

A Note on Transliteration and Translation

For the transliteration of words from Russian to English, I have used the Library of Congress method without diacritical marks. There are a few exceptions to this. In most cases, I have used spellings of proper names which do not fit this transliteration scheme, but which might be more familiar to the Western reader, e.g., Vysotsky, Zhenya, Melodiya. I have used an apostrophe to mark the soft sign in Russian words, but have not used it in the word *glasnost*, which is now part of the English language. I have made every effort to render translations from Russian into English which reflect the spirit and the tone of actual interviews and life histories. For instance, the Russian particle *to est'* is used constantly in speech, and I see it as equivalent to the word *like*, which often occurs in colloquial English speech. In addition, I have tried to use English slang which captures the meanings of the original Russian slang, which is so important in countercultural and musical life. For a sense of how I have rendered local meanings into idiomatic and slang English, see both the glossary and the notes.

Acknowledgments

A number of individuals and institutions provided me with crucial support at various points in this study. Wellesley College provided me with generous funding and sabbatical leave which enabled me to travel to Russia for extended periods to complete the research. Without this funding, the present study would not have been possible. The Pew Charitable Trust, which funded the Wellesley College Pew Summer Seminar Textual Strategies, provided extra funds for summer travel and for intellectual enrichment which has found its way into these pages. The faculty of the Harvard University Department of Sociology graciously invited me to offer a departmental colloquium; the presentation and discussion which followed helped me to crystallize some of the ideas which eventually found their way into this book. I am grateful to the St. Petersburg Institute of Sociology for inviting me to St. Petersburg in 1992 to complete the research for the project. Finally, the Harvard Russian Research Center provided me with office space and library privileges which were very beneficial in the course of writing this book.

Many people offered me conversation, criticism, commentary, and support which were crucial to this project: Stjepan Mestrovic, James Tucker, David Riesman, Gideon Sjoberg, Jonathan Knudsen, Liah Greenfeld, Igor Kon, Gregory Gomez, Murray Milner, Michele Rivkin-Fish, Tim Luke, Enric Bou, Carol Hartigan, Charles Simpson, Tom Hodge, and Luin Goldring. I am, of course, responsible for the points of view and any mistakes found in this book. A special thanks is in order for my colleagues in the Department of Sociology at Wellesley College: Susan Silbey, Jonathan Imber, and Lee Cuba. Their confidence in me as a person, scholar, and teacher provided moral and intellectual support during the research and writing of this book. These individuals define authentic and meaningful collegiality. I owe a special thanks to Elena Krasnoperova and Mariana Aleksandrovich for help in transcribing all the interviews, translating key passages, and proofreading. The research could not have been done, nor the book written, without the help of these remarkable women. Catherine Hudak also helped immensely with bibliographic and other matters related to preparing the manuscript for publication.

My greatest debt is to various members of the Petersburg musical community who invited me into their lives. Zhenya Leovin, Sergei Parashuk, Kolya Mikhailov, Dima Siderenko, Yuri Shevchuk, Viktor Sologub, and Misha Borzykin were particularly helpful in trusting an "intruder" from the outside. This book could not have been completed without their trust and confidence. This story is, quite literally, their story. I owe a particular debt of gratitude to Zhenya. When I first arrived in Petersburg to do fieldwork, he promised to help me "make a very fat book." Without Zhenya, I could never have gained the trust and confidence of the members of the Petersburg musical community whose stories are told in this book. Zhenya became a friend in the true sense of the Russian word *drug*, and it was through him that I first felt the depth of trust and warmth which defines the essence of Russian friendship.

A special debt of gratitude is owed to my beloved wife, Carol Hartigan, who offered unfailing support of my project in ways too numerous to mention. Most of all, I thank my little Sophie, who came along about midway through the writing of this book, and my little Eliza, who came along at the end. This book is dedicated to them because they have given authentic meaning to my existence in modernity.

1

A Recovery of the Senses: Toward a Critical-Interpretive Sociology of Russian Culture

We like to penetrate into the inner world of another man and to touch the most sensitive string in another's heart and observe its secret quivering; we strive to know its treasured secrets, in order to compare and confirm, to find justification, consolation, and proof of similarity.

—Aleksandr Herzen
My Past and Thoughts

A Theoretical Logic for the Interpretation of Russian Culture: The Dialectic of Structure and Agency in Social Life

While there are many differences among sociological theorists, a major strain of thought in sociological theory holds that society consists of individuals and social structures which exist in dialectical relation to one another. Social structures and forces do not rule completely over thinking and acting individuals and their subjectivities, nor are individuals completely able to change structural and historical conditions which precede them and which, in many cases, outlive them. While this theoretical logic has been discussed by a large number of contemporary theorists in a variety of ways (see, for example, Alexander 1987; Callinicos 1988; and Milner 1993),

1

perhaps one of the most prominent proponents of this theoretical position is British sociologist Anthony Giddens.

In a number of works, but most prominently in his book *The Constitution of Society* (1984), Giddens develops the idea that human action plays itself out in dialectical tension with the social structures which are, ironically, the historical products of that action. He claims that Marx's famous dictum, "Men make history, but not in circumstances of their own choosing," was perhaps the most important theoretical assertion in the history of social thought. Indeed, Giddens feels so strongly about Marx's assertion that a large part of his theoretical work is based on the simple insight contained within this seemingly innocuous passage. For Giddens, Marx's quote captured the dialectical relation between the individual and society which is the very basis of the constitution of society. Individuals are thinking, feeling, sentient agents who exert agency and control over and against existing social conditions. Their identities, selves, and actions unfold in relation to structural conditions and very often succeed in transforming those conditions. But these same conditions also limit and shape what actors are capable of achieving; as much as they may try, individuals never quite succeed in getting exactly what they want out of life. Indeed, life is a complex give-and-take in which actors get what they can from their surroundings, and their surroundings, in a sense, get what they can from actors. What human beings think, what they want, and what they are ultimately able to do are all modified by social-structural circumstances which are not "of their own choosing."

To the nonsociologist reader, such a view might seem a bit abstract. At one level, as Jeffrey Alexander (1987) has noted, sociological theory is concerned with the "abstract and transcendental, [and it is] a timeless search for the fundaments of action and order in human societies." At the same time, however, the formal, general, and abstract assertions of sociological theory are meant to frame and illuminate particular historical events which have occurred in particular times and places. An abstract view which emphasizes the dialectical interplay between human agency and social structure as the most essential process in the constitution of society provides the most basic starting point for rethinking and reinterpreting particular configurations of culture in the Soviet and post-Soviet context. From the perspective of such a view, rather than simply being the struggle of individuals against a "totalitarian system," expressions of Russian culture take on new meanings if we view them as instances which illustrate the more general, universal capacity of individuals to exert agency and control over structural conditions which limit and constrain them. It is not only in so-called totalitarian states that human beings have found themselves in confrontation with the structural forces which surround them. Simply being human means that one must struggle against structural conditions in order to express one's agency and to craft an identity and a self within the social-structural conditions which frame human existence (Giddens 1984, 1991). The dialectic of agency and structure is at the core of human social existence, and it is only the content and intensity of that struggle which changes across time and space.

Socialist Industrial Modernity and the Interpretation of Russian Culture

Giddens (1987) holds that it is the distinctive task of the sociological theorist to study "the social world brought about by the advent of modernity." His elaboration of the relation between structure and agency is meant to illuminate the particular qualities of the condition of modernity, a condition spawned by the advent of the Industrial Revolution and which has evolved up to the present. Giddens's work follows in the central tradition underlying the sociological enterprise which began in the nineteenth century: to understand the ways in which the subjective lives and consciousnesses of actors had changed under conditions of rapid transition from traditional to industrial society. Yet Giddens's discussions of modernity, as well as those of many other social theorists who examine modernity, are generally silent about socialist industrial society (but see Luke 1983; Arnason 1992, 1993; and Baumann 1992, p. 222).

It is difficult to find a place for a socialist industrial society such as the Soviet Union in Giddens's theory of modernity, or, for that matter, within the more general discourse on modernity in social theory.[1] On the one hand, Giddens (1984, pp. 294-341) sees the socialist industrial state as a particularly severe manifestation of industrial modernity characterized by a strong degree of surveillance and violence. On the other hand, in much of his other work Giddens presumes that capitalism is the decisive factor in the production of the general social condition which he calls modernity. In much of Giddens's work, capitalism is coterminous with modernity. This emphasis on market relations as one of the most fundamental characteristics of modernity seems to be a central underpinning of most social theories of modernity (see, for instance, Berman 1982; Poole 1991, p. 3; and Lash and Friedman 1992).

But is this actually the case? If one argues that the existence of market relations is a fundamental precondition for the emergence of modernity, how is one to view the historical development of the socialist industrial state, a social formation which was distinctly non-capitalist and even anti-capitalist? One way to resolve this inconsistency is by arguing that capitalism is not an essential precondition for the emergence of modernity. Emile Durkheim (1933) argued that it was the pace and intensity of industrialization which were the most essential underpinnings of modernity. Following Durkheim, I would argue that it is misleading to speak theoretically of modernity as if it were purely a phenomenon experienced in Western capitalist societies. Rather, I would like to make a distinction between two different trajectories of modernity in the twentieth century: capitalist and socialist.

The terms *modernization* and *modernity* have been used throughout the history of Soviet studies to describe the Soviet Union (see, for instance, Nettl and Robertson 1966; Lowenthal 1974; and Hough 1977). Arguments rage about how to classify the Soviet Union: Is it a modern, a traditional, or a "neo-traditional" society?[2] It is neither possible nor desirable to explore this issue in detail here. Rather, I simply wish to expand the discussion by introducing a more phenomenologically informed conception of the idea of modernity into the discourse on Soviet historical development. Let us begin by making a distinction between the terms *modernization* and *modernity*. Modernization is a social process consisting of industrialization, urbanization, and social differentiation which produces a "state" which we call "modernity" (Tiryakian 1992, p. 78). By extension, Soviet modernization, which was socialist in its design and implementation, produced a particular type of configuration which we might call "socialist industrial modernity."[3]

The historical pattern of the development of Soviet society was characterized by a number of profound social and cultural transformations, in particular its unprecedented and unmatched level of industrialization, the development of new roles and forms of social life, forms of culture, interpersonal relations, and communications networks, both mass and interpersonal (Lewin 1989, p. 302). While the progression of Soviet history represents a distinctive trajectory of modernity which shares many of the characteristics of capitalist industrial modernity, it also exhibits a distinctly different organization of time and social space, a pattern of intensity of industrialization, and a host of other structural and cultural characteristics similar to those which make up the infrastructure of Western capitalist modernity. Socialist industrial modernity is an amalgam of the global processes of modernization which began in the nineteenth century and of the particular historical events which occurred in the Soviet Union in the twentieth century. It is not a variant of Western capitalist modernity or even a deviant or perverse form of Western capitalist modernity as some have argued (see, for instance, Jowitt 1991, p. 34n). It is a form of modernity with its own social-structural configuration, cultural logic, and structure of experience. To be "Soviet" in the twentieth century was to be "modern" but in a different sense than what social theorists usually mean by the term *modern*.

The argument for viewing socialist industrial society as a particular type of industrial modernity allows us to move away from viewing cultural practices in Russia purely in relation to political structures and practices. This is the normal *modus operandi* of Western political scientists and historians and, to be sure, the sociologist of Russian culture would be naïve not to recognize that the political policies of the Communist Party did affect cultural outcomes. Yet, at the same time, the more general sociological meaning and significance of cultural practices in Russia are only intelligible in relation to the larger infrastructure of socialist modernity. As social historian Moshe Lewin (1989, p. 302; 1991, p. 258) notes, the party was the "smithy" for the modernization of the country and was itself a stultifying force which countered the forces unleashed by the process of modernization. The sociology of Russian culture situates Russian cultural practices within the larger framework of socialist industrial existence, as both a product of that existence and a force which resisted it.

While it is tempting to locate the birth of the socialist industrial modernity with the Bolshevik Revolution of 1917 (as does Habermas 1975), it is more accurate to say that the trajectory of socialist modernity was intimately tied to the growth of capitalist modernity in the West. Prior to the revolution, Russian society was primarily agrarian and lagged far behind the West in terms of the level of economic development. In the late nineteenth century, Russia experienced a modified form of capitalist modernization, but it never experienced the same degree of structural or cultural transformation as its West European counterparts. On the eve of the Bolshevik Revolution of 1917, Russia remained a predominantly agrarian society; what little modern culture existed was to be found primarily in St. Petersburg and Moscow among a small segment of highly educated intelligentsia. In spite of the transformative efforts of the Bolsheviks in the 1920s, Russian society continued along the path of capitalist rationalization, albeit in a modified form. And while the embryo of a socialist modernity was certainly contained within Bolshevik political philosophy and practice, it was not until the defeat of modified capitalism and the ascendancy of Stalinism that it is possible to speak of the birth of a distinct trajectory of socialist modernity. The modified Leninist formula for capitalist modernization as the path to socialism was replaced by the hyperrational ethos of instrumental rationality which infused all sectors of Soviet society, including the process of production and distribution of culture.

Many theorists of modernity (see, for instance, Giddens 1990) have conceived of it in terms of the metaphor of a juggernaut in order to convey a sense of the rapidity and flux of modernity. Yet it makes little sense to speak of the juggernaut of Western capitalist modernity when taking into consideration the degree and intensity of industrial development in the Soviet Union of the 1930s. For if Western modernity is a juggernaut, what metaphor are we to use to describe a society in which a "backward" country reached parity with the developed West in the space of less than twenty years, where, within only thirty years, whole cities were modernized, and the majority of a traditionally peasant population moved (either by force or by choice) from the country to the city? If we are to compare the trajectories of modernity in terms of which one deserves the metaphor of juggernaut, it is clear to which trajectory of modernity the metaphor most aptly applies.

A great deal more could and ought to be said by way of comparing these two trajectories of twentieth-century industrial modernity. What is important here is to see each trajectory of modernity as a structural framework of existence within which various cultural practices occurred and in which they took on their meaning. It might be said, to paraphrase Freud, that each type of modernity produced its own cultural discontents, its own particular experiences of disenchantment with the world. The Soviet trajectory of modernity was particularly acute; the pace of industrial development and its effects, as well as the permeation of all levels of social and cultural life with an ethos of bureaucratic rationality, profoundly affected individuals at the level of subjectivity.

Very few, if any, discussions of cultural dynamics in communist or post-communist societies draw on the theoretical logic of modernity theory (as distinct from modernization theory) in order to illuminate substantive aspects of culture in such societies. In Western sociology it is quite common to interpret cultural processes and practices in relation to the structural conditions which distinguish modern societies from traditional ones. From Weber, Durkheim, Simmel, and Marx onward through the twentieth century, sociologists have viewed youth movements (Mannheim 1956), artistic movements (Marcuse 1978; 1993), religious movements (Hunter 1983), and social movements in general (Habermas 1989; Giddens 1990) as responses to existential quandaries brought on by life in modern society. In discussing the consequences of modernity in Western capitalist societies, Max Weber (in Tiryakian 1992, p. 80) noted, "The fate of our times is characterized by rationalization and intellectualization and, above all, by the 'disenchantment of the world.' Precisely the ultimate and most sublime values have retreated from public life either into the transcendental realm of mystic life or into the brotherliness of direct and personal human relations."

Weber's understanding of the character of industrial modernity provides a useful theoretical logic for the interpretation of cultural counterprocesses and movements in the Soviet and post-Soviet social context. As Edward Tiryakian (1992, p. 78-79) argues, Weber's discussion of the dialectic of disenchantment and re-enchantment under conditions of modernity is central to understanding a wide variety of "counterprocesses" in modern industrial societies; indeed, he goes so far as to offer Weber's dialectical vision of history as a "common denominator" which unites all theories of modernity. Cultural counterprocesses (Tiryakian 1992) in communist and post-communist societies must be viewed, as they are in the West, dialectically in relation to the particular structural configuration of socialist industrial modernity.[4]

Culture and Counterculture in the Russian Context

What do sociologists mean when they speak of culture and counterculture? There are hundreds of definitions of culture in contemporary social science, and it is difficult to decide which one is best for an emergent sociology of Russian culture. In this book, the word *culture* is used in its sociological sense to describe a general process by which individuals collectively make sense of and find meaning in the world. German social theorist and philosopher Jürgen Habermas defines culture as the "stock of knowledge from which participants in communication supply themselves with interpretations as they come to an understanding about something in the modern world" (1989, p. 138). Habermas's definition—which is itself grounded in a long tradition of phenomenological and interpretive sociology—is the one which I use in this book. It stresses a sense of culture as a practical achievement, as the outcome of the concrete experiences of social actors in the social world. Culture does not simply exist; it is made and accomplished. People make culture, and culture, in turn, makes them. It is through the process of making culture that individual and collective identities are formed, and it is within the realm of culture that human beings compete, struggle, and exert forms of power over one another as they articulate different meanings.

What, then, do we mean by counterculture? If culture is the practical knowledge gained in the course of communicating with others in the process of living, then counterculture is simply practical knowledge which is the result of engagement in alternative forms of communication among actors engaged in the collective pursuit of alternative ways of living. A counterculture consists of a stock of knowledge which, quite literally, runs counter to the dominant stock of knowledge in a society. I use the term *Russian counterculture* to refer to a community of similarly situated social actors who share values, perceptions, beliefs, and cultural symbols and codes which stand in opposition to the dominant, "normal" culture of Soviet industrial society.[5] "Rock musical counterculture" refers to a group of individuals who share, first and foremost, a common commitment to the autonomous production and dissemination of rock music without overt or covert interference by "outside" political or economic forces. I exclude from the category of counterculture those musicians who are perceived by Petersburg rock musicians as being "popular" musicians, that is, musicians who are perceived as having been co-opted by either political or economic forces (although my account includes discussions of such musicians, not as members of the counterculture, but as figures which are used by Petersburg counterculturalists to define themselves as such). This book is not primarily a study of popular culture, but of counterculture, and the distinction between the two will become clear in the following pages.

The grouping of all musicians into the analytical category of "counterculture" is not meant to infer that all Petersburg rock musicians are completely homogeneous and united in their attitudes, values, beliefs, and preferences. Conflicts and differences exist among them; they are divided by differences in opinions, styles, attitudes, and beliefs. Yet, in spite of these differences, Petersburg rock musicians share a common perception of:

1. the value and worth of rock music as an authentic and autonomous art form which is equal in aesthetic value to other forms of "high art," such as painting or literature;
2. the importance of rock music as the major symbolic embodiment of a critical stance toward the values, beliefs, ideologies, and symbols of the infrastructure of Soviet modernity; and
3. the active use of rock music to claim a social role which is "outside" of the normal system of roles characteristic of socialist industrial society and, by way of this, the production of an identity and sense of self which also stands outside the normal, acceptable prescriptions for identity and selfhood characteristic of Soviet modernity.

Music, Meaning, and Modernity

At this point, an important sociological question emerges: Why is music such an important force in the formation of alternative communities and identities? The answer lies in an exploration of the sociological significance of music not only as an art form but as a form of communication which mediates experience in the world.

In sociological and ethnomusicological studies of music and musical subcultures, music is often seen theoretically as a "reflex" of the social world, and, in particular, of the social stratification system (Frith 1984; Willis 1990; Wicke 1991). Following this conception, many ethnomusicologists and sociologists of music have explored the role of music in facilitating communication between subordinate social actors and groups. Such communication is vital if the latter are to mount successful challenges to structures of social domination. Ian Watson (1983), for instance, has shown the importance of song in the formation of British working-class consciousness. In South Africa, music was instrumental in helping blacks to share their common experience of subordination and to carve out an autonomous cultural space in which they could redress their grievances (Coplan 1985; Erlmann 1991). During the American Great Depression, popular music was a major means of intersubjective communication among workers who found themselves subject to a common experience of social subordination (Lieberman 1989). In Jamaica, the development of reggae music, with its utopian themes of struggle and liberation, is directly related to experience of structural subordination among members of the Jamaican black underclass (Hebdige 1987; Cushman 1991). In a variety of social and historical contexts, popular music has served as a means of communication among actors, and this communication has had concrete political and social effects and outcomes (Manuel 1988).

Music is a form of expressive, aesthetic, "communicative action," a major means by which actors express and share the content of their "lifeworlds" (Habermas 1984; Lull 1985; 1987, pp. 10-12). The concept of "lifeworld" is an important one in the tradition of interpretive sociology. This tradition has its roots in the interpretive sociology of Max Weber and has been most developed in the phenomenological sociology of Alfred Schutz. Phenomenological sociology stresses the importance of exploring social life in terms of the meanings which actors themselves place on their own actions. In order to understand social life, we must enter into what Alfred Schutz calls the lifeworld of actors. The lifeworld is "the total sphere of experiences of an individual which is circumscribed by the objects, persons, and events encountered in the pursuit of the pragmatic objectives of living" (1970, p. 320). Music communicates a variety of experiences of being in the world. The communication of experience is a form of mediation which serves to establish common bonds between similarly situated actors. Music, perhaps more than any other form of aesthetic culture, allows for a sharing of the innermost experiences of individuals and their unification into a coherent "We" which is the foundation of all social groups and communication (Schutz 1951, p. 92; see also Dewey [1934] 1959).

Thus, music is not purely a phenomenon which emanates from human subjectivity; its communicative capacity is always framed, as Schutz points out, by the "objects, persons, and events" of the outside world. In the words of James Lull (1987, p. 12): "The potential for exercising the communicative capacities [of music] is influenced by the structural circumstances that surround their existence." Any phenomenological approach to music must be balanced by a view which takes into consideration the structural and historical circumstances which occur in the outside world—specifically, patterns of political and economic organization—which give rise to and, in a sense, "fill" the lifeworlds of individuals. Music is a meaning-making and meaning-sharing activity which allows for the formation of "affective alliances" among social actors. Yet music is also a cultural activity which is situated within particular social-structural conditions and which responds to and is affected by such conditions. A purely phenomenological perspective on music (as with a purely phenomenological approach to any form of culture) tends to focus too much on music as a subjective phenomenon and not enough on the external social, economic, and political forces in which human subjectivity exists.

Perhaps the most important recent theoretical work which avoids the solipsism of a purely phenomenological approach is that of Jürgen Habermas. Habermas's theoretical work is characterized by an attempt to explore the relation between the lifeworld and the social system. If the lifeworld is the world of subjective experience, then the social system is the "objective" world which gives rise to and frames such experiences. Habermas, like Max Weber, argues that the modern world is characterized by the dominance of instrumental rationality. It is this triumph of reason which is at once the driving force of modernity and a force which imperils and threatens to colonize the lifeworlds of individuals (Habermas 1989). Within a social framework characterized by the dominance of rationality, meaning is maintained through the process of intersubjective communication. Habermas's theoretical project moves away from the Marxian emphasis on the forces of production toward a view which stresses the importance of "communicative interaction" in social life (Habermas 1984, 1989; see also Poole 1991, p. 79). Marx erred, according to Habermas, in presuming that humans were essentially laborers. Instead, Habermas recasts the most fundamental "essence" of humans as communicators. What is more important is that we communicate our experiences of being in the world, for it is these shared experiences which "fill" our lifeworlds. The resolution of conflict in modern society has little to do with reclaiming the means of production, as Marx would argue. Rather, the central quandary of modernity is distorted communication, and this quandary is resolved by the rise of communicative movements which seek to protect the lifeworld from the forces of instrumental reason which are embodied in the structures which frame existence (Habermas 1989, pp. 394 ff).

Toward a Critical-Interpretive Theory of Russian Culture

Habermasian perspectives on culture have rarely been applied to the analysis of popular culture, most likely because so much of popular cultural studies is influenced by "postmodern" perspectives which are often seen as diametrically opposed to Habermas's commitment to modernism and the fulfillment of the Enlightenment project (Habermas 1981; Rorty 1985). Only in some cases has Habermas related his perspective to the dynamics of system and lifeworld in state-socialist societies.[6] Yet his framework is an important theoretical starting point for understanding the role and function of music in the Russian context. It allows us to conceive of music as a form of communicative action which allowed actors to retain a sense of inner autonomy and shared consciousness within the framework of Soviet modernity. Moreover—and this is a point which is central to this book—his perspective allows us to maintain a critical approach to culture in present-day, post-Soviet Russian society.

Habermas's primary purpose is to understand the relation between system and lifeworld in advanced capitalist society. A central question of concern to him is: To what extent is consciousness colonized by the logic of capitalist rationality in modern societies? Instead of accepting the simple equation between the expansion of capitalism and the expansion of freedom in post-communist Russia (a view which is present in so much rhetoric in discussions of the future of Russia), Habermas allows us to maintain a critical perspective on the relationship between cultural processes and the emergence of capitalism in contemporary Russia. Instead of asking, How can capitalism be made to work in post-communist Russia? we can instead ask, How will capitalism work on individual lifeworlds and the process of intersubjective communication in post-communist Russia?

Habermas's theoretical perspective forces us to keep the external world ever present in our analysis of Russian counterculture. Moreover, his perspective allows us to move from theory to practice in the

Russian context. While many aspects of his world view are utopian, I do accept many of his conceptions as important ideal-types which can guide the critical analysis of culture in post-Soviet Russia. Such conceptions allow us to address both the important issues of cultural freedom and democracy in present-day Russia, and the relation of the latter to fundamental processes of communicative action which are central to the democratization of Russian society.

Clearly, it is enticing to rethink the cultural history of the Soviet period—even at the risk of being accused of reductionism—as a series of attempts by Soviet actors to re-enchant the world in the face of what must be the most pronounced form of bureaucratic rationality in the twentieth century. It is precisely these processes of intersubjective communication which resulted in the formation of subterranean cultural communities within the context of Soviet modernity. Yet it is equally enticing to explore the fate of such communities within the context of the capitalist present. The Petersburg rock counterculture is an example of a moral community formed and held together by the form of communicative action known as rock music. As with moral communities in the West, this community was not immune to the effects of the logic of bureaucratic rationality. Nor is it now immune from the effects of a new spirit of capitalist rationality. The latter is experienced not so much as a force which facilitates freedom—although in some instances this is decidedly the case—but, rather, as a force which has brought with it a new set of dilemmas to producers of culture in Russia. The nature and social sources of these dilemmas will unfold throughout the following chapters. This critical project is rather new to studies of Russia, yet so is the qualitative sociological study of Russian culture. In what follows, I offer a brief elaboration of the qualitative methods which serve as the basis for this case study.

The Methods of the Study:
Interpretive Strategies for the
Analysis of Russian Culture

The Research: Qualitative Sociology in the Russian Setting

My exploration of the dialectical interplay between the lives of Russian counterculturalists and the course of history which frames these lives draws on some key methods of interpretive, qualitative, sociological research: ethnography, participant-observation, life-history analysis, and in-depth, open-ended interviewing. Using these methods, I have tried to capture the lived experiences and biographies of popular musicians in their own words and to understand their experiences as they have lived them across time and space. Ultimately, any view of Russian culture which does not have a firm grounding in the thoughts and experiences of members of cultural communities themselves is at best incomplete and at worst a gloss from the "outside" which confuses the reality of external sources with the more fundamental reality of culture which exists at the level of consciousness. While I have placed what I have observed and experienced into a theoretical context, I have done my utmost to ensure that these theoretical accounts do not become realities in and of themselves which supersede the realities which exist in the thoughts of the members of the Petersburg musical community.

There are many different definitions of reality circulating within the world of Russian musical counterculture. From the standpoint of interpretive sociology, it is what musicians think is real that is decisive for their own lives and cultural activity. In my opinion, one of the most important theorems in sociology is W. I. Thomas's (1966) notion of the "definition of the situation." Thomas claimed that "If men define situations as real they are real in their consequences." In a rapidly changing context such as Russia, in which everyone is unclear about just what reality is, thoughts and perceptions are perhaps the major shapers of human action and perhaps the only true reality that we can uncover. As much as Western researchers have tried to piece together the reality or truth of the Soviet Union (and many times out of very bad so-called facts), the sobering fact is that there are multiple truths and realities within this social space. The definitions of reality offered by musicians, excavated by the sociological imagination and refracted through the lens of sociological theory, offer us other views of reality.

As an interpretive sociologist who believes in the constructedness of cultural phenomena (including knowledge), I do not believe that there is any one truth about rock music in Russia. Old guard Soviet and American conservatives such as Igor Ligachev or Allan Bloom view rock culture as a pernicious evil which endangers the enduring values of their respective societies. Even among some left-leaning, progressive circles of intellectuals—both in Russia and in the West—rock music is often viewed as a simplistic cultural form which should never be put on the same footing as high culture by virtue of its simplicity or its crudity. Depending on which musician one talks to, rock music is any one of a number of things: a profession, a way to re-enchant a world, a means of self-expression, a serious form of high art, a labor of love, aesthetic stimulation, or just plain fun. This book draws on interpretive methods of social research to present the story of the world of the

Petersburg rock musical counterculture from the point of view of members of that community themselves. Through the use of interpretive methods of social research, I wish to place the study of Russian rock culture—and of Russian culture more generally—squarely within the tradition of interpretive sociology. What this means, to paraphrase the father of interpretive sociology, Max Weber (1978), is that the meaning and significance of rock music in Russia must be understood from the point of view of those who make it.

In all, over a period of six months of fieldwork carried out over the space of three years, I collected forty in-depth interviews with members of the Petersburg musical community (see appendix 1 for a detailed discussion of the methodological parameters and problems of the fieldwork). These interviews were not restricted to musicians, but included a broad cross-section of those involved in the production and distribution of culture in the city. Rock journalists and historians, group managers, and organizers of musical recordings and performances are all important within the musical community. Without them, there would be no musical community, because it is their activities which lie behind cultural productions and which make music into a cultural reality accessible to all (Becker 1982). In the course of interviewing members of the musical community, I selected ten individuals for more detailed study through the method of life-history analysis. I asked members of the musical community to elaborate their life histories in their own words. By letting these individuals freely roam backward and across their own lives, I wished to let them provide their own answers to important questions: How did they come to be involved in the world of rock music? What were the major events or "epiphanies" which caused them to choose music as a vocation?

These life histories were then followed by more pointed and focused questions about their musical experiences and their views on the role and function of rock music in Russian society, both in the Soviet and in the post-Soviet periods. Extended answers to the following questions, both by the larger sample of interviewees and by the smaller sample of life-history respondents, provided the major source of data for the present study: What is the meaning and significance of rock music in Russian society? How and why did they come to define themselves as musicians? Why did they choose rock music as an idiom of cultural expression? What does it mean to play the role of rock musician in Soviet and post-Soviet Russia? What do they see as the relationship between rock music and politics, and between rock music and the external world more generally? How does the social organization of cultural production affect the lives and work of musicians in what is perhaps the most culturally vibrant of Russian cities? How has the dissolution of the Soviet Union affected their creative activity? What are the prospects for cultural freedom and autonomy in a society which is increasingly infused with the spirit of capitalism and the impersonal ethos of the marketplace?

Answers to these questions provide the basic building blocks for the account of the St. Petersburg musical counterculture presented in this book. Yet the words of members of this musical community do not, in and of themselves, constitute the only social reality of rock musical practice in Russian society. While I have sought to construct reality as much as possible through the words of musicians themselves, I also present what Clifford Geertz (1973) has referred to as "thick descriptions" of the conditions under which Russian musicians live and of their activities. Thick description allows us to convey a sense of the "structure of feeling" (Williams 1981) of Russian society in different historical epochs. Only by understanding the structure of feeling in which cultural practices exist can we interpret their meaning and significance. The reliance on ethnographic observations which complement in-depth interviews and life histories of musicians does not mean, however, that I make the claim that this book represents a full-fledged ethnography of the Petersburg musical counterculture. Bronislaw Malinowski's famous injunction to "Grasp the native's point of view, his relation to life, [and] to realize his vision of the world" (in Nader 1993, p. 7) has guided my fieldwork to a great extent. Yet the aim of my fieldwork was to provide answers to a discrete set of important sociological questions rather than to describe completely and in minute detail every aspect of the way of life of Petersburg musical counterculturalists. As such, the book does not represent a complete ethnography of the way of life of the rock community. As Laura Nader (ibid.) points out, "Ethnographic is not ethnography." This study is ethnographic. Ultimately, the rich and detailed excerpts from life histories and interviews which I have presented provide, perhaps more than my own ethnographic "glosses," a profoundly more accurate sense of the "realities" of music-making in Russian society.

If the sociology of Russian culture (or the sociology of post-communist cultures more generally) is to have any future, it must be based on autonomous interpretive efforts which complement and draw on, but do not ape, the epistemologies and ontologies of other disciplines or put themselves in service of new forms of social domination. While the ultimate task of this chapter has been to provide a theoretical and methodological framework for the interpretation of one case study, I also offer it, perhaps presumptuously, as a model for future research efforts of interpretive social scientists who wish to understand culture in the sociological sense. This framework offers a way to excavate the realms of culturally constructed and shared webs of meaning which operate underneath the contours of the more obvious social-structural realities of Russian society.

2

Stories from Underground: The Origins of St. Petersburg Rock Music Counterculture

We always find something, eh, Didi, to give us the impression that we exist?

—Samuel Beckett, *Waiting for Godot*

Origins and Lives

The central task of this chapter is to explore the formation and the significance of the rock musical counterculture of St. Petersburg, roughly during the period between the early 1960s and the mid-1980s. The emergence of the Petersburg counterculture is a result of the intersection of an important Western cultural form—rock music—and the particular forms of consciousness which emerged in the course of Soviet historical development. Rock music came to the Soviet Union over thirty years ago, not long after its appearance in the West. This rather long history in a supposedly "closed" society raises a paradoxical issue: If Soviet society was such a totalitarian, closed society (the terms most often used by Western propagandists to describe the USSR), how was it possible that a vibrant musical counterculture—much less any form of counterculture—could develop at all?

The answer to this question lies in the examination of two intersecting cultural processes, one global and one local. In the post-war era there was a tremendous acceleration in the growth and diffusion of the media of mass communication in the global world-system. Not only was cultural information carried through these channels, it was also carried by an increasing number of citizens from Western industrial societies who enjoyed a historically unprecedented freedom of movement within the world-system. Radio, television, the possibility of individual ownership of the technologies of cultural reproduction, and the travel of citizens from new "information societies" to less developed societies allowed for a widespread circulation of symbols and signs throughout the world. This circulation of culture also reached the countries of the socialist bloc, albeit in a limited way.

Locally, the process of modernization unleashed social and cultural forces which simply could not be contained, even by the formidable structural barriers erected within authoritarian societies. Modern industrial societies—even authoritarian ones—need educated citizens to create and use new technologies and to engage in the complex tasks of industrial production. Education in the service of socialism, however, is a two-edged sword. An increase in verbal and technological literacy may lead to an increase in the productive capacity of a society, but it also leads to more sophisticated forms of cognition which enable the development of freedom of inquiry and a potential to reflect and think critically about the surrounding world. Indeed, as Anthony Giddens (1990, 1991) has argued, it is the capacity of individuals to think reflexively about their social surroundings, to imagine their own biography in relation to a world which they recognize as one of their own construction, which is one of the hallmarks of modern, industrial societies.

Ideologically, the Soviet state was organized at its very core to protect Soviet society from the "pernicious" products of Western culture industries which would contaminate the culture of the worker's state. Yet, in spite of the existence of a complex infrastructure designed to manage cultural expression and creativity, the sheer scope and complexity of changes within and outside of the Soviet society ensured that individuals living in this society would find ways to receive cultural information from the West. What was more important, individuals could actively participate in Western culture even from within the boundaries of the supposedly closed society, even though this participation took place, in most cases, in ways which were invisible to the West. No states have ever completely succeeded in monitoring all aspects of cultural life or in colonizing the subjectivities of its citizens. This is especially the case in Soviet-type societies. For if they had, the forms of resistant consciousness which were so integral in the transformation of socialist industrial society in the late twentieth century could never have emerged. The sheer complexity of global changes and of the inability of the Soviet state to police all spheres of a complex society ensured that some cultural information found its way into the space of Soviet society. And because actors are endowed with the ability to use culture creatively to evade and resist even formidable structural barriers, it was possible for people living in the Soviet Union to draw on Western culture "to make something out of what was made of them."[1]

An understanding of the origin and significance of the Petersburg musical counterculture, then, depends fundamentally on understanding this important intersection between the diffusion of Western cultural products into Russia and the ability of some people to rework and put such products to use in their local environments. Rock was born in Western capitalist society, and, more specifically, in England and the United States.[2] While it has diverse origins ranging from Africa to the American South and the American city, in the final analysis, it was the capitalist mode of production that organized discrete cultural practices into a cultural form which we now call "rock." Capitalism was the engine of rock's development as a global cultural phenomenon. Yet the development of Russian rock music culture within the context of socialist industrial modernity depended on the unique and creative ways in which certain Russians appropriated elements of Western rock culture and adapted these elements to construct an alternative way of life within the space of socialist industrial modernity. The sociological story of Petersburg musical counterculture begins with an exploration of the ways in which certain individuals adapted Western rock music as the basis for alternative ways of thinking, being, and acting within the infrastructure of socialist industrial modernity.

This chapter explores the origins of Russian rock music and rock counterculture through the life histories of those who participated in it. Through the particulars of these life histories we outline more general processes in the development of Petersburg rock culture. How was it that such a vibrant and unique island of meaning came into existence within the sea of socialist industrial modernity? What elements of Soviet existence and individuals' experiences of that existence led to the development of what might be called the "rock career" in Soviet society? What were rock musicians' ways of relating to the external world of normal Soviet existence? How was their cultural practice related to specific political and economic structures within the Soviet Union? The best answers to these questions emerge directly from the lifeworlds of participants in Petersburg musical counterculture themselves.

We begin with a rather lengthy life story, freely and eloquently given by Yuri, a guitarist who is a veteran of the Petersburg musical counterculture. It is appropriate to begin with Yuri's story, for his was the first life history collected in my field research. The particulars of his life guided my subsequent research and helped to frame the most important questions of this study. His story throws into relief some of the most important elements of the practice of rock music in Russia: a comprehensive and sophisticated knowledge of Western culture, the creative and often ingenious deployment of that culture as a means of crafting an alternative identity within the space of Soviet society, a commitment to a sense of individual calling as the source of creative inspiration, and a resistance to outside political and economic interference in one's life and creative activity are some of the central elements which define Yuri's identity as a rock musician. Like all life stories, Yuri's is unique. Yet no individual exists outside of history, and his life reflects patterns and processes which are to be found in the lives of other Petersburg musicians. Throughout this chapter and the rest of the book, we explore more deeply many of the issues raised in Yuri's story.

Yuri: A "Forty-Something" Veteran Counterculturalist

Where does one go to find out about the history of a countercultural community? To the veterans of that culture. And so I was brought to Yuri who was working in a small recording studio not too far off of Nevsky Prospekt, the city's major thoroughfare. Yuri sported long hair, which identified him as an "alternative" social type, and the wrinkles in his face identified him as someone who had lived a while, to be precise, since 1948. A native of the southern city of Ordzhonikidze (located in the Caucasus and now called by its pre-revolutionary name, "Vladikavkaz"), Yuri, like many other Petersburg musicians, was attracted by the culture of Petersburg and moved there permanently in 1973. By virtue of his age, experience, and talent, he is considered by many—even the young—to be one of the foremost musical personalities in the history of Russian rock. In addition to his musical talent, he is one of a small class of those whom others refer to now and then as a "poet." Later, I was to hear him referred to by some as a *staryi roker*, or "old rocker." This is a somewhat oxymoronic classification given the traditional association of rock culture with youth culture. Yet the label illustrates well the fact that rock culture in Russia has a long history—almost as long as in the West—and many of its practitioners are now members of the older generation.

Yuri has a varied past characterized by a number of musical adventures. He is clearly an individualist who held himself to high standards of musical quality and who refused to accede to the vagaries of public taste or to the pressure of the collective. After a number of various incarnations, Yuri found that he preferred the role of producing other people's music to playing his own. Yuri was instrumental in working "underground" in the early 1980s within the system of what musicians refer to as *magnitofonnaia kul'tura,* or "tape-recorder culture," the independently and informally produced and circulated Russian rock music that was the fundamental basis of the evolution of the city's musical counterculture. From independent rocker, to hippie, to born-again Christian, to practitioner of yoga, to rock producer, to folk bard, Yuri represents, in one person, practically all of the dimensions of countercultural existence.

In the summer of 1990, I met Yuri in a small sound studio where he was working as a sound engineer for the newly reformed state recording studio, Melodiya. He was surrounded by recording equipment which was noticeably older and of lesser quality than one might find in a Western studio of comparable size. On the wall was a large picture of himself standing with a guitar in Dvortsovii Square. Behind him loomed the huge, free-standing obelisk of Michael the Archangel. Here is Yuri's story:

> I ought to say that I lived earlier not in Leningrad, but in the Caucasus, in the city of Ordzhinokidze which is now called "Vladikavkaz." It returned to its old name. In the Caucasus the relations are nationalistic. If you go on the street and you bump into a bunch of Georgians or Ossetians, they can beat the hell out of you for any reason whatsoever. It's just that way. In just about any situation. Even if you're going around with a guitar, they jump you and break what you have into pieces. Well, such things are kind of bleak. It's the same kind of situation which I saw in *West Side Story* in which two parties were always at each other: the Sharks and someone else. Two bands, one Puerto Rican, they're always slashing each other. Here we've got the same situation, not entirely so, but something like it.
>
> To cut a long story short, it happened that I quit this game and was sitting quietly and playing the guitar, and our guys in that city, Vladikavkaz, didn't play or compose their own compositions, and I started to play in an amateur group at an institute where I was working as a builder. Well, we would get out on the stage, play the Beatles, the Rolling Stones, everything would be O.K. Then I would announce proudly, "Now—our own composition!" And somehow it wouldn't work. First, these compositions were in Russian—and [songs in] Russian didn't connect with the

audience at all then only in English. And if in Russian, then we had to sing something like the Singing Guitars (Poyushchiye Gitary)—there was a group like this, a Soviet VIA (*vocal'nyi instrumental'nyi ansambl*, or "vocal instrumental ensemble").[3] So, we had to choose from the repertoire of these Singing Guitars. If we played something different, nobody would even listen. All my undertakings were like this—I was struggling one, two years, composing, singing—they wouldn't interest anybody. At all. They didn't need our own compositions.

And then it happened so—my father was an officer. He was born in the Crimea, then lived in the Caucasus, and then moved to Leningrad. In Leningrad for the first two years I was totally in the underground. One day I went to the concert in the Arts Academy where the Myths (Mify) and the Russians (Rossiiane)[4] were playing. What struck me was that half of the things they played were their own and that people would listen and even applaud. All right. Well, I thought, that's it. Very quickly, I put together a small group, not a permanent one. I had two or three pals with whom I began to record, at home of course. At home— the drums, well the neighbors were having headaches all day long because of the thunder from the drums. Well, we adapted ourselves so that we played when people were going to work. By the way, many groups recorded like this—Kino,[5] for example. In the daytime everybody's away and we start crashing, shouting. By evening the creative mood appeared. In the afternoon it wasn't very productive . . . people begin gathering and knocking, "Enough! or we'll call the militia!" "One more minute!" "No, we'll call the militia right now!"

T. C.: Was it usually like this? Go on, I'm listening.

Yuri: Well, this lasted until I was drafted into the army. I had been evading our glorious Soviet army for a long time. For long enough—I was studying at the institute, and in those days they gave you an extension at the institute until your graduation. So, they gave it to me and I was evading them until the last minute, and then one day I was cornered like a beast and they led me away. Only for a year though. Those with a higher education served in the army for one year only. In the army I kicked up a group—I was serving in the radio regiment as a master repairman of equipment and was playing in a band all the time. I formed two groups there in succession, and I worked on the methods of working with people. Before I didn't play much on the stage—everything was such small potatoes, and here I was playing like crazy for dances, all these officers, grey-haired colonels were dancing to my rock-n-roll. Rolling Stones was already old hat. Ah, no, I was also performing Paul McCartney, great stuff (*v kaif*), you know, with such a roar. Nobody even understood the words, but these "granddads" (*dedy*) would always wake me up at night and say, "Let's get on with it!"

In short, in the army I cleaned out my throat, trained my voice, because at home I couldn't sing at the top of my voice—you know all our Japanese flats, the tiny ones. And there on the stage I shouted to my heart's content and started to give concerts. As soon as I returned from the army, I joined a band. This band was a nest for many groups. We had this super guitar player, Aleksandr L. He played in this band. He's playing in Akvarium (Aquarium) now.[6] There was also the keyboard player, Aleksandr A. In short, it was a quite professional, first-rate band. Aleksandr L. left it, and I came. Well, we played for half a year in the dance hall in a club for mentally defective teenagers. . . . I had a hit then entitled "I'm a Cretin and It's Great." I wrote that there's nothing terrible about being a cretin. On the contrary, everything's all right. And the people danced like crazy to this music. They liked it an awful lot. Well, I played for half a year, and then the stage, the same program every evening—it depressed me awfully. Every evening I changed the composition we were playing. I changed the arrangement all the time, just to make it a little different somehow.

And then I realized: I'm just bored with playing. And I performed there for the last time in 1978, twelve years ago. It was my last performance at such a big session (*seishn*). And at that time I played metal. I even have some recordings. Nobody played it at the time. They played hard rock. Rossiiane, more or less. And I had all this remarkable stuff. Everything played in overdrive with such outrageous riffs. People didn't get it at all. There was this audience there—after me Il'chenko performed, you know, lyrical songs like "Your Tears Are Like Rain." And the audience applauded him. I thought, "Damn it! Why the fuck should I play in this country when they're applauding such morons? I won't ever set foot on the stage again." I got so angry, because I felt that I was doing something new.

At the time we had groups like Time Machine (Mashina Vremeni),[7] the Russians (Rossiiane), the Myths (Mify). The Myths were more or less close to me in music. But all of them played rather lyrically. They had this kind of lyrical hard rock. And I emerged alone then, hard and heavy. After I quit, in a year or two appeared a group called the Ashes (Pepel). They were kind of following my traditions in another manner. And for ten years—for ten long years, until 1987—I gave up the stage and threw myself totally into sound recording. At home I had such a—I'm a radiomaster—I assembled tape recorders—such monsters—there was a huge iron plate hanging which I used as a reverberator—there are such plastic reverberators, they have huge plates, and I had this huge iron plate in my room, I sang in front of it—in front of the plate, into a microphone. Signals were coming from the plate and the microphone. It was a real strange environment. People liked to come to me then. They felt that a crazy person was living there. I was composing at home, and here I was already working in this studio. There was no multichannel old thing here—American ALPEX, by the way—it's a veteran of '70s. I started composing, quietly, in secret. Because in the studio I was working as an engineer, and only sound producers can compose, and the law requires that you have a musical education, and I, naturally, didn't have any musical education. I educated myself, learned the notes, but I needed an official document. Yet I stubbornly refused to get this document.

I repudiated the system then. I didn't want to play any games with it—like, I was on my own, making my own underground subculture. I had some people, acquaintances, followers. We had a circle. We wrote poems, prose. We had also this kind of pastime. We would gather at the country house of one of the friends and arrange compositions for many hours. He had a lot of instruments—drums, saxophones, piano, guitars, harps—whatever you wanted. He was a rich artist, the son of the artist Moiseenko. Have you heard about him, Moiseenko? He was well-known here. And we would come in at about six in the evening—there were four of us—and one would pronounce any word. "I see a Chinese boy walking." And the composition would begin. A kind of monologue and everybody playing on different instruments—somebody would play drums, somebody saxophones—then all would play together. And there was a development, some kind of a plot. And we formed this imaginary radio program *Radiosuyety*—we had these broadcasts, and all this took place in the village of Suyety (a Finnish village), and we composed about forty such broadcasts. Then we would listen to these broadcasts. Sometimes I listen to what we were up to. Such gibberish. But having listened to these broadcasts I realized that it was not just rock that I liked, but some kind of avant-garde, spontaneous music.

This is pretty much the way I recorded much music. Sometimes with any people—like this, we would sit and wait, and one of us, Mishka K., would run around the city, come up to a bunch of people and ask, "Hey, guys, anybody want to play?" Somebody would say, "I want to." "Well, come on." They would come to this house, instruments were all around. He picks up one, and we begin the composition. And so we recorded about six hours like this. It came out to be quite interesting music. I think it has passed its time, though. I have a cycle called *Night Jazz*. We recorded it a year before this trio Kornelin, Chekasin, Tarasov. When their disk was released it was like they had copied the music we had already played. They literally copied us—what we played, they did. And probably many people in the world played like this. We did it somehow independently. In short, I've toyed with the vanguard long enough, recorded my crazy electronic compositions—by myself this time, with superimposing. . . .

Around '80, I got seriously into yoga, and for five long years I buried myself in yoga. It was a very good period for me, I learned something, but [it was] also quite scary because I was fasting and weighed thirty kilograms less than now. I was so thin, I ate only raw products which were real difficult to get here. I spent all my time struggling to live. When I was walking I was counting every step because it was very difficult to walk. But at these moments I was composing much religious music. At that time nobody performed religious music. About five years later a group called Trumpet Call (Trubnyi Zov) appeared. But it was a kind of pop (*estradnaia*) religious music.[8] And I had this rock which was in the best rock tradition, but I was singing of the love for Christ, about an awareness of different truths. It sounded like an exploding bomb. Nobody had ever pronounced the word "Christ" seriously in any song. There was nothing like this.

And in 1980 I started to sing such things. They dragged me immediately to the KGB. They started to try to find out what kind of person I was. I came dressed in a military uniform, with a long beard and hair. And they see this "weirdo" (*stremnyi chelovek*) person and say, "We have information that you are a fascist." And they are just testing me. They haven't got any information. They just heard that I was a strange person. But they decided to start with this "I'm a fascist" crap. Maybe they thought I would immediately fall to my knees and cry, "Forgive me, I won't do it any-more!" I say, "No, somebody's deceived you, I'm not a fascist at all. On the contrary, I'm singing about the love of the people for each other. Down with war, I'm for pacifism." And pacifism here was also prosecuted. In short, they were dragging me in for quite a while. They ended up asking me for a recording. They said they had some recordings of very bad quality and that I must have some good ones. And all the time they tried to break me: Where was I recording, in the studio or at home? I was recording in the studio, but said, of course, that I was doing it at home. Otherwise they would have stuck me with some article for using state property illegally. And they'd throw me in jail. In short, they asked for a recording, and they have specialists who analyze what, where, and how it is made. Well, I made a tape for them. I recorded it about thirty times from the tape recorder to worsen the quality, to raise the level of distortion, all this kind of stuff. I also erased certain parts and superimposed some Indian music on it. A horrible mixture of the Indian music with mine, recorded thirty times. And I brought it to them. And after that it was like I was cut off. Didn't hear from them for about a year.

In short, I somehow got carried away by this role of a prophet and messiah. And I had three or four disks—the Scripture of Matthew. I was literally following in the footsteps of Jesus Christ Superstar, but it was my own, completely Russian under-standing of Christ. I started composing this, but somewhere in the middle I lost interest. I recorded half a disk but felt that I was starting to lose something, like this religious intoxication was pass-ing. I just started relating to things normally again. I think nothing should be done in the heat of passion—even belief in God. It should be more calm, so that it then comes out in a more true light.

Gradually I started returning to more traditional rock. It hap-pened somehow that after all those sweet hymns I felt like com-posing something "metallic." Then I recorded a disk, *Auto-da-fé*, which I myself like very much, a heavy, bulky thing. I like this kind of thing. And after this they again remembered me. They dragged me in again to the KGB. This time they were pestering me about yoga. Not about music, but about yoga! It was forbidden here as well. Just at this time they were putting all Hare Krishnas, Hindus, Muslims in jail. For some reason mostly Hare Krishnas (*krishnaity*). And I used to record Hare Krishnas. I even have recordings of myself singing "Hare Krishna" with them. In short, they again tried to do something . . . "We'll exile you!" they would shout, stamping their feet. "There is no Krishna, have you gone nuts? Are you a Soviet person or non-Soviet person? Here's comrade colonel—he exists, but there's no such thing as Krishna." Eventually, I maliciously told them to go to hell, and it worked, but they kept pulling my wife in, driving her to hysterics. They would stamp and shout, "You'd be better off marrying our lieutenant. Drop this idiot!" Such craziness.

But gradually I was returning to the traditional music, and before this the official press didn't pay attention to me. Because I was considered a freak (*urod*) and one newspaper—I still have it, *Leningradskaia Pravda*, about 1981—published an article which said something like this: "The youth who have reached the last stage of degeneration are listening to R., who sings suspicious songs, and to the religious maniac [Yuri]." I still have this little article. They lumped me together with R. who is real famous now. A real folk hero. Then the events progressed like this: a radio correspondent found me. She was considered the most erudite in rock music here, and suddenly somebody told her that there is this certain [Yuri], he is the father of rock music. For some reason they call me the father or grandfather of rock music, though in fact I am neither. In short, they told her there is such a "papa" who has two suitcases of recordings which no one knows about. He's fine (*krutoi*). She got in touch with me, listened to half of my recordings, recorded a lot, made some broadcasts. It was the beginning of glasnost then, 1985 or something. She pulled this off quite well— some letters came, asking if it was really true that we were hearing Yuri on the radio.

There were a lot of fans. They didn't know each other. . . . It was all in underground. Then there came a wave, there were delegations coming from Moscow, inviting me to give concerts. And I was heavily into yoga, sitting in the lotus position every day. It was difficult to combine concerts with yoga. I began hesitating— whether I should do yoga or concerts, only the devil knew. Then this club business started. The Rock Club came into existence, but they had strange things going on there. In the beginning, in the first years, they wanted to pull me into the Rock Club. I was actually a well-known person among our *tusovka*, and they needed some name, because there were no such names in the club at the beginning. There was no Kino, no Alisa, no Akvarium at that time. They existed, but they were not known—there were no decent recordings, nothing of the kind. And they needed me for prestige. Gena Z. organized the Rock Club. He came to me—he is a known hippie (*hippak*), a real *tusovshchik*—and said, "Join the Rock Club!" I say, "No." He says, "Why?" And I, after having suffered for so long with this communism, with all this communal creativity, with groups, communal flats, communism, I decided that there is one perfect way out—to show to the Russian musicians that one can play in a noncommunal manner, one can be an individual, a personality. Here they don't respect personalities very much. Everybody, since the times of communal flats, is accustomed to do everything together, in a crowd. And in music mainly—for example, Boris Grebenshchikov writes that the music contains lyrics by Boris Grebenshchikov, though in fact it was composed by the whole group. One would compose a line, the other a phrase, and I decided not to take this way but do everything myself, every part. On all my albums, I myself play all the instruments: drums, basses, keyboards, pipes, accordion, everything. And I, in my deep individualism, reached the point where I realized that I'm an individualist with a certain force and that there can be nothing more than that. I'm just the only one in the world. This idea warmed me up somehow and sustained me. People would always ask me, "Why aren't you in this *tusovka*? Why you are not in this informal society? Why not in that one?" And I would say, "Why should I be in some union, in some *tusovka*? Why can't you just be by yourself, just a person in this country?" They would say, "You can't. One has to belong somewhere."

And for these thoughts I was fighting with the Rock Club, arguing that there is no need for any organizations, especially for rockers. Rock in and of itself emerged as an alternative to the whole Soviet way of life. I was so fed up with this, that I just wanted to spit in the face of all of it. Rock emerges, and right away they start gathering everyone into bunches, making their own organizations, their own parties, their workers, their ministers. In short, I replied, "Not for anything." So Gena Z. tells me, "If you don't want to join the Rock Club, we'll destroy your recordings. Whenever we come across your recordings, we'll burn them." Such methods! I say, "Well, burn away. The people will judge us." He says, "Well you just wait!" He actually burned one tape in public, but only one. Maybe it wasn't even mine. Because I had very high-quality recordings and he would send them around. . . .

So, I was fighting with the Rock Club. Then I submerged myself in yoga, and in the meantime the Rock Club flourished. There were even such events—the concerts. Every concert was an event. And I was sitting there in solitude. This solitude lasted until 1987 when DDT[10] appeared [and] Akvarium became famous. By the way, as far as I remember the course of events, they became famous through America. Because this disk was released—*Red Wave*.[11] Before that they were known but weren't especially famous. And only when the disk *Red Wave* was released, here they decided—the local press, the authorities—to break up all the groups that were on that disk. They [the Rock Club] said it was not America, it was us who discovered them. America only did it later. And right after the *Red Wave* they ran to us, "We need to have Akvarium recorded, we need to have Kino recorded. We need this." I said, "You didn't need them for ten years, and now suddenly you need them." "Well, they've released this disk in America, we have to do this so that nobody will pay attention to the American one."

Voice: It was to the studio that they came.[12]

Yuri: Yes, they came to the studio and to the radio. I was hanging out at the radio already. Well, the fact that they were issued in America played a big role, and straight away all the four groups got real big, right off the bat. Well, I was continuing my individualistic activities until by chance I got pulled into some film. The film director had a good idea—to portray the musicians as themselves. There are meetings, conversations, going on in some ruins. Suddenly somebody would emerge from behind a wrecked door, another one would take a bath in ruins for some reason. Craziness, on the whole. And all of them are meeting, talking, then everybody is singing a song at the fire, or something. Such a dubious film. But that's not the point. The film director made me play there, and I did. DDT also were in this film, and we made friends. Though I had met Shevchuk [the lead singer of DDT] before, four years earlier. He had problems with his voice. He lost his voice. DDT was idle. DDT are very good musicians, they are not virtuosos, but they have a good drive (*draiv*). In concert they warm up to the audience almost like Rolling Stones. They play very powerfully. I liked this, and I suggested—or I was not the first to suggest, it doesn't matter—an idea occurred to us that while Shevchuk was resting with his voice for half a year, I would be playing my repertoire instead of him. They accompanied me, and we went on tour to the Far East. And I all of a sudden—I was sitting for ten years—now I started to tour throughout the whole country. Things turned out not so bad with us. And then

Shevchuk's voice returned, everything was O.K. DDT became a very well-known group, and I decided I was not going to be like a second soloist in such a second-rate group.

Well, I stepped aside, and since 1988 I started to perform in a duet with a guitar player. There's a poster over there. We started playing acoustic music, two guitars, a mouth organ. We were touring and playing for a while. I felt it was kind of boring. There is a lot of folk in my music. I should say, though, that we don't have any folk group or even any good, decent folk musicians in this country. I mean there are all kinds of music, vanguard and whatever, but no folk musicians. I tried to fill this gap, but one person cannot do it. Though I've written a lot of songs in a Russian style, not just "cranberries" (*kliukvy*), they seemed to me to be good songs.[13] And then I got bored again. I think, in the acoustic concerts it happens this way: if an audience comes, the concerts are very good. But if some unintelligent audience comes, it usually looks like this: you're playing, and they're shouting, "When will you take out the drums?" They don't understand that one can play the guitar only. We have two guitars. There are bards playing here. They play like this: one comes out and is strumming the guitar and singing. But if people are playing something, some instrumental stuff, they don't understand it. I remember in Volkhov: "Yuri! Shame on you! Where are the drums?" What a crowd! In short, I tormented myself over this and decided to play my electronic variations again. In the last year and a half I put together a new group consisting of young guys. Now, we're scattered in summer, so we aren't playing. One is composing music for a movie, another is playing in another group, and I'm here resting, waiting for better times.

Here is my life history in short. My musical life. There were a lot of nonmusical events, but I've given you the essence of everything. But I think that I proved my idea somehow. That a person here can be not in a group, not on the stage, but just an individual musician. Because there are many musicians who are composing at home by themselves. And they have a difficult situation—how to sell what they produce. There should be a market for it. Now cooperatives appeared, and there are groups which don't exist otherwise. Oblachnyi Krai, a known Arkhangelsk group, has existed for ten years only in recordings. They have never performed anywhere. They gave one concert here, but a weak one, because they are a nonconcert group.

But that's a group, and there are people who are individualists, because in our malicious communist state we need an idea of deep individualism. Because only through individualism can a true commune exist, a commune where the people don't gather into a herd, but are thinking individuals. And I, for example, in my yoga days, when I was into yoga—we had a team and went into the mountains for half a year. We lived for half a year in the mountains, in the tents. We were meditating, in the morning in the sun, in the evening by the fire, in a circle. And there were the guys there—all individualists who gathered. And we were living very nicely and peacefully for the whole half a year. I mean, with any other people it couldn't possibly have worked. And everybody did his own business. Some were writers, others were musicians, still others were religious philosophers. We had our teacher, though he died under mysterious circumstances—his body was found later in the forest.

I think the thing that musicians [in this country] really lack is individuality. . . . Our stars, for the most part—even the most famous stars—I'm saying this without any critique, I just noticed—Grebenshchikov gives an interview—he doesn't have much to say—he says some paradox, and people start thinking about what he meant. But in principle he has nothing to say. Well, he has something—of course, he's the best from all of this *tusovka*—but nevertheless it's a little on the difficult side. I used to communicate with him a lot before, so I know what kind of person he is. On the contrary, Western musicians have something to say. The way I see it in history, this is why many groups break up: because each of them has enough individuality of his own from the very beginning. Take, for instance, Phil Collins from Genesis, or the Beatles—this is the most vivid example, all of them except Ringo Starr turned out to be very successful. And even Ringo Starr struggled so hard that he actually came out O.K.

Sometimes when I recall that I had a real chance to be the first—not Grebenshchikov, but me, because I had everything—I think with satisfaction, "It's good that I didn't do that." For some reason I have a feeling that there is something better in store for me than simply to be in Grebenshchikov's place. And I'm quite happy about it, without any false modesty. I'm quite content with the role of one who is known only to music fans, to those who—they're rare in this country—love folk music, ballads. Actually, my folk music and ballads are of a pro-Western orientation. Of English culture, I would say. Here they appreciate more the sort of music of Zhanna Bichevskaia—Gypsy-romance music. All our folk music is Gypsy-romance. All these Gypsy harmonies—no, I like the real Gypsies very much, but all these city romances, Bichevskaia and so forth, I consider a kind of profanation.

I think that real rock music is possible only through the use of individual and national musical signs (*priznaki*). Rhythms. Harmony is of no big importance. You know, somehow—Berendiukov tried to do it in his time—with Kapura they began the folk Belorussian songs, and then he tried to prove that the structure and everything in there is a rock-n-roll one. And I once bought a disk of African folk music, of some tribe, listened to it. My goodness, there was pure unadulterated rock, Chubby Checker and everything. African folk music and Chubby Checker—these are the prototypes of English rock-n-roll culture. All musical folk cultures turn out to be similar. And there is a certain mix in rock-n-roll. But where the elite rock-n-roll things begin, or metal, pseudo-metal—Avgust in this country—they have nothing to do with rock. Their success is in the lights, in the show. If you had to listen to the recordings only, who the hell would need them?

T. C.: Where are you going in music now?

Yuri: Now I have a project going. I've embarked on some quite difficult musical projects. I'm afraid they might not get anywhere because our director may be replaced, and he had given me a green light. I wanted to make a disk, unite several of my ballads, the best, lyric ones, and to do it with the real symphony orchestra. The director told me that he would pay for the orchestra, and I've thought all the details of the arrangement over. All of the ballads will be connected by one thread, like one continuous symphonic score, two sides of the record, but everything will be done with a vivid folk-ballad structure. Folk, acoustic guitars, at the same time will accompany lightly and unobtrusively, while a large symphony orchestra is playing. It would be good if I could get the London Symphony. But the Soviet one will do also. This is my project.

The reason I want to come back to this? I have many rock disks. I did many disks in this style. I don't think this theme is going anywhere. It's already been explored well. I'm ready to be finished with rock. But ballads—why in America there are so many wonderful singers—folk, country. We have none, absolutely none. Just emptiness. . . .

Permutations

As one reads Yuri's story, one gets the distinct impression that he has
experienced the many twists and turns of life which one might expect in
the life story of a comparable Western musician of roughly the same age
as Yuri. The "opting" out of society, the retreats to communal living in
the forest, the spontaneous jam sessions all seem as if they could have
occurred in the forests of northern California during the late 1960s. His
move toward the mysticism of yoga and Christianity later in life suggests the careers of other notables in the world of Western music.
Indeed, there are many homologies between Yuri's life and the lives of
Western rock musicians. Yet these homologies raise a paradox: How is
it that the course of Yuri's life, his tastes in music and the permutations
of his life and interests can so closely resemble those of a Western rock
musician if the Soviet Union was a "closed" society? Indeed, Yuri's
very life history seems to clash with the conventional image of the
Soviet Union as a closed society. If it were a closed society, Yuri, at least
as he exists in his story, could not exist. His story tells us much about
the early history of rock in Russia, of its traveling to the Soviet Union, of
the formation of taste cultures. We shall return later to the many themes
and issues raised in his story. For now, however, his story allows us to
begin our exploration of the formation of rock musical counterculture in
Russia in general and in St. Petersburg in particular.

Symbolic Creativity in the Closed Society

One of the great myths prevalent in Western discourse about the Soviet
Union throughout its history was that Soviet society was a "closed"
society. Indeed, the dichotomy between open and closed society is of little analytical value for the analysis of Russian culture in the Soviet
period, since it obscures the sociological view of the dialectic of agency
and structure which exists across time and space. Surely, some societies are more open or closed relative to others, if we define open and
closed as the degree to which the free flow of cultural communication is
tolerated or unimpeded by structures of authority. Yet it is imperative to
stress that there are processes in supposedly open societies which make
them less open (or perhaps more closed) than Western rhetoric would
have us believe. Illiteracy (enforced by a social stratification system
supported in many cases by the rule of law), secret police activities,
market processes, and the normal processes of status relations in which
lower-status parties are fearful of communicating openly with status
superiors all have impeded free and open communication to varying

degrees at various points in the history of Western capitalist societies. Conversely, there were many communicative forces at work in the Soviet environment which made that society much less closed than it appeared in Western rhetoric and propaganda about the Soviet Union. The point is not to dwell on this debate—ultimately the debate hinges on quite unresolvable semantic issues about the precise meaning of the terms *open* and *closed*. Nor is the point to claim that the Soviet Union was more open than the United States. Rather, it is to crystallize the important idea that actors—even under the most repressive and oppressive structural circumstances—find ways to use culture products to evade structural impediments which stand in the way of cultural communication.

Paul Willis (1990) has referred to this process of the active use of culture by actors to make meaning in existence as "symbolic creativity." Indeed, there were many processes of both intercultural communication between the Soviet Union and the West and intracultural communication within the Soviet Union which were responsible for the flow of cultural information across national boundaries and throughout the country itself. In fact, it was precisely these mechanisms of communication that were responsible for the unique, specific cultural outcomes in Russia and the growth of underground urban communities in cities such as St. Petersburg.

One could push this idea even further and argue that the structural rigidity of the Soviet system actually facilitated creative and novel forms of cultural production and communication in the Soviet context. The lack of what Jürgen Habermas (1991) refers to as a "public sphere" of freely circulating cultural information served to push many people toward the development of private spheres of cultural communication. It was through these private spheres that, ironically, many Russians ended up being quite well-informed. What was lacking in formal opportunities for cultural communication was made up for by the evolution of informal networks of communication. The existence of distinct, alternative, informal patterns of communication in the Soviet Union forces us to rethink the forms and processes of cultural creativity and communication within this social space.

An anecdote from Russian cultural history which is quite unrelated to musical life (but actually offered by a musician) illustrates the paradoxical cultural outcomes which emerged from informal channels of communication. For many years, the study of Freud and the application of Freudian interpretations to social and cultural phenomena were severely circumscribed in the Soviet Union. Freud's voluntaristic positivism and his individualistic theory of the unconscious grated at the very core of Marxist epistemology and ontology, which stressed determinism and collectivism. His works were generally unavailable through official channels of cultural distribution, and their use was rigidly circumscribed, even for scholarly work. In spite of the dearth of Freud's writings, however, it was not uncommon to find communities of students and professors at Soviet universities who were quite conversant and knowledgeable about Freud's work.

Why was this the case? The answer is as interesting as it is relevant to the process of musical communication, which is of primary interest here. Knowledgeability about Freud—in some cases a quite proficient knowledgeability—was a result of patterns of informal communication which arose among networks of Soviet actors. Such patterns of informal communication were quite varied. Lacking open access to the broad range of Freud's works, one method of gaining knowledge involved the "mining" of critical works on Freud for concrete and substantive information about Freud. A typical scenario would be as follows: one interested in Freud would report to the library desk, where access to his works was controlled, and ask for particular articles by Soviet or Western researchers which were critical of Freud. Ostensibly, the use of such articles would be to make one's own contribution to, say, a "politically correct" Marxist criticism of Freud. Upon receiving the articles, the industrious scholar would then extract key quotations from articles and books. Such quotations would then be compiled into primers on Freudian theory, which could then be circulated among one's friends and colleagues in *samizdat*, or "underground" form.[14]

The result of symbolic creativity was, paradoxically, the formation of groups and networks of individuals who were quite knowledgeable about Freud in spite of the fact that public access to Freud was strictly circumscribed by official structures of authority.[15] The paradox can be stated in terms of a basic sociological proposition: the more limited the sources of cultural information in a society and the greater the structural barriers to access to such information, the more actors will seek to acquire and share cultural information informally. This proposition helps us to understand the creative and often ingenious appropriation of Western culture during even some of the most repressive periods of Soviet history. For instance, during the *Zhdanovshchina* (the period of cultural repression organized by Stalin's minister of culture, Andrei Zhdanov, after World War II to "protect" Soviet culture from the "pernicious" influence of the West), subcultures based on Western cultural practices emerged in Soviet society, especially in urban environments. As S. Frederick Starr (1983) has shown, Western jazz music was instrumental in the formation of well-developed urban jazz subcultures in Russia. Fans of Western jazz, often referred to as *stiliagi*, or "style hunters," combined Western styles of dress such as zoot suits, the "beat" jargon of Western jazz culture, and a voracious desire for the acquisition of jazz to form a vibrant urban musical subculture within a complex infrastructure of cultural repression. Such capacity for symbolic creativity was the most important process in the emergence of rock musical subculture in Russia.

The Command Control of Culture and the Formation of a Rock Music "Taste Culture" in Soviet Society

Historically, the raw stuff from which countercultural communities were created in cities like St. Petersburg came directly from the West and found its way into Russia through a number of mechanisms. At the end of the 1950s, during the so-called Thaw initiated by Khrushchev, the repression of the *Zhdanovshchina* gave way to a new policy of tolerance and openness to the culture of the West. In 1958, the Soviet Union hosted the VI Annual International Youth Festival. In addition, the Soviet Union participated in new and unprecedented student exchanges with the United States and relaxed restrictions on foreign travel to the Soviet Union. Young tourists, students, and participants in international events came to the Soviet Union bearing not only good will and a curiosity about the Soviet Union, but also the musical products of the West. Western radio broadcasts, while frequently jammed by state authorities, carried Western music into Soviet society. This was especially the case in Petersburg, which was close to European sources of radio information.

Gradually, throughout the 1960s, what might be called a rock music "taste culture" emerged in Russia. This taste culture was consumed and spread informally within "taste publics." Sociologist Herbert Gans makes a distinction between taste cultures and taste publics. A taste culture, in the broadest sense, "consists of values [and] the cultural forms which express these values" (Gans 1974, p. 10). Following Gans, a rock music taste culture is simply a cultural system consisting of shared values and meanings which are reflected in musical culture and communicated through a variety of media of both interpersonal and mass communication. A taste public, on the other hand, is part of a taste culture and consists of the consumers and users of the products of a particular taste culture. The emergent rock music taste public in Russia consisted of those individuals who developed a taste for Western rock music and expressed this taste through their consumption of the products and the adoption of the values that were circulating within the greater rock musical taste culture. Normally, in the West, taste cultures and their publics are formed by the circulation of culture products through formal systems of mass media. The interesting question is this: How did rock music become so widespread in a context characterized by extreme conservatism in culture and, most important, by the lack of any formalized mechanism for its production and distribution? The answer lies in an examination of the informal processes of communication which evolved in the Soviet context.

What is truly remarkable and historically unique is that such a taste culture was formed from such limited information and in such a short time. Indeed, rock music had diffused all over the Soviet Union not long after it had made its appearance in the late 1950s in the United States. The history of conservative Soviet cultural criticism of rock music is rife with metaphors of rock music as a bacterium or a virus which grows uncontrollably within a host culture (see Ryback 1990; and Stites 1992). From a sociological standpoint, such criticism is completely apt to describe the origin of a taste public for Western rock music within the Soviet Union. For this taste public emerged from a pool of cultural information so small that it was quite literally carried into the country in the pockets and suitcases of a small number of Western visitors to the Soviet Union. Like a virus, rock music grew into a nationwide taste culture consisting of both producers and consumers of rock musical culture.

In the context of the Soviet system, a rock music taste public could only exist in an informal or underground form. There are two reasons for this, both of which are related. The first is that the Soviet Union, increasingly after 1930, was characterized by a strong ethos of cultural homogeneity. A central aspiration of the Soviet state was to construct identities and personalities that would serve as the bulwark for the construction of socialist society. From the point of view of Soviet ideology, the development of socialism necessitated the development of a "socialist consciousness" and a socialist identity. In the task of constructing what is often called "the New Soviet Man," a great emphasis was placed on the development not only of Soviet values and morals, but also of "appropriate" aesthetic cultural tastes and values in the Soviet individual (see Marcuse 1958, pp. 231-43). There was only one musical taste culture that was legally and formally possible in the Soviet Union, and the aesthetic values within that taste culture were those values which were deemed to be important by the state.[16]

This value orientation was ratified and supported by the fact that the Soviet Union was characterized by a system of state "command control" of production and distribution. Since culture is a product, this command control extended to the organization of cultural production as well. The organization of culture in the Soviet Union is based on Joseph Stalin's dictum for production in general: "Demand must always exceed supply" (in Zassoursky 1991, p. 14). As Zassoursky (ibid.) notes, the idea of the commercialization of culture to meet the desires and demands of Soviet citizens was never used as a logic in the production of culture; indeed, the very idea of commercialization was one which had decidedly negative connotations. It is not possible to speak of culture industries in the Soviet Union, but of *a* culture industry that was controlled by the state and the cultural logic of socialism rather than by the logic of the marketplace. In the realm of musical culture, production was centralized in an organization called Melodiya. Melodiya represented in institutional form the state's monopoly over cultural production and, thus, produced and distributed only those products which reflected the values of the official taste culture. Since the state held a monopoly over the formal technological means of cultural production and distribution, it alone decided which elements of culture to produce and distribute in Soviet society. The result of this ethos of cultural homogeneity and an institutional infrastructure designed to promulgate it was that the possibilities for the emergence of independent taste cultures and taste publics in the Soviet Union were severely impeded.

In contrast to the logic of the Western cultural marketplace, the guiding principle behind Soviet cultural production was whether or not culture products were ideologically correct. In order for recordings to be recorded and distributed through official channels, they had to pass a litmus test to determine their degree of resonance with the values of the official taste culture. In such tests, rock music was generally doomed to fail since there was such a close relationship between the ideology of the state and the ethos of classicism in culture. One cannot underscore enough the alliance of specific cultural tastes with specific structures of power in Soviet society. Classical music—and more specifically classical music not "polluted" by Western influence—was "politically correct," while rock music was seen as a form of noise or dissonance (Attali 1985) that grated at the very core of the Soviet cultural cosmology.

The result of the ideological control of the major channels of the production and distribution of musical culture was that culture products which had little public demand ended up on store shelves. Indeed, one favorite issue of Melodiya was recordings of speeches by political leaders, especially Leonid Brezhnev. In Petersburg folklore, Brezhnev's whole persona was the butt of a huge number of jokes. Moreover, his difficult speech patterns and his inability to even pronounce the name of the Soviet Union clearly made the marketing of his speeches all the more humorous. One joke told by a musician in Petersburg sums up the Russian orientation to the ideologically laden cultural products of the Soviet culture industries:

> A *muzhik*[17] walks into Melodiya and says that he is looking for a record album which contains a lot of applause. The clerk suggests that the *muzhik* might be interested in a new release which features the greatest speeches of Leonid Brezhnev. The *muzhik* frowns and says he isn't interested in politics. The clerk, eager for the sale, suggests that the *muzhik* can play the recording at 78 rpm through the speeches and slow it down to 33 rpm when it gets to the applause.

In relation to rock music in the capitalist world, what is unique about rock music in the Soviet period is that the most popular forms of rock were not produced by those who controlled the means of cultural production. According to one prominent music historian and producer in Petersburg, until 1986, Melodiya, with the exception of one of its small Baltic affiliates, totally ignored what he refers to as "home rock" (*otechestvennyi rok* (Troitsky 1990c, p. 289).

The formal infrastructure for the production and distribution of officially sanctioned taste culture had a great deal to do with the formation of "informal" taste publics. The formation of a rock taste public in the Soviet Union was an informal process. By informal, I mean that its production and distribution occurred primarily outside of official structures and channels of information and as a reaction to the products produced and circulated by the latter. Initially, because rock music was a cultural import, every rock musician in the Soviet environment was more or less part of a rock music taste public. That is to say, before they became producers of rock music, they were consumers. Acts of consumption, however, gave birth to acts of production. Russian rock musicians were born, and in the process, so too was a rock music taste culture. Yet this was a taste culture which operated almost purely at an informal level outside of the state-owned infrastructure which protected the state-sanctioned taste culture. We now turn to an examination of how such a widespread taste culture arose in such an environment.

Networking Culture

Cultural information from the West was passed along through social networks of friends and acquaintances via two processes, one which

covered the productive aspects of culture and the other, the performative. One of the central processes of the production and the reproduction of music which evolved throughout the 1960s was known as *magnitizdat*. Like *samizdat*, or self-published literary works, *magnitizdat* was
an informal process for the production and distribution of rock music.[18]

As Gerald Smith (1984, p. 95) notes, the reproduction of music in
the Soviet context was somewhat privileged, since the technologies of
musical reproduction were much more widespread than those of other
forms of culture. Television and radio programs and films, for instance,
depended on access to complex technologies which were monopolized
by the state. The mass distribution of literature was dependent on print-
ing equipment and photocopiers, which were either unavailable or illegal to own. In contrast, as Smith (ibid.) notes, there were over a million
tape recorders in private hands in the Soviet Union by the end of the
1960s.[19] Still, supplies of tape were the biggest problem, since tape was
not produced or distributed in great quantities.

Magnitizdat was a rather creative solution to the problem of technological insufficiency in the Soviet Union. Indeed, an entire informal
culture emerged which was the product of existing technologies and
Western culture products that happened to end up in Russia. Such culture is referred to by musicians as *magnitofonnaia kul'tura*, or, literally,
"tape-recorder culture." Specific recordings, primarily of Western rock
music, were referred to as *magnitofonnye albomy*, or "tape-recorder
albums." Tape-recorder culture was the most important process upon
which the development of a rock musical taste culture in Russia
depended. Tapes were distributed through two distinct channels: the
black market and large, informal networks of friends and relations.
Black market prices for quality tapes or LPs from the West were often
quite high: one musician recalled spending forty rubles for a recording, which was at that time about one-quarter of the average Soviet
worker's monthly pay (about twenty-four dollars). Such recordings
were then spread among networks of friends. This informal spread of
cassette culture was enhanced by the overlapping of networks. Such
overlapping ensured that musical products were spread not just
throughout the city, but throughout the country as well. Music could be
acquired by a friend of a friend of a friend, and so forth, with the cumu-
lative effect that Western musical products achieved quite widespread
circulation throughout the Soviet Union. The quality of such home-
made tape recordings was decidedly inferior to mass-produced tapes
from the West. This problem was exacerbated by the poor quality of
tape decks and the poor quality of recordings which were literally
recordings of recordings of recordings, and so on, *ad infinitum*.

Because of the insular nature of Soviet society, most Petersburg rock musicians came to know rock music through their acquisition of recordings from tape-recorder culture. Said one musician: "Almost from the beginning, our rock culture was formed by the exchange of information among ourselves. Even in large cities like Leningrad and Moscow, we passed along information almost as soon as we got it so that we all knew very fast when something new came on the scene." Another musician noted that he had difficulty explaining the process to state authorities. While he is currently one of the most famous rock musicians in Russia, his fame was spawned through the simple act of giving one of his cassettes to a friend: "I gave a cassette to a friend, and pretty soon it can be found all over the country. And this they just can't understand." Indeed, the rapidity of word-of-mouth communication was remarkable given the large size of the city (over five million people). Interestingly enough, this pattern of communication, as perhaps the central type of communication, indicates the persistence of village culture within the context of a more technological infrastructure of mass communication characteristic of industrial modernity. Indeed, word-of-mouth communication remains an important type of informal communication even in the present day.

Cultural Fixation

While tape-recorder culture served as an important basis for the dissemination of rock culture throughout the Soviet Union, there was a more important aspect of the distribution of music through such informal processes. Specifically, the variety of culture products was both smaller and more unpredictable than in the West. The process of cultural diffusion is essentially unpredictable; it is impossible either to estimate what specific products of a parent culture will successfully diffuse and take root in a host culture, or to surmise how much of any given form of culture will spread within a host culture.[20] In considering the evolution of the Petersburg musical community, it is important to underscore the point that it is a culture which is based only on those elements of Western rock culture which managed to reach specific actors in Petersburg through the basically unpredictable process of cultural diffusion. While a great deal of cultural information from the West reached Petersburg—and indeed, it is astounding just how much did over the years—the entire range of musical products and information available in the West did not reach the city. Indeed, even though Petersburg was a major cultural center populated by some of the most creative artists in the country, the range of cultural information was rather truncated.

What this means is that the entire rock culture of the city was spun out of only a few threads of Western culture.

William James once made a distinction between two types of knowledge: "knowledge of" phenomena and "knowledge about" phenomena (in Park 1967). Knowledge *about* something is similar to the sense conveyed by the term acquaintance while knowledge *of* something is knowledge which is more comprehensive or in-depth. Petersburg musicians displayed "knowledge about" rather than "knowledge of" rock music. The process of cultural diffusion is fundamentally a process which has quite unpredictable ends. That is, we cannot know what the outcomes of the process of culture diffusion will be because such outcomes are highly contingent. In Russia, such outcomes were the product of unpredictable and random forces such as individual personalities, chance meetings and encounters in urban settings, whether or not the broadcasting that conveyed information from Helsinki to St. Petersburg was or was not jammed, and a host of other factors.

Throughout its evolution, the Petersburg rock music community followed the tracks laid by the initial configuration of Western culture present in the city as a result of the process of cultural diffusion. An example serves to clarify this process. In almost all interviews with leading musicians, the British band T. Rex was identified as a most important influence on their musical development. T. Rex (short, of course, for the dinosaur *Tyrannosaurus rex*) was a rock group led by British singer Marc Bolan. The band developed a style of rock which has come to be known as "glam and glitter rock," a form characterized by outrageous and shocking stage acts. Bolan's performances attracted considerable attention in Britain and in the United States and led to a considerable amount of popularity for the band. In the early 1970s, the band enjoyed a string of nine successive top-ten hits in Britain after which they experienced a precipitous decline—at least in the West. By 1977, Bolan was dead, and the group ceased to exist. Yet in Russia, long after the reputation of the group had waned and, indeed, long after Bolan was dead, T. Rex was still a major influence on the lives and music of Petersburg rock musicians. This musician, who was important for a time in the West, was central to the formation of musical tastes in St. Petersburg; even twenty years later, leading Soviet musicians claimed T. Rex as a major influence on their work in the present. This is the case even with musicians who claimed to be part of the "New Wave" or who were highly imitative of the most recent Western developments in rock.

The pervasive and enduring influence of seemingly obscure, or at least prosaic, musical styles was an important aspect of the Petersburg musical community. We saw, for instance, in Yuri's life story (and, indeed, we will see in many subsequent stories), that other important influences were the Beatles, Led Zeppelin, Deep Purple and, interestingly enough, the rock opera *Jesus Christ Superstar*. The Beatles formed the basis of a cult which exists very powerfully in the city even now. *Jesus Christ Superstar* is regularly performed in major concert halls even today, and it is difficult to find a musician who does not know its lyrics and music by heart. I would like to refer to this process of the deep entrenchment of specific forms of Western rock and their subsequent use as "maps" or "guides" for ongoing cultural production as *cultural fixation*. By cultural fixation, I mean that specific cultural products—in this case the music of an important, but limited range of Western rock groups—were seized upon early on and became the central objects upon which subsequent rock practice was based.

There are two basic explanations for this cultural fixation, one related to material factors, the other to ideational ones. The first has to do with the difficulties that Petersburg musicians faced because of the nature of the command-control structure of cultural production and distribution in Soviet society. In Western culture markets, products are made available to the public through the market. Once marketed, they are available almost immediately for a variety of uses by individuals and groups. They are also available worldwide, but their diffusion to other countries and use by actors in such countries are fundamentally dependent on the level of development of formal and informal channels of communication. There were no formal channels for the distribution of rock music in Russia which were not under the control of state culture managers. Therefore, the universe of culture products was not only smaller than in the West, but musicians had to work harder to acquire musical information. Unlike their Western counterparts, who had the luxury of developing taste cultures from among a diverse selection of culture products, Petersburg musicians not only had to make music, but had to form and maintain their own channels of independent communication through which to circulate musical products. In some cases, musicians were obliged to make even their own instruments. Even so, Petersburg rock musicians, so disadvantaged in relation to their musical cousins in the West, were relatively better off than their counterparts in the periphery. St. Petersburg is perhaps the most European of Russian cities, or at least, is closest to European sources of information. Cities in the periphery were dependent on what culture they could get from urban centers, such as St. Petersburg and Moscow, and in this sense were receiving cultural information which was still further watered down by the process of cultural diffusion.

The second possible explanation for fixation on a limited range of musical products has to do with the Russian fascination with Western culture in general, and the meaning and function of rock music in the Russian context in particular. I suggested earlier that rock's appeal in the Soviet Union lay in its function as a means of enchantment within the context of socialist industrial society. We will explore this function of rock music in more detail in the next chapter. The original infusion of Western music represented a kind of culture shock which reverberated through Soviet time and space. Throughout musicians' life histories, we find constant references to the revelatory character of their first exposure to rock music. They speak of the effect of music on their lives reverentially. In a sea of cultural homogeneity and ordinary existence, Western rock music became sacred to them. Their attraction to these early forms of Western rock was simply too strong to abandon, especially since so much of their craft and their own identity as musicians was so integrally tied to their early imitation of what, for them, was a very special means of relating to the world.

What I would like to suggest is that the forms of rock music which emerged in Petersburg from the 1960s to the present were a result of *cultural permutations* of culture products which were fixated on by the community of rock musicians in the early history of the formation of a rock music taste culture in the city. By cultural permutation, I mean the general evolutionary process of the transformation or rearrangement of Western rock music within the city such that, over time, we can begin to speak of a cultural form called "Petersburg rock music," which is highly contextual and specific to that city.

Cultural permutation is an open, uncertain, and unpredictable process. As a concept, it allows us to view large-scale, macrolevel cultural phenomena, such as the musical tastes and styles of the Petersburg rock music community, as a consequence of small-scale, microlevel actions, such as a cassette brought into the country by a visiting university student in the early 1970s, a radio broadcast taped from a Western radio station, or the exchange of musical information on a city street. No one can possibly know the precise mechanism whereby the music of T. Rex became a major template for the subsequent evolution of rock culture in St. Petersburg. The processes of fragmentary cultural diffusion and the development of erratic networks of communication congealed to create a situation in which T. Rex and other prosaic figures from Western rock-and-roll became important, ongoing cultural influences in the Petersburg rock culture. What is more important, while Petersburg musicians remained fixated at one stage of rock's temporal development, Western rock musicians and fans had moved along to develop new patterns of production and consumption of rock music. One might say, to borrow a Malthusian metaphor, that Russian rock grew arithmetically, while Western rock grew geometrically.

The process of cultural fixation defines the very essence of musical creativity in the Russian context. What were the concrete outcomes of this cultural fixation? The most important consequence was that musical innovation was slower in St. Petersburg than in the West. Indeed, the dominant form of making music (even in the post-Soviet period, as I shall discuss in a later chapter) relied on taking Western rock forms and working and reworking such forms rather than adapting ongoing cultural work to emerging developments and innovations in Western rock culture. Because of the shortage of cultural information, there was seldom any other strategy of musical production available for Petersburg musicians. The major result of such fixation on Western culture products is that a distinct "cultural lag" emerged between Petersburg and Western rock music. Such a lag is understandable given the difficulties in cultural communication between Russia and the West. Yet the real significance of such a lag is that it indicates that musicians became accustomed to taking Western culture products and working with them incessantly rather than abandoning such products to seek out new ones. The very definition of rock in Petersburg evokes specific styles from earlier periods of rock's historical development. In this sense, rock music in Petersburg was a much less fluid and changeable idiom of cultural expression.

Having outlined the most basic communicative processes which were the basis of the formation of rock counterculture in Petersburg, we now turn to the analysis of life histories of other Petersburg musicians. The words of musicians themselves add substance to the preceding outline of the communicative foundation of the Petersburg musical community. Their words also illuminate other important dimensions of rock musicianship in the city.

Epiphanies: Paths to Rock Careers

What follows are additional life histories of musicians which illustrate different experiences with different facets of Soviet modernity and different paths to what I shall later refer to as the vocation of rock musicianship. In the elaboration of each story, I present musicians' own words about the events which led up to their decisions to become rock musicians. These decisions can be seen as distinct "epiphanies," moments when individuals decided to pursue alternative musical careers within Soviet society.[21] Each of these histories also illustrates more general processes which were central facets of both the Petersburg counterculture and the dominant society and culture in which it was intermeshed.

Viktor: A Thirty-Three-Year-Old Bass Player

Viktor is a bass player and songwriter for a well-known band in the city. It is a band which—like most bands in the city—has been through a number of permutations of name and style. In all of its forms, the band is known for its innovative use of Western styles. Viktor himself is considered the brain behind the group, and he proudly declares its style to be "New Wave" (*novaia volna*). He speaks crisply and clearly in erudite, high-style Russian. Many other musicians often refer to him as "the intellectual." He is decidedly engaged during his interview and seems excited that an American is in the city asking questions that allow him to elaborate his own life history in an intellectual mode which will be appreciated by a "professor from the States." In his own words, "Nobody ever asked me questions like this before."

> My history is rather long and typical of our circle. It's a typical story, when in childhood peoples' parents wanted them to become musicians and enrolled them in a classical music school. It's also my own history. Then I became gradually fascinated by rock music. . . . I began to study the piano at age six. I went to the music school. I studied at the music school, but when I was twelve I began to study the guitar. This was because—this was at the end of the '60s and the beginning of the '70s—for the first time I heard groups like the Beatles. This was about the only album we could buy. I didn't like them very much. Then a little later, I began to learn more about other groups, I met a little older crowd, and they introduced me to groups like the Rolling Stones and, of course, I preferred the Rolling Stones. I remember that right away we decided to form some kind of group in school, and we began to play. This is a typical history. When I was twelve and he was eight, my brother, who lived with me, also began to play the guitar with me. At home we listened to songs, selected some, and played them. We formed a kind of "ensemble" in school. And then I finished school and applied to the institute and now, by profession, I'm a hydrotechnical engineer. . . .
>
> Yeah, while I was a student I played not only in school, but in other groups as well. We had a kind of "college" of musical

groups. I played the keyboards. It was funny because I played on this little synthesizer which was of a very bad quality. A kind of electric organ. I wasn't really too thrilled about the guitar. I knew how to play the piano. I even finished musical school. When I entered the [technical] institute, I met a black student from Madagascar, and he played the guitar. For me he was simply a copy of Jimi Hendrix. I didn't know any guitarists who were better. He himself was from a peasant family, very poor, and he was simply a genius of a musician. He didn't know how to read music, he just played by ear. He could play any song you wanted. He could listen on the radio to a Bach classical fugue played on an organ or, let's say, on a trombone, and then the next day he could play the whole thing on a guitar from memory. We studied together in one group at the institute, in one faculty. And I came to him every day at home, and I thought that I ought to play the guitar exactly like him.

Then I applied to the musical institute. I was already in a technological institute. But I began a kind of parallel study at the musical institute. And at first I studied the classical piano, and then I simply gave it up—it was a special jazz school, and I played Oscar Peterson. But I didn't want to play that. I understood that I ultimately ought to play the guitar. I already played the guitar because at home I listened to and liked—my favorite group was Led Zeppelin then. Also, one of my favorite groups was T. Rex. The first album in my life, the first one I bought (I was thirteen) was T. Rex. It was my very favorite group.

T. C: You bought it here?

Viktor: Yeah, I bought it here on the black market for forty rubles which was real expensive then. I sold my motorcycle in order to do it.

T. C: And then you decided that this would be "your" music?

Viktor: Yeah. The first group that pushed me to the serious study of music was T. Rex. And then, by chance, I gave my friend a T. Rex record to listen to, and he gave me a Led Zeppelin album to listen to. And I thought: I've got to listen to Led Zeppelin. And for six years, I listened to Led Zeppelin and I played it. I listened to the tape recorder, recorded songs, and played everything on the guitar. And in school, they said: "Wow, such a great guitarist!" As a result of this, I left the fortepiano department and was accepted quickly into the second-level guitar course. And I studied the classical guitar further. I didn't really get anything out of the institute because there wasn't anyone there who I could work with, and I found other people from other institutes, and we organized experimental groups in which there were people with a little more spirit. They were "higher" in the heart and in the mind. And there I played the guitar. Then, after only one year of existence of our group one of the people started using drugs and completely lost interest in music. And we ditched him. It was the bass guitarist. And this meant that we needed someone to play the bass guitar. I thought: "Well, I'll play the bass guitar." But I didn't have a bass guitar, so I bought myself a contrabass. And the first concert I played the contrabass. For me it was interesting because this was an entirely different thing, something quite new. For a long time I played this contrabass. This was in the early '80s. Then my musical tastes changed a bit, and my favorite groups were the Specials and Selector. And my brother who played the guitar in the group with me, his favorite group was the Sex Pistols. He's a little younger than me, four years younger.

T. C: You became a professional engineer?

Viktor: Yeah. I was glad to finally finish the institute, and I worked for seven years as an engineer. . . . There are plusses and minuses to it here. Because when I was working or when I was a student, I had little free time to study music. I had to study or work and only had free time in the evenings, and then I worked on my music. And now I have more free time, and I've become more lazy. Because when you've got a lot coming down on you, you're active all the time, doing something all the time, doing, doing, and in principle you get more done than you can do if you are only specializing in music.

In Viktor's life, we see the importance of spreading culture through networks of friends, through what Viktor refers to as an informal "college" (*kolledzh*) of friends. Unlike in the West where the major source of culture products is the market, Viktor received Western rock music through two important informal sources: friendship networks and the black market. The black market was a major mechanism for the distribution of goods—including cultural goods—in Soviet society. Many Western products were available on the black market at inflated prices. Yet, despite the fact that the black market offered Western culture products, the range of such products was small and not representative of the more general universe of rock music which existed in the West. Musicians and fans alike were pushed toward the black market simply because they had little access to new music or original LPs and cassettes. The black market met a strong informal demand for new Western music, but the demand was not highly specialized. Any type of Western rock-and-roll had value on the black market, and the rock taste public simply accepted what was offered, again with the result that the specific cartography of rock musical products was quite skewed and not representative of the greater universe of rock music which existed outside the Soviet Union, a universe which was the product of a greater number of individual consumer choices.

Viktor's classical music training enables his activity as a rock musician and his transformation from a consumer of rock music into a producer. Indeed, a large number of musicians came to rock music firmly grounded in a comprehensive classical music training, sometimes on more than one instrument. Classical music training was an important part of the Soviet educational system and was available to practically anyone who wanted it. Indeed, the Soviet welfare state's subsidy of the arts and art education made training in the arts easy to acquire. Parents often pushed their children toward classical music since, even within the context of a social system characterized by a leveling of social classes, to be a "cultured" (kul'turnyi) person was a very important form of cultural capital for achieving upward mobility. For many rock musicians, the formal rigidity of classical music reflected the similar rigidity of the official world. It was this homology—a homology which was ratified by the Soviet state's preference for classical music as the basis of official taste culture and as the most authentic of musical forms—together with the less formal and more open elements of rock which served to push musicians away from pursuing careers in classical music and to pull them toward alternative careers as rock musicians. While rock music is not without its formal elements, it is an art form which allows for a great deal more innovation, informality, and spontaneity than classical music. This is perhaps one reason why rock music appears historically in state rhetoric as an inferior or even dangerous form of culture. For in its very essence, it was a metaphor for the qualities which grated at the very core of the cosmology of Soviet society.

Personal and family influences also affected the transformation from ordinary person to rock musician. Musicians' interpretations and the meanings which they ascribe to cultural information are mediated by these influences. Viktor is inspired, for instance, by a most unlikely figure: a black musical virtuoso from Madagascar who, like Viktor, had carved out a musical career within the confines of his own restrictive circumstances and brought that career to Russia as a student. Viktor developed a friendship with this virtuoso, and their social relationship was a powerful force in the mediation of Viktor's own tastes. Other musicians were strongly influenced by family members, big brothers whose tastes became the standard for little brothers and, in some cases (as with Viktor), vice versa. Still others found fellow fans in school; almost all musicians had formed some kind of ensemble in school. Ironically, it was formal Soviet institutions such as the school which provided the sites where interactions occurred, interactions which resulted in the production of cultural values and products which went beyond the boundaries of official taste culture.

One of the most important outcomes of this process was the social construction of the aesthetic value of music. Musicians' interactions with one another were characterized by constant discussions and debates about what constitutes good or bad music. Through such negotiations, Petersburg rock musicians traded musical products and negotiated collectively the identity of music as good or bad, according to the standards of aesthetic judgement circulating within their community. Those musical products which were identified as "good" became the basis for musicians' own practice of rock music, and those which were defined as "bad" were excluded from the emerging discourse of the taste culture. It is important to stress the fact that the early history of rock music in Petersburg was highly imitative. Even in the West, rock practice is mimetic; Western rock musicians borrow musical styles and lyrical forms from one another, dress alike, and share general cultural practices. Yet it is safe to say that Petersburg musicians were even more mimetic than their Western counterparts. In many cases, if not in most, musicians focused almost exclusively on learning to play the songs of the most popular Western bands. Thus, Viktor fixated on Led Zeppelin for six years until he had mastered the group's music. Musical virtuosity was equated with a musician's ability to imitate and master the most popular Western songs and the specific styles of Western bands. Viktor and other musicians began their careers in rock-and-roll by imitating bands who were considered important, such as T. Rex, the Rolling Stones, and, especially, the Beatles. It was only later that rock-and-roll became "Russified," that is, inflected with a content that was specifically Russian in its linguistic and poetic characteristics. The process of the Russification of rock music was a significant step in its evolution as a unique communicative medium which could speak meaningfully to larger and larger audiences about the existential conditions of Soviet modernity.

Russification (*Russifikatisiia*)

Initially, because it was a product primarily of England and the United States, the pool of rock products which combined to form the Petersburg musical taste culture was characterized by English-language songs. Most musicians who began rock careers in the 1960s and early 1970s began by playing these Western songs and learning their English lyrics. As Yuri noted in his story above, attempts at singing in Russian were disastrous, because fans of rock music much preferred to hear rock music sung in English. English, as the language of rock, no doubt made rock more attractive and all the more oppositional in the Soviet context. Cultural homogeneity in Russia entailed linguistic homogeneity as well: the language of state socialism was Russian, and other languages, English in particular, signified danger and "otherness." English, after all, was the language of the United States, the Soviet Union's archrival during the Cold War. While it was perfectly acceptable to learn the language of the "enemy" for the purpose of furthering the interests of the Soviet Union, the themes expressed in English in rock music were hardly considered politically correct within the context of a highly circumscribed and homogeneous world of cultural forms.

The simple act of learning English-language songs and playing them was a kind of linguistic resistance, a mimetic act which identified musicians as having cultural aspirations and cultural tastes outside the purview of officially sanctioned taste culture. Yet rock music with purely English lyrics could not serve as a widespread vehicle of communication for complex thoughts and feelings about existence among a population of Russian speakers. Rather, its initial appropriation was a simple display of difference within the homogeneous Soviet cultural environment. While English was studied extensively in Soviet schools, the meanings of the songs, references to specific American and British historic events, and specialized slang were difficult to understand out of context (and, indeed, such things could not always be understood even by many Americans, particularly those who comprised the "establishment").

A central process emerged in the development of rock music culture in Russia which is best described as a process of the Russification of rock music. Gradually, throughout the late 1960s and early 1970s, an "authentic" tradition of Russian rock emerged which was characterized by the retention of the highly mimetic musical structure of Western rock, but which inflected Russian lyrics onto that musical structure. Normally, the term Russification (*russifikatsiia*) is used to describe the Soviet state's policy of political, economic, and cultural imperialism, particularly in the peripheral, national, and ethnic regions of the Soviet Union. Used to describe the transformation of Russian rock, the term Russification signifies a "colonization" of Western rock music syntax by Russian linguistic and poetic conventions. From a sociological standpoint, the Russification of rock music was a crucial step in the development of a rock music tradition which was not only a reflection of widely diffused forms of Western rock music, but which reflected local concerns in a language which could be understood. Russian rock music could now draw on important linguistic, literary, and poetic conventions which were particularly Russian in order to convey ideas more effectively to the larger community of Russian speakers. Russification brought about a greater realization of rock music's capability to serve as a meaningful medium for communication of information in the Soviet context.

Ultimately, singing in Russian—and singing well, not only as a musician, but as a poet and as a bard—became the most essential criterion for inclusion in the community of serious Petersburg musicians. Yet it is important to stress that while Russian rock adopted uniquely Russian musical and literary conventions in its lyrical dimension, it remained highly mimetic of the West in both sound and lyrics. Consider Viktor's account of the most important influences on his music, an account which gives us a glimpse of the mimesis of Western culture and a corresponding alterity toward things Russian:

> So we started to use texts from other authors. I was dispatched to the library to read a lot of poetry, and I found out that in general the problems which existed in our society in our time were just like the problems which were prevalent in the 1920s in the capitals of all Europe and in the whole world. So I began to use European poetry: French, German, Austrian, Swedish—all word for word. I simply found the leading poets who were, to me, of the highest quality and began to take their poetry. And in conjunction with our music this turned out rather interesting.

> T. C: Who has influenced your music? From the Russian tradition of rock?

> Viktor: From the Russian tradition of rock absolutely no one. Completely. I have never liked even one Soviet band. In general, not one. Of that time. When we were playing, I liked groups who played together with us. There was a period when I liked one group then another, a third. Now I like no Soviet groups. And if we're speaking about Western culture, which has had a much

greater influence, I can't name specific musicians. It isn't so much musicians as it is poets, writers, artists. I can say which Western writers I like best of all. It's in those writers that I discovered something for myself. Such as Ambrose Bierce. There was a period in my life when my consciousness was "adult" and when I began to study music seriously. And I was sad that I couldn't write poetry and that I couldn't convey the mood which he did in his novels. And then there's Flannery O'Connor and Edgar Allan Poe. And then I became interested in German existentialism. I very much like Swedish and Austrian writers. There's also Norwegian writers. Literature has had the most influence on me. And then, of course, from American culture, there's Andy Warhol. All this simply turned my world upside down.

As we can see, Viktor is an example of a musician whose songs were Russian in form but Western in content. More than that, he displays a strong sense of distance from both Russian philosophical and cultural traditions and emergent forms of Russian rock. Many other musicians simply tried to imitate the ideas and moods of Deep Purple, the Beatles, or the Rolling Stones. This was extremely common in early forms of Russified rock. It had moved toward Russian linguistically, but conceptually it remained closely connected to Western ideas and meanings from both "high" and "popular" sources. As a result, it remained outside of the well-developed tradition of what Gerald Stanton Smith (1984) has called Russian "guitar poetry." The latter was the tradition of "mass song," developed by important Russian bards such as Bulat Okudzhava, Vladimir Vysotsky, and Aleksandr Galich, which was known primarily for the quality of its poetic discourse. Gradually, rock musicians would move toward developing their own poetic, which was closer to indigenous traditions of guitar poetry and less overtly mimetic of Western ideas. It was to be a movement which was decisive in the evolution of Russian rock, and without which no serious appraisal of rock's significance in the Soviet environment can be made. We examine this more closely in the next chapter.

For now, it is important to stress that Russian musicians continued to draw on those forms of rock music which were made available to them and to imitate and reproduce what they heard. Nonetheless, there was an important exception: they used their own language to express their ideas. As such, Russified rock music was a kind of hybrid cultural form which had immense critical valence in the Soviet environment, at least in the minds of many prominent musicians. By the early 1970s it was possible to speak of the existence of something called "Russian rock-and-roll." It was with this Russification of Western rock music that it became possible for actors to form the close communicative bonds necessary to develop a counterculture which had the power to challenge the official world at the most fundamental level of subjectivity. It was with such Russification that rock music began to realize its cultural potential in the Soviet environment. This is not to say, however, that rock musicians lost their fascination with Western music. Rock practice in Russia has always unfolded in relation to rock practice in the West, and in particular, in the United States and Britain. Indeed, this fascination with Western culture has been constant throughout the history of rock in Russia, a fact which, as we shall see in later chapters, ultimately posed a challenge to the survival of authentically Russian rock music in the post-Soviet era.

Vitya: A Physician-Rocker

Vitya is a neurologist at a medical clinic in St. Petersburg. His father is a prominent professor of music at the Leningrad Conservatory of Music. His mother is the author of a book on the Czech composer Anton Dvorak. Vitya takes great pleasure in the fact that his own education in classical music provided a firm grounding for his rock vocation. Indeed, he often taunts his father with the idea that his movement from classical music to rock is a progressive one.

It is interesting that in a later interview with Vitya, his father and Andrei (an important underground producer of rock music) were present and participated in the discussion about the validity and autonomy of rock music as a cultural form. Such discussions allowed one to get a glimpse *in situ* of the types of debates which went on *v kukhne*, or "in the kitchen," about the meaning and significance of music. Vitya's interest in rock music was a great source of dismay to his father. During the conversation, he tried—most probably as he always had—to make the case for the aesthetic inferiority of rock music. Vitya and Andrei rebutted his points, arguing for the autonomy of rock music as a cultural form with its own aesthetic. As one would expect, the impasse was not breached, and to end the conversation, Vitya's father simply stated, "Well, all in all, rock-and-roll is a very interesting form of psychosis." Such a conservative attitude is in keeping with what might be expected from a professor at a conservatory.

Vitya is comfortable speaking about both high culture and low culture. His conversation ranges across themes as diverse as the musical activities of David Byrne in Brazil to the absurd poetry and prose of Daniil Kharms, an important influence on many Petersburg rock musicians. Like many other musicians, Vitya pursued a formal career in the real world—that of physician—but his avocation was that of rock musician, which first had its roots in the alienating milieu of the elite Soviet school and then in his frustrating attempt to participate in the "official" Soviet world as a neurologist. Vitya's story is short. He considers himself a minimalist in both constructing his own life history and in his musical activity:

> My biography is rather simple and not that interesting. I finished school. It was a school which was considered one of the best schools in the city and which was primarily for the children of party big shots. And so I got a pretty good education in English and in the humanities. Nevertheless, in my school there were basically very unpleasant kids. They were really the kids of high party bosses, used to living extravagantly, used to seeing themselves as being above everybody else, and therefore the psychological climate in school was very unpleasant. In principle, I had no friends among my own classmates, but between the ages of twelve and fifteen I made a number of friends from a nearby school whom I met in a literary club for children and at rock concerts which, for me, were rather more interesting things than school-related things. And in such a way, rock music which was highly popular among my circle of friends, became for me like some kind of alternative to my school education. And for me it was something which supported me during those unpleasant minutes which I experienced in school. This was at the end of the 1970s and the beginning of the 1980s, I'd say 1978 through 1981. I finished school in 1982.
>
> It seems to me that my biography after school was uninteresting. . . . I enrolled in the medical institute and studied basic neurology and psychology which were attractive to me. I became a neurologist, which is what I liked for myself, but the medical situation in the Soviet Union depressed me because I found it rather difficult to actually be a neurologist because the hospitals were so bad. There was a lack of medicines and good diagnostic equipment. And so, more and more my interest migrated toward music.

Vitya's case is interesting for a number of reasons. First, his story dashes any conventional wisdoms which exist about the relation between structural subordination and the choice of rock music as a career. Vitya is an elite in every sense of the word. Nonetheless, even as an elite, Vitya is disillusioned with his formal status and with other elements of the official world. Like other musicians, he found the experience of the school alienating even though he stuck through it to get a credential which would offer him some anchor in the formal world of Soviet statuses and occupations. Ironically, as he reminisces about the difficulties of being a doctor in Russia, he seems to remind himself of his own dissatisfaction. Such reminders push him more and more toward seeing music as an alternative way to make meaning in his life.

Many Petersburg musicians came from elite families. In fact, so many musicians noted that they came from "good families" and had high educational credentials, it is possible to argue that elite status in the Soviet Union was a factor which enabled and facilitated the choice of an alternative career and identity as a rock musician. The privileges of elite status included the possibility of traveling abroad, of going to the best schools and learning other languages, and of interacting closely with the most widely informed segment of the population about what was going on *za granitsei*, or "beyond the boundaries," of the Soviet Union. All of these benefits of elite status enhanced the ability of those who enjoyed them to learn about Western culture and to put that knowledge to work in their local environment.

Vitya's case is also interesting because it dramatically illustrates the duality of the social existence of many rock musicians. His story is similar to that of Viktor's, the bassist described previously. He simultaneously played two roles, one formal and the other informal. The general question of which social roles and statuses—formal or informal ones—were more meaningful in the Soviet social context is a difficult one to answer. Nonetheless, Vitya's story indicates that his general dissatisfaction with his formal status in Soviet society pushed him toward an informal rock music career which was more rewarding. Vitya was privileged, but the privileges of even those of high social status in Soviet society were decidedly less than those of high-status elites in the West.

Not all musicians held such high-status jobs. Indeed, many of them were decidedly suspicious of those who played formal roles and occupied formal statuses in the official world. Indeed, among musicians, there was a great deal of tension between those who played formal roles—thus indicating their willingness to participate in the Soviet world—and those who, despite their qualifications and abilities, voluntarily removed themselves from that world. The inherent danger and discomfort involved in pursuing independent musicianship meant that the boundaries between the formal world of the Soviet system and the informal world of countercultural existence were often rigidly demarcated. In many cases, people like Vitya voluntarily excluded themselves from full participation in the rock underground. Vitya kept his rock identity secret by avoiding public performances, and it was only later, during the glasnost period, that he emerged from this "grey zone" to fulfill the performative dimension of his true vocation.[22] People like Vitya were often excluded from the inner circle of musicians—that is, those who enjoyed the highest status within the rock community by virtue of their public demonstrations of their commitment to free and independent musicianship—because other musicians saw such participation as a form of complicity with a world which the practice of rock music was meant to resist. A mark of high status within the Petersburg cultural community was the conscious and purposeful rejection of the normal world in spite of the fact that one was an elite or had the credentials which would allow one to participate in that world.

At first glance, it is difficult to understand why rock musicians, especially the more serious and rebellious, would work in any formal jobs at all. While they could not make money from rock-and-roll (except if they chose to be state-sponsored musicians, a case to be discussed at the end of this chapter), time and time again musicians told me that it was possible to live almost free in Soviet society. One musician reckoned that before the advent of glasnost and perestroika he could live on three rubles per week, or roughly, at official exchange rates of the time, for about $1.80. Low prices and price controls, low rents, free medical care, and cheap transportation all offered, in theory, the opportunity (in complete contrast to the situation in the West) for rock musicians to develop their craft, ironically, at the expense of the state. Nonetheless, because some money was necessary, many musicians chose to work at jobs and in many cases low-prestige jobs. One musician referred to such rockers as "boiler-room rockers" (*kochegary-rokery*). Some chose such jobs because they simply could not accept the idea of conforming and adhering to the politically correct codes of conduct necessary to hold higher status jobs. Nor could they pursue what they saw as a cynical and hypocritical path necessary to get high-status jobs. There were also two important pragmatic reasons why rock musicians chose such jobs. The first is that, by law, Soviet citizens were required to be employed. Evasion of employment was considered a form of parasitism and was, technically, punishable by imprisonment. This policy of mandatory employment was enforced by a requirement that all Soviet citizens carry a "workbook" (*trudovaia knizhka*) in which their occupation and place of employment were prominently displayed. Most musicians were unwilling to go to jail for their activities, and many chose jobs to avoid harassment. They chose such jobs since they offered them the chance to work two days per week for, say, fifteen hours. This left the greater part of the week free for the pursuit of their craft.

Vitya's life testifies to the existence of rock careers within the space of normal Soviet existence. We shall return to Vitya's life and music at a later point. We turn now to the story of Misha, which illustrates in detail the relationship between a rock music career and alienation from different facets of Soviet existence.

Alienation (*Otchuzhdenie*): Misha

Misha is a thirty-two-year-old rock singer who describes himself as a "second generation" Petersburg rocker. By second generation, he means that he came after the early pioneers who had adapted Western forms of rock music into a Russian idiom. During the 1980s, Misha earned a reputation among his Petersburg musician colleagues as a "bad boy," a "provocateur" who pushed the limits of the tolerable in his music. Such provocations, according to some, made things difficult for musicians who were less political and had struck up a more symbiotic relationship with the state. In general, Misha disagreed with other musicians about the proper relation between music and politics. This often caused conflict between Misha and those musicians—some of them very famous— who defined their music primarily as poetry and encoded it with deep symbolism and cryptic messages about perennial existential themes. Like Vitya, the neurologist-rocker, Misha is highly educated. He attended the graduate institute of Leningrad State University, an elite institution, to study English. While his English is good, he sings and gives interviews only in Russian and disdains those who attempt to imitate Western rock musicians by singing, in his own words, "like monkeys in bad English." Misha sits and drinks beer with salt fish, or *vobla*, a favorite and traditional combination in Russia:

> Well, I lived my "conscious" youth on Reshitnikov Street in Leningrad. It was a proletarian, working-class street. My little family [note: Misha uses the diminutive form for the word family, *semeika*, to add irony to the description of his family] was from a stable, unsuccessful background. Dad was a complete and utter alcoholic with everything that goes along with that. A lot of time was wasted on family scandals, and I began to block out my home life, like I was always trying to escape somewhere. I eventually left home.
>
> I had these friends who had some of the first tape-recorded albums ever made. And since I already could play the piano—I

could play along by ear to any music I heard—and suddenly these recordings began to appear. Beatles, Pink Floyd—the whole circle—Beatles, Rolling Stones, Led Zeppelin. For us this was everything—they [the government] offered us nothing, and there was nowhere to go—on the radio there was nothing to be heard.[23] For us this was something completely new, and it attracted us with its sincerity, with its roughness. Even now I look back at this, and I think that this was exactly what rock-and-roll was all about. I mean this stuff was so lively. . . .

In the ninth grade, we decided to form a school group. We played everything. We played at school evenings, the Beatles, the Rolling Stones, Slade. It was an English school. Therefore we arranged songs a little in English. Just a little. We played Time Machine, and we began to make some of our own stuff. This was in 1977. I was in the ninth grade. I was born in 1962. This is where it all started. Then the Leningrad Rock Club appeared. It was real difficult to get in there. We were at the first concert—Strange Games, Aquarium. Like it was clear that one could sing in Russian no worse than in English. And then I began to come up with some new songs. My own. This was after the tenth grade. I got into the university. I didn't get in right away, but after two tries, I got into the philological faculty in the English department. I got in, but it was hard. And I continued to write songs.

During my fourth year at the university, it became clear to me that I didn't want to be a translator of English or an English teacher in school. And in general, I didn't feel like boiling in that porridge (*ne khochet'sia varit'sia v etoi kashe*), because at the university then there was a whole mob of careerists. People who were continually trying to trip each other up. The teacher was speaking some kind of ancient language that was used fifty years ago in England. We hung around with some other guys and saw that there was an entirely different language, that life was much different.

This gibberish was oppressive to me. In short, I somehow managed to find some musicians. They decided to try to do my songs. And then we did a program at a youth club, a club for adolescents. And we said that we'd make a discotheque. We had a tape recorder, but told them you have to give us a place to rehearse. And we sat there for three months, nothing coming out. I quit the university. I simply didn't go anymore, stopped attending sessions. And after that they dismissed me from the institute, from the fourth course. . . .

And at that moment we appeared at the Rock Club. They liked us, and right away we were invited to play in the 1984 rock festival which took place in May of 1984, and right away we managed to become prize winners. This all happened in three months, and to this day I don't know how it happened. It was just that kind of time. We played real lively, energetically. We played lousy, but energetically. We became prize winners, and we were raised up in our own eyes. I completely quit the university. They threw me out of there as a result of this, and to tell you the truth I was real glad they did.

T. C: You decided to become a musician?

Misha: Yeah, although then we couldn't get any money for this. Then for two years the military enlistment office began to hound me. They wanted to draft me into the army. So I went to the nut house. For a month I worked on myself [*sic*].

T. C: Better than being in the army, huh?

Misha: Yeah, I decided to work with my mother on this. I said, "Mom, they better not give me a weapon or I'll shoot an officer. You should come to the psychiatrist and explain to him that I can use a weapon the wrong way at any time." And I think Mom believed this. And as a result, they put me under observation. For thirty days they watched me, how I carried myself, whether I smiled or didn't smile. I was depressed. I really was. I had to be. I left there with a good diagnosis: schizoid psychopath. Article 7B stamped in my passport, excused from military service.[24]

And then I began to work in a boiler room. As a stoker. We had such good stokers then. "Rock stokers." A lot of people did this. Real comfortable. You work for four days, and then you rest for three. There was time to write songs. For two years I lived like this and then gradually because everything started to happen—I mean no one supposed it would. Everyone was against me. Mom was against me. All my associates came out against me. To be interested in rock music was considered to be in general kind of a foolish thing, as something which didn't have much payoff. It's all the same to me that no one was interested in it. Well, somehow people *were* interested in it because it was really interesting.

Attempts to evade the army were common among rock musicians. Many strategies were used—from attempted suicide (itself considered evidence of insanity within the world of Soviet psychiatry)—to

Misha's intentional decision to get himself declared "7B" by crafting a schizoid personality for public presentation to the authorities. Indeed, it is common to see scars on the wrists of musicians. The slashing of wrists was seen by many as the safest way to attempt suicide and be unsuccessful, yet to achieve the desired end, which was to evade what they felt to be the most horrifying and alienating institution of the official Soviet world—the military. On the other hand, many musicians did go into military service, and while there they often worked in trades that directly benefited their future rock careers. Other musicians used the army as a hunting ground for rock "fellow travelers," and it was in the army that many of them developed networks which they maintained throughout their lives. Still others, especially those with classical music training, were assigned to play in military bands and symphonies in the Red Army. Often such musicians, because of their special skills, were afforded special treatment in the army and indulged to a greater extent than regular recruits.

Misha's decision to leave the university was momentous, since university positions—especially in English faculties—were very hard to come by during this period. He found the careerism of his classmates alienating, and he could not stomach the idea of working with them in the standard jobs which graduates of such institutes could expect to get upon receiving their diplomas. His decision seems as much aimed at his relatives who meddled in his life from very early on. He sees them and their aspirations, as he does the rest of the "general mass" of Soviet society, as "Philistines" (*meshchanskie lyudi*) who prize and value conformity and stability at the expense of all else. The normal sequences of his life course (or what is called in Russian *zhiznennyi put'*, or "life path")—in particular the excessive concern with thinking about one's own future and security—are the essence of the Philistine orientation toward life and are particularly distasteful to him. What he sees as an obsessive concern of Soviets for the entitlements of the Soviet welfare state drives Misha away from such existence toward rock music. Misha chooses a profession which ensures that his future will have no particular form, and therefore he does not have to worry about its content.

> *T. C.:* Could you tell about the moment when you decided to be a musician? Was there a moment when you said to yourself, "I want only to play, to write songs?"

> *Misha:* There was such a moment. I decided for myself on this. On the one hand, as I already said, there was a moment when I just stopped going to classes and taking exams, like I simply

missed the whole term, and I knew that things would be unpleasant. But I decided for myself. I could be in the system for the rest
of my life: I'll graduate, get a good position as a translator in an
Intourist hotel, then go to England and live a good life. All the
time I'd be demeaning myself for the sake of getting hard currency, for the sake of traveling around all the time. I simply
decided that this was not me. It just wasn't me. I saw people who
were training for this. They were interested in high positions—my
classmates—any kind of respectable position. I looked at them—
well they were a different kind of people—they'd fall into some
rut, some normal, standard existence, you wouldn't change anything, even further you'd start to be afraid, afraid that they'd take
away your diploma, your work, then your wife, then your children, and then you'd die. Well that's serious business. There's a
need to travel around and to be free, but you need to buy it. Freedom doesn't come by itself. You need to buy it, and you buy it
with your own "model" conduct. That's tough. And this is how
the overwhelming majority of people live, and these are still considered to be "elites."

How I ended up there [at the university], I still don't understand because it's difficult to get into that elite club. They only
accepted one out of ten applicants. As a result, I made the decision
to become a musician because I was interested in music all along
anyway. But the university began to get irritated with me from the
time I enrolled in the second course. And my mother's circle of relatives were saying, "You need to study till the end. Only one year
remains. Get a diploma. With a diploma your life won't be
wasted." Well, I decided then to commit myself to getting the
diploma. Now I have it. I'm a specialist in the English language.

This was an inner responsibility which was so unnecessary.
I understood this in one beautiful moment and decided not to
care any further about any of these things. And I'm glad I did
because the more a person thinks about his own future and the
more a person reminisces sentimentally about his own past, the
older he gets. You need to grab hold of the reality of the present.
It's probably the most difficult thing, to begin to live in this reality.
Not in the future and not in the past. Rock-and-roll more or less
permits me to do this. And not music as music, but as a way of
life. All social laws seem funny. We live without having to go to
work. Now [1990] there is some kind of possibility to live like this,
while earlier there was never such a possibility. And now a lot of
musicians live like this. Because you really can get up in the morn-

ing and not think about your obligations to the state, but about what you've accumulated in your soul. And in this situation, you can develop any identity (*lichnost'*) you want in order to free yourself from the factory and from the state.

T. C.: So you see rock as a way of life against the government?

Misha: I look at myself now, and I understand that nevertheless the biggest role played in my life was the constant conflict in my family. Like for me my family was enemy number one. Dad, Mom—they were simply enemies. In school—enemies, practically the whole class, although I did have acquaintances, but nothing like friendship. And this all—it was all like everything was repression. And it beat down on me. The university too. Probably in order not to grow comfortable with existence, to become part of the "collective community" (*sotsium*), in this society you need at any moment to be the enemy of everyone.[25] At least that's where I've got myself, and in principle I'm glad I did.

T. C.: What do your parents think about you now?

Misha: Who? Oh. Dad's dead. Suicide. Mom has seen me a few times on television, and that's all. Now I'm a small medal for her to wear on her chest. She carries me to work on her chest, and everyone asks, "How's Misha getting on there? How are things there? Is everything all right with him in television?" I suddenly became proud of Mom. It's rather funny. An old person—what are you going to do with her? Well, accordingly, all my relatives have calmed down a bit. They see that something happened, although for them it wasn't exactly clear what. He appears every now and then on TV, which means that someone must be listening to him.

Well, all the same there's a general mistrust because things are unstable. Tomorrow there may not be a concert and there won't be any money. And the narrow-minded love (*meshchanskaia liubov'*) for stability scares people away. People of the level of the general masses. They go here and there, and then what? What happens tomorrow? Old age. I try never to let myself think about this, and this is why none of my relatives understand me—this not thinking about what the future holds, about old age, about how I'll provide a pension for myself. This is something which distinguishes rockers from everyone else. I never met one rock musician who thought about how he would live in ten or twenty years. Well, like that's when I decided for sure [to become a musician], and then everything just took its course. We took in various musicians. In principle there was a general conception [that] if there was one way to express it, if there was one concept that the group had throughout everything, it was simply the philosophy of alienation (*otchuzhdenie*). This is what's the most basic thing. Because all of these social phases, they come—today they're here, [but] tomorrow they're gone—and through all this only isolation exists. Most likely. You can't know today what will happen tomorrow. This is, perhaps, the main thing. Because everything is here today and gone tomorrow. But the thing which remains, the most important thing, is this isolation. It gave rise to this desire to go public and splash out my isolation and alienation (*otchuzhdenie*). Of course it's difficult to say what's going to happen next.

Misha's story suggests that a strong generational conflict often lies behind the choice of the rock vocation. In his own opinion, the problems with his family are at the base of his feelings of alienation from the world. A number of intersecting forces converge to push Misha toward the choice of rock as a career: a dysfunctional family and meddling relatives, careerists and opportunists at school. Misha carries negative feelings about these things with him, and they constantly cause him to "splash out his isolation and alienation." Importantly, his story suggests that it was family dynamics—and more specifically, dysfunctional dynamics—which drove him to seek solace in rock music. In the framework of a totalitarian theory of Soviet society, the Soviet family was often seen, to use a phrase coined by Christopher Lasch (1977), as a "haven in a heartless world." The pressures of life in a society in which the state attempted to colonize all aspects of life, so the argument goes, made families the source of strong affective feelings of trust and centers of open and free communication.

Is such a vision of the Soviet family fact or fiction? There is much evidence which suggests that the Soviet Union, like other industrial societies, experienced a high degree of family instability historically (see, for instance, Kon 1988). The idea of the family as a haven in a heartless world, though, is a somewhat romantic notion which does not always square with sociological realities, the principle one being generational conflict. Misha's history indicates that the family was, like other institutions in Soviet society, a potential source of anxiety and interference in individuals' lives, both because of the industrially produced pathologies which were acted out in the family and because of the family's willingness to stress conformity to official norms and values. The Soviet state went to great lengths to foster conformity in the population. Pressures to excel in school, to get appropriate education, and to quest after respectable careers within the Soviet system were all realities of Soviet existence. Contrary to conventional wisdom, Soviet families were all too ready to ratify a life path which was basically in conformity with official prescriptions. Indeed, this is why the family, rather than the state, at least in Misha's case, seems to be a veritable font for his alienation; it is a major site where he plays out his deep-seated feeling of alienation with existence.

Misha's story is important in that it points out that experiences of the socialist industrial order and responses to that order take place in various extrapolitical institutional sites, in this case within the Soviet family. Misha holds deep feelings of hostility toward his father, whom he describes at one point as a "completely Soviet man." He sees his father as a metaphor for the decrepitude of the Soviet system. His attitude of disgust toward his father is a stark empirical corroboration of Erich Fromm's (1941) Freudian-Marxian interpretation of alienation in modern industrial society. The working-class child, according to Fromm, sees his father debased by the industrial order. This debasement disqualifies the father as an appropriate model for the development of a strong ego in the child. The child, having no respect for the father as an authority figure, turns toward those in the social environment who offer him models of stability and authority. This turn toward authoritarian figures is, for Fromm, a key factor in the rise of fascism in the twentieth century. Fromm's interpretation of the rise of fascism may account for at least some of the consent to authoritarianism and fascism which has existed at various points throughout Soviet history. Indeed, the totality of Stalin's power emerged against a backdrop of a rapid process of industrialization which led to the massive proletarianization and debasement of huge numbers of people within such a short period.

The debasement of their elders by the Soviet system has been witnessed by members of the younger generation such as Misha. They are not angry at the authorities which caused it to come into being as much as they are angry with members of their own families who allowed themselves to be compliant "subjects" of the Soviet industrial order. Misha's anger is not projected directly toward fascist figures, but toward his own father, whom he sees as being a compliant cog in the wheels of Soviet modernity. Misha's father hides from debased existence in the bottle, while Misha lashes out both at the system and at his father through rock-and-roll. Consider one of Misha's most famous songs, a song which is an indictment of his father and the Soviet system, and which can be seen as a direct reflex of his own biographical experience:

Your Papa Is a Fascist

Don't tell me he is kind
Don't tell me he loves freedom
I saw his eyes—it's hard to love them
But your love is just fear
You're afraid to become one of the disagreeable
You know he can throw you out, he can kill.

Your papa is a fascist
Don't look at me like this
I know for sure
He's just a fascist.
Don't look at me like this.

Maybe, he's just cruel
Maybe, he knows nothing of Schopenhauer
But will and power is all he's got.
I won't follow him
I see the fruits of mighty illusions
I need my own sickle, my own cross.

Your papa is a fascist
Don't look at me like this
I know for sure
He's just a fascist.
Don't look at me like this.

And the color of banners does not matter
He can call himself whatever he wants
But the word lies if the hands are in blood.
I myself don't like labels,
But symptoms of the disease are too well known.
As long as he's up there, he'll be pressing.

Your papa is a fascist
Don't look at me like this
I know for sure
He's just a fascist.
Don't look at me like this.

There are ideas covered with dust
Others are clad in steel
What is in them does not really matter
More important is who is behind them.

Don't tell me he is kind
Don't tell me he loves freedom
I saw his eyes—it's hard to love them
But your love is just fear
You're afraid to become one of the disagreeable
You know he can throw you out, he can kill.

Your papa is a fascist
Don't look at me like this
I know for sure
He's just a fascist.
Don't look at me like this.

Your (*tvoi*) papa is a fascist.
My papa is a fascist.
Your (*vash*) papa is a fascist?
Our papa is a fascist.
Don't look at me like this!

Other songs reflect a similar concern to speak to the human condition within the context of socialist industrial society:

Humiliation

Your face is pretty
But it does not mean anything
Your body gives me pleasure
And I'm following you like a boy,
chasing you like a shadow
like a dog smelling a female.
You are my humiliation
And that's it!

Europe is pretty
But it does not mean anything
Your body gives me electric toys
And I'm following you like a boy,
chasing you like a shadow
like a dog smelling meat.
You are my humiliation
And that's it!

I am growing new skin
becoming covered with something extra

I have more and more of everything
I am getting shorter, shorter.
This world says in chorus
sternly, "On your knees!"
Life is just
Humiliation.
A Favor?
An Irritation.
Destruction.

My country is pretty
But it doesn't mean anything
Your body gives me inspiration
And I'm following you like a boy,
chasing you like a shadow
like a dog smelling kindness.
You are my humiliation
And that's it!

I'm growing new skin
becoming covered with something extra
I have more and more of everything
I am getting shorter, shorter.
This world says in chorus
sternly, "On your knees!"
Life is just
Humiliation.

A Dream of Suicide

I'm killing myself so light-heartedly
I'm drinking my fill,
smoking my thoughts.
I'll live without claims on eternity,
I'll take myself away from life.

Leave your phone, I am said to be solitary.
Don't call, I'll call you myself
When my body ceases to be my fate,
When I sing nothing anymore.

What a wonderful dance—one could not stop it.
Life is a dream, a dream of a suicide.
I am not tired at all, I want to pay off,
How much is the dream, the dream of a suicide?

Breathe deeply—the air is poisoned
It will make me understand, it will fill me
Look how innocently it's flowing as from the faucet,
pure poison, dazzling poison.

What a wonderful dance—one could not stop it.
Life is a dream, a dream of a suicide.
I am not tired at all, I want to pay off,
How much is the dream, the dream of a suicide?

And, finally, with the same theme of pessimism, Misha makes a direct comment on industrial society, indicting humanity for spreading pestilence over the earth and inviting it to die as a result:

When Will You Die?

When you die,
The Earth will sigh
Light rain will pour.
The gentle sadness
Of great infinite water
Will wash your footsteps away.

You have death under your feet
And this time you're disarmed
You have planet Earth under your feet
Which doesn't need you any longer.
When will you die?
When will you die?

The last accord
The last glance
Back, into remote antiquity
Your automobiles, your cities—
How long on this Earth
You've been building your family burial vault.

You have death under your feet
And this time you're disarmed
You have planet Earth under your feet
Which doesn't need you any longer.
When will you die?
When will you die?

When you die,
The Earth will sigh

Light rain will pour.
The gentle sadness
Of great infinite water
Will wash your footsteps away.

Misha's voice is the voice of alienation and marginality. It is an angry voice and one which, ironically, put Misha in conflict with many other members of the Petersburg rock community. We will turn to a more in-depth analysis of that conflict in the next chapter.

Yuri: A Russian Bruce Springsteen

Yuri is, at present, one of the most famous, if not the most famous, rock musicians in Russia. In spite of his fame, he has acquired a reputation for being accessible and is often seen on the streets of the city talking with ordinary people and fans. He is one of the few Russian rock musicians who has traveled to the West, having been invited by a New York producer to play concerts in New York and California. His experiences with Americans left, in his words, "a bad taste in my mouth." He is somewhat bitter that Westerners were only interested in Russian rock during the glasnost period as an expression of what he refers to as *russkaia ekzotika*, or "Russian exotica." One story has it that the American contract stipulated that the band would have to pay its way back to Russia from proceeds from concerts. These proceeds, however, did not prove sufficient, and the band was stranded in Los Angeles and forced to take on menial jobs to raise money for airline tickets home. As a result, while most musicians were extremely cooperative in offering help in my research, Yuri's approach was much more guarded. When another musician approached him on my behalf, he simply stated, "We don't need any Americans here."

Much of Yuri's bitterness can also be attributed to the difficult situation which Russian rock musicians faced during perestroika and afterward. Yuri's and other musicians' experiences with the West are very important and will be discussed at length in later chapters. I finally succeed in finding Yuri, not in Russia, but in Berlin in 1993 at a festival of Petersburg music. We sit on a park bench outside of the concert location which is at the Tränenpalast, the so-called Palace of Tears, an old checkpoint between East and West Berlin located across the street from the Friedrichstrasse Bahnhof in East Berlin. Yuri is in a "clean cut" phase at present, in contrast to the 1970s when he sported shoulder-length hair and the countenance of a hippie. Now his well-groomed hair, round wire-rimmed glasses, khaki pants, and polo shirt evoke an intellectual, almost "yuppie" persona. Yuri's attitude toward life and music has softened in recent years. He is wistful, ironic, and pensive about life. His wife died the previous year, and he believes this has led to a new creative mood and sense of seriousness in his life. He considers himself primarily a poet-musician, and he tells me that he would like to come to the United States again to give readings of his poetry and play his songs as a bard. He notes wistfully that he should come back to the United States because "After all, they're always calling me the Russian Bruce Springsteen." In Russia, increasingly, because of his gravelly voice, he is also referred to as the "second Vysotsky," a rock music version of a figure who is, arguably, one of the greatest bards in Russian history. Yuri is aware of his status. I tell him I live in Massachusetts, and he expresses a desire to meet Josef Brodsky, the Nobel Prize-winning Russian émigré poet who lives in the Western part of the state. Here is Yuri's story:

T. C.: Maybe you can tell a little bit about your history, biography. In your own words, because when I'm writing, I want to use musicians' own words.

Yuri: O.K. I grew up in blind, deaf, and dumb times [laughs]. The times of Brezhnev. I was born on the Kolyma River. My family suffered a lot from Soviet power. My grandfather was shot in 1937. And my mom and dad met each other on the Kolyma— that's in the North. Then we moved to the Caucuses, so I lived in the Caucuses. By the way, a war is going on there now.

As for my musical biography, it started in the city of Ufa, in the Southern Urals. Since my childhood I've had two loves—a love for painting, and a love for music. I first heard the Beatles when I was in the fifth grade. I was hooked at once. It was still in the Caucuses, somebody brought a magazine—there were some long-haired guys with guitars. Then I was tuning in to the *Voice of America,* trying to find something, and when I first heard it, I remember this state of shock. As a young man, I felt the energy of the time. I felt its formula. I just didn't know that it existed. But I needed it. I heard Beatles, Rolling Stones, Morrison, Lennon, and, of course, I was stunned. I thought, "How can this be? Somewhere in the rotten West, where everything is bad, as we are told—you know, I remember these child's thoughts of mine—where all the people are bad and bourgeois there are people who sing these wonderful songs that make me cry." That was the first anti-Soviet thought in my head [laughs].[26]

T. C.: When did you say you were born?

Yuri: In 1957. I'm thirty-five.

T. C.: And when did you become a musician? When there was a moment that you decided—

Yuri: I played back at school, at the dance parties.

T. C.: At school?

Yuri: Yeah, at school, yes. We gathered a group together called Vektor. We didn't write our own songs, but played Led Zeppelin, Deep Purple, Creedence, Beatles. . . . But we never played Soviet *estrada*. We played classics. By classics I mean classic rock-and-roll. And we studied [it], of course. And I tried to sing like them. I would put the tape recorder in front of me, you know.

And alongside with it I loved immensely our Russian poets such as Vysotsky, Galich, Okudzhava. These bards revealed a lot to me. Especially Vysotsky. He was just like a teacher of life, you know, without any sanctimoniousness. I was thrilled a lot in these days. By the Western rock-and-roll, the best of it. And then I was also into painting. I graduated from the institute.

T. C.: What institute?

Yuri: I graduated from the art and graphic department of the pedagogical institute. So by education I am an artist, a painter, you know. But all the same, music eventually won me over to her side. After graduation we gathered a serious group in Ufa, which we called X. It was 1981. We recorded four underground albums . . . started to write our own songs, got knocked around the head by the authorities. I was called into the regional committee of the party (*obkom*), to the ministry of culture, where all these guys asked me, "How come you do this? Why do you sing anti-Soviet songs?" Articles in newspapers appeared. I didn't have a job, anything. I was an *antisovetchik*. I had no privacy (*pod kolpakom*). And in Ufa, in 1985, I decided to record a new underground album, but I was told, "If you record even a single album, we'll throw you in jail immediately." Well, I did record this album in Moscow, with other musicians.

T. C.: But you made up your mind to go to Leningrad, yes?

Yuri: Yes, I did.

T. C.: Why Leningrad?

Yuri: For me it was the most complicated city. It was somehow easier in Moscow. I was accepted there, but in Peter I was not accepted at all. That is, at the beginning I was completely alone there, well, with two friends. . . . I was hanging around there for the whole year, without money, was just listening, walking, watching, and I realized that there would be a place for me there, for my world view (*mirovozzrenie*).

We got the group together for a whole year, and in 1987 we gave our first concert, in this Petersburg "group" (*sostav*), January 25, 1987, as I remember. It was such a serious concert for the public, in the Rock Club. We joined the Rock Club, and it supported us very much. In Petersburg at the time there was more freedom than in the periphery. In Ufa there was just feudal socialism.

Yuri's popularity spread, and he soon began to travel around the country giving private concerts in apartments and basements of buildings which served as "underground" performance halls. Such performances were integral to the development of music's fundamental identity as a communicative medium, especially in a society in which the ideas of gathering and socializing were so deeply entrenched.

I remember going to Siberia alone, with the guitar, or to Kazan'. A man who was meeting me would be standing at the corner. So the cops wouldn't take notice of us, he would say, "Yura, turn around that corner, and these other people will lead you further." I would go there, and then we'd enter a basement without electricity, but with hundreds of people. There were no microphones—otherwise cops can hear—candles are lit around. . . .

As long as we were playing Beatles or Led Zeppelin at dance parties, the authorities didn't pay any attention. We would play at a dancing party and say, "This is the song of an American orchestra." And that's it. As soon as they started to sing rock-and-roll in Russian, and, naturally, with the Russian language, the youth raised all the social problems, and the strangulation began to occur almost immediately. This "press" started in the '80s, such a strong one.

Yuri's life represents an important conjuncture between musical traditions which are specifically Russian—in this case Vladimir Vysotsky—and those which are Western—in this case rock music. The Russian tradition of popular song is characterized by a very distinct tradition of solo guitar playing as a poet and bard (see Smith 1984). Vysotsky was a Muscovite who sang and played the guitar in the Russian folk tradition of what is called *blatnaia muzyka* (literally "criminal music"), which is characterized by an affected pose of marginality and coarseness, both in life and music, which was meant to reflect the experience of life in Soviet society. Vysotsky's music was fundamentally Russian, both in its musical structure and in its poetic structure. He drew very little on Western musical traditions or conventions; he was a modern version of a centuries-old social type: the Russian guitar poet-bard. Vysotsky sang in the tradition of the *chastushka*, the village song which was a unique product of traditional Russian social structure.[27] His popularity led to the emergence of a veritable "cult of Vysotsky." As with all cults, the Vysotsky cult was characterized by the building of shrines and by pilgrimages to sacred sites related to Vysotsky's life and death, birthday celebrations, and deathday mourning.

Petersburg musicians, like all Russians interested in music, showed deep admiration for Vysotsky as a counterculturalist and as a poet-bard. Yet they did not directly emulate his bardic style. Rather, many sought to graft some of its poetic dimensions onto what they saw as a more energetic and powerful musical tradition: Western rock. While he is indebted to Western rock traditions, Yuri sees Vysotsky as an important teacher of life for him. His own gravelly voice, his emphasis on existential critique through poetry, and his often dramatic confrontations with state authorities are all highly evocative of Vysotsky's own style and biography. Yet Yuri combines this with what he constantly refers to as the power (*moshchnost'*) of rock music in order to raise the Russian bardic tradition to a new level of energy. It is impossible to overestimate the importance of the sense among Russian rock musicians that such a merging of traditions represented a progressive step in the development of music. Indeed, such a graft only served to strengthen the communicative and "infectional" capacity of their own craft. We will examine this important idea at length in the next chapter.

Yuri's life represented the importance of Leningrad in the cognitive world of musicians. It is the "big city," the cultural center of the country, a place which has its own geographical and temporal charms, and which encompasses the artistic lifeworld and gives it a unique character which, from the artists' standpoint, is unattainable in the rest of the country, even in Moscow. Indeed, historically, there is something of a *sorevnovanie*, or competition, between Moscow and Leningrad. At stake is the very definition of the cultural center of the country and the quality of the arts produced in each city. Musicians often write about the city in their music. Consider Yuri's song about Leningrad which illustrates the ways in which the experience of the city presented in his life story is reflected in his art:

Leningrad (The Thaw)

One degree above zero, zero, two degrees.
Winter has turned black.
January is blooming
With an ulcer of the sky—ah-ah!
From the south the wind has crawled up,
Incapable of running,
Sickly, it is devouring
The over-salted snow.

And behind it comes, like plague, spring!

And to Nevsky came flying down a flock of boots.
And on Nevsky such a commotion is reigning!
And above Nevsky is watching through a peep-hole a prison,
Consisting of lonely men
Who have not found reasons
For the free heat.

Spring is quite incomprehensible!

And in the canals water reflects the bridges,
And the precipices of the palaces, and the columns,
And the stacks of the domes, and a henhouse–flower stand
That gives away "for free" bunches of dried roses.
And the culture, sweating in the cellophane of rains,
Announces to everybody nights of "White Knives."
And we are all afraid
That we will end in a war.

Spring is to blame!

Hey, Leningrad, Petersburg, Petrograd,
Mars Field, Winter Cemetery,
Russia's offspring, not resembling his mother,
Pale, skinny, Jewish-eyed passer-by.
Herr Leningrad, overstocked up to the bellybutton,
Fried, stewed, given as a gift, stolen.
Monsieur Leningrad, marked by the revolution!
You have scorched the furniture, you have mutilated the Don,
With your windows, old women, lions, Titans,
Lindens, sphinxes, copper, "Auroras"!

Sir Leningrad, you are spoiled by the warmth,
Already in January you are over-kissed

By the greedy spring.
Your confidences
Have cleared my veins of anguish and doubt.
Sir Leningrad, I have fallen in love to distraction
With your eyes of steel.

Make me drunk, spring!

Musicians speak often of the freedom of "Peter" relative to regions
in the Soviet Union's periphery. As Yuri noted, the periphery was characterized by "feudal socialism." One musician from Magadan, a small
Siberian city, corroborated this notion, indicating that even as late as
1990, glasnost had not yet reached the periphery. He described the situation there simply as a "horror." The smallness of cities and towns in
the periphery, especially those which lacked a significant number of
cultural elites who would support some inkling of a counterculture,
were veritable crucibles of surveillance and cultural repression. As a
result, musicians often fled to Petersburg where they found not only
better structural conditions for the enabling of cultural expression, but
also a city which held for them a source of profound creative inspiration. Incidentally, while St. Petersburg did have a reputation as a conservative city, its sheer size and complexity (over five million population) served to some extent to impede the efforts of state culture
managers to thwart independent rock musicianship. Moreover, its
closeness to Europe, both culturally and geographically, made it a valuable source of Western cultural information which was the lifeblood of
Russian rock culture.

Yuri's initial training as a painter underscores the close connections among artists of various types in the city. Musicians make very little distinction between other types of art and rock music. Both are seen
as equally worthy, autonomous, and creative activities. A central aspect
of the Petersburg musical culture is its close connection with other communities of artists, with painters, photographers, sculptors. Indeed, it is
impossible to make distinctions between the status of such artistic communities since their situations *vis-à-vis* the state and their shared definitions of the social role of art were so similar. During one collective discussion among rock musicians and painters, fantastic plans for a joint
cultural venture between the Soviet Union and the United States were
being imagined. The fantasy grew by leaps and bounds; one artist suggested that American media mogul Ted Turner could be convinced to
donate an airplane which would be painted by artists from Petersburg
and New York or Boston and then used to fly American athletes to the

Good Will Games which were to take place in Moscow later in the year. Following this, a traveling art exhibit sponsored by American patrons of the arts would be put in place, featuring the work of artists from New York and Petersburg. Petersburg rock musicians would play in open-air concerts in conjunction with the exhibits. Those present found it difficult to understand that the same people who might fund exhibitions of "high" culture, such as painting, might be less inclined to fund concerts featuring "low" culture, such as rock music. Artists in Petersburg make very few distinctions between high art and low art. It is a distinction which they could ill afford in light of the fact that they were all, to varying degrees, faced with the similar position of subordination to the state.

"Philharmonic Rock": The Invention of a Soviet Rock Tradition

In the discussions above I have offered cases of musicians who, for one reason or another, did not play music professionally, that is, as an official occupation with the sanction of the state. Lest these discussions mislead, though, it is important now to turn to a discussion of the rise of what might be called a Soviet tradition of rock-and-roll. This tradition represents not only the historical attempt on the part of the Soviet state to co-opt the independent rock tradition, but the creation of a universe of "commercial" or "inauthentic" forms of rock music against which independent Petersburg musicians measured the value and authenticity of their own music and their own identities.

The Soviet state's orientation to rock music was a conservative and reactionary one. From the start, rock music was disadvantaged in relation to the official taste culture, since the latter tended to favor either classical music or musical forms which reflected particular realities of Soviet life in a positive way. Throughout the Soviet period, the most autonomous and independent rock musicians were subject to direct repression and harassment for pursuing their craft.

Yet overt and heavy-handed repression of rock musicians was only one of the more glaring tactics in the state's repertoire of culture management. As rock became more entrenched in Soviet society and became more visible, it became clear that any attempt to win the battle against rock music was futile, or at least relegated to the unreal world of rhetoric. In the early 1970s, the state added a new strategy to its repertoire of techniques for the management of rock music. This strategy is best described as a policy of "accommodation through co-optation." This accommodation through co-optation occurred through a strategy of what might be called the "invention of a Soviet rock tradition."[28] The root of this strategy was to infiltrate musical counterculture by offering musicians financial and material support in exchange for their willingness to refrain from writing songs with potentially troublesome content. The terms of this offer were simple: rockers were offered the right to claim the officially sanctioned role of musician (that is, given the official stamp of "musician" in their workbooks), granted membership in the Composer's Union together with all the rights and privileges which went along with such membership and, most important, were allowed access to studios, musical equipment, and space for public performance which was denied to all musicians who refused to negotiate with the state over the content of their music. The result of this agreement was the emergence of what many musicians refer to as "commercial," "popular," or "philharmonic rock."

Recall that, by law, no one in the Soviet Union was allowed to work in an occupation or profession which was not formally recognized by the state. Technically, only those who had been given an official imprimatur on their activity were legally considered to be musicians. The only way to play a public role as a musician was to submit one's culture products to inspection by state culture managers and yield to the latter's subsequent judgments of what was appropriate or inappropriate in the content of such products. From the point of view of the state, rock musicians who refused to accept state intervention in their music were not musicians at all, but potential "parasites" who were subject to sanctions provided for by Soviet law against any form of unofficial employment or idleness. Musicians who refused to participate within official structures of political and economic authority were referred to alternately as "independent," "underground," or "noncommercial" musicians. Conversely, musicians who participated within the formal structure of culture production were referred to as "commercial" or "state-sponsored" musicians.

The result of the state's decision to "barter" with rock culture rather than repress all expressions of rock *prima facie* was the emergence of state-sponsored rock groups. These groups were referred to as *vocal'nye-instrumental'nye ansambli*, or "vocal-instrumental ensembles" (hereafter referred to by the Russian acronym VIA).[29] Members of VIA were musicians who were specifically trained, groomed, or selected by state culture managers to perform songs which were stripped of any overt or even ambiguous critical content. Indeed, in many cases, the songs which were performed by VIA were actually written by members of the Union of Composers who had little to do with their actual performance. By name, the VIA was a watered-down euphemism for a "rock group" that retained the key elements of rock style—electric guitar and bass, drums, keyboards, light shows, and so on—but which allowed the state to engage in the production of rock music without having to identify its enterprise as such. Indeed, seldom were VIA ever referred to as "rock bands" in advertisements (*reklama*) or in discussions of music in official sources. The term *rock* simply had too much negative valence in the Soviet cultural context to allow its appearance in any formally sanctioned names for musical collectives. In the complex codes which were the most basic form of communication among countercultural communities, the term *rock music* came to be synonymous with independent music.

What the institution of the VIA represents sociologically is the attempt on the part of the state to allow the "noise" of rock music to be played, but to strip that noise of any actual or perceived critical or oppositional lyrical content. The VIA and their musical products opened up some space in the state's taste culture for rock music. It allowed for some acceptance of the "noise" of rock music, that is, its musical syntax, but stopped short of toleration of free and independent creativity in the lyrical dimension of music. Nonetheless, such a concession represented a transition from more overt forms of cultural repression to more subtle forms of management of culture through negotiation with musicians. The willingness of the state to negotiate cultural production is simply one example which is evidence for an emerging tendency toward cultural pluralism in the Soviet Union in the 1970s.[30] Yet it was a concession which stopped short of granting autonomy and freedom to the lyric content of rock music, the other "half" of rock music which is so central to rock music's identity as a powerful communicative medium.

The specific character of state-sponsored rock was not to propagandize overtly, but instead to offer alternative messages to the more potentially subversive messages embodied in independent rock music. Usually, these messages were not the same as the more blatant and overt state propaganda issued through a variety of channels. While it was a state-sponsored tradition, such state-sponsored rock could never have had any appeal had it grafted messages such as "Workers of the World Unite" or "Long Live the Communist Party" onto a rock musical syntax. Rather, messages about a whole host of adolescent concerns— love, relationships, friendships—replaced the more unrestrained and critical messages—critiques of the state, of Soviet existence, of Soviet modernity—encoded in independent rock. There is some sociological evidence that the VIA succeeded in their manifest function, which was to render rock music from a code of critique and resistance into a harmless form of "entertainment" (see tables 1 and 2 in appendix 2).[31] In

terms of musical intonation and content of lyrics, there were quite pronounced differences between rock groups and VIAs. The songs of the
VIA were much less likely to express parody, irony, or ideas about
sociopolitical phenomena. As one would expect, the overwhelming
majority of VIA songs contained themes of love and male-female relationships, which are central issues in adolescent existence.

The nature of the musician-state relationship for those who
decided to work under state sponsorship took the form of a Faustian
bargain. Musicians agreed to temper the content of their music—first
and foremost the lyrical content—in return for access to the means of
cultural production and reproduction (i.e., recording studios), the
means of cultural performance (i.e., state-controlled buildings), and
money. Moreover, such musicians were the only ones to appear on television stations, so ultimately they acquired social status among the
Soviet population (although they had virtually no status within the
community of independent musicians). Some state-sponsored musicians became, much like Western rock stars, cultural heroes and enjoyed
immense social status in the society at large. One Petersburg musician
who played in a VIA during the 1970s became so prominent that he
had to change his apartment regularly and put up heavy steel-rein-
forced doors to keep fans—especially female ones—from breaking the
door down in the middle of the night. He received love letters from all
over the country and mentioned one, in particular, in which a young
female author professed undying love for him and vowed to remain
faithful until such time as he would grace her with his child.

In Petersburg, many accomplished musicians made the decision to
accept state sponsorship of their activities. In doing so, they recognized
that they were "selling out" or, in the terms used by Petersburg rock
musicians themselves, "going commercial." Yet, at the same time, they
recognized that this was the only option which allowed them to retain
their self-definition as musicians. In this sense, they saw themselves as
not doing anything different than what their Western counterparts might
do if they were offered a lucrative recording contract in exchange for
following a producer's suggestions for changing some aspect of their
music or performance. In the case described below, a former state-sponsored musician noted that he had actually done a great service to rock
music by keeping at least the most basic elements of rock's musical structure alive in the public sector. While he ultimately made an exit from a
bargain which he found intolerable, in the early stages of his commercial
career, he felt as if he had actually won a minor victory over the state by
claiming some space for the noise of rock music within the historically
conservative and homogeneous state-controlled taste culture.

A Faustian Bargain: The Case of Igor R., Commercial Musician

We turn now to a case study of Igor R., an accomplished electric guitarist who accepted employment as a musician in a state-sponsored VIA in the early 1970s. Igor is an electric guitar virtuoso whom many consider to be one of the best electric rock guitarists in the entire country. Igor's technique centers on the development of astounding speed across a wide range of complex chords and chordal progressions. Because of this, he is attracted mainly to what is often referred to as "art metal," that is, heavy or hard rock which does not simply "thrash," but which allows the guitarist to use the guitar as an instrument for the display of technical virtuosity. By his own admission, Igor's own Western alter egos are the likes of Joe Satriani and Eddie Van Halen, two guitarists who are considered to be veritable virtuosi in the world community of electric guitarists.

In the 1970s, Igor made the decision to join a state-sponsored group in the city. He worked mainly as a guitarist, playing the compositions of others, but eventually came to play his own compositions, which were invariably inflected with his own "hard and heavy," "metallic" styles. While the details of his own life history explain his decision, it is necessary to stress at the outset the fact that Igor's decision to accept the terms of the state bargain was motivated, first and foremost, by his love of music. As a guitar virtuoso, he was more concerned with the technical and syntactical aspects of music. More than that, as a guitarist who described himself as a "metallist," he considered that he had had the "last laugh" through his relationship with the state. In his own mind, he was a metallist, and the fact that the state was paying him to play metal provided him with a *raison d'être* within an otherwise confining commercial career.

In the summer of 1990, with the breakdown of the state, all of the distinctions between independent and state-sponsored musicians began to blur. During this period, a young guitarist named Zhenya, an independent musician who was too young to have been faced with the difficult decision of whether or not to sell out, struck up a friendship with Igor. Igor is some fifteen years older than Zhenya. The basis of their friendship is a common commitment to playing the electric guitar. Zhenya grew up watching Igor play on television and never thought much about the political ramifications of Igor's decision to "go commercial"; he appreciates Igor simply for his musical virtuosity—he speaks only of Igor's talent and never of his politics—and he wishes to learn from Igor. For at least an hour before any serious sociological discussions begin, Igor shows Zhenya a new technique which he has developed for playing difficult chords on the electric guitar. The summer of 1990 is a time of forgiving and forgetting in Russia. There is no talk of politics, only music: how to make it well, and how to make it better than before. This is what most discussions which occur among Petersburg musicians are about: music. I came with Zhenya to Igor in his "room-and-a-half" apartment, and this is Igor's story:

In my childhood I attended a musical school, learned to play violin and the *baian*.[32] After that I started to play guitar myself. And then it happened that after the army I entered the musical college and devoted myself to music professionally. It was in 1975. The epoch of our first groups was about to end—there were a lot of groups in Leningrad until they were strangled by the government. Then there were fewer of them. Now there are more again. And then there was a lot of them—Galaktika, Sankt-Peterburg were considered the best. Also Mify, Rossiiane. I was engaged in this "musical college." And we were playing something in the dance clubs, like many groups did, because there were sessions (*seishny*) sometimes, and they paid us 120 rubles, 150 rubles for a *seishn*.[33] Not big money—but it was very rare. All the groups were playing in the suburbs at the dance parties, because they didn't have work in Leningrad, and all of them would play in Toksovo, or other suburbs about three hours' ride from Leningrad, to make some money. Not even money to live on, because everybody was working someplace else, but all the money we made playing we spent on the instruments. We would borrow money somewhere, buy the equipment, and then pay it back after the concerts.

In the college we had this musician, A. G. He was a keyboard player at one time in our group. He made his contribution there, introduced more classical themes into our music. And then some disorder started there. Zhora started drinking hard. Everyone started drinking. Andrei A. was a good drummer in his time. Sergey Z. was there—in short, the college gathered, and I was the last one to join them, me and Boris A. We played at dance parties in the suburbs and made art rock for the concerts. We played very complex compositions, complex progressions which lasted an hour, a kind of trilogy. One we made for a *seishn*. Though in the first part we performed simple rock songs, because we were afraid that the people wouldn't understand. But the second—it was like from the soul. We were playing for an hour. We were sitting and playing this complicated music.

So, we were playing this complicated music, but this group was still called Rossiiane. We were playing *seishny* at different institutes. We didn't exist in this form for very long. And again this not-unknown Comrade K. influenced our destiny. ["Comrade K." was an important producer of state-sponsored rock music in Leningrad. The use of the word comrade here is a satirical reference to Comrade K.'s role as a state culture manager.] We had quite a decent group. Many people liked it. To my surprise, people who came to the concerts preferred the complicated music, the music we made from the bottom of our hearts, rather than the commercial part that was supposed to please the crowd. Once we were playing a *seishn* and there were a lot of people. Our group was well-known then, and when we finished the first part, the audience received it in such a way that one man even came out onto the stage, took off his hat, made a bow, and left. We were so astonished. We thought if we started playing our hour-long improvisational piece, the concert would sure be a failure. After the break we took our seats and started playing. When we finished there was a pause for a half a minute, silence, and then the hall broke into applause, shouting.

Then it became clear to us that you should do what you feel like doing, what is your cup of tea, what you are doing from the heart, not for somebody else. And the musicians in the group were quite decent. All were professionals. And all of us had graduated from musical colleges, had a lot of experience, and paid attention primarily to the music, although the texts were interesting too. "Black and White World" was one of the compositions, about all our hopelessness (*bezvykhodnost'*).[34]

And then it happened that somebody was taken to the army, and here Comrade K. intervened. Someone somewhere listened to him. All these other guys play Led Zeppelin, somebody else's music, and he thought that here there were guys playing their own music, and that one should compose his own music. And he suggested, "Come to me, guys, I have instruments, everything." And Comrade G. took the bait. He was talking to him. I didn't want all this. Well, he signed. There wasn't anything I could do, not gather anything new. We lived together in such a community (*kostiak*).[35] As a result it came to nothing. I played one *seishn* with them, Led Zeppelin, and what of that? Then his Aprel' broke up. Thus, nothing came out of it. Neither decent nor interesting. As a result, the group just broke up. I played in different groups, at the dance parties, somewhere else, and then Comrade K. emerged once more in my life course and proposed to make Zemliane (the Earthlings). He said, "Let's play music." I said, "O.K., but why should we play Led Zeppelin, Deep Purple, who needs this?" We made up a program, all our own. We went on tour—by this time we had already become members of the Kemerov Philharmonic Society—and we were a big success. Back then nobody even wrote the word *rock* on the posters. That was 1979.

T. C.: And that was an official rock group?

Igor: Yes, well, we went the official route in order to be able to make some money, because we needed a lot of money for equipment and everything. We made our first tour, then Volodya found himself in Moscow, brought a whole bunch of all these Klavir, Shainski [Soviet composers of pop songs], etc. When I saw all this I told him, "Volodya, we cannot make such shit. Who needs it? We've got together to do something else. Who needs these songs? I'll make an arrangement and what then? Nobody needs this."

And then I left. I said that I wouldn't play such music, that we struggled not to play Shainski's "Village Stoves." And he got there. It was a horrible time, when he brought all these Soviet songs. There was this poet here, Pliatskovskii. He would jump up and say, "Yes, yes, yes. I heard your 'Red Comet.' We have a marvelous song, exactly for you. Tulikov and me have written it. He is on a drinking binge now." Tulikov was drinking, and this other guy was trying to sober him up and was telling him, "You're the standard-bearer, a model for others (*etalon*), so you'd better compose!"

And they created these works, the texts went like this:

> In washed-out modern jeans,
> In washed-out jeans you're walking somewhere.
> Like a little rain on the sea, like the sun in summer.

And then it went like this:

> I'm jealous of you.

What could I say to this? My face lengthened. Then he said, "And the refrain is just great":

> And airplanes-planes-planes.

I didn't know what to tell him because it was so terrifying. Comrade K. brought us these kinds of songs then. And I said, "I won't play this. I'd rather not do this at all. I'd better quit this." I had some work. I was giving guitar classes at a musical college. And we parted for half a year. The epoch changed. Then he [Comrade K.] found me again at the college and said, "Now it'll be for sure, we'll record a disk. We'll play music and record a disk." He was trying to persuade me for three days. I wouldn't agree. "No, Volodya." But eventually he did persuade me.

And then this epic with songs like "The Grass Near My House" started all over again. I worked for five years, and then it became just awful. It was too much for me. I looked back and thought, "My God, what have we been playing? What for? What were we striving for when we didn't eat and drink enough to gather this equipment? To sing these songs?"

T. C.: You were an official musician?

Igor: Well, what the hell does official mean?

T. C.: I don't know what it means [in this context].

Igor: It means that we are working officially, we have a workbook (*trudovaia knizhka*), the thing you don't have over there. Officially in our work record we are considered working in the Philharmonic Society, in Lenkonsert.[36]

T. C.: What did you think about this status? I know there was the state, and it said, "One has to play this way."

Igor: Yes, it was very hard then.

T. C.: How did you feel?

Igor: The thing is, we had this manager whom everybody knew very well. And in principle, he dictated the terms of our music. We played a lot of somebody else's songs (*chuzhikh*), used their arrangements. He had access to the television, the group was popular, it could work, and it did work with full houses. We tried to do something of our own, but it was difficult to explain it to Volodya. He was a very tough guy to fight against. We were popular, and after five years of work the whole country knew our faces. But I could never warm up to it. I didn't need that, I wanted the music itself to be interesting. I think many songs that we played were just songs which nobody needed. It was difficult then. To be popular, to be shown on TV, you couldn't play your own songs. It was practically impossible to perform your songs on TV. It had to be written by a professional author, someone who was a member of the Union of Composers.

During the time of Chernenko this atrophy (*marazm*) developed when all the groups working in official organizations had to be scrutinized by the State Artistic Council (Khudsovet). The Council would come, and all the groups had to perform two mandatory songs: "If the Guys of the Whole World" and "A Day without a Shot on the Earth." We would stand there like pigs in front of the microphone and sing songs that nobody needed. Somebody would play drums. Borya would press some keys occasionally. We didn't make any arrangements. Then the committee says, "What's wrong with you? Everybody else made arrangements." But since they considered these to be classics of Soviet song they thought it had to be performed in such-and-such a way. And we just became pigs.

You see, there was a lot of decay in the rock scene. For some reason Chernenko started a fight against the groups. He announced even at a plenary meeting that there were too many vocal-instrumental ensembles of dubious quality. And such ideology they brought to bear on us! He launched this fight. And then many groups were prohibited to work. And how could one not work—we didn't have any other means of subsistence. It was work. We had to buy instruments and all the rest just to live on. We were professional musicians. Nobody could do anything besides [make] music. We could only go play in a restaurant or someplace else. There was no other work for us. So I left this group at the very peak of our popularity. There was a lot of work. It was one of the most popular groups in the *Sovok*.[37] But nevertheless it became too much. And after that I started doing what I wanted to do.

While it is tempting to see Igor as a "collaborator" for his willingness to work within the state's framework for the production of rock music, his story indicates that his choice to do so was not an easy one for him, nor was his subsequent existence as an official musician. His experiences at the mercy of the whims of Comrade K. and Comrade G., two figures who were responsible for the management of people like Igor, indicate the basic incompatibility between a fundamental commitment to independence in rock music and the concerns of the state. In the beginning of his career in the early 1970s, Igor managed to find some meaningful existence as a musician, and he reminisces fondly about the time when an audience burst into applause after a moment of silence at the end of one of the group's compositions. "In every moment of silence, a militiaman is born," according to a Soviet-era Russian proverb.

Such moments of praise, however, were the exception rather than the rule. Generally, musicians—both state-supported and independent musicians—felt that they had to suffer at the hands of "unskilled," whimsical audiences who knew very little about music and who had been conditioned by the cultural uniformity of Soviet society to reject and be suspicious of any attempts at musical innovation. Musicians' own lives within the rock taste culture were characterized by an almost excessive concern to learn and play music well, while the taste public of musical consumers consisted of people who had very limited and piece-meal exposure to the wider range of Western rock musical forms. Such complacent audiences were the ideal of the state which had manufactured a kind of "star system" in which entertainment audiences came to expect a limited range of noninnovative music and reject attempts at novelty and innovation.[38]

Igor's choice was motivated by his desire to be a musician in a social context in which the conditions of musicianship were rigidly circumscribed and controlled by outside, extra-musical, political and personal forces. He found himself caught between a pragmatic desire to operate within the system and a commitment to the ideal of musical autonomy. Musicians such as Igor, who had been willing to barter some of their artistic autonomy away in exchange for some material support of their music, found themselves unwilling to continue when the terms of the agreement changed with the coming of a new regime. Even in the activities of those who collaborated with the state in the production of official rock music, the ultimate wellspring of rock musicianship was a strong and persistent desire to make one's own music and, in the process, make a meaningful life in the sea of socialist industrial modernity. Igor's life indicates that an autonomous musical career was not possible within the confines of the official political-economic infrastructure of Soviet society.

Conclusion

This chapter offered a glimpse into the lifeworlds of a number of Petersburg musicians in order to illuminate the varieties of musical expression, as well as some of the general parameters of the formation of rock counterculture in St. Petersburg. I have chosen to tell the general story of the emergence of the Petersburg musical community by articulating the particular life histories of key musicians in the city. In the next chapter, we move toward a more conceptual understanding of the meaning of rock music in the Soviet social context. Specifically, we focus on the ways in which musicians defined the identity of rock music and its privileged status as an authentic form of cultural communication. Such definitions were crucial to the formation of the individual identities of musicians, as well as to the formation of the collective identity of musical counterculture as an independent social group in St. Petersburg.

3

Musical Identity and Authenticity: The Local Meanings of Rock Music in St. Petersburg

Art, like speech, is a means of communication, and therefore of progress, i.e., of the movement of humanity forward toward perfection. Speech renders accessible to men of the latest generations all the knowledge discovered by experience and reflection, both of preceding generations and of the best and foremost men of their own times; art renders accessible to men of the latest generations all the feelings experienced by their predecessors, and those which are being felt by their best and foremost contemporaries.

—Leo Tolstoy, "What Is Art?"

The Identity of Cultural Objects

Many of the meanings of rock as a cultural practice and its relation to the formation of both individual and collective "counteridentities" within the context of socialist industrial society are implicit in the rich life histories presented in the last chapter. The purpose of this chapter is to explore the meaning of rock music as a cultural form within the Petersburg rock musical community. Before we can more fully understand how the practice of music-making serves as a basis for the development of alternative individual and group identities, we must elaborate in detail the specific "identity" of rock music as that identity was socially constructed by members of the rock community themselves. In the next chapter, we explore rock music as a means for the formation of both individual and collective identity in St. Petersburg.

Culture is an externalization of internal feelings, thoughts, and states of consciousness in objective forms which are then shared by other individuals (Berger and Luckmann 1966; Griswold 1986; Appadurai 1986). These objective forms have a degree of "facticity" which allows us to view them as cultural objects. Griswold (1986, p. 5) defines a cultural object as "shared significance embodied in form. Significance refers to the object's incorporation of one or more symbols which suggest a set of denotations and connotations, emotions and memories." Cultural objects, like individuals, places, and historical events, have identities. That is, they are inscribed with definitions of what they are, whether they are valuable or not valuable, beautiful or ugly, good or bad, worthy or unworthy, pure or dirty, auspicious or inauspicious, and so on. From a sociological standpoint it makes no sense to argue that any given cultural object is inherently good or evil, high or low, beautiful or ugly. Rather, what is important is to understand the process of the social construction of the identity of cultural objects as an outcome of the interaction of human beings across time and space.

The identity of cultural objects is highly variable from one society to another. What is considered quite valuable, pure, beautiful, or truthful in one society might be considered worthless, dirty, ugly, or false in another society (see, for instance, Douglas 1985; and Milner 1993). Communism was seen as evil and dangerous in the United States, while elsewhere people fought and died in its name. To make matters more complex, constructions of the identity of cultural objects also vary within societies: what is good, true, or beautiful for one social group or class can be considered to be quite bad, ugly, or false by others (Bourdieu 1984). As Griswold (1986, p. 5) notes: "The Black Hills were a cultural object for the Sioux, who saw them as infused with spiritual power, but not for the prospectors who regarded them only as a potential economic resource." Finally, even within groups there is often a lack of consensus on the meanings of cultural objects; individuals in specific groups are constantly engaged in negotiating the specific identities of cultural objects which are most important to the group. Within the Sioux nation, for instance, there might have been some general consensus about the "fact" that white men were evil or bad. Yet there were quite often disagreements and struggles over the issue of just how bad they were. Such struggles often led to infighting and factionalism within the group.

A major site of struggle both between societies and within societies is in the arena of competing definitions over the identities of a whole range of cultural products. One might view the entire history of Russian culture sociologically, for instance, in terms of the struggles among competing social groups and classes over the identities of specific cultural objects—art, music, ideas, architecture, ideology—in the Soviet environment. Like all other forms of culture, music is a cultural object; it has an identity which is socially constructed. In this chapter, as a way of speaking about the meaning of rock music, I would like to introduce the idea of musical identity. In this chapter, I focus on understanding the ways in which members of the St. Petersburg musical community constructed and negotiated the identity of rock music as a basis for their creative activity. The identity of rock music in this community emerged in the process of its production and circulation within the community of Petersburg rock musicians. Rock music was not simply a static cultural object which was produced and consumed, but an active code of resistance and a template which was used for the formation of new forms of individual and collective identity in the Soviet environment. Before we can understand such uses of cultural objects, however, we must understand how the specific identity of rock music was constructed in the Petersburg environment and elaborate the basic vocabulary which musicians used to talk about rock music in relation to other cultural objects in the Soviet social environment.

Musical Autonomy and Musical Authenticity

Among those who produce and consume musical culture and among those who analyze this process, there are very often debates about a central quality of music: its authenticity. Discussions about the authenticity of culture often hinge on the issue of music's relation to specific political and economic forces in a society. This explains why the debate about the authenticity of culture is such a mainstay of Marxian analysis and critique of culture. From a Marxian standpoint, the authenticity or lack of authenticity of a given cultural product is seen as a function of the relation of the artist and his or her culture to the means of production. Artists have always been concerned with finding ways to preserve their "authentic" art from external social forces. A most notable example in this respect is Bertolt Brecht, who was both an artist and a theorist of art. In his theories of art, Brecht sought to understand the social, political, and economic forces which "immobilized" art and eroded its potential to serve as an authentic means for the revolutionary transformation of society (Solomon 1979, p. 360).[1] In his own artistic practice, which was primarily theater, Brecht sought to counter such "inauthentic art" by the development of art which resisted co-optation by, and accommodation with, external social forces. It is in Brecht's sense that the authenticity of art is fundamentally related to the autonomy of art, that is, its independence from societal institutions and processes (Bürger 1992, p. 51).[2]

The identity of rock music in St. Petersburg during the socialist period was related to the specific encounters of Petersburg musicians with the dominant political and economic structures of Soviet society, and to the cultural objects which were the products of the latter. As we saw in the last chapter, the independent practice of rock music in this context was basically excluded from participation in the Soviet taste culture: it occurred, quite literally, outside of Soviet political and economic structures. From the point of view of those who were the "captains" of the Soviet culture industry, rock music was viewed as an inauthentic cultural object. From an official standpoint, music was seen as valuable and authentic to the extent that it worked to develop a sense of spirituality and to communicate ideas which would contribute to the building of a socialist society. From the point of view of state ideology, only musicians who worked within the dominant political-economic infrastructure of cultural production existed.

The Petersburg rock musicians whose lives we explored in the previous chapter, however, *did* exist. Moreover, from their point of view, it was the culture of the Soviet state which was inauthentic and their own music which was authentic. At the very base of the practice of independent rock musicianship lay a fundamental struggle to define rock music as an authentic form of artistic practice within the space of Soviet society. To begin, we turn to the analysis of an important issue: the relation of music to both the idea of politics and the specific forces of political domination which framed the existence of members of the St. Petersburg musical community.

Music, Politics, and Existence

Based on the evidence from musicians' own life histories presented in the preceding chapter, it is clear that the decision to embark on a "career" in rock music was a response to different experiences within the condition of Soviet industrial modernity. Yet rock was not simply a reflex of formal political and economic processes. Rather, it was an active means of relating to the greater condition of Soviet existence of which politics and economics were merely a small part. Very often, Western analysts of Russian culture tend to relate cultural expression to the world and categories of formal, conventional politics (see, for instance, Ryback 1990; and Stites 1992).[3] To ignore the intrusion of politics into the practice of rock would be, to say the least, analytically irresponsible. There is a great deal of validity in such an analytical strategy if one seeks to understand the politics of culture in Soviet society. In that case, what Khrushchev, Brezhnev, Andropov, Igor Ligachev, or Gorbachev thought about rock music and other forms of Western culture is extremely important. Yet at the same time, such an interpretive strategy conveys the impression that rock is a fundamentally political act or that underlying its expression is an overriding concern among musicians for the events of the official political world. While such concern was present among some Petersburg rock musicians, a more common idea emerged within this community which served as an important basis for the formation of the identity of rock music. That idea, strangely enough, is that rock music is "outside of politics."

The issue of rock music's relation to politics is a complex one. As was often said in the 1960s, "the personal is political," and to be sure, even the most isolated and seemingly apolitical acts of cultural expression have political ramifications. To study these ramifications is an important part of developing an overall understanding of the significance of rock practice in a variety of contexts in the modern world. Yet to see rock's significance purely in terms of its relation to the affairs of high politics conflates the outcomes of rock with its origins in the lifeworlds of those who make it and obscures its meaning as a more general cultural practice.

While some rockers saw themselves and were seen by others as "political" rockers, the very ideas of politics and politicized music took on decidedly negative connotations in the St. Petersburg rock community. While their lives were deeply affected by politics and economics, their own self-definitions of their craft, the meanings of their music, and the meanings of their own lives had little to do with the world of conventional Soviet politics. In fact, the primary identification of music as essentially nonpolitical was a value which led to the emergence of a norm within the Petersburg musical community which actively proscribed overt political content in rock music. In relation to the often-assumed relationship between music and politics, this is an interesting and even paradoxical finding. Yet, it is so central to understanding the identity of rock music and its practice in Soviet society that I have chosen to place a discussion of it at the very core of this chapter on the social construction of musical identity.

One day, in the initial days of my fieldwork, I was exploring the relationship between music and politics in an interview with Andrei, a guitarist from a well-known group. Andrei suddenly asked me in a somewhat angry tone, "Thomas, why do you always ask about politics? I'm sick of politics. I thought you wanted to talk about music." I replied that yes, I did want to talk about music, but that it was my belief that in the Soviet context the distance between music and politics was not that great. In fact, I said, my sense was that music in the Soviet Union was itself a form of politics. Andrei answered quite emphatically, "No, you are wrong. Music is outside of politics (*muzyka vne politiki*)." I was shocked by Andrei's statement, probably because I myself had come to the field armed with a politicized ontology of rock. Being entangled in the webs of my own presuppositions about the identity of rock music in general and rock in Russia in particular, I simply was not ready for Andrei's statement. I asked him to explain what he meant by the phrase "music is outside of politics," and he began to speak of rock music as a form of "energy" (*energiia*). I asked him to explain what he meant by "energy," and he simply said that he could not explain it to me. It was a feeling, he said, that just came over him when he played, and he could only describe this feeling as energy. When I persisted in asking him the ends of such energy and what drove him to play music, he answered by saying that he was simply following his "star" (*zvezda*).

The point of relating the foregoing anecdote is to stress that whatever else rock music was to Andrei, it was *not* concerned with politics. In fact, Andrei cared virtually nothing about politics. His observation was an important and fundamental starting point for rethinking the identity of rock music in St. Petersburg. Increasingly in the following months, his attitude was expressed over and over again in discussions with musicians. In very few cases (although in some) did members of the rock community talk about specific political personalities, ideologies, or events even though at the time—in 1990 during the period of glasnost and perestroika—Soviet society was going through a period of monumental historic change. To be sure, musicians had attitudes about the latter and did discuss them if pressed. Yet an overt concern with politics simply did not exist as a generalized sentiment within the rock community. Most musicians insisted on separating discussions of music from those about politics, or stressed the idea that I heard again and again in the phrase "music is outside of politics." This conscious avoidance of the reality of politics in the practice of rock is a fundamental starting point for understanding the local meanings of rock music in St. Petersburg. For it pointed to the fact that one of the most important qualities of rock musical identity is the idea that rock music is, first and foremost, an aesthetic practice which is primarily oriented toward crystallizing and communicating more general ideas about existence. We turn now to the words of musicians themselves in order to unpack this sophisticated relationship.

Gleb and Edik: Two Romantics

Many musicians who were most concerned to separate their musical activity from their political activity seemed to stress the romantic or artistic side of their music. In a discussion with Gleb and Edik, two members of a well-known band, the specific identity of rock music begins to take shape:

> *Gleb:* We want to try to play music which comes not from the gut, which is not carried through its loudness, but through something different. We're trying to make something. We're trying simply to make beautiful, romantic music. Romantic. . . . We just want— let's say, we just want the texts which we sing not to be political. We have a lot of groups who sing about politics. It's just uninteresting.
>
> *T. C.:* So are you saying your music isn't political?
>
> *Gleb:* Yes, we don't ever sing that way, except for maybe one song. We have a group [in Petersburg], Group X. They have a lot of political texts.
>
> *T. C.:* What do you mean by political music? Isn't it possible to say that all music is political?
>
> *Edik:* Well, not so much music itself as texts.
>
> *Gleb:* There are texts which are actually about politics. Let's say Group X, for instance, there's this song called "Your Papa Is a Fascist." We don't want to be like that.
>
> *Edik:* We're interested in universal problems which don't depend on this or that system, or on a particular time. In other words, they were here a thousand years ago, and they still exist—relations between people, the connection between man and nature.
>
> *Gleb:* We're not into protest music. We try not to do it. We want to sing about our own feelings. And, moreover, not about bad feelings, about things around us, but about good feelings and sensations, like, let's say, the morning breaks and the sun rises, and we feel good. We want everything to be beautiful. You just can't survive if you think only about how bad it is to live. You'll always be

going around depressed, in a bad mood. And people will avoid
you as a result of this. Things will never get better. We try to see
a little good in that which exists. . . . You know, my godfather
(*krestnyi otets*) has a priest who drinks a lot, and when they ask
him why he does this—why he drinks—he says, "You know, children, everyday I have Paskha [Easter]." You can imagine what
Paskha is? It's a church holiday, the day Christ was resurrected.
Paskha is the biggest holiday, you know, Christmas and Easter.
And he says, "I got through the whole war without even a
scratch. So every day I have a holiday. Sun: good. Rain: healthy.
All that happens is good." We like that idea, that all's well with
the world. There's nothing bad. And if it is bad, that means we
deserved it.

T. C.: So what, then, is politics? Simply something else?

Gleb: It's entirely different. People are interested in politics, and I
don't know why they are. If they weren't interested in it, I think
that they would live quite differently. . . . We wouldn't say, however, that if someone sings about politics that it's bad. Everyone is
interested in what makes them happy. Like if they feel like
singing about politics, about what's bad, let them sing. It's their
business, their life. We don't want it. We want to live a bit differently.

Gleb and Edik share a definition of music which places their craft
beyond the world of conventional politics. They tolerate politics in rock
music because they value freedom of cultural expression. Yet for them,
music addresses more perennial, global, existential issues and questions. When Edik quite off-handedly notes that music speaks to relations between people and connections between man and nature, he
identifies himself in some sense as a "cosmologist" who communicates
his cosmology, or perhaps more appropriately, his "countercosmology," to others by means of rock music.

The first sense in which music was seen as being "outside" of politics is that the practice of acquiring music, sharing it, and, ultimately,
playing it simply went on with little conscious thought about whether
or not such acts would be considered politically deviant. While the
political circumscription of rock music was quite strong, such circum-
scriptions were often ignored, or seen simply as an inconvenience by
musicians. Many musicians were much less concerned about the consequences of illegally buying and reproducing "illicit" forms of culture
than they were with a whole host of pragmatic problems: how to find

new forms of culture, how to reproduce them, distribute them, and perform them. Indeed, what is most striking throughout the hundreds of hours of conversations and interviews which comprise this study is not just the lack of discussion about politics per se, but the complete dearth of any expressions of fear on the part of rock musicians, either of the state in the abstract sense, or of the actual potential of it to intrude directly into their lives. Viktor's (the bass player whose history was discussed earlier) thoughts on the matter illustrate well the invisibility of the state and its proscriptions:

> T. C.: Tell me a little about the relations between musicians and the government. We [in the West] have heard a lot about this. What was the government's position on buying things like T. Rex? Did they think it was bad?
>
> *Viktor:* Well, it was at the end of the '60s, and then it was actually a criminal act. *I didn't even notice such prohibitions* [emphasis added]. I bought this recording, and it was prohibited music. There wasn't much of it around. There simply was a deficit of this music because it was difficult to buy, it wasn't produced, and it wasn't distributed. There was just a deficit. I didn't feel any clear political mood. There simply wasn't any. I began later to feel more political when I had already begun to study at the institute. It was in 1974. Even then, though, I only thought deeply about that what was going on in my circle of friends.

Viktor shows little concern about the attempts by authorities to thwart either the circulation of cultural information or the independent activities of musicians. Musicians speak of situations in which they or others were harassed by authorities; indeed, their descriptions of the intrusion of state culture managers into their affairs are vivid testimonies to the strained relations between the state and rock musicians. Seldom, however, did musicians react to such intrusion directly in their music. The state infrastructure of cultural repression certainly was an obdurate reality for them. Yet, by and large, musicians did not respond in kind, that is, by articulating specific critiques of the state or its policies. If politics spoke to the pragmatic affairs of the day, then music and other forms of art addressed more perennial questions about existence and the human condition. If the state attempted to colonize the lifeworlds of Russians with its ideology, then the response of the musician was to "retaliate" with an expression of more general critiques about existence. Such critiques were embodied in rock music, which was defined as a "special" form of cultural communication within the Russian social environment. It is important to delve into musicians' own definitions of art and music, because these definitions lie at the very basis of their practice and their identity as musicians.

The Importance of Higher Truth in Russian Rock Music: Rock as Art

The essence of serious rock music is intimately tied to rock musicians' definitions of rock music as an art form. Consider one musician's argument for the unique character of rock as an art form:

> I'll tell you one thought. In principle, rock music . . . well, since you're asking me to make some kind of crude distinction, imagine one of my English or American friends is sitting with me and we're listening to the B-52s. And suddenly, I say, "What's he singing about?" I'm interested to know. I like it, but I don't know what he's singing about. I don't even understand one word. And I feel like finding out what he's singing about. But even so, I still like it. Because I feel energy [of the music] without even knowing the thoughts [in it]. And it seems to me that it isn't important which language he's singing in because if a musician is very capable and there's energy there, then all the same you'll understand. You won't understand concretely my words that I sing on the stage, but you'll understand what I want to say to you only through the means of my energy. And that is what's most important in music.
>
> And I don't mean energy in order to dance. I mean energy in the sense of something meditative. Like when you listen to classical music. There are hardly any words, but you like it. You feel its mood, and you feel that it's conveying something good to you. And I think that music always should be so. And rock music as well. All art ought to be so. If you understand my words and they're good, well, so much the better. But it's not necessary, nor is it the only thing.
>
> And so when we performed in Italy in big stadiums, and I sing in Russian—no one understands one word, but they all understand. They feel as if they are communing through some kind of astral means. This is all meditative. It seems to me that true art (*istinnoe iskusstvo*) ought to be so. You can't explain why, but you like it. That is what's most important of all. There's no need to explain anything.

Thus, the most fundamental component of rock music's identity is that it is art. Music, in particular, is characterized by its musical energy (*energiia*) or drive (*draiv*). Good music displays energy and drive which is felt by the listener. Viktor continues:

Well, what the hell is rock music anyway? It's art. I simply think that what we do is some kind of variety of art, and I want it to be art. It's simply a form of art. Just like the Peredvizhniki, for instance, and the Impressionists.[4] It's a form which communicates simply because it *can*. I think that in the end there will be a differentiation of cultural forms, and rock will simply be considered art. It will be completely depoliticized, outside of politics.

T. C.: Do you mean that music will maybe be nonpolitical?

Viktor: Yes, I consider rock music to be the music of a generation which wants change. Yeah, maybe it's at a fixed stage. But music is music. It's for the creation of basic emotions, for the definition of the human condition. It ought to serve the advancement of the soul of man. All art ought to serve the purpose of making man's soul clearer and higher. It is outside of politics. Maybe at certain points in time art really must work to stir up the basic emotions. But in general it ought to tend toward moving humanity to a higher form of consciousness.

T. C.: So you see a music without political meaning?

Viktor: Well, for me sociality (*sotsial'nost'*) and ideology are different things.

T. C.: Could you explain this a little?

Viktor: I'll explain. Ideology is a fixed line which is held onto by the masses. My basic credo is that I want mankind to be purer and more spiritual. I want it to perfect the spiritual side, for it to live up to some kind of ideal, to some kind of absolute. I want man to live for others. This is the idea of sociality. When people live for others. This is a sense of life for all people. To be better, more pure and to live for all. And it seems to me that this is the idea of art in general. At some concrete stage one can use some concrete political steps, some kind of ideological texts. At the present moment maybe it's necessary. But in general it's all depoliticized. In general we [rock musicians] ought to propagandize spirituality and the soul.

Any musician you talk to will tell you the same thing. Because people who suddenly begin to be interested in music feel this "discovery" (*otkrytie*) when they play on the stage and when something lights them up. It happens sometimes when you're playing, and it feels like someone else is playing. You're holding the guitar, and someone else is playing. And someone else is singing. You feel that some kind of beam or ray is emanating from you. And when you feel subject to this feeling, you feel like someone is leading you, like there's some kind of light above you— this is the very best feeling in the moment of playing, in the moment of singing. And all musicians who've felt this will tell you the same thing as I have. In any discussion.

Viktor grounds his conception of rock as art in its difference from politics. Art is not politics, nor is politics art. His is a remarkably Aristotelian conception of art: art is special, and even privileged, by virtue of the fact that it expresses general and universal ideas and feelings rather than historical or particular.[5] This is not to say that in Viktor's world music cannot be political or even at times directly related to making commentary on politics or fostering political action. Rather, he offers a teleology of rock's evolution. The ideal end point of this teleology is a state in which rock music exists as an independent art form—outside of politics—which serves to develop the consciousness of humanity. Music is not necessarily unrelated to specific historical outcomes. Nor is "political music" necessarily seen as simply bad. Rather, as an ideal, rock music aspires to occupy its own existential space outside of politics. Viktor paints a picture of rock as a kind of *élan vital*, a cultural form which evolves creatively toward the expression of some form of more fundamental truths which are "above" or "more true" than the ordinary truths of politics and immediate history. Given the history of the Soviet Union and the intrusion of politics into the realm of culture, one might think that Petersburg musicians would be united by a common commitment to political change. Actually, the situation is quite the opposite. Rock retreats from the world of socialist industrial existence in order to occupy its own space within that existence.

Viktor's conception of rock as art and of its evolutionary movement from the political to the artistic is shared by many Petersburg rockers. It was evident in the life histories of other Petersburg musicians, in particular, in the experiences of Yuri, one of the most important musicians in the city. A central element of Yuri's lifeworld was a sense of constant alienation from Soviet politics which he considered to be the source of lies and hypocrisy. Early in his career, his music crystallized and communicated his political consciousness and rage. In his music, he did not hesitate to mention names and criticize specific aspects of Soviet political institutions or policies. His music met the world of politics on its own terms in the form of politicized music. Yet in one moment of epiphany, he recognized that an overtly political response to politics in music was not the most important quality of rock music. His realization of the "true" identity of rock music as a form higher than politics is stated in no uncertain terms as a kind of revelatory experience:

Yuri: I don't know, I always thought, back in 1984, 1982—the hypocrisy and lies were just suffocating me. Since school I've always been told lies, lies, lies, lies. I was just suffocating in these lies, and, naturally, I saw the world in this way, and I felt not just the imperfection of the system, but its horror and its mire (*boloto*). And I started reading anti-Soviet books which are being published only now, but I read them back then. For each book I could have been sentenced to eight years. In 1982 I read it all through, all the emigrant literature. My eyes opened. The first book that happened to come into my hands was Orwell's *1984*. Remember?

T. C.: Yes, yes.

Yuri: It stunned me. I read it overnight—I was given it for one night only, in great secrecy—and I came out into the street and saw what he described. I was shocked. I was in shock for a week. He opened up everything to me. And naturally, I began writing texts that were political in a way. I felt the necessity as a citizen to do this. I wasn't a politician. I was just a normal, living person who reacted to these lies. I couldn't just keep silent, sit and do art for art's sake, when everyone around me was just shouting for help. I just couldn't, I was unable to. . . .

A lot of people called me up: "Ah, Yuri—this is politics, it's primitive!" How can it be primitive? I was just stunned by this injustice, with everything that was going on. With these lies, these Lenins, with all this hypocrisy which I'd been hating since childhood. With the duplicity, double-dealing, and insincerity, everything was all just disgusting and horrible. Naturally, all this was pouring out in our work, and the first songs of [our group] were songs like "Don't Shoot," about the war in Afghanistan, or "The Pig on the Rainbow," or the song "Periphery," for which I was labeled an *antisovetchik* because I supposedly distorted the life of the Soviet village. Or the song "I Got This Role." They called me to KGB and asked, "What does this line in your song mean:

The sons are squandering on drink
the awards of their model fathers?"

And I said, "Isn't it so? Isn't it true? Why do you lie to yourselves and to others?" Can you imagine? I'm sitting there asking the KGB, "Why? Why lie? Look how you live!" Well, they fixed my ass.

There was a very serious moment in my life, when several articles were published in newspapers, in 1985, in Ufa. In plain words they just said that I was an agent of the Vatican, a CIA agent, and an *antisovetchik*, and I was leading the youth in the wrong direction with my political songs. I'll give you these articles as a present, very funny. And you know, I got so angry, I thought, well, I'll write something for you now. I'll return your evil. By that time a cycle of very angry songs was brewing. But then I thought for a while and stopped in time. I realized that it would do no good. And I just wrote a lyrical album, where on the contrary, I was crying out about life, about love. And all of the songs there are great (*v kaif*), speaking to the fact that everything will be all right, guys. The main thing is not to lose oneself. This turned me in a human direction, into a person. I realized that politics is only part of the world, and the world is large, and it's inside me. And Africa is inside me, and America is inside me, and this Berlin too. That's why, remember, I said before that I could sleep calmly in Berlin as well. The whole world is within us.[6]

Elective Affinities

Rock musicians, then, had very well-developed ideas about rock music as an art form. What is striking is the similarity or "affinity" between their conceptions of their art and the view of art put forth by Leo Tolstoy in his classic essay, "What Is Art?" Tolstoy's definition of art is important, not just because he was a Russian, but because it serves as a firm grounding for sociological understanding of the essence and social function of art. The purpose of art is

> To evoke in oneself a feeling one has experienced, and having evoked it in oneself, then, by means of movements, lines, colors, sounds, or forms expressed in words, so to transmit that feeling that others experience the same feeling—that is the activity of art.
>
> Art is a human activity consisting in this, that one man consciously, by means of external signs, hands on to others feelings he has lived through, so that other people are *infected* by those feelings and also experience them. (Tolstoy [1896] 1960, p. 51)

For Tolstoy, the content of art has little to do with assessing its authenticity. Rather, art is defined primarily by its form and function. In form, it crystallizes individual experiences and communicates them through a particular medium or media. Its function is to share that experience, to make consumers of art feel the lived experience of the artist. And, perhaps what is more important, consumers should feel art actively and be affected by it as by an infection (Tolstoy uses the biological metaphor of *zarazhenie*, which literally means "infection," to describe the effects of good art). Furthermore, Tolstoy makes a distinction between authentic art and "counterfeit art" (ibid., pp. 152 ff). Authentic art "infectiously" communicates experience to others. In contrast, counterfeit—or inauthentic—art fails to crystallize or communicate experience well. Tolstoy's theory of art is remarkably pragmatic and nonjudgmental. Art is what art *does*, and good art is that which does what art is supposed to do: infect others with the deeply held and authentically felt sentiments and experiences of its creators. Petersburg rock musicians' local definitions of rock music show striking affinities with Tolstoy's definition of art. These affinities are not conscious, but rather more of the sort of what Max Weber would refer to as "elective affinities."[7]

Tolstoy's pragmatic definition of art is particularly relevant to understanding rock music as an art form in the Petersburg context. It allows us to see why Petersburg rock musicians—most of whom are highly educated and classically trained musicians—chose rock instead of some other cultural form as their idiom. These individuals stood to gain little and to lose a great deal, both politically and economically, from the pursuit of their craft. The primary impulse which lay behind their activity was the desire to communicate experience in the most effective manner, to engage the listener with music which displayed *energiia* or *draiv* in its musical syntax and in the poetically inspired truths of its lyrics. The favorite metaphor of rock's most staunch critics is of rock as virus. Indeed, the essence of viruses is their infectiousness. Pernicious viruses are highly infectious, as is good art. The infectiousness of art, however, serves to construct alternative realities rather than to destroy existing ones. For rock to be authentic, it had to speak "beyond politics" to the human condition, to the human spirit and soul, and to the great questions of existence. This is what Petersburg musicians aspired to do in the practice of their craft.

The Importance of the Lyrical in Russian Rock Music: Rock Music's Identity as Poetry

Petersburg rock musicians saw themselves not only as artists, but as particular kinds of artists: poets. Indeed, if the form of what they did could be considered art, then its content was poetry. The definition of rock's identity as poetry became a generalized norm by which rock music and rock musicians were identified as good or bad, authentic or inauthentic. This norm can be stated even more clearly: rock music is an art form, and good rock musicians ought to be not only good musicians, but good poets as well. As we have seen, such ideas about the primacy of poetry in music did not always exist in the rock community. Early on, Russian rock was simply an imitation of Western rock music. Western rock music was seen as poetry and Western musicians as poets. In the early stages of its development, Russian rock—precisely because it was so imitative—could not be Russian poetry.

A key aspect of rock's identity as poetry emerged in the general course of its Russification. This Russification not only put rock in touch with Russian linguistic conventions, but eventually put it in touch with important Russian poetic traditions as well. At first, the poetic of Russian rock consisted of simple translations of Western philosophical ideas and poetry and the grafting of the latter onto a locally produced rock musical syntax. Recall Viktor from chapter 2 who described his activity as a translator of Western poetry and philosophy into Russian rather than as an original producer of poetry. The ideas of American, Swedish, and German philosophers and poets—but never Russian ones—were the most important formative influences on Viktor. Other musicians endeavored to translate the poetry of those who were considered to be the most important Western rock poets—Jim Morrison, John Lennon, Bob Dylan—into Russian as a lyrical basis for local rock. Gradually, however, the most important rock musicians began to see themselves as part of a unique and historically specific Russian tradition of lyrical poetry. The importance of this transformation was decisive for redefining the identity of rock music in Petersburg.[8] The idea of the fundamental identity of rock as poetry is captured well by Yuri, whose evolution from a politician to a poet was described above:

> T. C.: Can you tell a little bit about the relations between poems and music? Because you said that poems are very important—
>
> Yuri: Yes, yes. I consider that pure poetry—well, there's much music in it. I'm convinced that in the old times people didn't speak, they sang. There is this theory that ancient people sang first. Then speech as such became crystallized. They imitated birds' singing, etc., and they sang information. I believe in this very deeply.
>
> And in general, song is just a great Something (Nechto). It's more than just poems and just music. A good song—I don't

understand myself what it is, in the end. Sometimes, you know, you are sitting in the kitchen at night, in torn jeans, torturing the guitar, and suddenly—bang!—something starts flowing, streaming. Some harmony, a scrap of it, you suddenly heard it, realized, understood and put down. For me it's a very mystical thing, like meditation, when you're thinking for a long time, and you're continually banging the wall with your forehead. You have something, some sensation is ripening within you that you have to write something. And then you pass beyond this border, and you see everything at once, and you think, "Fuckin' A!" (*Pizdets*!), and you nearly cry with happiness. It happened!

T. C.: Yes, this is the Russian tradition. Sometimes I see Brodsky [giving readings] in the USA. He lives not far away, one hundred kilometers—

Yuri: Oh, say "Hi" from me [laughing]. I read his books.

T. C.: When he reads his poems, he reads in a Russian manner. And when you were doing this last night, it was very interesting, very similar [the reference is to a previous night's concert at which I was present]. Because these are poems, but also rock music.

Yuri: Yes, yes. The main thing is that before—during Khrushchev's "Thaw" of the '60s—the poets like Bella Akhmadulina, Okudzhava, Voznesenskii read poems and drew huge audiences. Now poetry has sunk into rock-and-roll. Real poetry lives in rock-and-roll. In Russia that's for sure. Especially in the '80s, because the official youth poetry was not poetry at all. But the best, the finest (*krutaia*) poetry was in rock-and-roll music. That is, the best, the purest, most sincere of everything went into rock-and-roll in the '80s. It speaks for itself. . . . To live is not boring for me, because the world is wide and interesting, and I am always interested in the person, just an ordinary person, who is sitting in a communal apartment, on a toilet in a bathroom. And I've been always trying to imagine the world as it is, and to tell him that the world is not just a communal flat, but that it is a whole cosmos, a whole universe. Even when he is sitting on the toilet in a dirty bathroom it's very important for him to understand this. That the world is a model of the universe.

Yuri declared that, above all, rock was poetry: "What's most important in rock music is poetry. The music is only secondary, and what you need to do is to make sure, first and foremost, that the quality of your poetry is the best that it can be. Only then you have to think about putting that poetry to music." Yuri's conception of rock music as pure poetry, as a commentary on the great "Something" (*Nechto*), was not always one which he held. Rather, it was an evolutionary step which was a product of his own life in Soviet existence. In a moment of epiphany, Yuri recognized that responding to political repression in kind through the development of overtly political lyrics would serve only to lower himself to the level of the guardians of the Soviet order of cultural repression and to run the risk that he would "become the other." For many musicians, the articulation of songs with overt political content and symbology was a quick road from a privileged existence outside of the alienating official world directly into that world. Another musician, also named Yuri, put it this way:

> *T. C.:* When I was in Washington three years ago [in 1987] during the meeting between Reagan and Gorbachev, there was an exhibition of Soviet culture there. I went there, and they had Russian rock blaring at the entrance. Five years ago, six years ago, it was impossible, because rock was still in underground. It seemed to me that it was a new form of propaganda.

> *Yuri:* A good idea.

> *T. C.:* Do you agree? Maybe it's a theory, or maybe it's true.

> *Yuri:* Why not? We've got a lot of rockers who do the same things themselves. They have their own political attributes. Alisa,[9] for example: red flags, sickles, hammers. On the one hand, they're singing against all this—if you listen attentively. But with their attributes they are only extolling that way of life. I made up my mind. No filthy *Sovdep*[10] attributes. To hell with that! It started three to four years ago, all these sickles, hammers, red flag on the butt or some place else—screw that! But many people have only got anywhere because of this. For example, Avia,[11] they have a show, people in jackets. . . . On the one hand, everything is very serious. They condemn stuff. But on the other hand, if you get distracted, look at this. God damn it! Without the text, without anything—what wonderful people in jackets they are, they're so independent, original, they're living, you see. *They think that they are fighting against this, but adapting such methods of struggle, they become the same. You see? This is interesting. What I'm saying is that when you begin fighting against somebody with his own means, you somehow grow like him* [emphasis added]. It's even

more funny to us than to somebody else, than to the Americans. Because we are stuck in all this, and the Americans look at this differently.

Yuri's sentiments were quite generalized within the Petersburg rock music community. Most rockers considered themselves to be outside of politics and, therefore, above politics. This purposeful distancing of the self from the official world is in keeping with the idea of rock musicianship as the pursuit of a more meaningful vocation within the alienating world of Soviet modernity. The conscious distancing of poetry from politics does not mean that rock has no revolutionary potential. On the contrary, many rockers believed that truly revolutionary outcomes could only be achieved by such distance. Ironically, their refusal to work with the terms of the system is highly reminiscent of Lenin's own resolve that his revolutionary program should never work within the system to effect change. As in revolutionary politics, the world which is the cause of so much consternation and alienation is banal. And to the extent that one uses the terminology, categories, or symbols of this world one runs the risk of melting into it and becoming the other.

Est' Pravda, a Est' Istina: The Truth and the "Real" Truth

Within the Petersburg counterculture, then, there was a great concern to maintain a distinction between musical activity and political activity. This is not to say that there were no "political musicians" or that the latter were not tolerated within the community. We shall discuss this issue shortly. It is to say, however, that the dominant criterion for the assessment of authenticity in music was whether or not it transcended everyday life by speaking in a sophisticated and poetic way about existence.

Since we have been concerned throughout this book to examine music in the terms which musicians themselves use to discuss it, it is useful at this point to discuss the linguistic distinction between the Russian words *istina* and *pravda*. The former word appears very often in musicians' own definitions of their craft. *Pravda* is the more common word used to describe the truth. A sense of a higher, more enduring, and even "truer truth" is conveyed through the use of the term *istina*. Thus, in Russian, there is a saying, *est' pravda, a est' istina*, which quite literally means, "There is truth, but then there's the 'real' truth." One could even say *istinnaia pravda*, which could quite literally mean the "ultimate truth," or more colloquially, the "simple truth."[12] Musicians often described their music as expressions of *istina*, as the embodiment of elemental truths about the human condition. They saw rock music as a means of achieving some sense of honesty and truth in personal existence within a social system which was, for them, Machiavellian and Hobbesian at its very core. Says Yuri, a veteran of the Petersburg counterculture:

> I had a main idea in music. It so happened that in society, in life in general, there was no way to be an honest person. When I was doing yoga there are eight principles in it. One of them says that one should be honest to the utmost. For example, to be completely honest for the whole day, not to say a single untruth. I tried, but it was very difficult. I don't know how it is in America, but I guess there is some hypocrisy there too. I mean, a person sometimes feels like doing or saying something different, but he does things in the way which is accepted in the society. I thought that if I had to torment myself so much in this life—to be hypocritical somewhere, to sometimes tell lies to my wife, at work—then maybe I would try to be utterly honest in music. I don't want a single note of mine to be false. And when I started to work like this, I had a certain style already which has been running through all my work, and I would suddenly realize that at some moments I wanted to play something completely different, and the circumstances demanded that I take this into account and play differently. Like if I play it in a ballad manner the audience will listen, and it will be accepted better. And at this point I realized that this was not a path which I could take. Once you've made up your mind to be honest, you don't do this, but what you feel like doing.
>
> Well, I started playing all this and found myself in such a maze where I'm singing about Jesus Christ. I'm not analyzing why I want to sing about him. I'm burning all over, and I think: I'll be singing this way while I feel like it. I'm singing for a year, two, three—I still feel like singing, everything's O.K. Though sometimes I would play some rock. Then one day I get up and think: Now I'm going to compose a song about Christ. But it doesn't work, [this song] about Christ. And all of a sudden I'm writing a song about a sixteen-year-old girl seducing me. And I'm almost forty. And I think I should throw this away. What about my fans? I have a lot of fans in the religious genre. People are always writing to me, sending me tapes from other cities to have religious music recorded for them. I think: God damn it, how will my new disk be with songs about Christ and about me with this sixteen-year-old? Not good. I should throw it away. And then I think

again: And what about honesty? Utmost honesty? I think: Let it be. I'll include it.

And this is why it happens that I'm consistent in my musical style. My consistency is as follows: I'm trying to be completely honest at least in music. I've tried to pursue at least one idea stead-fastly, all the time. And here lies my consistency.

Or, consider another Yuri's sense of the supraconscious element in music:

T. C.: Maybe you can tell about your philosophy of music. Why is music so important?

Yuri: Music. . . . How shall I put it. . . . Well, what is a word? A word is information coded by a certain symbol, right? Music is information of quite another kind than a word, or television or whatever. And here are we sitting and listening to music. This is a kind of information which is more transient, more natural, more primal. Because music is always from God, it's closer to the truth. That's why it touches everybody, and excites everybody. It's just Something (*Nechto*). And therefore in poetry I always seek music, melody, it's very important. Music is not only of the mind, heart, some level of consciousness, and from the gut. It's something "supraconscious." It's larger than the largest, because the main thing in music is its silence. This eternity. I like to be in the forest alone, wandering around and listening to this stillness. You know, like when its snowing for the first time—and there's complete quiet, this is music. Fantastic! This music—you're receiving infor-mation.

T. C.: Just to see is good, but listening is something else—

Yuri: Yes! Sight is not enough, but language is not enough either. Because language lies. The tongue can lie, because I think it's from the Devil in a way. The Devil has screwed everything up. A per-son seems to say right things about love in our "motherland" (*rod-ina*), about politics, people, and it's all lies. And somebody is believing him, somebody is not. In music you cannot lie, you know.

The notion of pursuit of fundamental truth and honesty in music is basically important to many musicians precisely because their own lives were so decidedly influenced by the institutionalization of lying as an

accepted form of communication in Soviet society. Musicians time and
time again spoke of the "big lie" of Soviet society and of the difficulty of
being honest in this society. They saw their music as a means of claiming
some authentic existence within the false existence which framed their
lives. To be less than truthful in music would be to follow the pattern of
normal Soviet existence in which the acceptance of a discrepancy
between fact and reality (or at least deploying different senses of the
truth toward pragmatic ends) had become normalized.[13] The true musician exists to inflect—or perhaps more appropriately to "infect" (in Tolstoy's sense)—ordinary truth, or *pravda*, with the more enduring, significant form of truth, *istina*. The category of *istina* in this case is filled
with alternative and independent experiences of the world, experiences
which were seen as more authentic than the reality of everyday life.

Petersburg musicians cared little about how the dominant society
received or adjudicated their search for truth. It was *their* truth,
expressed in their own language. And, indeed, the more those on the
"outside" castigated, vilified, and persecuted them for their vision of the
truth, the more they saw the necessity to "splash out" the truth in their
own vibrant idiom. One might say that the motivation of rockers—if
they had any clear political motivation at all—was to fight the state by
encasing the state in a more general critique of the existence which the
state itself had wrought. A simple stance of nonrecognition of the reality of the state and its ideology in music robbed the state of its totalistic
aspiration to colonize consciousness. But such ideas also provide an
intimation as to why rock practice was so rigidly circumscribed by the
Soviet state. It was precisely because rock musicians fled from the world
through music that their activity was seen as deviant. For independent
rock represented a refusal to hew the official norm that all forms of
individual expression should serve the project of Soviet modernity. The
practice of rock music was, ironically, politically deviant precisely
because of its apolitical identity. The dominant ethos of the Soviet art
world was reflected in the principles of socialist realism, which called
for art to be a reflection of the particulars of Soviet existence and a tool
in service of the Soviet modern project (Clark 1981). Unfortunately, the
pravda of the state could never square with the *istina* of rock music, for
each form of truth was the product of quite different motivations.

Ethereality versus Banality:
The Case of Misha, Musical Deviant

The denotation of rock as "poetry outside of politics" was a central
value which served as the basis for the emergence of a strong norm

which guided musical expression in Petersburg. Some musicians stead-
fastly refused to separate their music, or to combat the political by a
retreat into the ethereal realm of the lyrical. One musician, Kolya, for
instance, refused to separate musical activity from the act of taking a
political stance. His group was an important Petersburg band which
united music with choreographed stage shows which parodied official
life in a variety of ways. Earlier in our conversation, Kolya noted that he
was the ideologist of the group. Because it is a political term, I asked
him to explain what he meant by ideology:

> *Kolya:* One can't separate [the two]. The situation is that before
> 1985 it was—I am trying to find the right word—it was a form of
> opposition. Political opposition, opposition to the state, opposi-
> tion to "the press." Political not in terms of some political party. It
> was just a form of inner protest against what was going on, to put
> it in plain words. Just against that life, not that it was some dig-
> ging of ideological dogmas, communism or capitalism, it was just
> an opposition to dogmas, to the dull life which was simply sti-
> fling.

Kolya maintains semantically the standard connection between
rock and politics. Yet his very idea of politics is still seen as the articulation of a more encompassing critique of Soviet existence. The idea of
music as existential critique is maintained. Nonetheless, debates
between rockers over the issue of rock music's identity were a central
historical reality of Petersburg musical counterculture. And contrary
to any romantic image of the counterculture united in solidarity against
the state or communist ideology which might have been conveyed in
the above discussion of rock as art and poetry, such debates were a
source of sometimes quite pronounced conflicts among musicians.

As a result of the predominant view of rock as art and poetry and
as a means to the truth conveyed in the idea of *istina*, the label *political* to
describe music became something of an epithet within the rock community, and those whose music was defined as political were often
labeled as deviant within that community. We turn to the analysis of the
case of Misha, whose life history was offered in the last chapter as an
example of the alienated consciousness which underlies much rock
expression in Petersburg. Within the Petersburg community, Misha
was most often cited as an example of a "political" musician. What is
more important, Misha's politicized music was often used as a reference
point against which many musicians defined their own music as quali-
tatively better (that is, more artistic) and authentic. Misha deeply

resented the labeling of his music and his persona as political. He felt
that this label served to limit his freedom of cultural expression. He
found other musicians' appraisals of him ironic and even hypocritical,
since an important norm within the rock community was a spirit of toleration of each individual's right to articulate and communicate his or
her own vision of existence, to follow his or her "own star" (*svoia
zvezda*). Misha's own words best describe the process by which he was
"misunderstood" and labeled as deviant:

> I always hate it when [my group] is called a political group
> because it is entirely not political. If one listens to the texts care-
> fully and analyzes them deeply there always exists a second, con-
> cealed meaning (*podtekst*). They tell me "Three to Four Slimeballs
> (*gady*)" is a political song. Well there's a verse there: "Three to
> four slimeballs are always with me. Three to four slimeballs are
> tempting me." Well it's really about the Devil. It's about evil in
> general. And therefore it's funny when the label "political group"
> gets pinned on the chest of [my group]. We're no such thing.
> We're simply a group.

> T. C: Your music—is it political or social protest?

> *Misha:* Protest was never all of it. Just some songs kind of poured
> out, because the time was really so—like we came to the Rock Club
> and there were "bosses" [Misha uses the term *nachal'nik* which is
> usually reserved for "bosses" in the official world] like Akvarium
> and Zoopark. Everything for them was alright. They were con-
> stantly on tour, and at the time we saw that they didn't agree on
> anything. They didn't have a common understanding of things.
> They weren't expressing themselves fully in the sense that they
> were encoding their thought in their poetry, in their imagery. They
> were simply burying their true essence in what they sang about.

> T. C.: You said once that your music was not political. Before, you
> said that music was an internal struggle with reality.

> *Misha:* No. I said that it is an inner conflict of a person with reality.
> I still think so. I mean, pain. There is a kind of world pain [Misha
> uses the German word *Weltschmerz*]. And an individual reflects
> this pain. He absorbs it, and he must push it out of himself again,
> and I do this in the form of a song. I continue to accumulate this
> pain, then I spew it out. The ground for this pain is always some
> conflict, some disagreement with reality, a disagreement with
> everything going on around. This is what rock-and-roll is for me.

T. C.: Not only against communism?

Misha: That's a primitive idea.

T. C.: It's just that in the West people might think that if you sing about your father being a fascist that you are offering a criticism of communism [the reference is to one of Misha's songs, "Your Papa Is a Fascist," the text of which can be found in the previous chapter].

Misha: [Rock is] against any oppression of free will. It's very important. Freedom in all of its manifestations. What attracted me originally to rock music was that it didn't have its own little dogmas. I just felt that this was the way to allow me to preserve freedom in my life in this system and to preserve my relations with the system of humanity. In the world of rock music, I feel that I'm in my own element. I like everything about it. As for classical music—they tried to push me in that direction, to make me go in for classical music—there are much more formal elements there. Frames. The system is more strict.

Misha's ideas about the form and social role of music are hardly different from those whose thoughts about rock as a form of poetic vision of greater, existential truth were described earlier. His lyrics are not primarily meant to stand as forms of poetry, but as stark and even banal commentary on existence. This discrepancy between the ethereality of rock musicians' philosophy of art as described earlier and the banality of the actual cultural objects produced by Misha was the source of Misha's troubles within the rock community.

Misha is a "victim" of two related social processes. The first is the simple interpretive confusion which is a result of the fact that those who consume musical texts bring to their interpretations and evaluations of such texts their own values, beliefs, and norms. The second is that such evaluations and interpretations are the basis for inclusion or exclusion and the assignment of status within the countercultural community. For within the Petersburg musical community, rock music evolved as a deeply encoded, even cryptic form of poetic communication which sought to explore larger questions of existence. This was no mere convention, but rather a powerful norm by which musical authenticity was judged within the rock community. Adherence to such a norm was the basis for being granted status within the community. This relationship between conformity to group norms and status within a community will be explored at length in a later chapter. For now, it is important to focus on the fact that Misha was defined as a deviant for reasons which he found to be both unintelligible and unjust.

Misha's texts were identified as political by others, who, in Misha's words, "pin the label" (*iarlyk*) of "politics" on his band. In a community characterized by a strong belief in the apolitical status of music, Misha's music labeled him as a deviant. For Misha, the slime (*gadost'*) which plagued him could be any of the number of things which he viewed as the source of his alienation and anger: his alcoholic father, his meddlesome mother and Philistine relatives, the careerists at school, the boorish and tasteless audiences of rock music. Indeed, based on his story, one leans toward concurring with him, since he seldom mentions any concrete political figures or ideologies in his music. He sings mostly of his alienation from existence.

His lament gives credence to the perspective in contemporary literary theory which argues that there is no inherent meaning in texts, and that authors' intentions or motives have little to do with how their texts are interpreted by "active" audiences who form what Stanley Fish (1980) calls "interpretive communities." An interpretive community is simply a community which shares common definitions of reality and rules for interpretation of meanings of cultural texts. The Petersburg musical community is, first and foremost, an interpretive community. It has its own standards for the aesthetic evaluation of rock musical texts and for the judgment of the "authenticity" of rock music. It has judged Misha's songs—whether he likes it or not—as "political." And for many within that interpretive community, politics is a vile and pernicious sphere of social action from which authentic rock music seeks to escape. The mixing of politics and music grates at the fundamental identity of music as a higher form of truth, a truth which is above the sphere of politics. Misha's problem seems to lie more in the fact that he used more overt language to express his alienation, whereas other musicians, especially those from the older generation, tended to encode or encrypt their experience in a specialized and ambiguous language. Instead of the amorphous and anonymous reference to "they" used so often in Russian songs as reference to some ambiguous entity, Misha used the word *gad*, "slime," which people then took as a reference to the authorities. Instead of identifying a more general "press" of existence as the source of a search for alternative identity, Misha labeled the culprit: his father the fascist. Instead of offering a subtle dream of an alternative life, Misha offered the not-so-subtle act of suicide as a means of escape.

Within the context of the historical evolution of rock music in Russia, it is understandable that many members of the Petersburg rock community would view Misha as a "musical deviant." A key dimension of the culture wars between musicians and the state were debates about the meanings of the poetic of rock music. Very often, rock musicians deliberately made their lyrics cryptic and difficult to decode. This was because many of them felt existence was itself mysterious and cryptic. Yet opacity in lyrical content was also functional in maintaining rock's identity as a means of resistance within a system which demanded definition and homogeneity. The most important figures in the early history of the counterculture frustrated the agents of state surveillance by making their music deliberately cryptic and ambiguous. Over time, such ambiguity came to be a powerful means of resistance; indeed, it was seen by many to be the only means of evading the cultural arm of the Soviet industrial order and claiming autonomous space within that order. Consider the following lyrics by Boris, whom many consider to be one of the greatest figures not only in Petersburg, but in the entire history of Russian rock-and-roll. His poems defy easy classification or interpretation, and this is precisely what they are meant to do:

Counterdance

The century is soon over—how short is a century.
You must be waiting—or not?
But today it was snowing, and I can't get to you
Without leaving a trace—what do you need a trace for?

There's a reception there today—there's some refuge there today,
But we are unlikely to be expected as guests.
Look, someone has come through, and somebody's with him,
But they are they, you are you, I am I.

But there are no fortuities in this world
And it's no good complaining of my destiny.
He is playing for all of them—you are playing for him,
But who is playing for you here?

And I'm asking for one thing—if in your house
There is silk, and brocade, and ivory—
Forget about the house I lived in—
What the hell kind of a guest do I make.

I'll get drunk like a swine, fall asleep under the table,
In this society I'm unsociable,
I could never be the first among others,
But I hate to be the second.

But there are no fortuities in this world
And it's not me who should complain about the destiny.
He is playing for all of them, you are playing for him,

But who will play here for you?
He's playing for all of them, you are playing for him—
Let me play for you then.

The following poem is a scathing commentary on the Soviet common man as the bearer of the pathologies of Soviet modernity:

Watchman Sergeyev

A green lamp, and a dirty table,
And rules posted above the table.
Watchman Sergeyev is looking into a glass
And thinking about the past.
And his friends are coming to him
Interrupting the train of his thoughts,
And quickly they pour a liter of port wine
Straight into the watchman's mouth.

Friends have come not without purpose,
They've come many miles to see him;
They want to see him
At his battle post,
And watchman Sergeyev, having forgotten his duty,
Is catching the threads of the conversation
And puts chairs at the table for his friends
Since they have no place to drink.

And he is talking with them till dawn
Forgetting to inspect his yard.
He is drinking without looking at the door
Where a thief could have sneaked through;
But night is passing, day is coming,
As is the way of the world—
And watchman Sergeyev has fallen under the table
Having drunk the wine to the end.

And the green lamp is lit a little,
The replacement has been here for an hour;
Watchman Sergeyev can hardly stand up,
Blue from a hangover,
And, shaking, he steps out the door
Not knowing where to go yet,
He wants to have a beer and go to bed,
This modest hero of labor.

And finally, the following poem suggests that the desire to express anger can only be met by the sublime appraisal of a snowy morning, a morning which subtly, but provocatively suggests that even within Soviet society you can be someone else by thinking of something else:

It Was Snowing This Morning

Turn off the lights,
Leave a note that we are not in,
On tip-toes past the open doors,
There, where all is light, where all is silent.
You can be arrogant like steel,
You can say that everything is not the way it should be,
And you can pretend that you are playing in a movie
About the people who live under high pressure . . . but

It was snowing this morning,
It was snowing this morning.
You can be somebody else
If you want to, if you want to.

Do you remember—I knew myself,
My traces lay like chains
In a barbed wire of their own truth,
But there is snow and I again don't know who I am.

And someone is broken and doesn't want to be whole.
And someone is minding his own business.
And one can be nearby, but no closer than skin,
But there is something better, and it is so simple.

It was snowing this morning,
It was snowing this morning.
You can be somebody else
If you want to, if you want to.

Boris is one of the most famous of all Russian rock musicians. Over the years, he has developed a persona which is best characterized by a mystical, inner-worldly orientation toward the world. In his own words, "I don't talk to journalists. If I talk to anyone, I talk to priests." One other musician, upon hearing that Boris said this, satirically added, "And he also talks to God." His songs reflect a concern with general and ethereal truths about existence and intimations about alternative existences. Such truths may be considered anti-Soviet, but only by way of providing a commentary critique of Soviet existence. Indeed, they might serve as well as commentaries on existence within capitalist societies. In some ways, Boris most approximates the idealized image of the rocker as secular priest, the articulator of *istina*. Such an image is related to Boris's high social status and prestige in the Petersburg musical community. Because of his image and his status, he often found himself embroiled in controversies with other musicians who failed to preserve the integrity of music by sliding down the slippery slope from ethereal *istina* to the mundane world of ordinary *pravda*. Consider another important member of the musical community's view of Boris and his importance:

> They call B. G. "the father of Russian rock-and-roll," which is complete nonsense. He is at most the older brother. As for his merits—they aren't small, of course—I consider his major contribution to everything going on now to be the creation of a new song language. Yeah, he and Mike [another prominent Petersburg musician] invented this language which, though it's based on Russian words, seems foreign to many of our countrymen over forty but is understood by all rockers, birds, and beasts. Having jumped over the semantics, Boris came to the level of intonations and came into direct contact with the feelings and souls of his spectators and listeners.[14]

Surprisingly, many of the themes in Boris's songs reflect those of Misha's. What is different is his form of *poesis*. Boris's poetic is characterized by subtlety, metaphor, and irony. This emphasis suggests, in the first instance, why he decries overt, obvious, "political" music as banal and aesthetically unworthy. Boris castigates Misha, because his music simply defines reality rather than providing "intimations" of reality and utopian alternatives. To sing in a simple, unpoetic fashion about his own and everyone else's papas being fascists, or to suggest the bleak and pessimistic idea that Soviet existence is to be met by a "dream of suicide" is seen as banal. Misha's musical metaphors do not suggest reality, but present overt descriptions of reality which need no interpretation. Boris, like Misha, seeks to make commentary on existence, but he does so in a way which is less angry and bitter and, in the final analysis, less obvious. Most important, Boris—to use a phrase common among musicians—"has no need" for such music, for it simply identifies those who sing it as no better than the politicians who are responsible for the quandaries of Soviet modernity in the first place. Boris's own words convey the source of his dissatisfaction with Misha's music:

My sense of open horizons which I had earlier is disappearing. It disappeared in connection with all those spider-like battles against power and money which everyone has been interested in for a half year already [this is 1987]. If in the West musicians had been interested in these things, then there wouldn't have been anything—no Beatles, no Stones, nothing at all. If musicians want to be concerned with politics, then let them go into politics. Here's an example. Misha wants to be interested in politics. What would happen if all power were put in his hands? He would build still another totalitarian government. Misha simply hoists himself up on the stage and you can take him or leave him.[15]

Money and Music

The Cultural Contradictions of State Socialist Society

If playing politics was of central importance in gaining formal status and prestige in Soviet society, then making money was decidedly unimportant. Indeed, Soviet-type societies represent unique historical examples of industrial societies in which money and the acquisition of capital was of little importance in acquiring formal social status (see, for instance, Connor 1979). Ideologically, the ownership of private property was illegal, although a great deal of sociological research has indicated that elites did own private property and enjoyed distinct advantage in salary in relation to subordinate classes (Matthews 1978). However, ownership of private property was primarily a privilege which accrued from positions of formal status rather than a basis for the acquisition of social status. A more common basis for status attainment in Soviet society was the acquisition of appropriate formal political and educational credentials. These credentials were an important form of "symbolic" capital which could be used to achieve formal social status (see also Dobson 1980).[16]

We have already seen how some rock musicians distanced themselves from the acquisition of such forms of political capital either voluntarily by simple choice or involuntarily by the simple practice of their craft. Others acquired the forms of capital necessary to achieve some status in the formal system, yet retained a commitment to independent rock musicianship. Regardless of their formal identities, independent rock musicians were excluded from formal economic structures. Musicians could make the choice to do as Igor, the commercial rocker described in the previous chapter, and enter into commercial relationships with the state-controlled culture industries. But a commitment to autonomy in the practice of rock precluded such a move for most musicians. What is more important, making such a commitment meant that musicians excluded themselves from the possibility of making money from the practice of their craft.

Yet just because the state would not pay for rock music (more often it made musicians "pay" for their practice of it by harassing them) does not mean that the state did not enable musical activity in other, less obvious ways. The Soviet Union was a welfare state which provided some of the basic necessities of life such as cheap rent, utilities, and transportation; kept the rate of inflation and cost of living quite low; and provided free medical care. Ironically, such a confluence of processes actually served to enable the production of rock music in St. Petersburg. Within such a subsidized existence, members of the rock community could pursue alternative careers as rock musicians with little concern for money or other practical affairs of life.

This situation is in direct contrast to that which exists in the West. As we have noted, in Western societies, rock music is a product of capitalist culture industries. Rock musicians can achieve a degree of freedom from economic structures and financial worry primarily by achieving a measure of financial success from the sale of their cultural products. By and large, though, the vast majority of Western rock musicians cannot achieve enough financial success within the culture industries to exist solely as musicians. In fact, a good deal of Western rock musicians' day-to-day existence involves making a living in order to survive in their "authentic" vocations as rock musicians (Wills and Cooper 1988). In the terms of the Petersburg community, one might say that the "press" on musicians in capitalist societies is the capitalist system itself and the necessity of having to make a living within that system. That system requires musicians to expend a great deal of energy—energy which could otherwise be directed toward music-making—to meet the financial requirements necessary for their survival. To a lesser extent, Petersburg musicians had to do this as well, but many did so to avoid troublesome accusations of parasitism, or to secure the minimum amount of money necessary to support their craft. Ironically, while the greatest source of stress for Western musicians was the reality of having to make a living, Petersburg musicians were in some senses freed—both by their exclusion from formal processes of money-making and by their inclusion within the structure of the Soviet welfare state—to focus on what was most important to them: making music.

In the first instance, the lack of the necessity to earn money from music-making afforded many musicians a sense of freedom and choice in what they would play, where they would play, and for whom they would play. The very fact that they did not depend on music for their economic survival meant that they were free to set the terms of their own musical production and performance. Consider Kolya's description of the relation between lack of concern for money and autonomy in making decisions about musical performance:

> *T. C.:* You felt free then [in the Soviet period]? You could do whatever you wanted?

> *Kolya:* We had a choice, because then we were doing this as amateurs. Money to live on we earned in our steady jobs. Therefore we always did it for our pleasure. If somebody would say, "You are welcome to play at this concert, but you won't sing this and this song," we would answer, "O.K., we won't perform at this concert at all." Thus, we always had an opportunity to avoid censorship.
>
> Then tours to other cities began. Though there were some incidents, some idiotic articles—it's just laughable to recollect now, like an anecdote. For example, if the group Strange Games (Strannye Igry) appeared in sunglasses and leather jackets, it meant immediately that they are fascists.

> *T. C.:* Where was this concert?

> *Kolya:* In the Palace of Youth. We were to have two concerts. They ran up and said, "No sunglasses tomorrow! What is this?" We said, "O.K., we will not play." And we didn't.

For Petersburg musicians, the very idea of making money from music was quite foreign. This is not to say that money was not important for certain segments of the Soviet population—black marketeers are a prime example. Nor is it to say that those of higher status did not enjoy greater financial benefit relative to the population at large—elites often were paid in "special rubles" which could only be spent in "special stores" which featured Western goods. Yet, in general, the relative lack of importance of money as a means to status attainment meant that those living in Soviet society were much less concerned with making money than their counterparts in Western societies. Musicians were even less concerned, because they recognized that making money from the practice of rock was simply outside the realm of possibility. Consider Andrei's view of money, as well as the idea that rock music was fundamentally a practice in which one engaged because of some sense of service, or commitment to a higher ideal:

It's as if there's some kind of collective psychology [at work]. Well, for example, we traditionally found it unpleasant to talk about money. It wasn't that money was forbidden, but it was as if it didn't exist. In other words up to now there wasn't anything like this about which it was not possible to speak. . . . It was like some kind of object of silence. Even for me now, as an adult, it's sometimes tough for me to explain to my employer how much money I expect, how much I want to get for this or that work. In other words, for me it's complicated. I can't really even estimate how much I ought to be getting for work. You understand? Like this is such a very complicated psychology. For me, for example—I was shocked when I read ten years ago in some little book, that Ringo Starr chose the Beatles and not some other group only because they paid him two pounds more than some other group. You understand? For us this was absolutely crazy. Like for us it was as if everything was conceived out of some definite sort of idea of service (*sluzhenie*). And, accordingly, we all, at least illusorily, were devoted to some such idea.

Andrei was a producer of underground rock. In contrast to Western producers of culture (that is, those who control the means of cultural reproduction) who are defined almost exclusively by their concern to make money from culture, Andrei expressed little concern with making money. He recalls being starkly surprised that a member of the Beatles, arguably the most important foreign popular cultural influence in the history of Russia, was motivated by money, and a small sum of money at that. Traditionally, considerations of money did not enter into the matrix of factors underlying the production of rock music in Petersburg. Andrei articulates the notion that at the base of making music was "service to an idea" rather than financial consideration. The Russian word *sluzhenie*—which literally means "service," or more specifically, "service to an idea" (*sluzhenie idee*)—best captures the essence of the pursuit of rock as a vocation, or calling, rather than as a business.

Musicians had powerful fantasies about fame. Indeed, fame was the sole source of their informal social status. Yet fantasies about fortune were simply outside of the realm of possibilities. To be an independent rock musician in the Soviet context was to consciously remove oneself from the very idea of making money from music. In fact, making money from rock music signified the beginning of the end of creativity, autonomy, and authenticity in rock musical expression. Consider how Yuri's realistic appraisal of the impossibility of making money from his music leads to a definition of his situation as autonomous. Such autonomy he describes as a state of happiness:

Yuri: Do you know what life has taught me? When we gathered our present group, our guitarist once said, "Just imagine, we will record a disk, or come out onto the stage"—he was fantasizing like this—"and the master of ceremonies will come and announce, "Now the group [Yuri shouts the name of the group]!!!" And the audience would say "Woooow!!" And everybody started laughing loudly. Because nobody believed him. We laughed a little and sighed hard.

   We didn't get into rock-and-roll for the sake of money. We knew—and in saying this I'm honest before God—I knew I would never have a live concert, would never have records, would never have money, that I would always work as a street sweeper or shoemaker, that I'd be an outcast in society. But I knew that I would write songs and somebody would listen to them. And that was it. We came to rock the hard way, so money doesn't matter to us that much. . . . When I got my first record, I was just crying, you see. It was even greater than what I was dreaming of. And it is only natural that I'm philosophical about it all. We didn't get into rock-and-roll for the money. We were convinced that we wouldn't have any. What money? Well, you record a tape, give it to your friend, he records it for somebody else, to the third, the fifth, and the whole country is listening to your cassette. *That was the height of happiness* [Yuri's emphasis].

T. C.: I spoke to Andrei [a major underground record producer and intellectual of the rock scene who had worked extensively with Yuri on numerous projects]. He is a very strong person, in my opinion. And he is very keen on music. And he said he was working a lot but didn't receive anything, but that was just the situation.

Yuri: Yes, everybody knows that. Nobody counted on money. I'll tell you a story. In 1987 we went on our first tour and made two hundred rubles.[17] Our guitarist, Andrei, was holding his share and started crying. He said, "What am I gonna do with this huge sum of money?" And he immediately spent it on drinking, out of fear! We had never received that much money.

T. C.: Yet that's only a little money.

Yuri: It was a colossal sum for us. . . . We can't live if we're too comfortable, too rich, because it means that we have to compromise with our conscience. If you go into commercial ventures that's it, that becomes your cross to bear. *If you start making money*

*without thinking about the main thing—music—then it's the grave for
you* [emphasis added]. . . . We had such an experience of utter
poverty for an idea, that here everything is all right. I've been in
palaces, and I saw people who are unhappy in their palaces. But
one cannot buy love for money. You can drive a limousine and
just be Michael Jackson and wander like a ghost, with his made-up
face, absolutely disgusting. You can walk there like a dwarf,
Quasimodo, in your park, and be completely unhappy. And you
can be a simple fellow (*muzhik*), live your life simply, and be
happy. It's philosophy again. So, for me it doesn't mean anything.
Do you know what I need money for? To put our ideas into practice. We need money as a means of production. And so my family
won't be hungry. That's it.

Musicians indicated two important views about money which
were central to the Petersburg rock musical community. The first is
that musicians lacked concern with money, and, second, that they
believed that money corrupts music. The rejection of money signifies a
major difference between Western rock musical cultures and the Petersburg rock community.[18] What is significant, and perhaps even quite
ironic, is that Western rock culture, spawned as it was from the capitalist culture industries and integrally involved with money, served as
the template for the development of a musical counterculture in Russia
which was, at its very core, "noncommercial."

Commercial and Noncommercial Music

The relationship between money and music-making which evolved in
the Petersburg rock community can be stated quite simply:
autonomous, independent music-making was defined precisely by its
independence from the realm of formal economic structures of Soviet
society. In the course of making music outside formal structures of cultural production, Petersburg rock musicians came to make an important
distinction between "commercial music" (*kommercheskaia muzyka*) and
"noncommercial music" (*nekommercheskaia muzyka*). In the West, the
term *commercialization of culture* generally means the production of culture explicitly with success in culture markets in mind. The idea of noncommercial culture is more in keeping with the idea of art for art's sake,
or the production of aesthetic cultural objects according to individual or
collectively shared ideas about aesthetic quality and authenticity.
Petersburg musicians share this distinction, with the added touch that
rock music, by definition, could not be produced within official eco-

nomic structures. If it were to be, it would cease to be rock and would become something else entirely. It is possible in the West to speak of "commercial rock-and-roll"—indeed, all successful rock in the West is by definition commercial. In terms of the local definitions of rock music in St. Petersburg, however, the idea of commercial rock is oxymoronic.

One musician captures the elemental distinction between commercial and noncommercial music and the idea of how the former process affects rock music:

> We have a notion of commercial music. We have such a notion, though I'm not sure that now it means the same that it meant before. At first pop music (*popsa*) was considered the sort of music that was played in the restaurants. I never played in restaurants. There is a certain repertoire in a restaurant that everybody plays. A pop (*popsovyi*) repertoire. A song from Deep Purple, one from here, one from there, from different Italians, kind of like disco music. And this is called "commercial music" because of the fact that in the restaurant they pay money for it. You want your favorite disco music, you give ten or twenty-five rubles to the musicians, and they play it for you. This well-paid music—it also sold well in the cooperatives. You can say—Laskovyi Mai. Do you know this group? They are sixteen- to seventeen-year-old guys. They compose very primitive computer music. But it sold very well in the kiosks. We have these little stands, kiosks, where they sell recordings. By virtue of the fact that this music sells well, it's called "commercial." Then you've got music which everybody pays respect to, and they say, "Yeah, that's great. That's hot (*kruto*)." This is called "noncommercial" music.

Another musician corroborates the idea that music for money is commercial music. But more than that, commercial music is regarded as contrived and artificial, while noncommercial music comes from the heart:

> *T. C.:* What does it mean in this context, commercial music?
>
> *Igor:* It means making money. Just making hits. Just sitting at the computer with your head only, without your heart, calculating a song—these words can go here, those there. This is all nonsense, gibberish. We are writing everything from the heart, and this is what matters. So, even if we are rich some day, we will never be commercial. You see, never.

T.C.: Yes, of course.

What was most important in the practice of separating music-making from moneymaking is that it led to the emergence of new criteria by which to evaluate the authenticity of rock music. In addition to a commitment to the poetic expression of truth, or *istina*, the identity of rock music came to be defined in relation to its proximity to official economic structures and practices. The closer music was to such structures, the less it was seen as being authentic. Of course, some active members of the underground music community—mostly producers and concert organizers—did not share such a conception and saw nothing wrong with making money from independent rock music. Such individuals were seen by musicians as a source of constraint *within* the musical community itself. Witness, for instance, an attempt by a very important figure in the Petersburg musical community to convince a very important musician, Yuri, to make some money from his music:

> *Yuri:* My reputation is like this: I'm known to those people who are very interested in music. But for the wide range—everybody, for example, knows Grebenshchikov. Not everybody knows me. Only those who really know music, rock music.

> *T. C.:* Maybe you don't want to be famous, but then something may happen with your music or life.

> *Yuri:* I never wanted to be famous and a star. I had such a credo— from 1980 to 1981 my fame started to spread, and every day I was defending myself against visitors, autographs, was recording kilometers of tape. Before, we had this kind of home concert system. That is, the fans gather, and since there were no halls, they'd put in some little apparatus at home, pay you fifty, one hundred rubles. You'd come, and you'd play. And I swept all this aside, because through my individualistic creativity, I came to the conclusion that if I'm turning into a real rock star—and at that time I was irritated very much by the rock of Makarevich from Mashina Vremeni (Time Machine), everybody was just idolizing him, not a rock-and-roll audience, just the public in general. And I thought, God damn it, if I were to become like him, so that such morons (*mudaki*) were idolizing me, I would have better gone and gotten myself drowned in shit. I disliked it strongly.

> And there were attempts to pull me into this course. Andrei [a key underground producer in Petersburg], this great manager here—then he was manager of Mashina Vremeni—arranged con-

certs and this and that. He came to me once in 1980 or 1981, took a seat on the sofa, and said, "Let's do your concerts." He was interested in commercial success. A lot of people would have come to hear me. I say, "Let's not, Andrei." He says, "Why?" I say, "I'm interested in neither money nor fame." I say this to him quite in earnest. He looked at me like this and said, "Are you an idiot or what?" And I say, "Look, I'm confessing to you. I'm sitting here hungry, skinny, and the idea of how to get closer to our Almighty Lord, Jesus Christ, interests me much more than concerts." He says, "Come on, forget this shit. I don't have anything against Christ, but think, it won't hurt you to have three thousand rubles, or even five thousand." I say, "It is very possible that it will hurt." He never persuaded me.

Rock versus Pop: The Relational Identity of Rock Music

The qualities that defined musical identity tended to occur in pairs. That is, the positive qualities of musical identity, such as its authenticity, goodness, auspiciousness, and purity, tended to be paired with negative qualities, such as inauthenticity, badness, inauspiciousness, and impurity. A commitment to making music outside of formal economic structures conferred upon the products of such musicianship these positive qualities. Conversely, the commercialization of music, a process which brought music into contact with money, was seen as "polluting." Very often, for instance, musicians described those who were in the business of music specifically to make money as *nechistye liudi*, or "dirty people." Another common reference to commercial music producers was "shark" (*akula*). Music which was the product of a cooperation with political-economic structures was seen as being "spoiled" or "dirty."

These binary classifications were constructed by musicians themselves in the course of thinking and talking about the identity of rock music in St. Petersburg. There are a number of words which musicians used to describe such spoiled cultural products, but the most common is the Anglicized Russian word *popsa* or *pops*, which simply means "pop." Another word used to identify commercialized music is the untranslatable word *estrada* (or less commonly, *estradnaia muzyka*). Still another term used to convey an even more desperate attempt to commercialize music is *restorannaia muzyka*, or "restaurant music." The Russian term *estradnaia muzyka* is not purely equatable with the idea of *pops*. According to one prominent Russian rock critic—himself a part of the countercultural musical community—pop music is seen as a bit more stylized than traditional *estradnaia* music, since it uses more modern instruments and practices of modern rock (Troitsky 1990*b*, p. 271). Pop music is considered to be music which "is created with the sober calculation (*s trezvym raschetom*) of commercial reward" (ibid.). From this comes "a dance rhythm, a melodiousness [*melodichnost'*] (often with 'inoffensive texts' [*uklonom v odessku*])." "Pop-poets," as pop musicians, are characterized "not only by an inability to create anything intelligent, but also by a complete unwillingness to intimidate art councils (*khudsovety*), the administration and directors of cultural enterprises . . . without radio and TV, pop is doomed and simply does not make any sense" (ibid.).

In contrast to pop, authentic music which is specifically described as *rok* comes "from the soul." It is a product of pure consciousness which is made without any consideration of commercial reward or success. Moreover, in contrast to "pop-poets," the authentic rock musician is not frightened by the consequences of making music, and fears neither the official organ of cultural surveillance, the *khudsovet*, nor the economic privation which is the inevitable consequence of the practice of independent music-making. As such, rock music is more pure than pop music, is considered aesthetically superior, and, therefore, more authentic than pop music. Yet this does not mean that rock musicians do not grant that some pop musicians are, in the words of one commentator "very talented" (ibid.). We have seen previously that some rock musicians felt that even pop musicians could display some *draiv* or *energiia* in their music. Ultimately, though, the authenticity of pop was questionable since one could never be sure whether the products were a result of outside political or economic influences or the products of individual consciousness and conscience. In granting some legitimacy to pop and attributing to its creators some talent, rock musicians corroborate the fact that music can be a form of entertainment. But rock music is never defined as entertainment, in spite of the fact that it obviously entertains audiences.[19] Rather, rock is seen as serious artistic work in the service of an idea.

What is important in the above distinctions is that the very use of the specific word *rok* to describe a musical product evokes all of the positive qualities of musical authenticity. *Rok* is the opposite of *popsa*, and its very identity is defined in relation to the latter. This is significantly different than in Western rock communities in which the word *rock* does not infer an explicit relation to commerce or the market. It is quite possible for rock to be wildly successful from a commercial standpoint and still be defined as rock. Of course questions remain among musicians and analysts about the degree to which rock is spoiled or made less authentic or popular as a result of its commercial success (see, for instance, Frith and Horne 1987; and Walker 1987). Yet such questions were not within the realm of the discursive possibilities of the Petersburg rock musicians: music for money is pop, while music for music's sake is rock.

It is fascinating that some Petersburg musicians use the verb *popsovat'* to convey a sense of interference or spoiling of their authentic musical form.[20] *Popsovat'*, literally "to make something into pop," is quite interesting from an etymological standpoint. The word is found in everyday Russian language as early as the nineteenth century. The famous Russian lexicographer, Vladimir Dal', offers the following definition in his *Explanatory Dictionary of the Living Russian Language* ([1980] 1955): "youth term: to spoil [*isportit'*], manipulate [*iskazit'*], or mess up [*ispakostit'*]."[21] This word was used as early as the nineteenth century to describe a situation characterized by interference and, what is more important, interference which results in spoilage or the "pollution" of some autonomous form of activity. It conveys a sense of the idea of the intrusion from outside forces which is at the base of all discussions of the distinctions between rock and pop as they are used among Petersburg musicians. The same word is used to connote a sense of spoilage of rock products a century later: business spoils the authenticity of rock music as an art form.

It is extremely important to underscore the fact that independent rock musicians in Petersburg defined their activity in opposition not only to the dominant political and economic structures, but in relation to the very cultural objects which were the products of such structures. If rock music was outside of political and economic structures, it was also outside, or superior to, the culture which came from inside such structures. Western analysts have made a serious analytical mistake in lumping together forms of culture produced within the system and those produced outside of it and referring to the whole as "popular culture."[22] Indeed, independent musicians in Petersburg felt themselves to be rather esoteric, cryptic, and not desirous of the kind of cheap popularity accorded to the progenitors of *pops*. To refer to rock music in the Russian context as a form of popular culture is to insult the Petersburg countercultural musician who sees his activity as fundamentally and essentially noncommercial.[23]

The category of the popular is one against which Petersburg musicians define the authenticity of their own rock music. Such a relational definition of rock music's identity, however, was bound to lead to a contradiction. On the one hand, rock music was seen as an esoteric, secretive, and even cryptic form of art which aspired to convey deeper truths about reality. On the other hand, it had appeal to wider and wider audiences, thus making it "popular" in the sense that the term popular has been used to refer to the *vox populi*. Rock musicians were thus caught in between a definition of their product as special and even esoteric (similar in many ways to the ways in which many artists see their art) and the fact that they often became famous and "popular." The tension which resulted from this contradiction could be resolved somewhat by the fact that musicians' popularity would never be formally and commercially rewarded in Soviet society. The structural realities of that society obliged musicians to live simply and in service of the idea of rock music as art. For many, this was less an obligation than one of the "fringe benefits" provided by the socialist welfare state. The situation was to change, however, when the social structure of the Soviet Union began to move toward a market economy. The basic effect of this movement was increasing movement of money into the practice and production of rock music. This movement, which we shall explore in detail in chapter 5, was to have profound consequences both for the identity of rock music and for those who made it.

The Identity of Rock Music:
A Summary of the Vocabulary of
Rock Music Authenticity

We have seen that defining the identity of rock music in Petersburg during the Soviet era consisted of two fundamental processes:

1. the construction of musical identity according to the relation of the latter to formal political and economic structures; and
2. the assignment of the label of "authentic" or "inauthentic" to musical products to the extent to which they adhered to particular categories which comprised the fundamental qualities of music.

In the evolution of its identity, rock was judged as authentic to the extent that it adhered to constructed categories of aesthetic judgment which circulated within the rock community. By way of summary of this chapter, I would like to provide a summary of the "vocabulary" of the qualities which were used to define musical identity as either authentic or inauthentic within the St. Petersburg rock musical community. First, a word is in order regarding what might be called the "vocabularies of motive" which musicians used to describe their music and their lives.

A Note on Situated Activities and Vocabularies of Motive

In the course of answering a wide range of questions about why they became musicians, what rock music meant to them, or the relation of music to economics or politics, musicians articulated a specific vocabulary. More specifically, what they articulated was what C. Wright Mills ([1940] 1963) referred to as a "vocabulary of motive." According to Mills, when individuals are asked to explain their actions, they articulate explanations for what they do. Mills refers to such explanations as "motives." For Mills (ibid., p. 443), a motive is that which "tends to be one which is to the actor and to the other members of a situation an unquestioned answer to questions concerning social and lingual content." St. Petersburg rock musicians lived in a common situation and engaged in the practice of rock music outside of formal political and economic structures. Their answers to questions about the sources of their rock careers, the meaning and identity of rock music, and their relation to formal structures of political and economic authority constitute a vocabulary of motive. Why does a rock musician choose to be a rock musician? Because Soviet existence is alienating. Why does a rock musician choose rock over, say, painting? Because rock is a unique and energetic cultural form which crystallizes and communicates ideas about the truth, or *istina*. Why do they not wish to make money from their music? Because money corrupts music and musicians. All such explanations are constructed from a vocabulary of motive which explains, not only to individual musicians themselves, but to sociologists and other outsiders, the nature of the world, the identity of rock music, and reasons for what they do.

Ultimately, we have to ask four questions: Did Petersburg musicians really believe that rock music was a means for the embodiment and communication of ultimate truth, or *istina*? Did they really believe that they raised themselves above politics through the practice of their craft? Did they really not wish to make money from rock music? Did they really believe that rock music was pure to the extent that it remained distant from the corrupting factors of power and money? From a sociological standpoint, it is fruitless to engage in speculation about the "real" motivations of Petersburg rock musicians. The search for "true" motivations leads us into a psychological abyss from which we cannot possibly understand the process of the social construction of reality and meaning within the Petersburg rock community. We are not concerned here with discovering what the "true" desires, needs, or psychological needs of musicians were in this situation. Instead, we focus on the explanations offered by musicians about the identity of their music and the explanations which they themselves offer for their activity. The central sociological reality which emerges thus far in our account of Petersburg musical counterculture is that in the course of talking about their lives and the meaning of rock music as a cultural practice, Petersburg rock musicians constructed a specific vocabulary of motive which served as the basis for their ongoing activity as musicians. Vocabularies of motive are situated, which means that they explain and make intelligible to all actors in a situation a certain reality or realities. The reality which we have been most concerned with in this chapter is the reality of the definition and identity of rock music.

Table 3.1 presents a vocabulary of the fundamental categories which musicians themselves used in the process of constructing musical identity. I have presented the categories in binaries, since, as I have argued, the social construction of musical identity is fundamentally a relational process. As with all binary classification schemes, the qualities

TABLE 3.1
A Petersburg Vocabulary of Musical Identity

(Authentic)	(Inauthentic)
+ ◄———— Musical Objects ————► −	
Rock (*Rok muzyka*)	Pop (*Popsa*)[24]
Autonomous	Controlled
Spontaneous	Planned
Noncommercial	Commercial
Complex/Coded	Obvious
Experientially/Existentially based	Invented
Ethereal	Banal
Otherworldly	Thisworldly
Art	Entertainment
Vocation	Job
Sensible	Nonsense
True	False
Strong	Weak
Energetic	Asthenic[25]
Difficult	Simple
Unique	Standardized
Open	Closed
Creative	Hackneyed
Esoteric	Mass
Innovative	Redundant
Valuable	Cheap

listed in the table represent ideals according to which musical products are measured. There is no such thing as perfectly authentic music. Conversely, no music is absolutely inauthentic. Rather, authenticity and inauthenticity represent two poles of a spectrum of possibilities of musical identity. The positive qualities of rock music represent the positive end of the spectrum, while the qualities of pop music represent negative ideals of musical identity. Authentic musical products are those which are discussed in terms of the vocabulary on the left side of the table. Conversely, inauthentic products are those which are identified with the vocabulary on the right side of the table. As with other binary classifications, elements of the vocabulary appear individually or in clusters with other elements. That is, vocabulary from one column can be combined with other categories in the column in the process of the identification of music. Musical objects in St. Petersburg existed in social space between two poles of musical authenticity, one positive and one negative. The concrete activities and interactions of Petersburg musicians pushed musical objects toward one pole or the other, that is, identified musical objects as being authentic or inauthentic.

In the next chapter, we examine the ways in which the pursuit of the ideal of authenticity in the production of musical objects led to the construction of both individual and collective forms of identity within the context of socialist industrial modernity. In the process of striving to create authentic musical products, musicians also constructed alternative and authentic selves within an existence which they viewed as inauthentic. More than that, in the process of making music together, musicians created a community which stood as an island of meaning in the sea of socialist industrial modernity.

4

At Play in the Fields of the Soviets: Individual and Collective Identity in the St. Petersburg Rock Music Community

Von der Gewalt, die alle Wesen bindet,
Befreit der Mensch sich, der sich überwindet.
(From the force all creatures heed
He who transcends himself is freed)

—Georg Simmel
The Transcendent Character of Life

Der Gegenpol von Zwang ist nicht Freiheit sondern
Verbundenheit. (The opposite to coercion is not
freedom, but fellowship.)

—Martin Buber
Freedom, Power, and Democratic Planning

Music and Identity

We saw in the last chapter that Petersburg musicians conferred upon rock music a very special identity. From their point of view, rock music was a special and extraordinary form of culture, a privileged form of communication which articulated and conveyed heartfelt ideas about reality and existence. Serious rock musicians' lives reflected a basic commitment not only to producing this special form of culture, but also to protecting rock from threats by outside forces. They did this by resisting accommodation to political and economic institutions. In the process of producing and protecting such special cultural objects, rock musicians also carved out for themselves "existential spaces" within Soviet industrial existence. As opposed to the identity of rock music, we might begin to speak of the identity of rock musicians. In this chapter, we explore the process of how rock musicians, through the pursuit of independent musicianship, came to see themselves as special, both to themselves and to others. Yet, as we have argued, music-making is a collective enterprise. Producing rock music was much more than a simple act of the creation of aesthetic cultural objects: it led to the emergence of a cultural community in which individuals could construct alternative and subjectively meaningful identities within the space of socialist industrial society. In the course of making music, Petersburg musicians formed a special group which we have referred to throughout this book as rock music counterculture. This counterculture shared a distinct way of life which consisted of its own norms, values, beliefs, symbols, language, rituals, and practices of everyday life. And what is most important, this counterculture was marked by its difference from and opposition to the dominant culture of socialist industrial society.

In this chapter, we focus on two related processes. First, we explore the identity of the Petersburg rock musicians as a special kind of identity within the context of socialist industrial society. Second, we explore the ways in which the activities of each individual, each pursuing his own identity, combined to form a distinct culture— a counterculture—with its own collective identity. Finally, we explore the significance of this counterculture in relation to the dominant culture of socialist industrial modernity. In addition to presenting a picture of the general way of life of the St. Petersburg rock counterculture, this chapter draws on important sociological concepts such as the idea of the sacred, vocation, and community in order to make sense of the significance of the practice of rock music at both the individual and the collective levels. We begin by examining one of the most important ideas in the history of sociological theory: the idea of the sacred.

The Sociological Meaning of the Sacred

The idea of the sacred is perhaps one of the most basic and important in the history of sociological thought. Emile Durkheim ([1915] 1965), one of the founding fathers of sociology, made the study of the sacred a central task of the discipline. At the basis of Durkheim's sociology of religion was the idea of the separation between the sacred and the profane which exists in all societies. All societies classify things according to whether they are extraordinary and endowed with special qualities or whether they are ordinary and mundane. The former he identifies as sacred, the latter as profane. Because they are special, sacred things are separated from profane things and a good deal of social activity is based on maintaining that separation. Durkheim says that "sacred things are those which interdictions protect or isolate, profane things those to which these interdictions are applied and which must remain at a distance from the first" (ibid., p. 56). Showing the influence of a binary and relational way of thinking which was to influence much of later French social theory, Durkheim stressed that the identity of sacred objects is defined in relation to those things which are defined as profane, and vice versa: "The sacred thing is *par excellence* that which the profane should not touch. To be sure, this interdiction cannot go so far as to make all communication between the two worlds impossible; for if the profane could in no way enter into relations with the sacred, the latter could be good for nothing" (ibid., p. 55). We know what is sacred by virtue of what we know to be profane. The sacredness of sacred things is actually strengthened to the extent that the latter come in contact with ordinary things. All societies make distinctions between sacred and profane things. Yet while this formal distinction is constant, the specific content of the sacred and profane is highly variable.

There are two important points regarding Durkheim's distinction between the sacred and the profane. The first is that the idea of the sacred is not limited to the description of supernatural phenomena. In normal usage, the term *sacred* evokes images of gods and deities, of supernatural and magical forces beyond worldly control, or of experiences of transcendence and grace. This is because the term is often used to describe the special character of religious phenomena. Yet, for Durkheim, sacredness is not only a quality used to describe religious or supernatural phenomena. Objects from the secular world—people, places, things, nations—can also be seen as sacred, depending on the specific social context. Durkheim (ibid., p. 427) says that "there can be no society which does not feel the need of upholding and reaffirming at regular intervals the collective sentiments and the collective ideas which make its unity and personality."

The second important point regarding the sacred is that it is not purely equatable with objects which are defined as good, benevolent, or positive in a given context. As Durkheim sees it, any inherent qualities of objects have little to do with whether or not they are considered sacred in a society. This is a point which is highly relevant for our discussion, and it is worth quoting Durkheim at length:

> The idea of [the sacred] is in no way made up of the impressions directly produced by the thing upon our sense and minds. Religious force is not only the sentiment inspired by the group in its members, but [is] projected outside of the consciousnesses that experience them and objectified. To be objectified, they are fixed upon some object which thus becomes sacred; *in principle there are none whose nature predestines them to it [becoming sacred] to the exclusion of others; but also, there are none which are necessarily impossible* ([1915] 1965, p. 261; emphasis added).[1]

Sacredness depends more fundamentally on the projection of certain feelings and sentiments of what Durkheim calls "religious force" on objects. In Durkheim's view, anything can be considered sacred.

The focus of the last chapter was on the identity of rock music as a special cultural object in the Soviet environment. In light of the previous discussion on the nature of the sacred, it is useful to begin by thinking of the local identity of rock music among Petersburg rock musicians as a sacred cultural object within the context of Soviet society. It is particularly fortuitous that Durkheim often used the French word *objet*, "object," to identify that which is made sacred. For rock music in the Soviet context was a cultural object upon which the religious force which makes things sacred was projected. In the course of the production of rock music, specific positive qualities of rock music emerged which defined its identity as a sacred cultural object. Conversely, negative qualities emerged which defined the identity of certain musical objects as *popsa* and *estrada* and, therefore, profane. The making of rock music was fundamentally conditioned—even constrained—by an emphasis on maintaining distinctions between sacred music (*rok muzyka*) and profane music (*popsa*). Profane musical products and the forces which produced them continually threatened to come into contact with rock music and make it profane. Recall the important connotation of the verb *popsovat'*, "to meddle," "interfere with," or "to spoil." *Popsa* and the social forces which produced it were omnipresent forces which, both actually and potentially, came into contact with rock music and threatened to pollute it or spoil its special identity. Such profanation, however, only served to strengthen the sacred identity of rock music. Indeed, independent rock musicians worked constantly in the shadow of the profaning influences of commercialism, and it was the constant threat of such profanation which made music even more meaningful and sacred as a form of privileged cultural communication.

Sacred Objects, Sacred People

At this point, an important question emerges: Why is it necessary to reconceptualize the identity of Russian rock music as a sacred cultural object? The answer lies in an examination of the relations between sacred cultural objects and those who produce them. In the process of constructing and protecting the identity of sacred musical objects, musicians came to see themselves and to be seen by others as sacred. The example of rock musicians in the West is instructive here. Historically speaking, it is clear that many Western rock musicians—both the living and (especially) the dead—are seen as extraordinary. It is difficult to argue with the fact that certain Western rock musicians enjoy a measure of esteem and veneration which practically no other class of individuals in Western societies enjoys. The example of Elvis Presley is useful here. In the wake of his death, Elvis's identity became sacralized to such an extent that, for all intents and purposes, he ceased to be purely human. Massive numbers of people celebrate Elvis's birthday and deathday and make annual pilgrimages to the sacred site of Elvis's grave at Graceland to pay homage to him. All around the world (even in Russia), Elvis has "appeared" both as an apparition and as a human being who was still alive, for death happens only to mortals (see Marcus 1991). There are many other cases which illustrate the process of what might be called the "sacralization of rock musicians." The identities of Jim Morrison and John Lennon have both become objects upon which sacred feelings have been projected and reinforced through various types of social action which are highly religious in nature.[2]

What accounts for the deification of Western rock musicians? An answer to this question lies in an examination of the relation of musicians to the sacred cultural objects which they produce. Here, Durkheim is again our guide. Sacred objects do not simply exist and float around in social space: they are made sacred through the social interaction of individuals and are used actively by people in the course of day-to-day living. One of the primary uses of sacred cultural objects is as a basis for the formation of both self-identity and social identity. Self-identity is an individual's own definition of who he or she is. Social identity is the sense which others have of an individual. Ordinarily, sociologists speak of this sense of identity as social status. Those who are highly esteemed by others have high social status, while those who are held in low esteem by others have low social status. In the formation of self-identity, individuals often measure the value of their selves by the cultural objects with which they come in contact. For example, Thorstein Veblen (1934) demonstrated that rich people conspicuously consume cultural objects not only to demonstrate to others, but to themselves, that they are special. Individuals often use such sacred objects to define themselves as special or as different.

In a recent work on the formation of status groups in India, Murray Milner (1993) notes that a major source of social status is the association of individuals with sacred objects. Those who regularly come in contact with sacred objects are generally considered to be of higher status than those who regularly commune with profane or ordinary ones. In other words, individuals who associate with sacred objects come to define themselves and be defined by others as sacred. In traditional Indian society, the identities of those who associated with sacred Hindu objects or participated in special, sacred events took on the qualities of such objects and their status as members of higher castes was strengthened. Status, for Milner, is itself a particular kind of sacredness. Important statuses are not simply positions from which those who occupy them enjoy immense privileges in relation to others. Rather, individuals who enjoy such status are often treated as special, extraordinary, and not of this world: they are treated as sacred.

The above arguments are a useful starting point for understanding both the individual and the collective significance of rock practice in St. Petersburg. We have seen, for instance, how, in the course of making music and talking about it, musicians constructed a special identity for their cultural products. Yet, at the same time, their very sense of their own identities was fundamentally conditioned by their constant production of and relation to their own special cultural products. By virtue of their "communion" with rock music, members of the rock community came to see themselves as having a special identity—a sacred identity—and were seen by others as occupying a special status—a sacred status—in relation to the rest of the world. Both self-identity and social identity were fundamentally related to rock musicians' close association with special musical products.

I do not wish to convey a sense that this relationship between cultural objects, self-identity, and social identity is a causal one. It is neither possible nor desirable to attempt to specify relations between these phenomena in such a way that one or the other phenomenon is seen as antecedent or causal to the other.[3] At base, the relationship between these phenomena is a processual one. Surely, the production of sacred music may lead to the definition of one's self-identity as sacred and to a sacred social identity in the eyes of others. And surely those who are in regular communion with those who are considered sacred may come to see themselves and be seen by others as sacred. Yet, those who see themselves as sacred and are seen by others as sacred are also in a position to produce sacred objects. It thus becomes difficult, if not impossible, to determine the precise source of the sacredness of either objects, selves, or statuses. The sacredness of objects, of individual identity, and of social identity are related in a processual way. Each is a product of and contributes in an ongoing way to the production of the other. This "triangle of sacredness" is depicted in figure 4.1.

We might restate the above argument as a series of questions: Are musical products sacred by virtue of the fact that those who produce them are considered to be sacred or consider themselves to be sacred? Or are those who produce them sacred by virtue of the fact that the objects which they produce are considered sacred? The answers to such questions will become apparent as we explore the relationship between cultural objects, self-identity, and the collective identity among mem-

FIGURE 4.1
The Triangle of Sacredness

Self-Identity

Cultural Objects

Social Identity

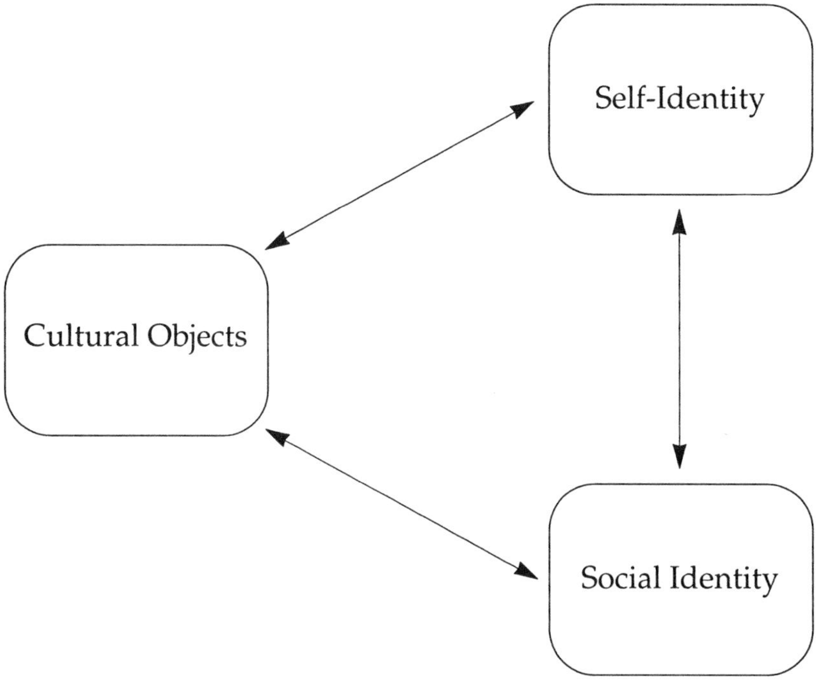

bers of the Petersburg musical community. We turn first to the examination of the relationship between making music and making personal identity within the context of socialist modernity. Our guide here is not Durkheim, but Max Weber. For this idea of making one's own alternative and subjectively meaningful identity within the space of socialist modernity is best seen as the pursuit of what Weber called "vocation."

Authentic Music, Authentic Lives: Rock Musicianship as a Source of Individual Identity

Play and Transcendence

In the second chapter, we examined some of the varieties of musical experience which evolved in St. Petersburg during the Soviet period. We saw that among Petersburg musicians there were numerous paths through life which led to the choice of rock musicianship as a career. Musicians' experiences in "normal" existence, in the world of *Sovok* with its norms of social and aesthetic conformity, mediocrity, complacency, and anti-individualism, served to push them away from that existence. The path to an alternative individual existence lay in the playing of rock music. This playing of rock music was, at the most fundamental level, a way of transcending elements of Soviet existence. We must never lose sight of the fact that rock music—despite the seriousness of those who made it—was a form of play.

Yet rock music was a form of "serious play." Indeed, the degree to which many musicians pursued their craft with the utmost seriousness and without a hint of recognition of any idea that music was a form of entertainment is striking. In any case, what musicians did was play music. Hence, it is useful to begin our discussion by seeing music as a form of "serious play" in the Soviet context. This paradoxical and oxymoronic sense of play as a serious enterprise is captured well by Johan Huizinga, whose work focused on the central importance of play in human societies. Huizinga's definition of play is worth noting in detail:

> Summing up the formal characteristics of play we might call it a free activity standing quite consciously outside "ordinary" life as being "not serious," but at the same time absorbing the player intensely and utterly. It is an activity connected with no material interest and no profit can be gained by it. It proceeds within its own proper boundaries of time and space according to fixed rules and in an orderly manner. It promotes the formation of social

groupings which tend to surround themselves with secrecy and to stress their difference from the common world by disguise or other means. (1950, p. 13)

For Huizinga, the "charm" of play is enhanced by the fact that it is secret. The central element of play is the "abolition of the ordinary world . . . what the 'others' do 'outside' is of no concern" to those who are playing (1950, p. 12). Play, for Huizinga, entails a "stepping out" of ordinary reality into a "higher order." Play establishes and maintains independent and collective forms of identity. Huizinga's conception of play allows us to view a whole host of cultural practices, ordinarily viewed as "not serious" or as "fun," as being vitally important at both the individual and the collective levels of social existence. Play, especially in restrictive or confining social situations, becomes a means of transcending the world, a means of subjectively removing oneself from the world while still remaining in it. It is in this sense that "play-ing" music was a practice which lifted individuals out of the normal world of Soviet existence. By understanding music as play we can begin to understand the true meaning and cultural significance of rock music as a form of individual search for transcendence, a form of "play in the fields of socialist modernity." Yet more than that, the play of rock musicians can be seen as the pursuit of a meaningful vocation within Socialist industrial society.

The Quest for Authentic Identity: Rock Music as a Vocation

In the course of thinking about and discussing their individual lives, rock musicians continually described their own identities as the pursuit of what is called in Russian, *lichnost'*. Generally, the word *lichnost'* is translated as "personality" or "individuality." Yet in a social scientific sense, *lichnost'* has also been used—mainly by political elites and their acolytes in social science—as a concept referring to "identity" (see, for instance, Strutinskii 1987; and Shavel' 1988). *Lichnost'* is a very important word in the Soviet political vocabulary. The Soviet state aspired to develop the personalities and identities of its subjects along the lines of the norms and values of its own culture. To be a good Soviet citizen was to display a communist identity (*kommunisticheskaia lichnost'*), and this identity would serve as the subjective bulwark for the construction of a communist social order.

The Soviet state's attempt at developing a "socialist personality" can be seen in theoretical terms as an attempt to forge what Italian social theorist Antonio Gramsci called "cultural hegemony." Gramsci

(1971) defined cultural hegemony as the process by which the ideology of a dominant class or a group comes to be viewed by members of a society as "common sense" and as the natural, right, or legitimate "way of things." Ideally, cultural hegemony is achieved to the extent that individuals in a given society—especially those who are members of subordinated social groups and classes—come to think of the society and their place it in as legitimate, right, or deserved (Gramsci 1971; see also Crowley 1988; O'Sullivan et al. 1983, p. 103; and Cushman 1993, pp. 35-38). The development of a socialist identity was a central aspect of the overall strategy of the Soviet state for forging cultural hegemony and legitimacy at the level of individual existence. Yet, as Gramsci notes, hegemony is only an aspiration; it can never be fully achieved in reality because subjects invariably find ways to resist the supplication of their subjectivities by dominant ideology through a variety of creative and industrious means. Indeed, in modern industrial societies, hegemonic aspirations could never be completely successful. Such societies, even those of the Soviet type, are simply too complex for states to steer at both the institutional and subjective level without the emergence of systemic crises (Habermas 1975). There are always means of escape, and in Soviet society a primary means of escape was through the practice of rock music, a practice which fought prescriptions for communist identity by enabling a sense of alternative identity.

Many rock musicians retained the politically laden word *lichnost'* to describe the ends of their own cultural practice. This fundamental ability to reclaim conventional categories is somewhat enabled by the existence in the Russian language of the reflexive possessive pronoun *svoia*, a word which conveys a sense of "one's own," as opposed to someone else's possession of some object or quality. Time and again, while talking of the ends of their musical activity, musicians referred to the pursuit of *svoia lichnost'*, or "my own identity." In some cases, musicians used the more mystical idea of following their "star," or *zvezda*, to describe the ideal individual end point of their musical activity. The word *lichnost'* itself is strongly evocative of politics; yet musicians stripped the word of its official meanings and connotations and invested it instead with a content which was more subjectively meaningful. For the musician, the making of authentic music became an important template for the construction of an authentic sense of one's own personality and identity based on values held to be special to the individual.

The pursuit of independent and autonomous identity through the playing of music can be viewed, in Max Weber's terms, as the pursuit of a vocation. There are many senses—both religious and secular—of the idea of vocation. The notion has been used both by religious and socio-logical thinkers to emphasize a simultaneous retreat from the world and a pursuit of a course of action or belief grounded in one's own beliefs and values, or what might be described as a "calling." The voca-tion, or calling, of the Christian meant that the individual was, quite literally, "called out of the world" and "called out against the world" (Weber 1930). In addition to describing the Puritan work ethic as a call-ing and as the pursuit of a vocation, Weber (1946a, pp. 115 ff; 1946b, pp. 152 ff) also used the term *vocation* to describe the idea of an indi-vidual's commitment to politics and science as a passionate, dutiful, sincere, and authentic way of life rather than as a means toward satis-fying one's own self-interest. Weber used the idea of vocation to outline the possibility of participation in the political world based on the indi-vidual's own sense of inner calling and sense of values and morality. The pursuit of a vocation signifies an individual choice of a path through the world, an attempt to find some way of participating mean-ingfully in the affairs of the world. But what is so wrong with the world that would make Weber argue strongly that meaningful identity could be achieved only in spite of it?

At the very core of Weber's sociology is a fundamental distinction between different types of social action. Weber (1978, pp. 24-25) argued that action can be oriented in four ways. Action can be instrumentally rational, or oriented toward achieving rationally defined goals through rational means. Action can also be value-rational, or guided by con-scious beliefs in some aesthetic, moral, religious, or ethical values which are independent of and often in conflict with considerations of rational self-interest. Finally, Weber makes a distinction between affectual action and traditional action. The former is action based on the individual's emotions and states of mind, and the latter is simply action which is based on habitual ways of doing things.

Weber's typology of social action makes us aware that people do what they do for very different reasons. A good portion of Weber's sociology was based on this fundamental typology of social action. He sought to examine and compare historical manifestations of social action based on different types of subjective orientations. Yet Weber was also concerned with understanding the changing patterns in the predominance of one or the other type of rationality. What concerns us most here is the distinction between instrumental rationality and value rationality. For Weber the phenomenologist, value-rational action was the primary type of action through which individuals achieved some sense of meaning and value in their personal existence. For Weber the historical sociologist, modernity was characterized by the increasing displacement of value-rational action by instrumentally oriented action. Modern societies, he argued, were increasingly guided by the ethos of instrumental rationality. The result of this was the growth and entrenchment of structures of political and economic domination, or what Weber described with his famous metaphor of the "iron cage." The incessant emphasis in modern societies on the pursuit of rational goals through rational ends made it difficult for individuals to engage in actions based on their values and beliefs rather than on rational self-interest. Modernity, for Weber, ultimately led to a crisis of meaning.

Weber's own response to the domination of instrumental rationality in the modern world was to argue that individuals should accept what is inexorable and devote themselves to the pursuit of vocations based on their own ethical values and beliefs. Such pursuits would serve as a means of re-enchantment in a world which had been disenchanted by the logic of instrumental rationality. For Weber, the process of the bureaucratic rationalization of the world had led to a practice of politics which was often self-interested and cynical. He argued that in the modern world too many people were living *off* politics as a vocation rather than living *for* politics (1946, p. 84). Yet he offered the idea of "politics as a vocation" as a means by which individuals could retain some sense of individual meaning within the world. Indeed, the survival of meaning in the modern world depended fundamentally on the existence of individuals who felt morally bound to pursue their duties within the bureaucracy according to the dictates of their own values and beliefs rather than the brutal logic of instrumental rationality (1946; see also Sayer 1991, pp. 92 ff). Such a pursuit involved an acceptance of the outside world, but also enabled individuals to achieve a sense of "inner distance" from the bureaucratized, rationalized "outer world."[4] For Weber, individuals could find some measure of personal meaning and authenticity in existence through the practice of politics as a vocation.

Weber accepted the idea of an authentic and meaningful practice of politics within the world of industrial modernity. What possible relevance, then, could the term *vocation* have for Petersburg rock musicians who felt that the only possibility of moral or ethical action lay outside of conventional, institutionalized politics? The answer is that the triumph of instrumental rationality in Soviet society extinguished the possibility of the practice of politics as a meaningful rather than a self-interested vocation. The historical development of socialist industrial modernity was characterized by the triumph of the ethos of bureaucratic rationality and the infusion of that ethos in all spheres of social life. Indeed, what distinguished so-called totalitarian states from those of the capitalist West was the degree to which the ethos of instrumental rationality came to serve as the predominant guideline for almost all types of social action in such societies. Even the prescient Weber did not anticipate the severity of the forms of domination which would result from the increasing infusion of instrumental rationality into more and more spheres of social life in the twentieth century. What is more, he could not anticipate that the triumph of instrumental rationality in Soviet society would, indeed, extinguish the very possibility of the practice of politics as a vocation in this society.

Weber's idea of vocation remains important in a formal, ideal-typical sense for the analysis of forms of authentic and meaningful identity in socialist industrial society. The search for meaning and authenticity in existence was played out through actions based on the values, ethics, and beliefs of actors rather than on the pursuit of rational self-interest. In social contexts such as the Soviet Union, individuals did pursue vocations. Yet such vocations, if they were to be meaningful and authentic, were expressed outside of politics. Indeed, it could be no other way, for the practice of politics in the Soviet Union had become a pragmatic affair which was defined primarily as an arena for the satisfaction and protection of self-interest. Indeed, the idea expressed not only by musicians but also by many Russians that "honest people suffer in the Soviet Union" testifies to the inability to pursue meaningful vocations within the formal structures of Soviet society.[5]

Music was a vocation which offered musicians some meaning and sense of purpose in what, for them, was an essentially intractable and alienating world of Soviet modernity. Rock musicians simultaneously rejected the official and empty world of Soviet modernity, but remained fundamentally within that world—and rather noisily at that. Indeed, paradoxically, they could not exist without it, for it was the very condition of Soviet modernity which was the wellspring of their craft. What distinguished Petersburg musicians from their conformist comrades was that, rather than remain within a world in which each individual pursued his or her own self-interest against everyone else, they translated their subjective feelings of disenchantment with the world into the practice of rock music as a vocation. Rock musicians felt called away from the world and called toward music. They saw music-making as a means of mediating between fundamental existential truths and a public which had been subject to the various evils of Soviet existence. There is a certain duality to the rock vocation, for, like other vocations, it sought to escape from the world precisely by projecting itself onto the world—in this case through the creation of special, sacred forms of music.

The vocation of rock musician was only one part of a greater universe of vocations which emerged in relation to the hyperrational world of socialist industrial modernity. One has only to think of individuals' commitments to religion, to ideas of nationhood, or to the family as alternative pursuits of a sense of meaning and purpose within this world. The usual picture of Soviet society is one characterized by images of a deadened lifeworld, of abjectly alienated actors living in fear, without meaning, without *raison d'être*. If actors in the Soviet world exhibited any life at all, they did so in hidden and more contemplative and private ways. There is little doubt that Stalinism and the Stalinist legacy produced radical forms of alienation and corresponding flights of individuals from the official world. Yet, on the other hand, the history of consciousness and cultural practice in Soviet Russia (and in communist-type societies in general) is not simply the history of retreat into the private realm of subjective disenchantment. That history also includes forms of resistant consciousness which actively rejected the existing world while at the same time projecting themselves onto that world. Soviet history is characterized by sometimes rather poignant efforts by individuals to define their own realities, to distance themselves from the world precisely through the creation of alternative forms of culture which conveyed alternative meanings. Rock music was only one such vocation which served as an alternative technology for the construction of alternative selves. We now turn to an examination of the relationship between the pursuit of personal identities and the formation of the social identities of rock musicians in St. Petersburg.

Sacred Objects, Vocation, and the
Social Identity of the Rock Musician

Until now we have framed our discussion primarily in terms of the meaning of music-making at the level of individual subjectivity. Yet individual identity means nothing if it is not converted into social identity. For the ways in which individuals see themselves is fundamentally conditioned by the ways others see them. To paraphrase Charles Horton Cooley ([1902] 1956), society is like a looking glass in which individuals see themselves reflected. For Cooley, human communication was the very source of the formation of the self. People communicate messages to others, and the subsequent conceptions they have of themselves are formed and re-formed according to the messages that are reflected back to them by others. Self-identity is a social product which emerges in the course of human interaction. The pursuit of vocation is vital in producing a meaningful sense of one's own self-identity. But the individual pursuit of vocation, as Weber stressed, is precisely that—individual. Self-identity must be transformed into social identity if it is to have a viable social existence outside of consciousness. Social affirmation of one's own self-identity is fundamentally important if one is to be taken seriously outside of one's own mind.

Rock musicians' self-identities as "mediators of truth"—arguably the most important aspect of the successful rock vocation—were strengthened by the fact that others agreed with such self-identifications. Rock musicians saw themselves as others—both within their community and their audiences—saw them: as sacred mediators and arbiters of more fundamental truths about Soviet existence and the place of individuals within the latter. In what follows, two cases are presented which illustrate the social identities of musicians. These cases are of two Petersburg musicians who were, arguably, the most revered musicians in the period of late socialist society. They dramatize well the process of the sacralization of the social identity of the Petersburg rock musician.

Kostya and Viktor: The High Priests of Russian Rock

Kostya was one of the pioneers of the Petersburg rock community. According to most accounts, Kostya was one of the most famous rock musicians in the entire country throughout the 1980s. Viktor, together with Kostya and Boris, whom we discussed in chapter 2, was probably one of the three most famous and highly regarded musicians in Soviet society. These vignettes are primarily based on limited interaction with the musicians involved. In the case of Kostya, this has much to do with his image as a "black" figure, a proponent of the musical style of *chernukha*, or "cruel theater," which emphasizes the cruel, dark, and absurd qualities of life. While I enjoyed a unique opportunity to travel around with Kostya, he was not as communicative as most other Petersburg musicians. Yet watching him "in action" and watching how individuals acted toward him, provided impressions which were important for interpreting the formation of his sacred social identity in St. Petersburg. In the second case, that of Viktor, no primary information was possible at all: in the summer of 1990, Viktor died in a car crash. The social reaction to his death, however, offers us a glimpse into the nature of the sacredness of his status, a sacredness which permeated not only St. Petersburg, but the entire country. For in death the sacred identity of important figures is seen most clearly.

Kostya: Anti-Modern Prophet of the Black Ethic

Kostya is in his mid-thirties. He rejects official categories of existence and is somewhat distrustful of any attempts by those from the outside to get inside his lifeworld. He talks hesitantly and cryptically. He does not expound much on his life history and refers those who are interested in it to his music, in which the messages which offer clues to his life are encoded. Yet he does not mind inquiries into the meaning of his music. Kostya lives hard. His wrists show evidence of scars from suicide attempts to escape military service. Members of his group have a reputation for using narcotics, and at our first meeting during a concert rehearsal hashish is omnipresent. Kostya denies the use of hard drugs, yet many members of the official world—especially those who work with troubled adolescents—feel that Kostya uses hard drugs and that he is a negative role model who fosters alienation and nihilism among youth, which in turn leads to drug use. Kostya does not deny that accusation, except to say that "If they are that way, it's the system, not me, who made them so." In 1993, the guitarist of the band—a known alcoholic and heroin addict—committed suicide by jumping from a window.

Although he is widely known to all (and especially to the guardians of public order who see him as a provocateur), Kostya is most popular among youth. He grew up in Moscow, but lives most of the time in Petersburg where he was a great source of consternation for authorities over the years. After one concert, fans ran wild through the streets, committing acts of vandalism. At subsequent concerts, the militia were especially on guard to ensure that similar incidents would not happen. After overt bans on Kostya's concerts were lifted during the glasnost era, his group played a concert in Moscow at the Olympic Stadium. As a prophylactic measure, city authorities trucked in over one thousand police to form a corridor from the exit of the stadium to the nearest subway station. Everyone leaving the stadium had to walk through what musicians called the *krasnyi korridor*, or "red corridor," in order to get from the stadium to the subway.[6]

Kostya responds to his popularity, as well as to his ability to incite riots, in a very nonchalant way, claiming that he doesn't care how the audience receives his music or what they do afterwards. What he does care about is articulating a persistent and mystical critique of Soviet industrial existence through a style which he describes in one word: *chernukha*. As one author defines it, *chernukha* "means the highest expression of cruel realism, which criticizes all sides of contemporary life and dethrones social mythology, as if it were a funeral procession for the ruined destiny of the 'little man'" (Kniazeva 1991, p. 35).

Kostya's musical poetic emphasizes what he calls the "dark" (*chernye*) aspects of existence in a highly personalized message which sets him apart, both as the voice of the alienated young generation and as an object of attraction for members of that generation:

My Generation

Two thousand of the thirteenth moons
are given away to the ridiculous game.
But the light from the extinguished star is still light.
It's so difficult for you to believe in your way
from this wall to that wall.
Answer!
Do you understand me or not?
Unfortunately, I am weak, as was the eyewitness
of the events on the Lysaia hills.[7]
And I can foresee, but cannot foretell.
But if you suddenly saw
my eye in your window,
know—
I came to disturb your sleep.

This is my generation that keeps silent in the corners,
my generation does not dare to sing,
my generation feels the pain,
and puts itself under the whip,
my generation looks downwards,
my generation is afraid of the day,
my generation cherishes night,
and in the mornings eats itself.

The green-blue day
appeared where the thunderstorm passed.
What a wonderful holiday,
but it definitely lacks us.
It is so difficult for you to decide,
you are used to weighing the "pros" and "cons."
Understand!
I'm giving you a chance.
To be alive is my trade.
This is daring, but it's in my blood.
In the clouds, I can read the names
of those who are able to fly.

If one day you
feel the pulse of great love,
know—
I came to help you stand up!

Hey, generation, answer me!
Can you hear me? I am here!

Come to Me

Come to me,
if it happens to be night, we won't drink tea.
Come to me,
I will explain to you the meaning of the word "farewell."
Come to me,
if snow falls, you'll go to bed a little earlier than me.
Can you hear? It's me speaking to you!

To me!
Come to me,
when it is senseless to sing and you're anxious from waiting.
Come to me,
I will lift you up, I can fly.
Come to me,
if the mechanism of the years breaks off into colorless days.
Come to me,
I'm starting to count: one, two, three. . . .

Come to me—
this new moon takes vengeance on those who have waited.
Come to me,
I'm still wondering how I dared.
Come to me,
the forest goes on living, the forest feels the movement
    of the spring.
Come to me,
I hear the voice, I know—you are calling me.

To me—
this is me who is saying this to you.
To me—
it is you who is calling me.
To me—this is me who is saying this to you.
To me—
it is you who is calling me.

Kostya's poetic is characterized by a critique of the emptiness and isolation of the world and the setting up of himself as the object of enchantment and attraction. When asked what the major influences on his art are, he answered tersely, "Tolstoy, Dostoevsky, Hermann Hesse, Bulgakov, and Jim Morrison." Mikhail Bulgakov represents a particularly strong influence on Kostya. His *Master and Margarita*, an important novel written in the 1930s, chronicles the actions of Wolin, the embodiment of the devil who has come to Moscow to wreak havoc on the city. In the course of the story, Wolin elaborates his dark philosophy and offers a harsh critique of Soviet society. At the end of the novel, Wolin meets Christ on a rooftop. The latter decides that the Soviet people are beyond salvation, and Wolin decides that they are not worthy of corruption by him. Indeed, Wolin even informs Christ that he and his evil exist in order to make the Soviet people good. Wolin eventually takes leave of the city.

While in Moscow, Wolin lives in Apartment #9 on a particular street in Moscow. Both the street and the apartment actually exist in the present day, and the latter has become a sacred site which is visited by followers of Bulgakov's philosophy of *chernukha* as it was articulated by the protagonist Wolin. More than that, the walls of the apartment building and the stairwell have become a site for graffiti which stresses particular messages from the novel, quotes from Wolin, and artwork portraying characters and scenes from the novel (see Bushnell 1988, 1990). As Bushnell (1988) notes, the site expresses, through the idiom of graffiti, "popular readings" of the themes in Bulgakov's novel. As such, it became an object of concern to state authorities. The latter would come and whitewash the walls, but the next day Bulgakov's popular interpreters would come and reinscribe their messages on the walls in a variety of new forms.

The readorned public space of Apartment #9 served as a site of pilgrimage for Kostya and his group. As a site, it was a stark symbol of the spirit of *chernukha* and a place where those who felt that spirit as sacred and special could go to ratify their central beliefs. Indeed, Kostya's own music is heavily inflected with the demonic symbolism of the novel, and his own persona evokes Wolin who is a master debunker of Soviet existence. Indeed, it appears that Kostya saw himself as something of a modern-day Wolin, although, unlike Wolin, he has not yet given up on his countrymen. What is most important, Kostya saw himself as the evil which is necessary for any good to come from Soviet existence, and herein lies the most important connection between his own self and Bulgakov's character. Kostya's pilgrimages to Apartment #9 both affirmed and strengthened the connection between himself and Bulgakov, who, through the protagonist Wolin, presents a scathing critique of Soviet society. Such visits not only confirmed in his own mind his status as a priest of the anti-modern ethic of *chernukha*, but worked to solidify that image in the minds of the public as well. Indeed, at a later point during the glasnost era when he produced an album through the restructured organization of Melodiya (to be discussed in the next chapter), the album featured a picture of Kostya and his group at Apartment #9 in Moscow. In the picture, Kostya stands quietly next to a graffiti portrait of Wolin. Between pilgrimages, the group goes on the road, putting the themes in Bulgakov's fiction and other themes in the genre of *chernukha* to music.

What is most important about Kostya's image as the high priest of *chernukha* is that he represents in one figure a merging of two traditions of nihilism. One tradition is from the West in the form of the alienated rock poet who criticizes and aims to destroy all conventional forms of existence. In this regard, Kostya is highly imitative of nihilistic Western rock poets such as Jim Morrison. Morrison conceived of himself and was seen by others as a modern Dionysus, who came to wreak havoc on the world of Apollonian propriety and rationality. Kostya has confirmed this connection by making a pilgrimage to Morrison's grave in Paris. Yet, as we have seen, rock music in Petersburg was not simply a carbon copy of Western philosophies as they are embodied in Western rock music. Kostya's debt to Bulgakov, and the very idea that he uses terms such as *nihilism* and *chernukha* to describe the essence of his rock practice, place him squarely within a more local tradition of Russian nihilism.

Nihilism has a deep history in Russia. As a political philosophy, it was much more influential there than in most countries of the West; indeed, it is virtually impossible to speak of any serious nihilistic tradition of thinking in American political philosophy. Traditional forms of Russian nihilistic thought in art, literature, and political philosophy not only expressed a profound sense of doubt and uncertainty about formal social institutions such as the government, the family, and the church, but also aimed at destroying them (Gubankov 1989, p. 120). Like Russian nihilist revolutionaries and artists, Kostya's music aims high: at the negation of Soviet existence itself. Also, like the philosophical themes of earlier Russian nihilists, the content of his music is characterized by a strong ethic of egoism which locates the source of authenticity in the self rather than in the social (ibid.).[8] He encourages his alienated fans to "listen to him" and "come to him." Kostya illustrates the fusion of a critical and a negative (in the sense of negation as the term was used by Russian nihilists) tradition of Western rock with a deep-seated tradition of Russian nihilism which is familiar to Russians historically. Combined, these traditions transformed Kostya into a modern-day nihilist, a debunker of Soviet existence, an identity which he displays proudly, both in his persona and in his music.

Living as a participant-observer among Petersburg musicians offered many opportunities to see the sacredness of their status as the latter was expressed *in situ* on the streets of Petersburg itself. In spite of their sacredness, figures such as Kostya were much more accessible and approachable than their counterparts in the West. In the West, famous rock musicians are quite hidden behind mansion doors or behind phalanxes of the agents and promoters in whose hands their destiny lies. In Petersburg, musicians often traveled on subways and walked on streets like everyone else. Although as sacred as their Western counterparts, they were the opposite of Western rock musicians in terms of their financial situation. As a result of their distance and exclusion from formal political and economic structures, the most famous Petersburg musicians were, as a rule, quite poor. The source of their sacred social identity lay almost purely in their socially affirmed function as arbiters of the truth.

This combination of "ordinariness" and their sacred status produced a unique situation in which the "gods" of Russian rock often mingled with ordinary "mortals." In an urban environment which was quite homogeneous in comparison with the West, figures such as Kostya stood out as beacons of difference. A very common mode of transportation in Russia is to flag passing cars and offer drivers money to take one to one's destination. Kostya very often did this, and people would stop. Upon realizing who he was, they would excitedly offer Kostya a free ride anywhere he wanted to go. In one case, a bus full of passengers on a normal route stopped for Kostya and took a detour from the route to take him where he wanted to go. Lacking a limousine or even a car, Kostya would often ride the tram or the subway and be immediately identified by those on the train. Sometimes this caused great commotion among passengers. Yet, for the most part, Kostya's presence was met with silent admiration and awe. His presence was mostly acknowledged with silent whispers, which, like a chain reaction, spread the news to other passengers that Kostya was on board. In no case did people scramble to touch Kostya, shout, scream, or faint—the normal responses to sacred musicians which we have seen historically in many Western contexts. Kostya's response to such actions was simple inattention or quiet discussion with his girlfriend, who accompanied him practically everywhere.

The high priests of Russian rock culture, such as Kostya, in contrast to those in the West, played their sacred roles in close proximity to those ordinary people who considered them sacred. What is important is that even people who did not particularly like his music responded to him, either to corroborate his special social identity or to sanction him for his musical activities. In either case, whether as an object of attraction or an object of danger, he was considered a special and sacred entity. Since the major themes and messages of so much Petersburg rock music echoed a concern with existence in Soviet society, it is only fitting that those who articulated such themes and messages participated with and were seen by those who lived within that existence. But what is even more important about Kostya is that this modern-day exponent of nihilism was considered to be one of the most important figures in rock music in the entire country. His sacredness was conferred upon him because of his ability to plumb the depths of alienation, despair, and disillusionment that were so common among those who lived in Soviet society.

In terms of the inner dynamics of the Petersburg rock community, Kostya's existential critique was an important factor in the determination of his high status within the Petersburg rock community. His high status indicates the degree to which rock music was seen as good and authentic to the extent that it mounted a critique of existence. While some musicians viewed Kostya as a political musician, the overt political symbology of his performances—torn Soviet flags, inverted hammers and sickles, and so on—was a rather minor part of more general anti-systemic symbology which aimed to create an entire countersystem featuring Kostya himself as its high priest. It was this aspiration which made Kostya special, both within the community and with fans. Yet it also made him, in the eyes of the guardians of the existing social order, all the more dangerous. For not only did Kostya present the most bleak assessment of Soviet existence, but he succeeded in creating around himself a new countercultural cult of personality. In anthropologist Michael Taussig's (1992) terms, Kostya was sacred precisely because he represented, from the standpoint of the dominant culture, a *maleficium*. In this way, we can begin to reinterpret the state's response to such musicians as being motivated by much more than a simple concern with controlling independent expression. Rather, the state viewed Kostya and his music as the embodiment of a wholly different conception of the sacred than that which existed in the dominant culture. This conception, crystallized in both the persona and the music of Kostya, represented what might be called in the Soviet context, the "countersacred." We shall return to this idea at the end of this chapter.

God Has Died and Flown to Heaven: The Cult of Viktor

Our next case is, again, one which examines one of the most famous rock musicians in Russian history, a musician to whom I will refer by his first name, Viktor. Viktor was killed in a car crash in the summer of 1990 while on a summer tour in the Baltic republics.[9] Historically, his death was highly significant, for as one musician put it: "You know, this is so significant because this is the first time one of our Russian rock musicians has died." The fact that Viktor was the first famous Russian rock star to die illustrates the relatively "young" character of Russian rock culture; Western rock stars such as Jim Morrison, Elvis Presley, and John Lennon had died relatively long ago. Another musician, in a more critical stance, offered the opinion that "Viktor is dead because he wanted money." This attitude will be of great significance in a later chapter in which we discuss the creeping commercialism which affected even the most sacred heroes of the Petersburg musical community during the glasnost era. For now, we are mainly interested in Viktor's very special social identity, an identity which is best understood by examining the reaction in St. Petersburg to his death.

By all accounts of members of the Petersburg musical community, Viktor was not considered to be an accomplished or sophisticated musician. Most of his songs consist of a series of three or four chord progressions which were repeated over and over in simple variations. Yet the lyrical content of his music was a different matter. Its poetic was characterized by a fundamental concern to express basic truths about everyday existence and interpersonal situations and problems. Given this fact, many musicians felt that Viktor's special appeal was due to his ability to make commentary on some of the complexities of Soviet existence in a way which was accessible and simple. Consider the texts of Viktor's most famous songs:

There Is Time, But No Money

The rain has been pouring since morning, it has been, it was, and it will
And my pocket's empty and it's six o'clock
No cigarettes, no light
And in the familiar window the lights are off

There is time but no money
And no friends to visit

And everyone is gone all of the sudden
I got in with some strange crowd

I want to eat, I want to drink
I just want to sit down somewhere

There is time but no money
And no friends to visit

Sunny Days

Horrible white stuff lies below the window
I wear hats and wool socks
Everywhere I'm uncomfortable and I drink beer till I'm drunk
How can I help missing
You
Sunny days

Hands and feet are freezing and there's nowhere to sit
These times are like continuous night
I want to climb into a hot bath
Maybe that can stop me from missing
You
Sunny days

I am crushed by the winter and am getting sick and I sleep
And now and then, I am certain that winter is forever
It's still so long till summer, and I can hardly wait
But maybe this song will stop me from missing
You
Sunny days
Sunny days

My Friends

I came home, as usual, alone
My house is empty, but suddenly the phone rings
And suddenly a knock on the door and shouting from
    the street yelling
It's enough to sleep and a drunk voice will say, "Give me
    something to eat"

My friends always go through life marching
Only stopping to buy beer

My house was empty, but now it's crowded
And as many times before, my friends drink wine there

And someone broke the window long ago and got stuck
    in the bathroom
To tell the truth, I don't care

My friends always go through life marching
Only stopping to buy beer

And I laugh, even though it's not always funny to me
And get very angry when they tell me
That you can't live like I do now
But why? Don't I live
But to this no one can respond

My friends always go through life marching
Only stopping to buy beer

I Walk Down the Street

I walk down the street wearing a green jacket
I like my shoes
And I also have a pretty tie
I ironed my pants for two hours
Sat in the barber shop since morning
And now I walk down the street alone
Down the street I walk
Down the street alone

My friend has new records
And I'll walk into a cafe and drink a cup of coffee
And then go visit him
And in the store windows, I look like Buddy Holly
Papa will soon let me drive his car
I walk
Down the street alone, I
Walk down the street alone

I Want to Be With You

We haven't seen the sun for a few days already
Our legs have used up their strength on this trip
I wanted to come into the house, but there is no door
My hands are looking for support, but can't find it
I want to come into the house

Many picks have been worn away from my grating
    against the strings

I've seen many streams, but haven't yet seen the sea
The acrobats under the circus dome can't hear the waves
You are behind this wall, but I don't see the door
I want to be with you

My birthday fell between astrological constellations,
    but I cannot live
The wind is twenty meters per second at night and during the day
Before I read books, but now I burn them
I want to go further, but I'm knocked off my feet by the rain
I want to be with you

Good Night

The roofs of houses are shaking under the weight of days
A celestial herdsman is herding clouds
The city is shooting at night with pellets of light
But the night is stronger and her power immense

Those who go to sleep
Pleasant dreams
Good night

I waited for this time and this time has come
Those who were silent are no longer silent
Those who had nothing to wait for are now mounting their horses
One can no longer catch up with them

Those who go to sleep
Pleasant dreams
Good night

The neighbors come home and hear the thunder of hooves
Not letting them sleep, disturbing their dreams
Those who have nothing to wait for embark on their way
Those who are saved
Those who are saved

Those who go to sleep
Pleasant dreams
Good night

Teenager

You look back but what can you bring back?
My friends one by one turned into machines

And you already know that this is the fate of the generation
And if you can run, that is to your benefit

You could have been a hero, but there was no reason to be
You could have betrayed someone, but there was no one to betray
The teenager who has read a truckload of romantic novels
You could have died if you had known what to die for

Try to save yourself from the rain when it rains inside
Try to save yourself from the desire to get out
You are a pedagogical failure and you just
Were not stopped in time
But now you to try wake up, but this is not a dream

In these songs, we see a simplicity which preserves the identity of
rock music as a form of poetry which crystallizes and communicates
important ideas about Soviet existence. What is more, it does so simply,
which testifies to one aspect of rock's paradoxical identity as a cultural
form which is accessible, while at the same time addressing more perennial and important issues: the experience of being alone; the importance of
friends as a source of sustenance; the general problems of being a teenager
in Soviet society; and simple desires for love, belonging, and companion-
ship are all central features of his poetic, a poetic which is starkly apolitical.

Viktor's sacred status was poignantly dramatized in the reaction
to his death. In St. Petersburg, soon after news of his death spread
around the city, major figures of the rock community and his fans began
to congregate in the center of the city at the Leningrad Rock Club. In the
courtyard to the club, a shrine in memory of Viktor was set up which
consisted of flowers, pictures of him at various points of his life, and a
large tape recorder which played his songs over and over again.
Around the shrine, fans gathered, wept, and prayed. Some of those
passing by on the street outside the courtyard where the club was
located stopped and came in to pay their respects. Many people put
money into a basket in return for small buttons with an image of Viktor
and his birth and death dates. While those gathered were primarily
young people, the audience consisted of people of all ages. Nearby, a
group of elderly people was crying and lamenting, not over the death of
a rock star, but over the death of someone who was so young (Viktor
was twenty-eight when he died). Inside the Rock Club, the inner circle
of rock musicians, managers, rock critics, and other close associates and
friends of Viktor gathered around candle-lit tables and drank vodka,
one bottle after another. Periodically, around the courtyard, young people would erupt in gestures of violence, smashing walls with their fists

and sometimes each other as well. One angry young man threatened his girlfriend with violence until he was told to stop by one of the club's administrators. He did so and went silently into a corner, buried his face in his hands, and cried uncontrollably.

Such violent reactions appeared to be somewhat generalized around the city. Some bands of young people reacted by running around the city committing acts of vandalism, especially against state buildings. Such activities provoked a response by city authorities. Even as late as 1990, the still state-run media had little to say about any aspect of rock culture. In this case, however, the city evening news presented a brief report on Viktor's death, but the report focused less on the particulars of his death or on presenting a retrospective of his life and work (something which one can imagine would be what might occur on American television in the event of the death of a major Western rock star) than it did on advising young "comrades" to maintain control over themselves and their actions. Like the fans, city officials recognized that his death was a significant event, and they were aware of the degree of spiritual reverence and awe with which many fans regarded Viktor. Days later, the official national press reported Viktor's death, but offered no retrospective or analysis of his place in Russian cultural history or his significance as one of the most prominent icons in the history of Russian popular culture.

A few days later, Viktor's body was returned to the city and interred in the Bogoslovsky cemetery during a mass funeral which was attended by thousands. The grave was decorated in the traditional Russian Orthodox fashion with a likeness of Viktor in the form of an enlarged picture (Viktor, interestingly enough, was not Russian at all, but an ethnic Korean). This likeness was later replaced by a carved stone statue of Viktor. His grave now remains an important site of pilgrimage; it is the most often visited and decorated site in the otherwise nondescript graveyard. Heartfelt letters written to Viktor and important personal belongings offered to him are strewn by the thousands around the grave site. Near the grave, a tent is pitched in which a group of young people—about six or so—live and keep a vigil over Viktor's grave. At no time is the grave left unattended; if someone has to leave, someone else remains to keep watch. According to one source, the girls in the group, almost like vestal virgins, have sworn themselves to celibacy in memory of Viktor. These cemetery dwellers maintain the grave, watch over the belongings left there, and forbid people to intrude on the sacredness of the place. Photographs of the grave are prohibited by these young guardians, and they refuse to talk to "outsiders" about their feelings for Viktor.

What might be called "the cult of Viktor" was quite strong in the Petersburg community and, indeed, throughout the former Soviet Union. The best evidence of this is to be found in the huge volume of letters which poured into journals and newspapers in the days and weeks following his death. The content of these letters offers a strong sense that Viktor was viewed not simply as a great musician, but primarily as a sacred figure who was an important reference point in individuals' search for meaning in life. The texts of two of these letters are presented below. In them we can see the ways in which the devotion of fans, Viktor's personal meaning to them, and their feelings about his death express themselves as worship. The language of the letters themselves reflects the authentic sense of sorrow and lamentation which is usually reserved for more religious figures:

There has never been a bigger sorrow in my house. The 16th of August my husband came home from work with some kind of deathly pale expression on his face. I understood right away that something terrible had happened. And when he explained what he had heard on *Maaku* [a radio program] about the death of Viktor, I just couldn't believe it. I tried to prove to him that it's just some stupid rumors again. But the next day when my husband brought home the newspaper, opened to the page with a photograph of Viktor and an article, there was no hope left, and we stood by the window, behind which were the gloomy skies without the sun shining, and cried. There's usually a deficit of masculine tears. In fourteen years of knowing one another and ten and a half years of marriage, it was the first time I saw him cry. Not one or two miserable tears, but real, bitter sobs into his folded hands. I'm not even speaking of myself. In these few days, my eyes became red and swollen—I can hardly see what's around me.

I don't want to believe in that which actually happened. They can't, they shouldn't die, such poets, such singers. They shouldn't die—from the height of my thirty years I can see this well—such young people. Twenty-eight—that's not the age for death. That's just not fair.

I can't believe that there won't be any new songs, new albums of Viktor, no new parts in films. I can't believe that "A Star in the Name of the Sun" [the name of one of Viktor's more well-known early underground recordings, here transposed to refer to Viktor himself] has set. How can one live without the sun? These days the pressing feeling of awful unfairness possesses me.

What will happen with [Viktor's group]? A new Leader? Or will the group no longer exist? . . . It seems to me that Yuri K. could take Viktor's place and try to save the group. He has a good voice, and can sing melodies well. Of course, problems could arise with the lyrics. . . . But David Gilmore was able to reanimate Pink Floyd when, after Roger Waters left, the group almost fell apart. And Pink Floyd is at the height of success. Or could they all go to other groups? It can't be that [the group] will no longer be? One wants to count on at least something. . . .

My God, how heavy it is on my heart. The death of Viktor— that is my personal sorrow. When a star dies, its light shines much longer on our earth. Whatever may happen, whatever may take place, Viktor will always remain "A Star in the Name of the Sun." For me, in any case.

—Irina J. (Krasnotyrinsk)

It is as if life inside of me has ceased. These past few days I tried to refute this, but I only found ways to confirm it. Then I saw a flier for "Needle" with the inscription "In Memory of Viktor," and that was the end of the last hope. In the room sat some girls, giggling after hearing the word "screwing" (*trakhat'sia*) and I could not understand—was it not sorrowful for them, were there actually people for whom it did not matter? Why, for God's sake, is it so unfair? He takes away those who are the best and most loved. "And we know that it has always been that way. . . ." Yes, we know this, but it is impossible to accept it.

In the spring, in April, I could not have predicted that this would happen, but for some reason it was then that I started to catch myself on the fact that in every newspaper with horrible stories, I would look for the obituaries. Other than that which was in the black frames, I would not look for anything. And I found it. . . .

Excuse me please, if I am hurting you, but I just don't have anyone with whom to share this grief. And the worst pain—the pain of the soul will live in us forever, until the last day. The only thing I pray for right now is that God will love Viktor just as much as we love him, and that He will take care of his soul, now that we are unable to take care of his body.

Good-bye, and God bless you!

—Julia L. (Krasnoyarsk)[10]

We can see through such letters how individuals responded to Viktor as a sacred entity and in doing so actually sacralized his identity to an even greater degree. There are other cultural practices which lend a religious dimension to the commemoration of Viktor. Each year since his death, concert promoters stage a large concert in Moscow featuring important bands from around the country. Locally, in St. Petersburg, smaller concerts are also held in his memory. In both Moscow and St. Petersburg, on his birthday in June, people gather and lead street demonstrations in his name, replete with all the iconography of a Russian Orthodox religious procession. The processions lead to a wall in the Arbat section of Moscow, a wall which is now called Stena Viktora, "Viktor's Wall." The wall is emblazoned with graffiti and other objects which commemorate Viktor's life and work. The most noticeable inscription there, one which offers us a true glimpse into the sacred nature of Viktor's identity, simply proclaims: "God has died and flown to heaven." It is in such inscriptions that we can truly see the extent to which, for many, "true" rock musicians commune with the gods.

From Identity to Community:
The Petersburg Rock Community as an
Alternative Moral Community

The previous discussion of rock music as a vocation within Soviet existence evokes images of an almost religious commitment to the practice of that vocation. Using the term *vocation* to interpret the meaning of rock practice at the level of individual subjectivity, however, does not mean that Petersburg musicians were a society of individuals each pursuing their craft only in private. Rather, they constituted a community. As Ross Poole (1991, p. 87) notes: "[The] concept of individual identity presupposes a certain form of social life—a 'community' . . . in which individuals recognize that certain relationships are constitutive of their own self-awareness." As makers of alternative meanings, Petersburg musicians could not develop meaningful identities without forging and maintaining social relationships with other individuals. The fact that music is a collectively produced cultural form meant that individual musicians had to forge and maintain social relationships with other musicians. This consciousness of kind and the sharing of a common culture brought musicians together as a cultural community.

The Petersburg Rock Counterculture
as an Elective Community

Making rock music is not necessarily an individual and solitary act. As a cultural object, rock music is created with others. As a communicative act, it must be done for others. In the process of creating and communicating rock music, a cultural community of musicians was formed in Petersburg. This was a community of individuals each pursuing their individual commitment to the vocation of making music. The community was united by its common rejection of the official world and by its common appreciation of musical practice as a way to apprehend an alternative sense of the sacred within the context of Soviet society. As a way of speaking about communities united by a common perception of the sacred, I would like to introduce the idea of elective community. The term *elective community* was first used by French sociologist Roger Caillois to describe a "form of secondary organization that possesses constant characteristics and to which recourse is always possible when the primary organization of society can no longer satisfy all the desires that arise" (Caillois 1988, p. 149).[11] According to Caillois, an elective community is a community which has its origins in and is held together by a common disillusionment with the dominant sense of the sacred and, conversely, united by an alternative and shared definition and sense of the sacred which is articulated in a specific way of life. Caillois posits a fundamental desire among human beings for authentic sacred experience. It is the lack of such experience (especially in the modern world) which drives people to "elect" to seek it in tandem with others who also desire sacred experience but who find that modernity offers them little by way of fulfilling such a desire.

At the very base of the elective community of St. Petersburg musicians was an alternative sense of the sacred, expressed through the form of rock music. What is most important is that musicians elected to come together as a group and share a way of life. The question that emerges at this point is how this feeling of community was expressed collectively in the everyday lives of musicians. Answers to this question lie in an examination of the musicians' own sense of their collective relationship with one another and the vocabulary which they use to express this relationship. They also lie in an examination of the collective ways in which musicians expressed their music and in examining some of the "extramusical" forms of cultural practice in which they engaged. Counterculture does not consist solely in the creation and distribution of cultural objects, but in sharing a system of more general values, beliefs, and practices which constitutes an alternative way of life. We begin with a discussion of the most fundamental idea of collectiveness discussed by Petersburg musicians, the idea of the *tusovka*.

The Sociological Meaning of *Tusovka*

An understanding of the collective significance of the practice of rock music in the Soviet context is contingent on the understanding of a word which rock musicians constantly use to describe their activities and experiences as rock musicians. That word is *tusovka*. *Tusovka* is not translatable precisely into English, nor is there consensus on the etymology of the word.[12] Even Russians have some difficulty in explaining exactly what it means in English. Generally, the word is used to describe a number of phenomena. First, it describes a group of people who are simply united by a common interest in something. For example, it is possible to speak of a *futbol'naia tusovka*, "gathering of football fans," or a *mashinnaia tusovka*, "gathering of motorcar enthusiasts." Petersburg musicians speak of a rock-and-roll *tusovka* and, within that *tusovka* there exists a number of discrete *tusovki*, such as a hippie *tusovka*, a heavy metal *tusovka*, and a punk *tusovka*. The second sense of the word *tusovka* describes a discrete happening, event, or gathering.[13] Thus, one can refer to a certain experience as "a great *tusovka*" (or use the reflexive verb *tusovatsia* to say that "we really had a great *tusovka* together," or *my tusovalis*). A final use of the word is to describe an event or experience which was simply "great" or truly memorable. Thus, the word is broad enough to describe specific events such as a rock concert, a special scenario or place, or a broader sense of an important time or phase in the collective life of an individual or social group. As such, it is a potentially confusing term. Fundamentally, though, the term as it is used by Petersburg musicians generally describes a collective gathering or time which was held to have special significance to those participating in such a gathering or time. As such, it is perhaps one of the most important concepts in Petersburg rock musicians' vocabulary, for it crystallizes in one word the sense of "we-ness" and *communitas* which was the very essence of music-making as a form of collective action.

Earlier, I argued that the pursuit of *lichnost'*, or identity, best captures the idea of rock musicianship as an individual vocation. Here, I would like to argue that the idea of *tusovka* best describes the sense of collectivity which musicians feel as a result of their common activity as counterculturalists. For making music together was a special task, and living together as counterculturalists was a special way of life. The idea of *tusovka* best captures the essence of musical counterculture as an authentic, alternative, and meaningful collective experience of the sacred within Soviet existence. For most rock musicians, *tusovka* is used at present to describe their past activity together during the socialist period, a time when the boundaries between "us" and "them" were clear and the meaning of rock music as a form of opposition was unquestioned. One musician, Yuri, puts it this way:

> Especially in the '80s . . . the best, the finest (*krutaia*) poetry was in rock-and-roll. That is everything best, purest, most sincere went into rock-and-roll in the '80s. It speaks for itself. All the underground were just colossal people. Now it's not like this any more, of course. Now painting, theater, everything is permitted. Then there was only rock-and-roll. And all the power was there, in rock-and-roll. The best people I saw were in rock-and-roll only, in these *tusovki*. That was a real rock-and-roll. . . . We created it, and the communists could do nothing about it. It was our language. We would gather at night, at somebody's flat. . . .

As a cultural moment, Petersburg rock musical counterculture can be described in the broadest sense as a *tusovka* engaged in by *tusovshchiki* who appreciated, valued, and shared alternative experiences or happenings within the world of Soviet modernity. The *tusovka* is a special time, place, or gathering, which is sacred simply by virtue of the fact that it occurs outside of everyday, ordinary life. The very idea of *tusovka* connotes an alternative collective, a meeting of individuals who are united by common interest in something which is not part of the official Soviet world. In the simplest sense, the *tusovka* was a negation of the idea of collectivity, or *kollektivnost'*, which was a central component of official Soviet culture (Cushman 1988). Interestingly, unlike the idea of *lichnost'*, a category which musicians invested with their own content, musicians seldom used the word *kollektiv* or *kollektivnost'* to describe their collective life.

It is important to note at this point that the musicians' descriptions of their collective identity as a *tusovka* did not mean that they constituted a utopian community without conflict. The idea of the *tusovka* was precisely that: an idea, or more appropriately, an ideal. Yet it was an ideal of collectivity which was authentic in relation to the ideal of *kollektivnost'* prescribed by the dominant culture. Not every musician subscribed to this ideal. We saw in the beginning of chapter 2, for instance, that one musician felt that the idea of *tusovka* represented still another source of constraint on his individuality. Yet in actual practice, the rock *tusovka* did offer individuals a chance to express their individuality, even if they were sometimes harshly judged for not hewing to the norms of musical authenticity. There were very clear differences between members of the community about the meaning of music and the proper relation of the musician to the outside world. Nonetheless, Petersburg musicians shared a recognition of rock music as a vocation, of rock music-making as an autonomous and legitimate form of artistic expression. It is within the context of this bounded moral community that a more general culture and way of life was created and circulated. And it is this system of alternative meanings which stood in opposition to the system of meaning of the dominant culture of Soviet society.

In an important work on boundaries in moral communities, Michele Lamont (1992, p. 11) notes, "Boundary work is an intrinsic part of the process of constituting the self; they [boundaries] emerge when we try to define who we are: we constantly draw inferences concerning our similarities to and differences from others, indirectly producing typification systems." Significantly, the boundaries of the Petersburg musical community did not simply mark off differences with such things as communist ideology. Rather, in the act of stressing their difference from the dominant society through the creation of music and an alternative way of life, musicians created a bounded community which marked itself off from the dominant society. Social activity within the boundaries of the music community served to strengthen and maintain those very boundaries. We now explore these practices as a way of articulating a cartography of the way of life of the Petersburg rock community.

The Norms of Friendship and the Norms of Rock Practice

Making music was not the only source of authentic and meaningful collective sentiment in Russia during the Soviet period. In Soviet society, friendship was an important form of social action based on strongly held feelings and sentiments rather than on pure self-interest or rational calculation (Shlapentokh 1984; Kon 1987). Friendship was an important source of meaning-making between individuals, a kind of interactional haven within the bureaucratic world of Soviet industrial society. The culture of friendship was extremely intertwined with the culture of music-making in St. Petersburg. The affective force of music-making was buttressed by the affective force of friendship.

Friendships in the Russian context are not without conflicts. Yet it is clear that some conflicts between friends, in what Allan Silver (1990) has called "commercial society," are due to the intrusion of rational calculation and the spirit of capitalism into the affective world of friendships.[14] It is also clear that the political-economic institutional forces of "commercial society" had very little influence in the Soviet social context because such institutions were not highly developed. On the contrary, it was the very rigidity of the bureaucratic world, a world which even sought to administer friendships along its own lines through the imposition of norms of "comradely relations," which ensured the strength of affective ties between friends. In the Russian context, friendship was a social sphere with its own norms, values, and beliefs which guided the actions of individual friends in relation to one another. While rock musicians may have had conflicts with their families, the sphere of friendship was a special one in which one could experience strong feelings of trust and belonging. Adherence to the norms and values of friendship was part of the experience of the rock *tusovka*. Experiences making rock music and living the rock lifestyle were fundamentally enhanced by the fact that rock music was made and shared among friends.

While those within the rock *tusovka* were not all friends—indeed, there were quite pronounced conflicts among some musicians—they at least maintained a common commitment to the way of life of the community. Another way of putting this is that while not all musicians may have been friends, they at least recognized that they had a common enemy and, as a result, were united collectively by this fact. Friendships among musicians were an important basis for the formation of individual rock groups within the community. Within small groups, musicians not only made music together, but acted as friends as well. An example of the importance of friendship in rock practice is found in the case of Zhenya, a young guitar player. Zhenya is classically trained as a French horn player. For Zhenya, music is, first and foremost, an affective experience. Yet his music has been of specific pragmatic value to him. For instance, his classical musical expertise (like his rock music expertise would later) allowed him to escape some of the more dismal parameters of Soviet existence. Military service remains compulsory, even in post-communist Russia, and Soviet military life is considered to be exceedingly bleak and something to be avoided at all costs. In Zhenya's case, his expertise on the French horn paid off for him; he was recruited by the leader of the Red Army Orchestra as one of the French horn players and thus escaped a litany of inane tasks as a recruit and the banality of living in the military on five rubles a month in any number of strange and hostile places. When speaking about his "service" in the orchestra, Zhenya reminisced fondly about the tactics of evasion he and other musicians used to escape the pain of having to play instruments—especially brass ones—in sub-zero temperatures at public gatherings. Four years after military service, Zhenya still expressed a fondness for the French horn and indicated that he still liked to play it, especially when he was sad. But his real musical epiphany occurred when he "discovered" the electric guitar and began to teach himself to play rock music. He soon became a rock composer and lead guitarist and joined the group to which he still belongs.

Zhenya is a bit unique in the Russian context. He is twenty-three years old and has a British father, a rarity given the close circumscription of contact with foreigners through much of Soviet history. During the "Thaw," Zhenya's father came to Russia to start a business venture, married Zhenya's mother, a Russian, and returned to England after Khrushchev was ousted. With such a powerful foreign connection and enticement of such a high standard of living, one would expect that Zhenya would have emigrated much earlier. In fact, Zhenya had very little desire to emigrate. His family in Petersburg consists of a mother and a very old grandmother. Zhenya's mother travels often to Britain to be with his father. He talks a great deal about his father, but almost purely in disdainful and negative terms. His father has always pressured him to move to England to join him in his business there. Zhenya has no desire whatsoever to emigrate and even less of a desire to join his father in business. His father is contemptuous of his musical activity and of his stubborn refusal to leave Russia. Zhenya is equally contemptuous of his father, as is witnessed by the following quote. For Zhenya, his father is a metaphor of normal existence: "He's old, and he's always going 'bah-bah-bah' in my face. He's so puffous [sic] and full of shit.[15] He wants me to come to England and take over his business. What am I going to do in England? Be an English businessman? All of my friends and my life are here. You know, they're always talking about the *rodina*. You know, *rodina* for me is where my friends are. If my friends were in Africa, then my *rodina* would be Africa."

Rodina is usually translated as "homeland " or "motherland." The idea of *rodina* was one of the most important in the repertoire of official Soviet culture, for it worked to connect the Soviet system—a creation of the twentieth century—with a more timeless and affectively meaningful sense of "Russian-ness." In case anyone had any doubts about their commitment to the Soviet motherland, the idea of "Mother Russia" was there to remind them of their common collective identity as Russians. Like the category of *lichnost'*, or "personal identity," discussed previously, the word *rodina* was used by many musicians to describe their sense of place. Yet it was stripped of any official connotations and instead invested with a private, more subjectively meaningful content. In this case, Zhenya defined his *rodina* as the place where his friends were.

Zhenya's statement shores up the fact that the St. Petersburg musical community consisted of networks of close friends. To be a good rock musician, to play well with others, one had to adhere to the basic norms of friendship as they were defined in the Soviet context. At the base of the Petersburg musical counterculture was the ideal—not always realized of course, but stressed nonetheless—of friendship as a value rather than as a means toward a specific end, such as money or power. It could be no other way, for to associate with other counterculturalists was to place oneself outside the dominant culture and, therefore, into a position of economic and political privation. Friendship has long been among the most important forms of sociation in Russian society and a form of sociation which offered individuals some interpersonal refuge within Soviet industrial society. The friendships among musicians, who were marginal figures in Soviet society, provided an affective bulwark underlying the act of making music. The overlapping of friendship and rock musicianship made the latter an even more meaningful and potent form of cultural communication.

Place and Identity: Being in Petersburg and Being a Musician

Zhenya's statement about the importance of friendship also shores up another point which is central to Petersburg musicians: the importance of being in Petersburg. As many sociologists have shown, place is fundamentally related to the formation of one's personal identity (see, for instance, Cuba 1987; and Cuba and Hummon 1993). Petersburg musicians are not only Russian and ought to remain in Russia, but they are also Petersburgians. The city was their home and was the site of their cultural activity and a major source of their self-identity. As such, their ongoing cultural activity was fundamentally conditioned by simply being there. Zhenya himself on one occasion noted, while walking along the banks of the Neva River in the early morning hours during the White Nights, "We can go to Paris or Hamburg or anywhere else, but we return here because it is our city."

Members of the Petersburg musical community were profoundly and integrally tied to the city of Petersburg. The city was the site which made their rock practice meaningful. Many musicians recognized very early on that their music was a special and contextual Russian cultural form which would have little significance in the primarily English-speaking world of Western rock. Indeed, many found it strange that a Russian rock musician would want to leave the city to pursue a career in foreign lands. Ironically, musicians' strong, voluntary ties—in addition to the fact that they were not physically allowed to leave—served to confine them to Russia. The city represented a unique historical source which made their rock *Petersburg* rock as opposed to just ordinary "home rock" (a common description for Russian rock). Their whole way of life was conditioned by the fact that it occurred within the bounded space of the city. A common conventional wisdom among Westerners through the ages was the assumption that all Russians desired to "escape" from the Soviet Union. There is little evidence to suggest that this was the case with Petersburg musicians either before or after the dissolution of the Soviet Union. Indeed, as we shall see in chapter 6, even in a world of increased opportunity *za granitsei*, or "beyond the borders," those Russian rock musicians who decided to emigrate abroad lost their status within the community. In some cases, the latter were seen as traitors to the cause of Russian rock music.

The city of Petersburg itself, then, enabled the specific forms of musical practice which emerged within it. Yet we must not lose sight of the fact that the city was also a major center of Soviet industry and an arena of formal political activity. It is also important to emphasize the fact that St. Petersburg—despite its high-style, European elements—was a Soviet industrial city. As such, the city itself, and many of its components—its architecture, structural layout, and the temporal patterns of movement of its citizens—was a cultural metaphor of Soviet industrial existence. Western cultural analysts have focused a great deal on exploring the cultural activity of people in relation to the spatial and temporal patterns of the cities in which that activity occurs (Giddens 1984, 1990; Soja 1989; de Certeau 1984). Modern industrial societies are characterized by distinct patterns of temporal and spatial organization which serve as the basic locales which frame human agency and cultural expression. Giddens (1984, pp. 145-58) argues that the patterns of time and space in modern societies represent "nets of discipline" which frame expressions of human agency. It is important to view musical activity and countercultural existence in relation to the temporal and spatial frameworks which characterize the city of St. Petersburg. Such frameworks constituted the very locale in which countercultural practices were, quite literally, played out. What is more important, countercultural practices resisted such patterns of social and temporal organization of the city.

Let us begin with a temporal dimension of the city which has little to do with politics or history: geography. Since Petersburg is located at a high latitude, the summer months are characterized by almost constant daylight. During the so-called White Nights, the sun never really sets. As Dick Hebdige (1988) has argued, counterculturalists and bohemians depend fundamentally on the cover of night to "hide" their cultural activities. The lack of night in the summer months posed a distinct problem not so much for the making of music, but for the more general public assembly of rock musicians and other artists in the city. The lack of night cover in the summer months made it a problem for musicians to come together and to meet with other groups which constituted the more general countercultural community of the city. The lack of private places for counterculturalists to congregate made it difficult to conduct countercultural activity. The following case illustrates the ways in which Petersburg counterculturalists accomplished the very important task of being with each other in public spaces that were under a very high degree of surveillance.

The Taking of the Bridge

Musicians constituted a specific group within the more general community of Petersburg counterculturalists, which included artists, bohemians, and others who pursued alternative vocations and identities within the space of socialist industrial society. It is difficult to separate the activities of musicians from those of other counterculturalists, for they very often did things together and considered themselves to be part of a greater urban counterculture of the city. The event described here occurred in 1990, during a time which was characterized by a much greater degree of cultural openness and a corresponding relaxation of the state's surveillance of countercultural expression. Yet this case crystallizes the ways in which public gatherings among members of the counterculture occurred throughout the Soviet period.

St. Petersburg is divided into a number of regions that are linked by a series of drawbridges which span the Neva River. In the months when the river is not frozen (usually from about late March until about November), these bridges are raised every morning between 1:00 and 5:00 in order to allow transport ships to pass along the river from the industrial sections of the city to the Bay of Finland and out to sea. Each bridge is raised at a different time, according to a schedule which is published in local newspapers. The raising of the bridges begins at 1:00 A.M. and proceeds until all are raised at approximately 1:30 A.M. They remain raised until about 4:00 A.M. whereupon they are lowered in succession. By 5:00 A.M. all of the bridges are lowered and they resume their normal function as connectors for traffic flowing to different regions of the city. If the flow of boat traffic along the river is heavy, the bridges are lowered later, and if light, they are lowered earlier. The most immediate effect of the raising of the bridges is that movement between different sections of the city by residents is effectively constrained for a period lasting from two to three hours. Since the population of Petersburg exceeds five million people, the number of people actually affected by the bridge-raising each night is considerable. The constraint on movement is enhanced by the fact that the city's metro system, a major source of transportation in the city and the most common mode of transportation beneath the river, stops running at 1:00 A.M.

The raising of the bridges is a constant of the urban environment of St. Petersburg, and it exerts a major influence on the rhythms and patterns of movement and interaction during the nighttime hours. In expectation of the raising of the bridges, public and private social gatherings break up before 1:00 A.M., and cab drivers scurry to be in a particular region where they will not be cut off from fares. In short, all those who have chosen to be outside in the early hours of the morning must orient their activities in anticipation of the raising of the bridges. In Western capitalist cities, the organization of urban space is more oriented toward accommodating the freedom of movement of individuals. In spite of the fact that mass transportation systems of Western cities often shut down in the early hours, inhabitants of the Western city are still afforded the opportunity to move freely about the city by other means. Indeed, it is difficult to imagine a modern, capitalist, urban context in which movement within urban space is thwarted to such a degree. In contrast to the Western city, the organization of space in Petersburg is a metaphor of the cultural logic of socialist industrial society. This cultural logic is rooted deep within the history of the rapid industrialization of the Soviet Union and expresses symbolically the collective needs of "the system" over and against the needs of individuals to move freely about the city. The impact of the bridge-raising on movement within the city is more pronounced in midsummer, since this is the period of White Nights, a period during which many city residents move about the city in the dusky daylight of the early morning hours.

The raising of the bridges entered into the folklore of Soviet urban life as a "cultural event," and various bridges, especially those in the center of the city, served as meeting places for various groups. In fact, the gathering of people around certain bridges emerged as a kind of urban ritual which is quite historically unique to St. Petersburg. Groups of school children in summer camps outside the city often took midnight field trips to the Neva to watch the bridges open. On their wedding nights, newlyweds could be seen ambling toward the bridges to solidify their commitments to one another as the bridges were raised. Thus, even though the raising of the bridges did effectively alter the movement of people from one region to another, it also provided a locale which enabled a number of other conventionalized activities to occur. Such conventionalized activities were seldom of much concern to city authorities, for they were a normal part of the rhythm of the city.

In the raising of the bridges, however, resides a powerful metaphor of the cultural logic of socialist society. In the most obvious sense, the bridge-raising is a metaphor of power, but power of a different kind, power which limits the free movement of the body and speaks the fact that the spatial and temporal organization of the city is oriented toward fulfilling the needs of the system rather than the needs of its citizens to travel freely from one region to another. The raising of the bridges signifies in a regular and standardized fashion the potential of the system to determine the movement of individuals who inhabit the space of the city. The practice reinforced and reasserted in visible fashion and on a nightly basis the particular cultural logic which infused the social organization of the socialist city.

Early one Sunday morning in July 1990, I was informed that there was to be an exhibit of underground art which would take place at approximately one o'clock on Monday morning at the raising of the Dvortsovyi Bridge, which is located in the central part of the city and which connects the city's main thoroughfare, the Nevskii Prospekt, with the region on the north side across the Neva River. My informant told me that the exhibit would be taking place *on* the bridge—he used the Russian phrase *na mostu*. Knowing that the bridge was a drawbridge, I was curious about the use of the preposition *na*, which indicated that the exhibit would take place, quite literally, on the bridge. My sense was that my informant meant that the exhibit would take place on one or the other river bank. Upon arriving at the bridge later in the evening, however, I found no exhibit on either side of the bridge, and upon asking where the exhibit would be, I was informed by people in the crowd that it would actually take place, true to my informant's word, *on* the bridge. Upon inquiring further, I discovered that the artists who had planned the exhibit were members of a new, independent artist colony which was located in an abandoned building in a central location of another section of the city. According to my sources, the artists who were planning the exhibit had no connection with any official organization and, in this sense, could be considered independent cultural producers. The artists had secured permission from city authorities to attach their paintings to the road on the bridge so that when the bridge opened, one of the open sections of the bridge (the one facing the northern region of the city) would serve as the physical backdrop for the exhibit, displaying artwork to the people who were gathered on the north side of the river.

For approximately one hour before the bridge-raising, artists pre-
pared their paintings on the side of the road, while the usual intense
stream of cars passed trying to get to different regions before the bridge
was raised. City police monitored this activity, kept the artists off the
roadway, and ushered along people who had stopped to see what was
going on. The usual groups of schoolchildren, newlyweds, and others
gathered on either side of the bridge. In addition to these groups, a
number of members of the city's counterculture also arrived—allies
and friends of the artists, rock musicians, and other bohemians who
traditionally inhabit the Petersburg night. About five minutes before
the bridge was raised, the artists were allowed onto the bridge where
they quickly fastened their large murals and paintings onto the asphalt.
The Dvortsovyi Bridge was raised at 1:00 A.M., and one section of the
bridge was transformed into a freestanding exhibit of contemporary
Petersburg art. Spotlights mounted on trucks, which had been secured
by the artists prior to the exhibit, were driven up to the north side of the
bridge and accentuated its colorful art against the grey Petersburg sky.

The art exhibit remained in place for about one hour. During this
time, the usual crowds and members of the city's cultural community—
artists, famous and not-so-famous rock musicians, and other noncon-
ventional types—arrived and gathered around as close to the exhibit as
possible. The exhibit was particularly well-attended by members of the
city's underground rock music culture. They met, chatted, drank,
smoked, stood silent, played music, and joked. Crowds were kept from
approaching the bridge by members of the city militia, both uniformed
and plainclothed. After about an hour, and after considerable dickering
with the artists, the authorities demanded that the bridge be lowered
and ordered the artists to take their paintings off of the road. After they
had removed their creations and their spotlights, the bridge was raised
again, as usual, unadorned and grey against the dusky Petersburg sky-
line. Gradually, the crowds began to disperse and the normal pattern of
activity which usually occurred on either side of the river—people and
cars waiting for the bridge-closing—recommenced. In short, St. Petersburg space and time returned to normal.

From the standpoint of the observer from a relatively pluralistic
Western social context, the art exhibit at the Dvortsovyi Bridge seems a
rather ordinary event, a simple display of public art which one is likely
to encounter in any Western capitalist city. Yet in the context of St.
Petersburg in 1990, the exhibit was rather extraordinary. Within the
traditional context of cultural expression in socialist society, such public expressions of unofficially sanctioned art had seldom been allowed.[16]
In the past, had such an event occurred, political authorities would

have inspected the art in order to ensure that it was within the bounds of what was considered publicly expressible. Within the context of the Soviet Union in the late 1980s, the exhibit was just one of many cultural moments occurring around the city which were increasingly eroding from below a system of historically entrenched political practices designed explicitly to monitor and control cultural expression in Soviet society.

In a more fundamental sense, the exhibit can be seen as an active expropriation of the dominant use of a prominent fixture of the public space of St. Petersburg. Petersburg bridges were not the products of socialist industrial development. As architectural forms, they predate the Soviet period of historical development. Even before the Soviet period, elements of the built environment of St. Petersburg, such as the bridges, were actively and intentionally used by political elites to circumscribe the movement of revolutionary groups. The use of the bridges to control movement in urban space seems to have been continued by the new class of Soviet elites who seized power in 1917. The meaning of the bridges is thus not embodied purely in the structural appearance of the bridges themselves (although in many forms of architecture which constitute the Soviet-built environment one can, quite literally, read the cultural logic of socialism in, for example, the great mass of apartment buildings which Russians themselves refer to as *stalinskoe barokko*, or "Stalinesque baroque"). Rather, the metaphorical significance of the bridges emerges in how the bridges were used in everyday life to facilitate industrial production and, by way of that, to disable individual freedom of movement in the city. It is in the official uses of the bridges that the latter take on their ideological meanings as metaphors of the built environment of the city. Louis Althusser (1969) notes that "Ideology is indeed a system of representation, but in the majority of cases these representations have nothing to do with 'consciousness': they are usually images and occasionally concepts, but it is above all as *structures* that they impose on the vast majority of men. . . ." While Althusser is referring specifically to political, social, and economic structures such as the state, the family, and the market, it is also possible to speak of ideological meanings which are inscribed in the temporal and spatial organization of the urban environment.[17] In this sense the bridge represents, in an almost pristine form, a metaphor of the ideology of socialist industrial modernity, a physical manifestation of the ideological principle that the requisites of the system outweigh the needs of individuals to move freely about urban space.

In contrast, the act of "taking the bridge," of aestheticizing it, represents an alternative use of the bridge, an act of excorporation which rejects the dominant, hegemonic meaning incorporated into the space of the bridge and replaces it with counterhegemonic meanings which spring from the consciousness of actors in the urban environment. This alternative use of space serves as an example of how counterculturalists accomplished the act of coming together publicly in order to ratify their sense of collectivity. There is little question that such activity might have been more rigidly circumscribed in earlier times—the artists who adorned the bridge, for instance, would have had to have been members of official artistic collectives. Yet the case illustrates well the ways in which counterculturalists used public space as a site in which to come together to display the symbols and enact the practices which united them as a community. The bridge-raising was, in every sense of the word, a *tusovka*.

The case also illustrates another important aspect of countercultural existence: the negation of ordinary patterns of time in Soviet society. At base, the general patterns of movement of musicians and other counterculturalists were characterized by alternative rhythms which resisted the normal patterns of movement through the city which were the product of the historical development of socialist industrial society. Industrial labor in socialist society, as in capitalist industrial society, is organized around an eight-hour workday in which the primary hours are between 8:00 A.M. and 5:00 P.M. The normal rhythm of life in St. Petersburg included a five- or six-day workweek which ranged from Monday to Saturday. Sunday is a traditional day of rest. The exhibit described above took place during the "deadest" period of the Soviet week: the early hours of Monday morning when the majority of the population was at home, sleeping or preparing for a new week. While some conventional groups and individuals were present, the event of the bridge-raising was for them a special event which they engaged in on special occasions: a birthday, a wedding, an annual trip to the city from the countryside. Yet for counterculturalists, movement about the city during the "non-normal" times was the preferred rhythm of life. For them, an activity such as that which occurred at the Dvortosvyi Bridge was, in fact, quite normal. In industrial society, whether capitalist or socialist, night (even if it looks like day) means sleep, and day means work. Those who must work during the day must sleep at night, and the industrial order depends to a great extent on individuals' conformity to this cyclic progression of sleep and work. A key aspect of the existence of Petersburg musicians was their overt rejection of this rhythm of the Soviet industrial order. Indeed, because they had placed themselves outside of normal existence, their own movements were determined by the logic of their own counterculture. The fundamental stance of Petersburg musicians' countercultural community was one of alternative uses of public space and alternative uses of time. Such negations were alternative "ways of doing" and, ultimately, led to alternative "ways of being."

Style and the Body

In contemporary social theory, a great deal of emphasis has been placed recently on understanding the relationship between society and the body (Turner 1984; Freund 1982; Foucault 1975). In his analysis of the practice of modern medicine, Michel Foucault, for instance, placed great emphasis on exploring the body as an object upon which the practices and the ideologies of the dominant culture are inscribed (Foucault 1975). For Foucault, social control and domination do not consist merely of the exertion of the overt power of the state over individuals. Rather, control and domination are achieved culturally through the constitution of the body. Cultural practices regarding the proper adornment and carrying of the body in the social world are important practices which build consent and hegemony at the individual level of existence. From a sociological standpoint, Foucault's and others' observations on the importance of the body as a site where cultural hegemony is negotiated are important for understanding both the maintenance of "normal" Soviet existence and the rejection of such existence in the form of countercultures.

In this regard, it is important to note that consent and dissent within the Soviet framework are not measurable simply by standard categories of political science, i.e., voter turnout, demonstrations for or against the government, political participation, and so on. Rather, as Dick Hebdige (1979) notes, consent and dissent are often expressed through style, that is, through the adherence to or rejection of cultural codes which prescribe and proscribe practices of bodily adornment and movement. We have already seen above that a principle means of resistance among Petersburg musicians was the movement of their bodies in alternative ways through the space of the city. Such individual movements constituted an alternative rhythm of everyday life which worked to extract musicians from the temporal and spatial "nets of discipline" which characterized the St. Petersburg urban environment. Yet, in another sense, it might be argued, following Foucault, that another strand of this net of discipline consisted of prescriptions regarding appropriate bodily adornment. Part of the process of forging cultural hegemony in the Soviet Union involved "inscribing" specific norms of bodily adornment on the bodies of its citizens. Thus, wearing short hair, dressing in the khaki work uniform and standard black shoes prescribed for the Soviet worker, and a host of other practices signified a certain degree of acceptance of the system at the level of everyday life. What is more important, adherence to particular bodily conventions was related to the ongoing reproduction and functioning of the Soviet system. Conversely, a rejection of such conventions represented a form of dissent within the Soviet system.

A fundamental part of the more general way of life of Petersburg rock musicians was the articulation of and adherence to a set of conventions for the adornment of the body. There is nothing new in pointing out that Russian rock musicians rejected formal conventions of dress and bodily adornment. After all, rock musicians everywhere are characterized by the substitution of dominant sartorial styles with those of their own making (see, for instance, Hebdige 1979). What is new in the context of conventional studies of Soviet society is seeing conventional styles of bodily adornment in Russia at some level as a metaphor of tacit consent to the official Soviet world and rock musicians' alternative styles as a rejection both of the larger system and of their "comrades" who have let their bodies be inscribed with the dominant practices prescribing bodily adornment. The development of independent bodily styles represents a rejection of conformity to systemic norms at the most fundamental level of everyday life. It is this system of stylistic conventions which Petersburg musicians rejected in their elaboration of an alternative bodily style. If the average *Homo sovieticus* wore short hair and was clean-shaven, the rocker wore long hair or sported a beard. If *Homo sovieticus* wore a tie or a work uniform, the rocker developed his own "uniform" which consisted of a pastiche of sartorial styles taken mostly from the consumer products of Western capitalist society. In short, members of the musical community did everything possible to ensure that all codes for bodily adornment which they saw as complicitous with the dominant culture of socialist industrial society were rejected.

In many cases, the rejection of prescribed styles of bodily adornment, perhaps more than any acts of music-making, served to mark musicians as nonconformists in the public space of the city. Since most musical performances were quasi-public, they occurred outside the gaze of the state organs of surveillance. Yet musicians inscribed their difference and otherness as counterculturalists on their bodies as they moved through the city, and this often served to provoke a response from the local militia. This was most evident in the case of punk rockers whose sartorial style was perhaps the most outrageous in the Soviet context. One young punk rocker, Alexei, for instance, recalls his harassment at the hands of the local militia purely on the grounds of his bodily style rather than as a consequence of his music-making. Like Western punks, Alexei dressed in torn shirts (or "cut-ups"), sported tattoos and earring, and wore large black military boots. He was constantly harassed by the militia, who asked him questions about why he dressed this way and threatened him with jail for wearing military dress, an infraction of the Soviet legal code. One day, Alexei was picked up four different times by four different militiamen and brought to four different militia stations for questioning. He denied that his dress was an indication of anti-Soviet attitudes and explained that he dressed that way because he wanted to.

Most musicians did not experience such overt harassment because of the fact that, even as early as the 1980s, less outrageous bodily styles such as simple long hair or jeans had become more tolerable in the otherwise homogeneous cultural framework of the city. Such styles were simply seen as youth styles, problematic from the point of view of state authorities and state-sponsored sociologists of youth culture, yet hardly worth policing on an ordinary basis. Yet rock musicians' alternative styles often evoked a response from ordinary Soviet citizens who conformed to dominant cultural practices and wore that conformity on their bodies in the form of what might be called Soviet "conventional style." A major point of Foucault's sociology of the body is that it stresses the fact that social control is maintained by actors themselves in the course of everyday life. In other words, the policing of those who displayed alternative bodily styles was often carried out by those in the local environment who followed the dominant conventions and prescriptions for "proper" bodily adornment. This fact is illustrated in some of the experiences which musicians had not with state authorities, but with ordinary Soviet citizens.

In some cases, certain groups in Russian society have organized around maintaining traditional bodily and sartorial styles as expressions of a commitment to a "normal" (i.e., Soviet) way of life. One such Moscow youth group goes by the name of *liubery* (based on its origins in the Moscow suburb of Liubertsy).[18] *Liubery* are characterized by their defense of traditional Soviet values, and they express this through their own set of cultural codes which reflect the themes of the dominant culture: bodily strength and health, short hair, conventional styles of dress, the use of official Soviet symbolism, and so on. These codes were, symbolically, the opposite of those used by Petersburg musicians as a whole. The usual method of *liubery* was to visit "bohemian quarters," parks, and concert squares of the city searching for anyone who might be considered different. Upon finding such people, they would create a disturbance and beat them, sometimes severely. The *liubery* were convinced of their own moral superiority and saw themselves as vigilantes whose task was to restore cultural order and normalcy in their cities. They defended traditional Russian and Soviet values and official policies and saw rock musicians as metaphors of Western decadence and the erosion of Russian/Soviet status and respect in the world-system. According to one prominent chronicler of Russian counterculture, the *liubery* were particularly hostile toward hippies and heavy metal rock bands (Troitsky 1990a, p. 244). While *liubery* in their original form existed only in Moscow, youth groups who were analogous to them existed in other Soviet cities and practiced a similar defense of Soviet culture by engaging in battles against their more modern counterparts (ibid.).

Such groups emerged in Petersburg and are still prevalent, according to one source, especially in Kupchino, the distinctly working-class section on the outskirts of the city. In Petersburg, these *liubery* seldom engaged in direct confrontation at concerts or other collective cultural events. Rather, they practiced a form of what might be called guerrilla warfare on rock musicians and other countercultural types in the city. One strategy was to go to concert areas and wait until concerts were over and people were dispersing. Upon finding an individual or a small group which they identified as the enemy, they engaged in harassment and sometimes even beatings. In one case, after a concert in an outlying area of the city near a popular lake, Zhenya, a musician, was approached by a number of young men who were dressed in normal Soviet clothes and sporting traditional short hair. They began to call him foul names, pull his hair, and demand money from him. Recognizing that he was in danger, Zhenya quietly tried to ignore them and told them that he had no money. Their answer was that since he was a rock star, and since he had such a pretty girlfriend, then he must have money. His girlfriend intervened and asked them to leave Zhenya alone. After harassing him for a few minutes and lightly shoving him around, they left, calling him foul names.

This encounter illustrates that it is not just city officials and militia who see countercultural types as a threat, but ordinary rank-and-file city dwellers as well. Zhenya felt that rock musicians and other counterculturalists were more often harassed by conservative youth gangs than by the state. Further, he theorized that the local authorities left youth groups alone because they agreed with their critique of alternative lifestyles and saw them as an ally in their fight against more antisystemic countercultural elements. Such conservative "shock troops" were often more immediately dangerous to the day-to-day affairs of Petersburg musicians than state officials who resorted to more subtle means of cultural repression through accommodation and surveillance.

A Note on Sex and Women

Since we have been discussing practices of the body, a note on the sexual behavior and attitudes toward women is in order. The practices we have described above are primarily male practices. It ought to be clear at this point that in our discussion of the Petersburg musical community women have been noticeably absent. The reason for this is that the Petersburg musical community primarily consists of men, with women on the periphery. In general, women were actively excluded from full participation in the countercultural community. In only one instance did I see a female group; in most cases in the course of the research females were present only as witnesses to events and interviews. There is one exception, though, and that is that women were very often group managers. This role involved organizing the affairs of men and, in many cases, keeping them from pursuing their own self-destruction from alcoholism or drug use. In this respect, female rock managers were simply playing a traditional Russian female role within the counterculture itself.

A good indication of the "maleness" of the musical community lies in the attitudes of many musicians, especially younger ones, toward women and sex. Worldwide, rock musicians are often associated with lewdness and sexual promiscuity (see, for instance, Bloom 1987; and Pattison 1987). The raw energy of rock music often leads its critics to project those qualities on those who make the music. In the case of many Petersburg musicians, this is clearly true. As in all male cultures, derogatory comments were sometimes made about women. For instance, upon being asked why there were so few women in rock music, one musician simply answered that they did not have enough energy, or *energiia*, to be good musicians. Another chimed in that if women were rock musicians "they would no longer be good for fucking." Whereupon still another added that I had seen for myself "the weakness of female musicians" at a concert earlier in the day at which one group featured a female drummer. Such views were expressed by a minority of musicians, and when they were expressed, they appeared to be related more to traditional Russian patterns of male culture and ways of thinking and joking about women than they did to the norms and values of the musical community as a musical community.[19]

What is striking is that a great number of musicians were either steady family men or maintained (ostensibly) steady monogamous relationships. This was even more the case as rock culture matured and became less dominated by young people. As rock musicians progressed through the life course, many assumed more traditional roles, such as husband and father. This fact demonstrates that the countercultural thrust of the musical community was more directed toward alienating aspects of Soviet existence and less at those aspects, such as romantic love and friendship, which, like music-making, were potentially authentic and meaningful experiences.[20] The emphasis on sexual promiscuity which existed among some members of the community could be explained by the fact that official Soviet morality included strong proscriptions against polygamy and correspondingly strong prescriptions for monogamy. Such norms were often fundamentally reinforced by the Soviet family, a fact which, again, demonstrates a certain degree of closeness between the state and the family which many musicians resented very deeply. In this respect, sexual licentiousness and promiscuity might be seen as a way of striking back at the moral nexus between the state and the family.

Cultural Performances: Rituals of Solidarity and Difference in the Petersburg Musical Community

We have examined some of the practices which constitute the countercultural way of life of Petersburg musicians. These practices might be seen as rituals. All communities have rituals and celebrations which crystallize their culture, beliefs, attitudes, and values and, in so doing bind their members together (Durkheim [1915] 1965; Turner 1969; Eliade 1959; Douglas 1985; Tambiah 1985; McLaren 1986). The literature on ritual in the social sciences is vast, yet Stanley Tambiah's (1985, p. 128) definition crystallizes the essential aspects of ritual as a "culturally constructed system of symbolic communication [which is] constituted of patterned and ordered sequences of words and acts, often expressed in multiple media, whose content and arrangement are characterized by *formality, rigidity, condensation,* and *repetition.*" Rituals are highly patterned forms of social activity which condense and crystallize the sentiments and beliefs of a group and communicate the latter in a meaningful way. They are at the very core of the reproduction of the culture of a community, group, or nation. We have already seen in the case of the taking of the bridge outlined above that the Petersburg musical community periodically met to identify and communicate with each other. We explore such collective rituals and other types of rituals in this section.

It is possible to speak of three levels of ritual in society: the linguistic, the interactional, and the collective. The first level of ritual is the linguistic and involves the use of specialized language to communicate more general cultural values and norms. Every group has its own language which members use to communicate with each other. Very often, social groups, especially subordinated groups, develop their own slang, jargon, or argot which they use to identify each other and talk about reality. In an important work on the relation between language and group formation, Basil Bernstein (1975) refers to such shared systems of language as "linguistic codes."[21] The use of the word code is important, for it conveys a sense of secrecy and opacity in language which makes the latter unintelligible to outsiders and more meaningful to those inside the group. The sharing of such meanings strengthens the solidarity of the group. We have already seen the ways in which Russian rock music's lyrics served as a code for the communication of important ideas. In this sense, we can see the very act of playing music as a ritual which circulates meaningful, coded messages (Supicic 1987, p. 295; Bergesen 1979; Attali 1985; Cushman 1991). But such cryptography also occurred in the more general, everyday language which musicians used to talk about their lives and their music. The use of such language identified people as belonging to the rock music community, but it was also an "anti-language" (Halliday 1976) which identified those who used it as standing in opposition to the dominant culture. The very idea of describing a collective experience as a *tusovka*, for instance, resisted the more formal idea of *kollektivnost'* and placed the individual who used it within the boundaries of an alternative community. Similarly, one did not refer to one's fellow musicians as *tovarishchi*, or "comrades," unless he meant to infer that they were complicitous with social forces outside the community. As another example, the language of the music community was characterized by the incessant use of Russified English words which were used as markers of the culture's Western rather than Soviet orientation. Such words were quite widespread in Soviet youth culture in general; in the music community, Russified English musical terms were a common part of everyday usage. The vocabulary of specific words which combined to form a grammar of resistance in the Petersburg community is quite extensive and was used on a regular, ongoing, everyday basis as means of group and self-identification (see appendix 1).[22]

The next level of ritual is the interactional level. Sociologists often make a distinction between microlevel rituals and macrolevel rituals. The former are the small-scale rituals of everyday life which convey beliefs and values among individuals in a group or society. Erving Goffman (1973) referred to such rituals as interaction rituals. While small-scale and seemingly insignificant, such interaction rituals are important for conveying generalized and widely held beliefs and values. A very important activity for musicians was simple interaction with one another in private circumstances. Again, the norms of friendship described earlier were ratified and reinforced primarily through microlevel interaction rituals. Merely being with one another and engaging in rituals of everyday life, such as smoking and drinking together, were important rituals signifying group membership. In the Petersburg musical community, the simple act of passing time with friend-musicians was an important interaction ritual. Indeed, hanging out together was a fundamental act which presupposed the ability to make music with one another. Such hanging out and idling was done when others were pursuing more serious ventures in the conventional world. Rather than go to work or prepare to go to work the night before, musicians would simply be together even if they were not playing. Such interaction rituals occurred with an almost complete disregard for the normal rhythms of everyday industrial life. The most common question one heard among musicians was: "What day is it?"

Finally, an important form of ritual is the collective ritual. As we have seen from the case of the bridge gathering above, collective rituals were perhaps the most important form of ritual in the St. Petersburg musical community. Collective rituals consisted both of the celebration of special days, such as birthdays or even deathdays, and of occasions of musical performance. The former were important for reaffirming common identity and status as musicians in the context of some other important event. Yet musical performances were important in defining individuals as members of the musical community. For it is in musical performance that the true identity of music as a special form of communicative action is most fully expressed. James Peacock (1990, p. 208) notes that "the sacred only becomes real as embodied in form" and the form which communicates the sacred is the performance. The performative act of making music with others was an important ritual in and of itself; it was the act which rendered ethereal conceptions of music's special quality into tangible, audible sounds. Music was experienced as most sacred during the performance. Such musical performances were important in identifying musicians as musicians to others and were the very events which allowed musicians to display a public commitment to the vocation of music-making.

In Petersburg, perhaps the most common form of celebration was the quasi-public rock concert. Since, as a rule, public space was denied for the purposes of rock performance, members of the rock community celebrated their culture in much the same way as they existed: behind closed doors. We have already discussed how the individual practice of rock occurred *v kukhne*, or "in the kitchen." In contrast to Western societies where there was at least the possibility of performing in public venues, many musicians created their culture with the knowledge that it might not ever be performed openly. The most important venue for the public performance of music was the *podval*, or "basement performance." Such performances were themselves rituals which celebrated the secret and elect nature of rock existence. Consider one musician's testimony as to the sacred nature of the *podval* performance:

> I remember going to Siberia alone, with the guitar, or to Kazan'. A man who was meeting me would be standing at the corner. So the cops wouldn't take notice of us, he would say, "Yura, turn around that corner, and these other people will lead you further." I would go there, and then we'd enter a basement without electricity, but with hundreds of people. There were no microphones—otherwise the cops can hear—candles are lit around. And I'm singing, you know. *Those were like last suppers* [emphasis added]. A bottle of port wine being passed around—what a rock-and-roll it was! . . . those were the finest (*krutye*) moments in my life. It was ten years ago. And all of us are raised on this, you see.

Indeed, the clandestine nature of such performances corroborates Huizinga's notion that the very power of play as a means of enchantment and transcendence lies in its secrecy.

One very important aspect of these performances was their timing. Often concerts were held in honor of a community member's birthday. Very often, they took place on important official holidays which were occasions for large-scale public rituals (see McDowell 1974; and Lane 1981). While the formal world attempted to ratify a sense of what it considered to be sacred through the staging of elaborate rituals, rock musicians would prevent such an occupation of their consciousness by such rituals by staging their own musical events on various sacred days of the Soviet calendar. Lenin's birthday, May Day, or Revolution Day became occasions for the celebration of alternative events or ideas such as the birthdays or deathdays of famous Russian or Western rock musicians. One extremely important day on which concerts would be held was the anniversary of the death of John Lennon. Curiously, Victory Day, the day on which the Soviet Union celebrated its victory over Germany in World War II, seemed to be a day on which not even the musical community would engage in its usual practice of the subversion of official ritual through musical performance. There appear to have been some elements of an "authentic" sacred event which were shared by the dominant society and the Petersburg musical community.

Such quasi-public performances—which might be called "alternative festivals"—took place in opposition to official holidays, but not in an antagonistic or directly confrontational way. Like many forms of performance and festival, the replacement of formal and subjectively meaningless rituals by more subjectively meaningful and informal ones took place quietly and clandestinely, in their own time and space. Rock performance, like all performance and festival, in Mikhail Bakhtin's (1973, p. 295) words, "built its own world versus the official world, its own church versus the official church, its own state versus the official state," all at the level of consciousness far away from the contours and practices of everyday Soviet existence. Rituals which occurred at every level of social existence served to build a sense of what Victor Turner (1969) refers to as "communitas" among Petersburg musicians. Such communitas was the fundamental spirit which defined musicians as a collective which stood outside of normal Soviet existence.

All of the elements of the way of life which we have described in this chapter—the norms of friendship, the importance of place and practices within Soviet time and space, bodily styles, and rituals—fused together into a whole which we have described as Petersburg musical counterculture. Adherence to each element of this cultural system served to define musicians as members of this elective community. If Lenin was to be seen everywhere, on subway walls, buildings, and in offices, then the visage of antiheroes such as Kostya and Viktor were to be seen on the walls of private homes, in the personal space of one's automobile, or inscribed as graffiti in public places as acts of resistance which reclaimed public space for the self. If the dominant sartorial style of Soviet society demanded a simple khaki shirt and pants, black work shoes, and short hair, then the countercultural style was bound to include elements which sought to reject these dominant styles at every juncture: Sex Pistols tee shirts, headbands made from Soviet flags, spiked cowboy boots, long hair. Moreover, if the normal expectation of the workday was eight to five, then counterculturalists could be found either on the street, in the rehearsal studio, at home sleeping—in short, anywhere but at the office or the factory. And it is this system of homologous codes which constituted a counterculture. In the last part of this chapter we explore the collective significance of the Petersburg musical counterculture as an elective community which stood as a collective expression of the sacred in relation to the dominant culture of Soviet society which expressed itself as sacred.

The Sacred and the Countersacred:
Competing Cosmologies within Socialist Industrial Society

The Cosmology of Socialist Industrial Society

Like other modernizing industrial societies, the Soviet state grounded its trajectory of development in a system of beliefs and values about its own history and about the world in general. Indeed, one of the defining characteristics of Soviet society was its attempt to render elements of its own history—important people, places, events, and times—as sacred. Over time, such activity yielded what sociologist Robert Bellah (1967) referred to as a "civil religion." Civil religion is simply the replacement of the content of traditional religion—supernatural deities, forces, and spirits—with a content derived from historical events, places, and personalities of modern society. The formal qualities of religion such as the observance of holidays to commemorate important people, places, and things; the reservation of special times for the contemplation and worship of the sacred; and the deification of important historical figures were all retained, yet invested with a secular content. This historical process of transforming the events, persons, places, and ideas connected with the modernization of Soviet society into sacred entities represented a distinct effort to sacralize the secular. In the Soviet Union we see, historically, a most dramatic attempt by secular authority to render elements of the secular world sacred, to make, quite literally, a religion out of politics (Lane 1981; Sironneau 1982; Luke 1987).

This process of transforming the secular into the sacred was a hallmark of Soviet history and had its origins deep within the aspirations for a total transformation of society and culture which followed in the wake of the Bolshevik Revolution of 1917. The Russian Revolution as a cultural revolution was characterized by a high degree of cultural iconoclasm which aimed to destroy the Russian historical past and replace it with a new world order (Stites 1985). The course of Soviet historical development was characterized by rapid industrialization, urbanization, migration, and other phenomena which we consider to be the central aspects of modernization. Lying behind these concrete processes were fundamental ideas which defined ideal relations between man and other aspects of the cosmos: society, other individuals, the supernatural. Most analysts of the Soviet system refer to such ideas as "ideology" which is part of the Soviet Union's "political culture" (see, for instance, Tucker 1987; White 1979). Clearly the state was the driving force behind such ideas, but such ideas defined a more global and universal set of relations among entities in the spiritual, physical, and social world of socialist industrial modernity. Although one could speak of the belief system of socialist industrial society as ideology, for the purpose of conveying a sense of the totality of the belief system of Soviet society, I have chosen to use the more encompassing term *cosmology*.

Anthropologist Stanley Tambiah (1985, p. 130) notes that "All societies have cosmologies which relate man to man, man to nature and animals, and man with the gods and demons and other non-human agencies." This is no less the case in modern societies. Tambiah defines cosmology simply as "the body of conceptions that enumerate and classify the phenomena that compose the universe as an ordered whole and the norms and processes that govern it." Johan Galtung (1981) characterizes the dimensions of social cosmology—that is, a society's overall cultural definitions of reality—as consisting of five fundamental categories: space, time, relations between actors and nature, relations between actors and other actors, and relations between actors and the transpersonal or supernatural.[23] Each of these categories is filled with a specific content which is evident in ideological pronouncements, macrolevel and microlevel rituals, and the institutional and individual practices of everyday life. What is more important, the latter are products of the concrete historical development of the society in which they occur. Table 4.1 offers a summary of the formal categories of cosmology with examples which illustrate the specific ideals of the cosmology of socialist industrial modernity.

Cosmology is a more encompassing term which allows us to understand the totality of the Soviet modern experience as opposed to a more restricted view of Soviet history as a reflex of politics. Elements of the cosmology of socialist industrial society were expressed in numerous social and cultural practices of Soviet society, and it is at the level of practice that cosmology makes itself manifest to people. The ideals in the above categories were evident across a wide range of Soviet social, political, economic, and cultural practices.

Using the idea of cosmology to describe the belief system of socialist industrial modernity by no means infers that the categories were actually adhered to or believed in by Soviet actors. The categories of Soviet cosmology represent ideas which were considered sacred within Soviet society. Recall that a central element of the sacred is that it is capable, by virtue of its extraordinary qualities, of intimidating and instilling fear in those who apprehend it or come in contact with it. Politicians use guns and terror to get unwilling subjects to do things, but power is inherent in the idea of the sacred: those who are officially allowed to be close to the sacred benefit from their association with it. Mere mortals, however, cannot tangle with the sacred, for the results could be quite dangerous. This line of thought can explain a great deal of conformity and order throughout Soviet history.

One could spend a great deal of time debating the issue of the extent to which Soviet citizens actually perceived this sacralization of the profane as an authentic, meaningful sense of the sacred. There is little question that special personalities such as Lenin and Stalin, special events such as the Revolution or the birth of Lenin, special places such

TABLE 4.1
The Cosmology of Socialist Industrial Society

Category	Example
Space	Definitions of center and periphery, the relation of one's own society to others. The Soviet Union is the center of the world communist movement, and the rest of the world is defined by its position in relation to that center. The farther another society is from the center, the more threat it poses to the center.
Time	The idea of progress, evolution toward specified goals. The end of time is a utopian ideal, a desired state of affairs toward which all social action in the present is oriented. The Soviet Union aspires to be a communist society in which people are liberated from the constraining ties of the mode of capitalist production and inequality in productive relations.
Actor-Nature	Relations between humans and nonhumans. In general, humans are superior to nonhumans, and it is the task of humans to master nature through science and technology. The building of communism requires the mastery and exploitation of nature.
Actor-Actor	Ideal conceptions of proper relations between actors. Ideally, Soviet people are collectively oriented, cooperate with one another, and work together. Conversely, individualism is a negative quality associated with capitalism.
Actor-Transactor	Relations between actors and suprahuman, supernatural forces. Religion is seen as a mythic superstition which supports unequal, individualized social relations. The Soviet Union unmasks religion as myth and offers atheism as a facilitator of socialist development.

as Leningrad or Red Square were both constructed and perceived as being endowed with extraordinary qualities. In relation to other ordinary people, events, and places, the aforementioned were sacred. The real significance of the Soviet Union's proclivity to sacralize the secular throughout its history does not so much lie in the effects which such sacralization had on the consciousness—either individual or collective—of Soviet actors. Rather, the sacralization of the secular on such a grand scale demonstrated that elements of the profane world could be elevated to a position of sacredness. The only step for individuals was to find an appropriate content with which to fill the category of the sacred and thus render it truly and authentically meaningful at the most important level: the level of subjectivity. Soviet history is instructive for indicating the extent to which the idea of the sacred was detached from the supernatural (its usual attachment in traditional societies) and attached to various realms of the mundane, non-supernatural world.

What interests us here is not consent and conformity, but dissent and resistance. For members of the Petersburg musical community, the cosmology of socialist industrial modernity did not provide meaningful categories for personal or social existence. At the most abstract level, musical counterculture was a collective effort to invest existence with a degree of authenticity which was subjectively meaningful to those involved. The countercultural activity of Petersburg musicians was a way of articulating a countercosmology. Musicians negated the dominant conception of space by locating the center of their counterculture in the rock culture of the West. The idea of a linear progression toward some fixed social goals through fixed social means was negated by the celebration of "hanging out" and articulating alternative uses of time and space. The idea of man's dominion over nature was rejected. Even though the practice of his craft depended fundamentally on the products of technological society, the rock musician countered the ethos of the technological domination of nature through a poetic which stressed harmony with the existing world and a critique of the Soviet Union's attempts to tame that world with instrumental reason. Rock musicians accepted the idea that collectivity was important, but invested this category with their own sense of authentic communitas through the practice of the *tusovka*. Finally, the emphasis on ethereal truths, the sacredness of music, and the speciality of musical performance came to have an almost religious significance which countered the idea that the world was purely of man's own making. Music-making in Petersburg did not just resemble a religious experience. It was, in William James's sense, a variety of religious experience. While the object of contemplation in rock music may not have always been religious in nature, it is clear that the practice of rock music was an alternative means of spirituality within the context of socialist industrial society.

The Petersburg musical counterculture sacralized a new cultural cosmology, a "countercosmology," which was the very source of alternative individual and group identity in the context of socialist industrial modernity. This culture stood against the dominant culture and its cosmology. As a collective phenomenon, it was born of a failure of the dominant sense of the sacred to do what the sacred is supposed to do, namely, to offer individuals meaningful frameworks which they can use to guide and orient their lives. Counterculture constructs a sense of the countersacred, which is the antithesis of a sacred gone bad, a sacred polluted by the logic of instrumental rationality. The Soviet state's attempt to make a civil religion out of elements of its own secular history was an attempt to render the products, people, and places associated with the ethos of instrumental rationality into sacred entities. Such a project could only fail, for the sacralization of rationality itself could only lead people to search for ways to re-enchant the world, to "resacralize" it through the creative construction of alternative modes of thinking, being, and acting.

5

Notes from Underground: Glasnost, Perestroika, and the St. Petersburg Rock Music Community

> Spiritual authority differs from political authority in that it only grows stronger from opposition and controversy. It's a good thing if an idea produces heated opposition at first. A creative intellectual who doesn't provoke irritation and even hatred is not so creative as he thinks. If the time comes when everyone loves him and respects him, he is finished.
>
> —Gyorgy Konrad, *Antipolitics*

> Contra Franco vivíamos mejor. (Against Franco we lived better.)
>
> —Manuel Vázquez Montalbán

Back to Reality: A Return to Political Economy

The view of rock music and rock counter-culture presented thus far illustrates well the sociological idea that music-making, and culture more generally, are accomplishments. From what we have seen so far, it is amazing that music was accomplished at all in St. Petersburg. The lack of instruments and sound equipment, the lack of reliable sources of cultural information, the inability to secure space in which to perform, and a deeply entrenched infrastructure of surveillance and cultural management all worked against the orderly and routine practice of rock music. Ironically, though, it was this very disorder that made rock music even more oppositional and resistant in the Soviet context. Musicians often expressed their disgust with the technical aspects of organizing performances or advertising themselves. Yet rock was accomplished, and the fact that it was done under adversity made its practice all the more special to those who made it and to those who consumed it.

Up to this point, we have been speaking primarily of the ethereal ideas, values, and beliefs about both music and life which lie behind the practice of rock in St. Petersburg. However, it is important to stress that culture is accomplished through structured practices of production and distribution. The focus of this chapter is to outline in detail the social organization of the production of rock culture in Petersburg from roughly 1980 until the dissolution of the Soviet Union in 1991. First, we examine the institutionalization of rock practice which occurred during the early 1980s with the formation of two important institutions: the Leningrad Rock Club, which primarily organized rock performance, and an underground production studio, which produced and distributed independent rock music. Following this, we explore the macro-level structural changes which occurred in Soviet society as a result of the state policies of reform known as glasnost and perestroika. The central purpose of this chapter is to explore the ways in which the changing institutional contexts of cultural production affected the process of music-making, the identity of rock music, the identity of individual musicians, and the collective identity of the Petersburg musical community.

In the second part of the chapter, we turn our attention to outlining the basic dimensions of the process of cultural perestroika, or the restructuring of cultural production according to the principles and practices of capitalist economics. We delve into the lifeworlds of musicians themselves in order to throw into relief the ways in which structural changes began to affect the lives and work of rock musicians. The reforms of the glasnost era enabled the free expression of rock music in previously unimaginable ways. Yet such openness was part of the problem. For the structural changes brought on by glasnost and perestroika began to erode and efface the historically developed and highly contextual meanings of rock identity, the identities of Petersburg rock musicians, and the collective identity of the rock community.

In 1991, the Soviet Union as a formal entity was dissolved. In the wake of its dissolution, the process of the capitalist rationalization of Russian society was accelerated. This chapter focuses on rock culture under conditions of "late socialism," that is, the period from roughly 1980 until the dissolution of the Soviet Union in 1991. In the next chapter, we turn to an examination of the fate of the Petersburg rock counterculture under conditions of what might be called "post-socialism," or perhaps more appropriately, "early capitalism." Thus begins our exploration of the ironic and paradoxical story of what happens to music and musicians when they "come up from underground."

The Social Organization of
Rock Music Culture in St. Petersburg

The Informal Production of Independent Music:
An Underground Culture Industry

The Petersburg music community developed its own practices for the production and distribution of musical products and performances. These practices constituted what might be called an "informal infrastructure" for the production and distribution of independent rock music. This infrastructure met the informal demands for independent rock music of the Russian taste public which were unsatisfied by the formal products of the state-controlled Soviet culture industries. The first way of satisfying such informal demands was through the informal production and distribution of independent musical products.

During the late 1970s and early 1980s, in a Soviet "House of Pioneers"[1] not too far from Nevsky Prospekt, Petersburg's main avenue, a very important cultural activity was occurring. In the basement of the building was a small recording studio in which a man by the name of Andrei produced tape-recorded albums of certain independent Petersburg musicians. Here is how the system worked: a group or a musician would come to this producer and audition, whereupon he would decide whether they would merit recording.[2] Upon making his decision, the producer would make recordings of the music, reproduce them one by one on tapes, and distribute them to rock music aficionados in the city. In turn, these rock products were reproduced and distributed through the communicative channels of the tape-recorder culture which were already firmly in place in the city. Because of the lack of access to the means of mass reproduction, such forms were inherently limited in their diffusion. Yet it should be pointed out that, ironically, as with other *samizdat* products, the demand for informal musical products was much greater than the demand for the products of formal institutions for the production of culture such as Melodiya.

Normally, sociological understandings of large-scale cultural processes do not stress the role of specific individuals in such processes. Until now we have worked against stressing the role of great men in the history of Petersburg rock culture by focusing on rock music as something practiced by particular types of individuals in relation to more macrolevel structural and institutional forces. Yet in this case, it is impossible to ignore the central role played by Andrei, the underground producer whose system was just described, in the ongoing operation of the Petersburg musical counterculture. Arguably, without Andrei, there would have been no systematic production and distribution of Petersburg rock music. As such, his history and thoughts about rock music are extremely important.[3] Unfortunately, despite persistent efforts, Andrei refused to be interviewed for this study. The reasons for this are not mysterious: Andrei became the president of Melodiya during the glasnost era and later went on to be a full-scale participant in the illegal reproduction and distribution of both Russian and Western rock music—or what is usually called "piracy"—after the dissolution of the Soviet Union. Andrei's career as a musical pirate will be discussed at length later in this chapter and in the next chapter. Stories about Andrei's career abound in the folklore of the community. The following explanation taken from a close colleague of Andrei crystallizes the central elements of the nature of Andrei's enterprise:

> Formally he worked with schoolchildren, taught them how to use soldering irons, how to assemble electronic equipment from schematics, about electric circuits. He himself was connected with the rock music scene and was always interested in it, and it occurred to him to assemble and disassemble not only radio sets, but also some recording equipment. Actually, it was not a criminal deed—a person could assemble a tape recorder at home and use it as if he had bought it in a shop. So, some equipment he bought on the black market, some in the shops. Since he had friends in the Melodiya studios, through them he bought salvaged obsolete equipment, refurbished it, and installed it. In this way after a while he made quite a decent studio which he would renew regularly. That is, when Melodiya was getting new equipment, the old stuff was almost automatically bought by the House of Pioneers. For his part, Andrei also helped Melodiya with some projects, since he had a business mind, certain abilities, and he participated in some business. . . . And I think it was known to the authorities, but for some reason it was more advantageous to keep this source open, so as not to lose contact with others by closing it. Because it was clear to some that rock culture would disperse, and then it would be somehow more difficult to control.

This complicity between formal and informal organizations of cultural production shores up a central point: the activities of each sector were not so rigidly separated from one other. Andrei needed at least some technologies of mass production created by the state in order to make his recordings. In a material sense, Petersburg rock culture—even though it was ideationally distanced from the external, material world—was fundamentally dependent on the technologies of socialist industrial society for its very existence.[4] Underground cultural production was not overtly proscribed by the authorities since to do so would literally close off the option of further surveillance of such productive activity. The reality of so-called unofficial production is that it was directly enabled by the official materials and the political practices of the dominant social order.

To understand Andrei's vision and motivations, we must rely on an interview which he offered when he was engaged in underground production. The interview offers many glimpses into the lifeworld of this most interesting "Gutenberg" of Russian rock music.[5] The following segments of the interview reveal not only the deeply encoded ways of speaking characteristic of members of the Petersburg rock community, but also some important historical facts about the informal production of rock music in the city and Andrei's own conception of his place in that history. The interview also offers glimpses into Andrei's own conception of his work and his importance in the rock culture, his relations with fellow counterculturalists, and key elements of his personality and world view which played a key role in cultural outcomes in St. Petersburg. The interview is presented mainly as a monologue, the elements of which presumably occur in response to questions by the interviewer, Gena. It begins with an introduction which stresses Andrei's importance in the development of the Petersburg rock counterculture:

> *Gena:* There are people about whom we can safely say: without them much would not happen. . . . I'm far from thinking that it's time to collect scrap metal and immortalize Andrei Vladimirovich in bronze—he hasn't invented anything, and besides, gone are the times when it was possible to have such a "portrait" in one's lifetime in, say, Dnepropetrovsk. . . . But note: there is no monument to Gutenberg in Moscow. Instead there is a perfect sculpture of Ivan Fyodorov who, one would think, didn't invent anything new either, but is considered a printing pioneer just the same.[6]

Presumably in answer to a question about his age, Andrei notes:

> I'm old enough. I understand this is not an idle question. Indeed, not everyone in our circle is called by name and patronymic. The

fact is, I'm running a sound-recording workshop in the House of Pioneers and Schoolchildren. Just imagine, the director comes and sees overgrown rockers and moreover hears that they call me "Andriukha." Everybody understands that this is nonsense. As for my year of birth. . . . Till I was thirty, I've been Pisces, and now I've become Aries. When Christ was born, an opposite change occurred: Aries was replaced by Pisces. Usually at such moments, which occur very rarely, they are waiting for a messiah . . . (Gena: Take into account that Andrei explained to me everything connected with the mystery of his birth, stated his attitude to the Gregorian and Julian calendars, accused the Nicaean Council of 630 of heresy and devilishness, and also explained his last-year procrastination by the lunar and solar cycles. I will venture to tell you that he was born in 1951 and refer those interested in sacred and astral matters to the article in *Context*, 1978.)

[My studio] was not born all of a sudden. At one time I tried to find some literature on sound recording and finally realized that in the whole world music is being composed under awful conditions—nobody has achieved ideal conditions so far. Allan Parson's phrase, "Give me a good room and two microphones and I will record whatever you like" remains only fine words. In the West heaps of good equipment are piled up in sheds. Here we've got the same sheds plus poorer equipment. But the main conclusion from this inspired me: even with the minimum means one can achieve good results. For some time I was engaged in the organization of the concerts, mainly of Mashina Vremeni (Time Machine), and no wonder that there was a number of recordings, though they were concert recordings. Thus the appearance of the album *The Birthday* in 1978 was a natural result. There was no studio at that time, and *The Birthday* was not an album in the true sense of the word. On the whole at that time one could have observed a surprising situation: the groups that came to the studio for a recording session tried to play a concert, i.e., at the count "one-two-three" they started to thrash away (*thresh*) just like they did on stage before the audience. Such an approach had nothing in common with creating an album as a work of art. The surviving albums from that time now draw nothing but smiles. Thus, we are deprived of the opportunity to evaluate, or at least evaluate the contributions to the rock movement of such groups as Flamingo, Galaktika, Nu pogodi! and many, many others. Whole trends have died out, the most interesting people were gone without leaving a trace. . . . It's a pity, of course.

. . . Then I started to make attempts to record. Mify (the Myths) . . . well what can one say about them. . . . The group of Yuri Stepanov (Andrei is singing). I lost my interest in Mashina Vremeni by 1980. As I see it, Makar [Andrei Makarevich] ruined rock, the work of the group ceased to be collective. But, having refused to record Andrei as a group, I suggested that he be recorded as a bard. Remember, "The Cow," etc.? The equipment in the studio at the time: tape recorders "Tembr-2M" with rearranged circuits—"one track reads, the other records"—and MES-28 with Speed 19.

. . . How were my musical tastes formed? It began very long ago, and so to say, in two directions. On the one hand I was learning to play guitar (and now I'm performing quite complex musical pieces), and from the sixth grade on, in addition to listening to recordings of symphony music, I started to listen to rock. The Beatles began it for me with the *Sergeant*. Before that I liked Shadows, Platters. Now I listen to music with some difficulty—the perception of a producer interferes, it's impossible just to relax and enjoy—the analysis is going on against your will in your head. Here is some guy singing out of tune (*lazha*), here's a guitar that's overdone. You know. . . .

How did my musical tastes influence my work with groups? I see what you mean. I myself have heard what they say: "Andrei is imposing his opinion on the musicians." Yes! I'm a dictator in the studio, like the conductor at the concert or the captain on a ship. Well, judge for yourself: B. G.[7] suggests that we record fifty (!!!) guitars by superimposing them on one another. I, of course, suggest that he look for another studio to perform such marasmatic (*marazmaticheskie*) experiments.[8] Or the same Akvarium—I don't like the song "Wild Honey," and I will not record it because I consider the text to be mere bragging. Many musicians, especially the young ones, have a poor orientation even to their own performances—everybody knows only his part, which is, on the one hand good, since it gives a collective character to the work, but this is the very thing that requires my supervision. Artem [an important underground rock critic] once told me that I'm not a sound producer at all, but a true producer. Quite probable.

Andrei is a producer in every sense of the word. Given the complete lack of recording opportunities in Russia, musicians relied almost solely on performance as a means of musical expression. Such performances, which were usually quasi-public, served to enhance the sacredness of rock music. Because of their emphasis on performance, musicians simply had no experience in making recordings. Andrei took it upon himself to separate the act of musical performance from the act of musical recording. In such a way, he began to teach musicians that there is a difference between the two: the elements of successful performance do not always constitute a good recording. Andrei's self-professed dictatorial temperament suggests that musicians were quite at his mercy if they wished to be recorded and take their place within the underground star system of St. Petersburg. Andrei's autocracy tempers somewhat any idealized notions that Petersburg rock musicians had complete freedom to play whatever they wanted. They could, of course, do so, but this would exclude them from acquiring further status in the rock community since status was dependent to some extent on the objectification of music through the process of recording it. Andrei's intrepid productive activities, combined with the deeply entrenched networks of distribution, helped to define St. Petersburg as perhaps the most important site for the production of independent rock music in Russia.

Andrei's totalistic personal control over artistic production indicates that even within a context in which there was no discernible profit motive (as is the case with Western culture producers), producers still maintained a great deal of control over artistic production. Western producers' control over artists is based primarily on their assessment of the economic viability of artistic products and styles. In Petersburg, the major criterion of artistic control was simply the personal taste of Andrei, who had access to the only means of cultural production outside of state control. Andrei controlled the illicit means of cultural production and did so in accordance with his own aesthetic proclivities and whims. Thus, Petersburg rock musicians, while independent of the state, were quite dependent on arbitrary forces beyond their control. What is more important, such forces existed even within their own informal cultural community. Conflicts between producers and artists are a universal aspect of the mass production of music no matter where such production occurs. From the point of view of Petersburg musicians, though, the dictatorial stance of Andrei—who was after all one of their own and whose activities put him in personal danger—was infinitely preferable to the dictatorship of outside forces which offered even less compromise and the lack of opportunity to record anything at all. Andrei was the lesser of two evils; without him, musicians would have been condemned to obscurity.

The basic parameters of the taste culture for rock music in the city, and eventually in the country at large, were determined almost single-handedly by Andrei, who used the state-owned means of cultural production to make musical products. It is important to stress here that the ownership of musical products lay completely outside of any individual or institution, formal or informal. The very act of declaring oneself as an independent musician ensured that one would have no control over one's own cultural products. Soviet copyright law (which we shall discuss at length later) only protected the rights of ownership of cultural products of those who worked within the state-controlled institutions of cultural production; all other cultural products were, by definition, illegal and were subject not to protection, but to prosecution. Even Andrei had no rights of ownership. By all accounts, he made very little money from his recordings in the early stages: his motivation seems to have been a commitment to music for music's sake. In all of the stories told by musicians about Andrei's activities, he was never described in pejorative terms as a black marketeer or a speculator (*spekuliant*) in cultural goods. According to one source, Andrei made some money by distributing his albums and organizing underground concerts. Yet there was no way he could control the informal process of cultural production and distribution which occurred in the population at large. Once they left his studio, musical products became public goods to be reproduced and distributed by a population which was hungry for such products. Musicians themselves had no control over either the production or the distribution of their own music. They were guaranteed no income from its distribution. Indeed, the more widespread their musical products became, the more chance they had of actually being harassed. The returns which musicians received were personal, in contributions to the development of their own individual and social identities as rock musicians. The objective existence of their recordings was an important first step in building their social status within the rock musical counterculture and the taste public at large.

The Leningrad Rock Club:
The Institutionalization of Cultural Performance

Andrei's efforts were primarily oriented toward the production of musical culture in the strict sense of the word *production* as the making of objective forms of culture. His work solved a very important problem for musicians: the problem of how to transform their practice into objective cultural products. Yet this left unsolved the equally important problem of cultural performance which is a crucial aspect of rock's identity as a form of aesthetic cultural practice (Wicke 1991). Traditionally, performances were rather chaotic and unpredictable. Without formal opportunities to play, musicians could not become visible to a widespread public; they would be destined to wander from basement to basement and, ultimately, would run the risk of falling into obscurity.

In 1980, a resolution of the problem of performance emerged in the form of the Leningrad Rock Club, located on Rubenstein Street off the city's main avenue, Nevsky Prospekt. Many attempts to organize independent rock practice had occurred earlier. These had failed either because of lack of resources or because of direct government prevention of such attempts. The Rock Club emerged as the first functional institutional entity for the widespread organization of public musical performance in the city. It was to become the center of the city's musical counterculture, a central meeting place for members of the community and a veritable font of musical performance.

We shall address the various theories offered by musicians as to why the club emerged at that particular moment in the city's history. First, though, we can examine its foundation in the terms offered by the directors of the club in an "underground press release." This press release offers us a glimpse into the ideology behind the club's formation, but it also gives us some intimations about its connections with formal political structures, which rock musicians had traditionally resisted:

> The Leningrad Rock Club was founded in March of 1981 under the auspices of the Intercouncil House of Artistic Activity. This amateur organization presently has over sixty groups. Attempts to found a club like this were undertaken earlier but for a variety of reasons they were unsuccessful. The most obvious explanation was that the Leningrad rock movement in the 1970s through 1980 was notable for its instability and chaotic nature. Concerts occurred from time to time, the structure kept changing, and there was a lack of constant contact with audiences.
>
> Up till 1981 many rockers of the old guard (*staroi zakalki*) began to vanish from the stage. At that time, many talented young musicians began to appear, wishing for "a long life in rock-and-roll." To ignore this situation was impossible, for the situation demanded that crucial changes be made.
>
> The club opened on March 7—it's difficult to convey the diverse range of the most defiant feelings which were reflected in the faces of the numerous rock music fans who gathered on Rubenstein Street. In a rather short time, a lot had changed—groups got the possibility to appear, gradually the professional level of musicians was raised, the criteria of evaluation changed, the public became more discriminating, more strict in their judgments.

Unfortunately, it's impossible to say that with the appearance of the club all the problems will be solved in a flash. Previous problems like the lack of high quality equipment, the fact that many groups don't have a place to practice etc., etc. What are we supposed to do, we live in a material world! But since the coverage of these and related problems is not at all obligatory on the pages of our album [a reference to the underground journal in which the release appears] then we will not cover them. As if there never were problems, the club will continue its activities![9]

The club was founded at the initiative of members of the city's musical community who were not primarily musicians, but fellow travelers of the rock *tusovka*. It was organized much along the lines of formal Soviet bureaucratic institutions with the exception that, in general, the activities of the club were more firmly under the control of the club organization. The club's organization consisted of an artistic council (*khudsovet*) led by a president. The *khudsovet* consisted of leading musicians, rock intellectuals and journalists, and rock fellow travelers. The membership of the club consisted of groups who were granted member status based on an audition for the club *khudsovet*. Once admitted, members paid dues to the club, and such dues were a major source of the club's funding. Membership in the Rock Club was also an important symbol of status in the local music community and in the country at large. Such clubs were organized throughout the country, in most cases, after the club in Petersburg. By all accounts, the clubs in Moscow, Petersburg, and Sverdlovsk (now Ekaterinburg), were considered to be the most important in the Soviet Union as a whole. Throughout the 1980s, the club membership gradually increased. By 1990, there were sixty groups who were registered as members of the club.[10]

Unlike Western clubs, which are usually privately owned venues for rock performance for profit, the Rock Club was an organization which was designed to solve the difficult problems of musical performance in the city. As one of the club's founders put it:

It's necessary to make a fundamental distinction between the understanding of what "rock club" means in the West and what "rock club" means in the Soviet Union. A rock club in the West is a place like a rock cafe, where musicians congregate, play, meet each other. In other words, it's a place of rest and concerts. But in the Soviet Union, not only in Leningrad, but in other cities, a rock club is an organization which tries to solve the problems of musicians. In other words, it is a "production firm" (*prodiuserskaia firma*).

The club's most basic function was to "produce" performances for members in local concert halls, in its own small auditorium, and in other Soviet cities. A most important event was the annual Rock Club Festival which featured bands that were considered most important in the city. By virtue of Petersburg's historical importance in the country at large, these annual rock festivals became something of an "All-Union" event which were attended not only by fans, but by other groups and club organizers from other parts of the country.

Repressive Tolerance or New Forms of Symbiotic Inequality?

The formation of the club represented a very real force in the enabling of rock practice in Petersburg. Nonetheless, the club was run by what many musicians referred to as "rock bureaucrats." In light of what we have already learned about the idealistic and ethereal nature of the rock counterculture, it is understandable why musicians would use such an ironic oxymoron to describe the club leadership: musicians had always resisted the bureaucratic ethos of Soviet society. The important issue at this point concerns the relationship between the Rock Club and the state. The fact that it was allowed to form in 1980 meant that the government must have been involved at some level in its formation or operation. The press release above notes specifically that the Rock Club was formed under the "auspices" of the Intercouncil House of Artistic Activity, an official organization of the Communist Party. Yet what exactly was the relationship between the Rock Club and formal institutions of culture management in the city? And, what is more important, what was its effect on the practice of independent rock?

Many musicians believed that, in addition to member dues and outside donations, the club received direct financial support from the state. Their main reason for believing this was the simple fact that the club existed in such a central location and was housed in state property. In addition, some musicians could not understand why the club always seemed to have more money than it could have received from membership dues alone. They reasoned that it would have been impossible for such a club—consisting almost exclusively of musicians who were not employed by the state and who had been defined in most cases as provocateurs—to exist in the social environment of the early 1980s.

The club served the very important function of centralizing the most popular independent musicians in one area where they and their activities could be kept under surveillance and, if need be, controlled. Prior to the foundation of the club, there had been a long history of state surveillance of rock musical activities, and such an act on the part of the KGB would certainly be in keeping with this tradition.[11] From a theoretical standpoint, such state cultural practices of "repressive tolerance" (Marcuse 1965) were central parts of the overall repertoire of more subtle and efficient, and less overtly repressive, state techniques for the management of oppositional culture.[12] At the time of the formation of the Rock Club and during the initial years of its operation there was no way to verify the extent to which the state was involved in its formation and operation. Musicians simply made deductions from what they knew about what was possible in their society at the time. During the glasnost era, more concrete evidence for this relationship between the state and the club emerged, and we shall discuss this later. The important sociological fact is that musicians felt that the state was involved in the organization of the club, and this knowledge affected their subsequent musical activity. While there were musicians who overtly traded their musical autonomy for material support, even independent musicians became involved with the state simply by virtue of their affiliation with the club and their participation in its affairs. In this respect, it is not accurate to speak, as many Western analysts of rock music in the Soviet Union have done, of an absolute distinction between "official" and "unofficial" music (see, for instance, Ryback 1990; Ramet and Zamascikov 1990; and Stites 1992). The official was already in the unofficial as early as 1980 in a more sublime form of state management of rock expression at the Rock Club.

The relationship between the rock community and the state which emerged in the formation of the Rock Club is best described as one of symbiotic inequality. A condition of symbiotic inequality is one in which two parties coexist in a mutually beneficial situation, although one party enjoys greater advantage, privileges, and power over the other (Milner 1980). In the case of relations between rock musicians and the state, the state obviously maintained the upper hand in relations with musicians; it alone retained the power to intervene aggressively if cultural expression moved beyond the parameters of what it deemed to be tolerable. While remaining highly critical of Soviet existence, many musicians accepted this situation simply because the state's policy of what might be called "guarded neglect" seldom intervened in their lives. Because of the Rock Club, Petersburg musicians were able to expand the public performance of their music. This enabled them to fulfill one of the most central requisites of rock music's identity as performance. In pragmatic terms, public performance enhanced their individual and social identities as rock musicians in the minds of the Russian taste public.

The Rock Club enabled public performance of independent rock, but at the same time it also facilitated surveillance of the rock scene by the state. This sense of paradox was captured well by Andrei, another underground producer and rock intellectual who worked closely with Andrei, the underground producer discussed above:

> The rock musicians who formed the independent element were organized into the Rock Club which was a kind of safety valve (*otdushina*) formally permitted from above, partly for show (*pokazukha*), partly in order for it be more easily controlled. And there were certain forms of communication—we had our own magazine which existed in fact illegally, but on the other hand, was not prohibited by anybody either. Then there was Andrei's studio [see above], which did not exist officially. But again, it was not prohibited either. Nobody permitted it, nobody prohibited it. Such a paradoxical situation.

Andrei's observation shores up a central point related to situations of symbiotic inequality: each party pursues its interests with a guarded but relatively relaxed recognition of the interests and actions of the other party. Relations are rather unrestrained, as long as each party acts according to the terms of the symbiotic relationship. This was the central reality of relations between the state and the Petersburg counterculture which existed in the early 1980s: in Andrei's terms, "Nobody permitted it, nobody prohibited it." Independent rock music culture had evolved to a point which made its overt circumscription by the state impossible. And the state had evolved to a point which made overt circumscription undesirable. It is beyond the scope of this book to delve into the reasons for the emergence of the state's ambivalent and even tolerant position toward independent rock.[13] It is worth noting, though, that by the end of the 1970s and during the early 1980s, the Soviet social system was experiencing a number of "steering crises" (Habermas 1975) which were far more serious than the threat posed by rock musicians. The escalation of the Cold War by the United States, the crisis in Afghanistan, and the management of large-scale movements for ethnic and national autonomy were just a few of the international and domestic crises which took precedence over the control of independent cultural expression in the Soviet Union.

This symbiotic relationship between musicians and the dominant social order was problematic for both parties. The profound differences between each party ultimately led to conflicts. State culture managers set boundaries on cultural expression and exerted constant control over the content of music and the style of its performance in order to keep rock practice within those boundaries. The actions of rock musicians are best characterized by an incessant push from below to extend those boundaries without overtly endangering the basic identity of their music, their own identity, or the identity of the group. In formal terms, the Rock Club was a site characterized by an ongoing tension between competing interests and objectives of two parties whose styles of practice were fundamentally at odds with one another. Both sides accomplished, at least to some degree, their own objectives: the state could maintain some semblance of control over rock musical expression, and musicians could engage in cultural performances.

After the formation of the Rock Club, most musicians who were affiliated with it were not harassed or repressed overtly so long as they exhibited some semblance of control over their public performances. During the Chernenko period there was a conservative reaction against rock music. Rock musicians speak of this period as the intensification of what they often called "the press" or the "strangulation" (*dushilovo*) of the state.[14] While we have not been interested in second-guessing the motivations of Soviet political elites, we should at least point out that this "press" might have been a reaction to a perceived trend toward cultural pluralism, a trend of which the Rock Club was a glaring example. The press was most likely an attempt to reverse such a trend and is quite in keeping with a historical tendency of Soviet political elites to reverse and delegitimize the policies and practices of their predecessors as a step toward implementing and legitimatizing their own. Nonetheless, there are very few stories offered by musicians themselves which would indicate that the rhetoric of cultural conservatives was always translated into large-scale practices of repression within the rock community. Some musicians did experience an intensification of the intrusion of the KGB into their lives even after the Rock Club was formed. Recall, for instance, Yuri, the veteran counterculturalist from chapter 2, who was pressed not only by the state but by the actual organizer of the club. Yuri's troubles with the state have much to do with the fact that he refused to participate in the *tusovka* of the Rock Club (which in formal terms was not exactly a *tusovka* since the very idea of *tusovka* resists institutionalization and formalization; Yuri seems to have grasped this in his rejection of the club).

How did patterns of state control over independent musicianship manifest themselves? And how did musicians react to such control? Since the club was a site of struggle, very often serious conflicts would emerge which laid bare the underlying conflicts between rock and the state. Normally such conflicts would occur as a result of musicians' overstepping the boundaries of what was deemed permissible by both the club art council and the state culture managers. The normal process of musical performance occurred as follows: organizers of Rock Club festivals would invite certain bands to play at scheduled concerts and at annual festivals. The latter were the most important, and competition for the right to play at them was particularly keen. At some point in the process, bands would be asked to submit their songs' lyrics to the club *khudsovet*, ostensibly so that the latter could make and print a program of events in order to sell advance tickets to the performance. The club *khudsovet*, however, was ultimately responsible to party organizations in the city which were in charge of the management of aesthetic life. The club's council could never tell when there would be intervention; state culture managers could intervene at any time and inform the *khudsovet* that they felt the content of some songs was questionable. Such censorship was expressed in the euphemism "Such songs are not needed." Of course, from the point of view of musicians, such songs existed precisely because they were needed, and therein lay the source of conflict between the state and the musicians. Normally, as a condition for performing on state-owned property, bands would have to agree to tailor their performances to some degree in order not to provoke the authorities and jeopardize the whole event and future ones. Yet very often, musicians overstepped the boundaries which were at the base of their symbiotic relationship with the state.

One example of this overstepping of bounds can be found in the experiences of Yuri, a well-known Petersburg musician, whose life we have discussed in earlier chapters. Early in the 1980s, Yuri was still in what he calls his "civic phase." He had agreed to play a certain program of songs which had been approved by the club *khudsovet* in advance and which, therefore, had been "cleaned up." During the concert, he changed the program to include a song which had not been approved beforehand. The song is a rather scathing indictment of Soviet existence, an almost pure embodiment of the critical existentialism which characterized much Petersburg rock of the time:

> The country cooed to me of its filial love
> Wiping dry eyes with its hanky
> Blowing its nose in the dawn's bloody udder
> Mentioning heroic names
> Fastening medals on a chest full of holes
> Charting a path of progression in work
> Pouring more tea in District Committee (*raikom*) heaven.
>
> Everything's normal!
> Everything's fine!

But I'm still crawling, crawling, crawling.
Crawling along the sand, along Nevsky Prospekt
Crawling along the steps of Red Square
Among the black front entrances, the screeching weeds
Crawling along the eyes of de-electrified ladies.
I'm not a human being. I'm a rabid hound
Crawling in the footsteps of indifferent leaders
Crawling and shoveling the shit of their ideas
Crawling in the dreariness of the subway at night
Crawling around beer halls, crawling around theaters.

Bury Fedyka in the Kremlin wall!
Give him what you didn't give me.
Immure the truth, together with him.
He knew how to shoot at the national anthem.

Aren't you the people?
The words aren't the people
Words aren't the world, the world is not medals.
It's not a smooth surface all around, it's a whirlpool.
I'm not driftwood, here I'm a fish
I don't like life, I want it
I hate yours as I hate mine
For me the whole world is tragic, I'm sad
But my heart, my heart.[15]

The lyrics of this song express an existential lament, but one which is clearly inflected with specific references to the official political world. After the song was finished, a state culture manager appeared from backstage and began a verbal attack on Yuri. According to Yuri, this person had not intervened during the song for the simple reason that riots might have ensued within the excited crowd. Knowing that there would be no intervention had given Yuri the confidence he needed to sing the song. Through such rational calculations of risks and adaptations to specific situations, musicians like Yuri tested the boundaries of the permissible during this period and ensured that the Rock Club, despite the best efforts of Soviet culture managers and the compliant club *khudsovet*, remained a site of struggle and opposition. Yuri was later to avoid such conflicts by changing from civic music to more lyrical music.

Another musician, Dima, recalls the tenuous and arbitrary relationship between the state and his group and offers us an idea about just how unpredictable state intervention in musical affairs could be. Like many other prominent Petersburg groups, Dima's group stressed the identity of rock music as art, and its performances were characterized by absurd stage shows which seemed to have no meaning whatsoever. Dima, the group's major ideologist, was deeply influenced by Daniil Kharms, an absurdist poet, dramatist, and writer who lived in Petersburg in the 1920s and is often described by musicians as the Russian Kafka. His lyrics defied easy classification which made it difficult, if not impossible, for the state to find any reasonable grounds to harass the group. In fact, his group was one of the first to be allowed to go abroad in the mid-1980s. The story below testifies to the ways in which the harassment of musicians had its sources in the most arbitrary activities of the state:

> *T. C.:* Did you have conflicts [with the state] when you were beginning?
>
> *Dima:* We had fewer conflicts than the others. Because our texts are mostly very subtle. Very subtle and crazy. That's why those above us either didn't understand anything, or said, "What can you make of these songs? They are just crazy. Just singing some nonsense." And it was difficult to find fault in something, because almost every phrase in a text had not one, but two, three, four, five meanings. And they would ask us, "Are you singing about this?" We would say, "No, not about this at all."
>
> Only once we had a more or less serious conflict, though it was not our fault. We have a dancer, and when we went to France for the first time, we were working with these French managers, and our dancer was stripping on the stage, and we played some songs to accompany this clowning, this schizophrenic, absolutely idiotic striptease. He was taking his clothes off and remained wrapped in a bandage only. You know, a bandage like in ballet? And they considered that in ballet it was decent, but in a rock concert it was indecent, even though he was a classical dancer by education.
>
> But the conflict was caused not by this. The conflict was very funny. Some people from the Soviet embassy in Paris came to our concert. And our managers didn't let them in. I don't understand why, but they just didn't let them into our dressing room. They wanted to speak to us. I think they got into the concert, but they were not let into our room. We didn't even know about it. When we were done with the concerts and returned to the Soviet Union, a scandal in the press started. We had our passports for going abroad issued by the Ministry of Culture, and we were prohibited

from working by the Ministry of Culture, prohibited to work in one organization, in a third, in a tenth. And everything was because Volodya danced with naked buttocks. But in fact it was just a pretext to find some fault with us. The real reason was that some big people were not let into our concert. On account of this several of our concerts abroad just didn't take place, because we couldn't get our documents ready in time. Such strange conflicts. But we didn't even know that some big people from the Soviet embassy were not let in to speak with us. They took offense, and since they were serious people, they started trouble (*zavarili kashu*).

Dima's experience illustrates the highly unpredictable nature of relations between the state and musicians and the degree to which arbitrariness was a key facet of musical existence. Quite often, state interference in musical activity had very little to do with the content of any music or musical performance at all.

From External Censorship to Internal Censorship: *Raison de Club*

Beyond the fact that the club represented a site in which a functional relationship of symbiotic inequality was forged, there remains the important question of why Petersburg rock musicians—who by their very nature were committed to a stance of radical independence from outside sources of interference in their lives—would consent to such a relationship. Many musicians felt that *some* performance was better than *no* performance. The live performance of music was a fundamental ritual which served to create individual identity as a rock musician and to place the musician within the greater collective which was the counterculture. To put it bluntly: no performance, no status as musician. Yet there is a deeper explanation, and one which illuminates just how much the Soviet system limited consciousness about what was possible and what was impossible to accomplish culturally within its confines. Petersburg musicians, like many other citizens of Soviet-type societies, simply believed that they were accomplishing as much culture as they could accomplish within a framework of Soviet existence which they felt to be essentially unchangeable.

As we mentioned in chapter 3, it is difficult to understand the true motivations of any individual. All we can know is that individuals use vocabularies of motive to explain why they do what they do in particular situations. Understanding vocabularies of motive is often difficult because certain individuals often refuse to elaborate such vocabularies to researchers. This was the case with the early organizers of the club. Seldom would any of the members of the administrative apparatus of the club speak freely to me about their activities during this period. So we are left to deduce their motives by examining their situated activities as rock musicians in the Soviet context. On the one hand, the organizers of the club were bona fide *tusovshchiki* who had demonstrated a commitment to rock and the rock lifestyle in their own biographies. Many considered themselves to be the veterans and pioneers of rock music, the guardians and protectors of an authentic tradition of Russian rock-and-roll. The strength of the norm which prescribed a distinction between music and politics prompted them to consider overly political expressions in music as deviant within the community of serious, artistic rock musicians. For them, rock music would have political outcomes, but these outcomes would be achieved like everything else in Soviet society—slowly and through deeply encoded forms of communication which would encase politics in a more general critique of existence and which would, ideally, work to efface the more general institutional infrastructure of Soviet modernity.

By engaging with the state in the formation and operation of the Rock Club, a certain segment of the Petersburg musical community lost some of the autonomy and independence of spirit which characterized its traditional and earlier orientation toward the world. Some members of the club's council had no faith in the possibility of change in the Soviet system. Their compliant attitude was justified in the interest of what might be called *"raison de rock"* or *"raison de club."* A similar logic was at work historically in many sectors of Soviet society and, indeed, throughout the socialist world. In the early 1980s, for instance, when social movements from below began to challenge the legitimacy of the Polish state, Polish political elites countered such movements with the argument of *raison d'état*. While they agreed that reforms were necessary, they argued that the revolutionary aims and rapid pace of change put forth by worker and intellectual movements would jeopardize the very existence of Poland as a national entity. According to this logic, the Soviet Union would intervene in Polish affairs, and the situation would become infinitely worse.[16] A similar logic seems to have prevailed among the dominant members and leaders of the Rock Club. Many felt that what they had accomplished in forming the club was truly revolutionary in the context of Soviet history. Some concessions on the issue of autonomy were viewed as a legitimate compromise. Some recognized that the presence of overt and caustic political themes—themes which were at odds with rock's poetic identity anyway—might endanger the very existence of the Russian rock tradition.

From the point of view of those who had fought so hard to gain some measure of success in the organization and public performance of rock-and-roll, the club represented a significant step in the evolution of the Petersburg rock community. The result was that many members of the rock community—in particular the club organizers and rock journalists—took what might be called a "conservative" approach to music. From their standpoint, they had achieved the upper hand in their *kulturkampf* with the state. Even though the state retained power of intervention in their affairs, they recognized that it seldom did intervene unless musicians violated the condition of symbiotic inequality upon which the foundation of the club was based. This fact, coupled with skepticism about the likelihood that glasnost and perestroika would bring about enduring change, created a situation in which some members of the Petersburg rock community tried to protect what they saw as a good thing. They recognized that to accept this structure was not to capitulate to the domination of the structure. Rather, they saw it as a kind of modified victory. Moreover, they were able to reduce the level of what psychologists call "cognitive dissonance" by keeping the important distinction between music and politics ever present in their minds. If the state centralized them for purposes of surveillance, they could simply ignore such surveillance by stressing that they now had the opportunity to perform and spread their messages to a larger number of people.

The Enemy Within

The result of this precarious peace with the state was that overt conflict between the state and the musicians was reduced. Yet the overt intrusion of the state was gradually replaced by a new pattern of social control within the rock community: that of musicians policing each others' activities. In chapter 3, we examined a case of conflict over the proper identity of rock music which occurred between Misha and Boris. Recall that Misha was labeled as a political musician and that this label was reinforced by Boris, who was perhaps the most sacred figure in Russian rock music. Because we had not discussed the structural organization of the Petersburg community, we could not yet understand how this conflict played itself out in the site of the Rock Club. Yet, this conflict was a direct example of how informal social control occurred among certain Petersburg musicians. The club was a site in which high-status rock musicians bore down on musicians whom they considered to be deviant. In the early days of the Rock Club conflicts emerged over the scope and pace of rock's evolution in the Soviet context. This conflict revolved around competing answers to the question: Just how fast should the musical community evolve? Those musicians who defined the identity of rock music as poetry and took on an identity in keeping with that definition felt that the pace of change should be slower. Those who were more outspoken and radical in their music felt that rock music should seek to expand the boundaries of the tolerable beyond those set by the state, or for that matter, by any entity—individual or institutional—outside the rock community. The latter refused to accept the idea that the system was unchangeable; indeed, they felt the very point of rock music was to change the system.

Many of the club's most radical members merely acted in the spirit of cultural independence which was presumably the basic ethos of the club. Yet they found themselves in trouble, not from the state, but from the other club members. Moreover, the methods of social control used to sanction "musical deviants" were starkly reminiscent of the most repressive of the state's repertoire. There are a few poignant examples of this which we have already seen. Recall, for instance, how Yuri, the veteran counterculturalist, was told by one of the key club organizers that he had better join the club or else they would burn his recordings! Recall another Yuri, from Ufa, who received phone calls from people admonishing him for his political music which was primitive and therefore "not needed." And recall how Misha—the embodiment of the alienated rock musicians who sang of fascism, suicide, and humiliation—was banned from playing at the club not by the KGB, but by the club *khudsovet* itself. Misha felt that the latter was in complicity with "their KGB." He felt that the club had failed in its central task: to fight for and guarantee the right of freedom of expression in music regardless of its content. Reminiscing in 1990 about the situation in the early 1980s, Misha clearly viewed the Rock Club itself as the new censor, no better than the state, and indeed, complicitous with it:

> We made a program in 1986, collected some songs to use, but they called us into the center and said, "Guys, don't sing these songs please, because otherwise you won't be prize winners anymore, you won't have anything, and we'll generally just ban you from playing." But we played the songs, and then it began, like because we made a provocation, someone there at the club received a reprimand. The curator of the Rock Club got a reprimand for what we did from the House of Amateur Activities (Dom Samodeiatel'nosti). We were kept out of the way for half a year—for half a year they banned us from playing. But we played all

the same. It's kind of funny to hear all of this now. And they've all understood that what they did was wrong, but they're never going to own up to it publicly.

[They would say] "Guys, these songs aren't needed, here's a bad phrase," And everything began to get irritating, and as a result they didn't get many songs from us because we felt that they were against us in the first place. Naturally, as you would expect. And when we showed them these texts, they said to us, "Don't sing them, otherwise there'll be a scandal." The *khudsovet* ought to have stood up for the rights of musicians, just like all of one's friends. And X [an important musician member of the club]—we got along well with him. But nevertheless, at a critical moment they turned against us. . . . We tried, on the one hand, to urge on this process. We tried, on the other hand, to urge on this process so that the Rock Club *khudsovet* wouldn't be afraid, so that they would protect musicians. But they tried to hold back musicians, so that their KGB wouldn't come down on their heads. The Rock Club was organized by the KGB.

Simple declarations of the complicity of the *khudsovet* with the KGB were often made in this way, not expressed as theory or conjecture, but as simple fact. It was a fact which musicians such as Misha deduced legitimately from the pressure of the *khudsovet* which made itself felt directly in his life:

T. C.: Yes, I heard this, and I read the interview with the General Major [Kalugin].[17]

Misha: And I was looking at the scene, and I was sure that there's no close cooperation [between the *khudsovet* and the KGB]. To a certain point, everyone hung together, but as soon as it smelled fishy everybody headed for the hills. They started accusing us of everything: we're untalented, we're provocateurs, we're trying to pull down the Rock Club from the inside, we're young Turks, we don't know how to play. But you know we got somewhere anyway. Time passes. It's funny. Now this doesn't make sense. But in principle, I think that not one creative personality ought to have to say to itself something like, "From now on I won't sing political songs. It isn't fashionable." It seems to me that everything ought to develop naturally. If you feel like it, if a political song bursts out from you—let it. Put it down. Make an arrangement. If tomorrow a lyrical song bursts out from you—welcome it. Do the same thing. I don't think one should restrict oneself in anything. Otherwise you immediately become the slave of the audience, which is the most dreadful thing.

The Rock Club facilitated the expansion of rock musical performance. But at the same time, it also served to constrain the independence of underground rock music. In an ideal-typical sense, some of the characters whose life histories we presented earlier were the embodiment of what might be called "musical charisma." Their popularity and their sacredness emanated from what audiences and other musicians felt to be their innate and special ability to make commentary on existence through music. In spite of the fact that the Rock Club was a potentially subversive organization within the context of Soviet society, it was at least a subversive organization which could be kept monitored and which could be at least partially controlled in its activities. The Rock Club, in some senses, represented the first source of paradox in the history of rock culture: it was an organization which allowed independent rock expression to exist and in some cases even thrive, yet which also served as a site for the surveillance and control of such expression.

With the formation of the club, the older dichotomies between "us" and "them"—so much a part of the world of the rigidly bounded rock culture—began to break down. Going into the 1980s, the spirit of authentic collectivity expressed in the idea of the *tusovka* was quite strong among musicians. The Rock Club, however, represented the first step in the process of the institutionalization and formalization of a culture which was, at its very core, united around values and ideals which were inimical to the logic of instrumental, bureaucratic rationality. In the early 1980s, rock culture began its confrontation with social forces which contradicted some of the most basic norms and values of countercultural existence. Increasingly, as the pace of social change picked up through the 1980s, the social forces which were unleashed began to have a profound influence on rock musicians and their music.

Glasnost and Perestroika

In 1985, the forces of reform inherited political power in the Soviet Union. Social reform was to be carried out on two fronts: one structural, and one cultural. The structural dimension of reform was known as *perestroika*, or "restructuring." The aim of perestroika was to reform Soviet political and economic structures according to the basic principles of market economics. Perestroika was never meant (at least by those who initiated it) to transform the Soviet Union into a carbon copy of the capitalist societies of the West, much less to dissolve it as a national entity. Rather, it was meant to preserve the best elements of the Soviet welfare state, but with a modified market economy which would be based more on satisfying the demand for a greater supply of goods and services. Glasnost, the cultural dimension of reform, advocated openness in the realm of culture. This openness was meant to facilitate freedom of cultural communication in the service of the structural transformation of Soviet society. The term *glasnost* is usually translated as "openness" in the Western press and scholarly literature, but more literally it means "publicity." As an ideal, it called for the publicity of new and critical ideas about the Soviet past, present, and future which had been repressed in the previous era.

In both the Western and the Soviet consciousnesses, the term glasnost came to serve as a metaphor for an ongoing process of radical reformation of Soviet social institutions and culture. According to reformers, the result of the social and cultural changes wrought by glasnost would result in the democratization (*demokratizatsiia*) of the Soviet Union, not only in the political sector, but in all institutional sectors of Soviet society. A concrete end of glasnost was to realize the potential of Soviet economic and political structures through the expansion of freedom of cultural discourse. Such freedom entailed a stark reappraisal of the Soviet collective memory as well as the tolerance of new forms of criticism of traditional political and social practices (Nove 1989).

A central task of the rest of this chapter is to explore the concrete effects of the dual policies of glasnost and perestroika on the practice of rock music in St. Petersburg. In particular, we focus on how social and cultural changes affected the traditional practice of rock musical counterculture as this practice was described in previous chapters. As we have seen, musicians were guided by the assumption that music was an expression which came from within; musical counterculturalists acted as if the outside world did not exist. Nonetheless, musicians were continually aware of the political and economic changes around them and knew that even if they did not participate conventionally in such changes, the latter would invariably affect their music-making and their more general lifestyle. The most immediate effect of the rapid economic, political, and cultural changes brought on by reform was that previously underground musicians were forced to come up from underground, to exist publicly within the maelstrom of social and cultural changes which surrounded them. While cultural freedom was certainly a desired ideal of musicians, their previous existence made them ill-equipped to face a set of radically new political, economic, and cultural conditions which were the result of the social reforms of the late 1980s. The emergence of openness in cultural expression facilitated an unprecedented expansion of the possibilities for unimpeded public expression of rock culture. Yet, at the same time, the extensiveness and rapidity of such reforms deeply affected the practice of music-making in St. Petersburg.

We begin by exploring musicians' experiences with glasnost and then turn to an examination of ways in which the changing political economy of cultural production affected their lives. The dual processes of cultural openness and restructuring profoundly affected the very identity of rock music, rock musicians, and the Petersburg musical community.

Initial Responses to Glasnost

William Faulkner once noted that "the past is in the present." One sociological interpretation of this is that individuals meet the present with the experiences of the past firmly in mind; try as they might, individuals cannot always transcend past experience, for it is such experience which constitutes and "fills" the very lifeworlds of individuals. Drawing on past experiences, individuals construct typifications (Schutz 1970) which they use to orient their ways through the present and anticipate action in the future. Without such typifications, social life would be impossible, for individuals would have to re-learn the sum of their previous experiences every day, which is an impossible task. In the course of living, Petersburg musicians developed a number of typifications about the way their world worked, about what was culturally possible and what was culturally impossible. Indeed, culture is really the summation of all these typifications which are constructed and shared in the process of living. Schutz (1970) referred to the summation of typifications as a "stock of knowledge." The Petersburg musical counterculture consisted of the aggregate, shared experiences of similarly situated individuals in the Petersburg environment, a stock of knowledge which musicians used pragmatically to guide and orient their musical activity and more general conduct of life. Rock music was the cultural form which crystallized such experience and made it available to others.

It was with this particular stock of knowledge firmly in place that Petersburg musicians confronted the new and drastic political and economic changes which began to occur around them with the advent of glasnost. These changes were treated initially with a healthy degree of skepticism. As with other elements of the external Soviet world, glasnost and perestroika were things which were going on in the background, but which were not seen as directly related to their everyday lives. If musicians thought about the world outside their community at all, they tended to think mostly about the practical issues of securing the technologies necessary for making music and gaining access to the space necessary for performance. Alienation from conventional politics was such a central aspect of the *Weltänschauung* of Petersburg musicians that many of them simply had a difficult time believing that any policy of change which originated from above could bring about any meaningful changes. This skepticism was understandable since the very essence of rock practice was its distance from the external world. When asked to describe their initial attitudes toward glasnost and perestroika, many musicians simply saw them as policies which were doomed to fail. One metaphor which many musicians used to describe the hesitation of others was that it was like a horse race in which the starter had fired the pistol but all the horses remained in the starting gate waiting to see which of their comrades would be the first to run. Another metaphor to describe the situation was that everyone was fearful of sticking their necks out for fear that the blade would fall on them if glasnost turned out to be a sham. One rock manager, Misha, conveyed a sense that glasnost was a cultural ideal which, at best, was incompletely realized in the Soviet environment. He notes, "Oh, you know we have a funny story about glasnost, well not really a story but a kind of image. If you write the word glasnost and take out all the vowels, what you have left is '*glsnst.*' That's what we have at the present time." Misha's statement adequately captures the mood and the spirit prevailing in many quarters even as late as the summer of 1990, a mood which can best be characterized as cautious optimism.

Given what we have seen about the way in which the majority of Petersburg musicians lived their lives, their skepticism was understandable. Musicians simply could not believe that Soviet political elites, whom they typified as Machiavellian by nature, would actually jeopardize their power and privileges by attempting a real cultural reformation. This cynical typification of politicians was deeply ingrained in the lifeworld of musicians. As one musician put it, when asked what he thought about Gorbachev: "They're all assholes, Brezhnev, Andropov, Chernenko, and Gorbachev. He's the biggest asshole of all." While Gorbachev was emerging as the darling of Western liberals, he was simply seen as another in a line of General Secretaries who would preserve the infrastructure of untruths which musicians felt was the cultural bulwark upon which the Soviet social system rested. Some of Gorbachev's concessions to cultural conservatives provided some support for their view: in 1989 a law was passed which made it illegal to defame the President of the Soviet Union.[18] Such laws were seen by many musicians as evidence that the spirit of glasnost was not always evident in reality, and that new Soviet laws were, like earlier ones, designed to protect the power and interests of communist political elites.

This skepticism concerning glasnost led musicians to be cautious. This caution was particularly evident among older members of the rock community and among the leadership of the Rock Club. Musicians who had been raised in a situation characterized by constant attempts by officials to colonize and thwart their activity were skeptical about the motivations and intentions of these same officials who now seemed almost overly supportive of rock practice. For example, Yuri had a significant history of harassment by state culture managers in the early 1980s and offered a distinctly Machiavellian interpretation of the motivations and interests of political reformers. His rhetoric (as well as that of those who were present at the interview and who chimed in) indicates the degree to which many musicians shared this skepticism about glasnost and perestroika. Glasnost was seen not as a genuine ideal for the reformation of Soviet culture, but as a strategic ideological move, a throwback to the earlier Bolshevik strategies of implementing "emergency measures" when they felt their power threatened:

> *Yuri:* Now the Komsomol members are the main rockers. Before, our Komsomol members would walk in the streets with scissors—in the '60s when these style-hunters (*stiliagi*) began to appear in tight pants—they would come up to a person and cut his pants with the scissors.[19] Now when you go on tour the first people to meet you are the Komsomol members. I was in the Far East—they brought VCRs with pornography—all Komsomol members—they're producing home-distilled vodka (*samogon*)—they have a dry law there—and then Sasha [a guitarist] once said, "And where are the women?" The Komsomol members say, "We're bringing women right away!" And they went off for women. Now the Komsomol members are in the vanguard of rock culture, serving us. *The point is, they are adapting themselves. They see where the wind blows, and they trim their sails to the wind. The wind blew that the party had to kick everybody's ass—they kicked ass with the party. Now the wind blows that one has to make money. Tomorrow they might kick ass again or cut trousers again, or even the person in the trousers. This is the way they are* . . . [emphasis added]. It seems to me that the state

is simply under siege now. It was besieged by rockers—the whole country rose as one—first Vysotskii, then tape-recorder culture, then rockers. They were constantly getting put down, going to jail for drugs, for this, for that, but they kept climbing back up. So, what happened is this: the state is besieged. It is forced to compromise. It doesn't have any other way out.

By the way, in our studio the former director . . . it was like this. Remember, they released the first record of the Rock Club? The very first, a mix—each group had a song. When the disk was being released, we had this [Soviet] artistic council (*khudsovet*)—all of them were sitting there listening with wry faces and saying, "What kind of lousy stuff is this?" And the director says, "Don't worry. I think it's just temporary. This is the first and last record. And then everything will be O.K. We have to throw them a sop." That's the way they all think. Not that it's a policy of some kind. They are just besieged. They feel like they are in a besieged fortress and throw sops. And this policy is the same up to this day. Only now this fortress has almost surrendered, but they still act according to this principle.

Voice: Or pretend to.

Yuri: Yeah, pretend to. There are those Komsomol members who adjust very quickly. They are the best friends of rock-n-roll now. You are welcome, guys. Do whatever you like. But in reality these are all just emergency measures.

Voice: NEP number two. The repetition of NEP.[20]

Yuri: Actually, yes. Musical NEP.

Voice: They need to gain time.

Yuri: Exactly. While they are collecting their party groups for fight . . .

Voice: Or to go underground.

Yuri: Ligachev [a powerful conservative communist and opponent of social reform in the 1980s] is the leader of the underground organization.

T. C.: I've noticed that Ligachev says many negative things about rock.

Voice: He has a funny type of face.

Forcing Glasnost from Below

Not all musicians were ruled by such skeptical typifications about the prospects and possibilities of social and cultural reform. Some musicians saw the new situation as an opportunity to force the social system to live up to the stated ideals of openness and free expression for all which were embodied in the policy of glasnost. This brought such musicians into even further conflict with other members of the rock community, especially those of the older generation who had defined themselves as the protectors of rock culture in the city and who had supported a less confrontational, more symbiotic relationship with the state in the early 1980s. Even as it became clear that glasnost was not simply an ideology, but was actually allowing for more openness in culture, many old guard counterculturalists continued to be guided by their typifications as to what was possible and what was impossible in the Soviet context.

The nature of the emerging conflicts is dramatically illustrated by the case of Misha, the young musician discussed earlier in this chapter, who had experienced so many difficulties with older members of the community who had labeled him a provocateur. Because of his unwillingness to water down any of the angry and revolutionary themes of his music, Misha was constantly sanctioned by his more cautious and ethereal colleagues. Recall that Misha (by his own description a member of the second generation of Petersburg musicians) saw rock music as an outpouring of sentiment about alienation in Soviet society. His very definition of rock music was that it was an "internal disagreement with reality," and his view was that rock musicians had an obligation to inform the world publicly about that reality. How musicians did so, from his point of view, was their own business. When glasnost was proclaimed as the new law of the land, Misha took this proclamation at face value and tried to translate the ideals of glasnost into his own rock practice. Yet, even after glasnost, many members of the rock community continued to thwart Misha's style of rock music on the grounds that it was provocative and dangerous to the interests of rock. Misha's description of these events offers a sense of what it felt like for him to be banned from playing, not by state authorities but by his own fellow travelers in the world of rock music:

> Well, glasnost and perestroika came around, and things took such a turn for the better. They came rather slowly though. Previously everything was happening only because I myself made it happen. We weren't interested in money. We didn't give commercial con-

certs, therefore we didn't have any desire to get in with the public. We didn't have any desire to get on the bandwagon and sell ourselves because we had never sold anything anyway. For a concert we were getting about twenty rubles per person. You can't even survive on that.

So things were happening like this: we were writing programs. We were participating in the festivals of the Rock Club, and at that time they were allowing us to play. They allowed us to play, but then we were banned for half a year. Everybody was allowed to play, and we were prohibited. We were so bewildered—how come? I heard then from this one guy: "It's profiteering. You're deliberately gaining cheap fame." But as I recollect, what I was doing couldn't have been considered profiteering at that time. It couldn't have been for the sake of getting famous, because we were deprived of an opportunity to earn any money. We didn't believe in glasnost at all. Though we wanted to do something ourselves, to really achieve something, we didn't believe that there would be any fundamental changes in the world outlook in the country as a whole.

That's why for a half year there was a real strike against us. It's foolish to speak about some interests, that some person thought beforehand, deliberately arranged a political scandal in order to make money later. I remember it now. I was afraid when I was going to that concert. I just closed my eyes. "Well, I don't care. We've decided to perform these songs and we will." My musicians told me, "Maybe we better not, Misha? Maybe we better not kick against the pricks (*lezt' na rozhon*)? We won't have any concerts afterwards, and now they are surely going to punish us. And we won't become prize winners (*laureaty*), and they won't write about us in papers." Then there was such a system. You become a prize winner—they write about you in newspapers. . . . Yet it happened that we ventured such a step anyway, and it proved fruitful.

In Misha's view, the "pricks" were not the culture managers of the state, but those very individuals within the rock community itself who had taken upon themselves the task of sanctioning music which they felt would jeopardize the entire club. Even after glasnost began, the earlier pattern of the social control of musical expression from within the rock community continued. Older musicians, tempered by their own experiences, failed to understand that the intrepid scope and pace of change brought on by glasnost meant that the state had little time to be concerned about the activities of rock musicians. Perhaps this was because older musicians simply could not imagine a historical scenario in the Soviet Union in which the state could be unconcerned with independent cultural expression. Yet, as early as 1986, this was exactly the case. Ironically, while the state began to forego the repression of rock music, many musicians continued to act as internal censors because they were still guided by typifications upon which their very identities were based.

The reality of state-culture relations after 1985 was, quite simply, that the state no longer cared about circumscribing rock music, or for that matter, any other form of cultural expression. Rock musicians were free to sing what they pleased; the state would neither help nor hinder them. They were now responsible for themselves. This very fact was, in the first instance, the source of an initial crisis for the rock community. For the very identities of rock music, rock musicians, and the rock community depended fundamentally on the existence of a state cultural apparatus which, both actually and potentially, circumscribed musical activity. The state had been a central structural "term" against which musicians defined themselves and their music as resistant and oppositional. For most musicians, the disappearance of this structural impediment was not lamented, but greeted as a situation which would take some getting used to. Musicians simply had no experience in making music in situations where the specter of state intervention was not continually hanging over them.

Seizing the Day

By 1990, musicians—even if they retained some skepticism—began to realize that glasnost was somehow different from earlier periods of cultural reform. There were many concrete reasons for this. In 1987, party officials sponsored an official "Rock Panorama" in Moscow which included fifty-one rock bands from all over the Soviet Union. The festival encompassed a number of different rock styles, from traditional rock to heavy metal to punk rock. Official newspapers began to print schedules of rock events and interviews with members of the rock underground. Official, state-controlled publishing houses began to publish books on rock music, and a new *Encyclopedia of Rock Music* was issued. Petersburg musicians began to get invitations to tour abroad, sometimes more than they could handle. Musicians who had played in small auditoriums or under the gaze of both internal and external censors began to play quite freely to curious audiences in France, Denmark, Germany, Holland, and in some cases, even in the

United States. One prominent Petersburg musician made a recording with a large American production company. Western rock stars also began touring the Soviet Union, drawing huge crowds. To top all of this off, the formerly state-sanctioned musicians were literally turned out on the street; culture managers who had sponsored them earlier refused to book concerts for them and instead booked concerts for previously underground rock musicians. As one musician put it: "It's a paradox. The musicians who were playing in the concert halls five years ago are now playing in the basements, and we're playing in the concert halls."

These occurrences happened with a startling rapidity, and the city's musicians seized the day by declaring themselves "professional" musicians. Kolya, a self-described "art-rocker," recalls how this cultural transformation affected his own life course:

> And then this perestroika started. And everything started opening up. And an opportunity to work professionally appeared, because the censorship was eliminated—I mean the censorship in state concert organizations. . . . And right at this time a large festival, "Rock Panorama," was being organized in Moscow. It was the first of this kind, where musicians came from all over the Soviet Union, both professional and nonprofessional—by that time, some musicians appeared who could already be called professionals. And we were quite a success there. We received some invitations for tours, performances, and we decided to turn to a professional existence. Though it was not the easiest step, because I, for example, had been working as an engineer for about five years and had carved out a small career for myself. Yet at this point, I just had to choose. Everybody dropped their jobs and became just musicians.
>
> It was interesting when the invitations started to come after this Rock Panorama, but there was still a trace of this old system, and many funny anecdotes were caused by it. We never saw the first nine invitations in the first year, because naive Western people sent them to the Ministry of Culture. And the Ministry of Culture looked through the lists of groups that work in state concert organizations, and we were not in them, naturally. And that's it. Then somebody had the sense to send them directly to us. And again they were like, "You haven't been to a socialist country yet. Go there first." At first we were allowed to go to Czechoslovakia, then to Finland, which is capitalist, but closer. And then all the rest began to occur.

Because previously underground musicians had been most in demand in the informal taste culture, they became the ones most in demand in new formal concert venues. Compared with their previous situation of economic privation, musicians initially began to make considerable amounts of money from their concerts, in some cases more than they had ever made before in their lives. One musician recalls being paid two hundred rubles for one concert, a sum of money which he had never before had all at once. Those musicians who toured in Europe were paid in hard currency, often in small amounts by European standards, but huge amounts by Soviet standards. Dima, the keyboard player and songwriter for a prominent art-rock group, reminisced how, by 1988, he had made enough in the West from just a few concert tours to live comfortably in Petersburg for a year:

> I paid off my debts, paid for my instrument. It was impossible for me to buy my instruments in this country. They cost there [in Europe] about four thousand dollars. For the Soviet Union that's just a fantastic sum of money, and when we were touring for the first three to four years, practically all my money was spent on the instruments I acquired. And now, I have a decent salary. The money we make in the West—in principle, we can go there twice a year, we have just come from there and can go in the fall—after these two small tours, five, ten concerts each, I can live here very well for the whole year. I mean, three, four, five times better than the average Soviet person lives.

The disappearance of impediments to cultural expression allowed musicians to express what had been a private vocation as a public profession. Indeed, what was most significant about glasnost was that, for the first time in recent history, musicians could declare themselves as professional musicians. Like other Soviet citizens, they still had to carry the ubiquitous workbook, but with one major difference: one's stamp could say "musician," and this status was not subject to confirmation by any state authority.

In one sense, the years of glasnost and perestroika were a kind of golden age for Petersburg rock musicians. They stepped into existing infrastructures for concert performance and reaped the financial resources which had previously been reserved for state-sponsored musicians. They basked in public acclaim of their music, acclaim which previously had been expressed privately and clandestinely. What is most important, musicians' lives were made easier by the fact that the basic parameters of the Soviet welfare state were still in place. They could still live cheaply and save money to buy much-needed instruments and pay for travel. In nearly all accounts of their experiences from 1986 to 1989, musicians were euphoric about the fact that they could now follow their calling openly and even be supported in it.

In another sense, though, as the social, cultural, and economic processes unleashed by social and cultural reform began to accelerate, musicians increasingly began to see that their new status as professional musicians was not without its difficulties. For glasnost had unleashed a plethora of cultural voices of which rock music was only one. And as perestroika accelerated, the welfare state's subsidy of existence began to decrease. As time wore on, musicians found that their new-found freedom came at the cost of giving up some of their uniqueness as the embodiment of critical consciousness. More than that, the concrete structural changes in Soviet society meant that making music depended fundamentally on making a living from music. As social and cultural change accelerated, musicians began to face what they themselves referred to as a "crisis." We now turn to examine the roots of this crisis and the paradoxes which musicians faced as glasnost and perestroika defined a new set of terms for countercultural existence.

The Paradoxes of Glasnost

Strange Bedfellows: Emerging Homologies between Official and Unofficial Cultural Discourse

We have seen that, even before glasnost, the state's attitude toward rock music was one of increasing tolerance which resulted in a limited form of cultural pluralism in Petersburg. Yet, such tolerance stopped short of allowing complete freedom of musical expression. Musicians developed forms of internal censorship, and state culture managers intervened just enough to keep musicians aware of the limits of the tolerable. With the advent of glasnost, however, a documentable efflorescence of critical cultural discourse emerged more generally in Soviet society (Nove 1989). This efflorescence was particularly pronounced in Petersburg, one of the most important cultural centers in the country. In the realm of music, the initial reforms completely restated the terms upon which the state related to previously censured forms of oppositional music. State policies toward culture not only changed from a position of intolerance toward oppositional cultural forms, but also expanded to include the actual promotion of a variety of forms of oppositional music, including such forms as rock-and-roll which were previously anathema to Soviet authorities.

What was most significant about these changes was that they represented an emerging homology between the cultural content of independent rock music and the content of official political discourse. A cursory examination of the rhetoric of legitimation which undergirds glasnost and perestroika reveals the emphasis on the falsity, tyranny, and alienation of the Stalinist and Brezhnevian eras. Yet the components of the official ideology which served to legitimize reforms were, in many ways, a reiteration by the state of the themes which had been articulated in oppositional cultural forms such as rock-and-roll music for decades. Simply stated, the reformist state made a matter of official discourse what had long been expressed unofficially in the Soviet Union. Increasingly, throughout the late 1980s, musicians found that there was very little difference between the themes of their oppositional discourse and the discourse of glasnost put forth by the state. The emerging resonance between rock discourse and the discourse of Soviet political elites resulted in the transformation of the structural relation between the musicians and the state from one of opposition and mutual antagonism to one of cooperation and mutual benefit. This homology of discourses suggests a blurring of previously antagonistic positions, an ironic agreement between oppositional discourses and official political discourse which called into question the viability of rock music as a unique form of social critique within the late Soviet social context.

This homology of critical discourse was a factor which began to erode rock's privileged position as a means of cultural critique in the Soviet context. The critical themes of rock music and other forms of culture were mirrored by the state and served to efface rock's privileged status as a form of cultural critique. Recall that musicians felt that it was their critique which was special and authentic in the Soviet context, even more so than other forms of oppositional culture. Recall that a major source of the collective identity of the elective community of musicians lay in its secrecy and the shared belief that rock musicians were special people who had a special ability to articulate and communicate special truths about Soviet existence. Glasnost, in effect, began to efface the "speciality" of rock music, rock musicians, and the rock community, first, by obligating musicians to go public and, second, by appropriating the special themes embodied in rock music and making them part of the official discourse of the state. It might be said that glasnost was concerned with making the real truth, or *istina*, about Soviet existence a basis for a reformed socialist system. As such, the state had become a competitor of rock musicians. What is more important, it was a competitor which enjoyed a decided advantage in having its voice heard. Unfortunately for musicians, as the state elaborated its critique of Soviet existence, it still controlled the major sources for the dissemination of cultural information, in particular the media. People could now hear Gorbachev and other reformers on the evening news articulating many of the existential critiques which had long been embodied in rock music.

Yet the emerging homology between the discourse of the state and the discourse of rock was not the only challenge. For if glasnost really meant the advent of authentic cultural pluralism in the Soviet Union, it also meant that rock musicians would have to compete with the variety of other cultural voices which were the outcome of such pluralism.

An Embarrassment of Cultural Riches:
Cultural Efflorescence and Cultural Obsolescence

In any pluralistic situation, producers of culture must compete with other parties for the attention of the public. Indeed, the very idea of a free marketplace of ideas, expressed so eloquently by J. S. Mill, is predicated on the idea of the competition of ideas; the ideas which win are, presumably, the best ideas because the public has adjudicated them as such relative to other ideas. In the pre-glasnost era, musicians enjoyed a rather privileged status within the Soviet marketplace of ideas which existed primarily underground. In a sense, this status came to them by default because there was so little competition from others for the public's attentions and affections. Yet glasnost increasingly enabled the emergence of a number of cultural voices. Rock musicians began to realize that they were no longer a privileged cultural sphere. Rather, they found themselves in fierce competition with others who had "seized the day" by taking the idea of glasnost as a guide for their own action. In Petersburg especially, numerous new political parties, associations, magazines, journals, and newspapers were formed which crystallized in different cultural idioms—for example, political ideology, literature, visual art—the sentiments which rock musicians had long expressed in their music.

Alec Nove (1989, p. x) has referred to this flowering of discourse during the glasnost era as an "*embarras de richesses.*" Increasingly, there emerged in the Soviet urban environment such a plethora of cultural information in so many different sources that people had a difficult time choosing among so many alternatives. In the face of the expansion of critical discourse in many different media, the privileged position of rock music as the voice of oppositional consciousness faced an impending obsolescence. Musicians felt this obsolescence increasingly in their own experiences with performances and audiences. While the initial years of glasnost had thrust them into immediate prominence, the momentum of glasnost eventually made it so that their voice was simply one more among others. As one musician put it succinctly: "Now that everyone can pick up a journal or newspaper and read anything they want about politics, they aren't interested in rock music as a source of information anymore." One former underground musical producer put it this way:

> Earlier, musicians were a substitute for magazines and newspapers. Today magazines and newspapers have completely got the better of us and now serve our function, although the masses have kind of turned on them too. Well, at least it's kind of funny to search for some kind of news, some kind of truth in the songs of musicians these days. Before it was as if musicians had some kind of spiritual message and people were ready to take this message. But now everybody's got a message. In general, that's the way it is in consumer-oriented relations.

Still others recognized that the situation had become competitive and that rock was no longer the privileged voice which it once had been. Speaking of the situation in 1990, one musician noted:

> Now the situation is very complicated for everybody in the Soviet Union, if we speak about how the interest in rock music has fallen off. The interest in art has fallen off in general. Before, the word *rock* itself used to draw a crowd. The group could be completely unknown, but if there was a poster, people went there. We experienced this ourselves when we were first performing. When we came, nobody knew us, but there were posters with some costumes, instruments, and the words *Rock Club* on them. And we were playing to full houses in that region—Kemerovo, other big industrial cities with millions of people. We gave fourteen concerts to full houses at one place, though nobody knew the group before. People would come just because it was rock.

Another musician, Viktor, expressed his sense of the impending obsolescence of rock music in the late 1980s with a bit more philosophical complexity. Viktor felt that in the new cultural context, rock was bound to be ignored if it merely reiterated what everyone already knew:

Earlier, musicians could use the stage for propagating any idea because we could speak to many people openly about problems which they knew about but were afraid to talk about. We did this when we were an underground group. And after this, the militia would kick our asses. Now the situation is a bit different. We can say the very same thing, but no one will arrest us. Now it's a different situation. But people are worried about something else now: they feel that there's evil (*zlo*) in the world. And if we tell them about it, about this evil, it will be too much for them. Because everyone already sees this misfortune.

Viktor himself refused to capitulate to the fact that history was rendering his idiom obsolete; instead, he continued to advocate that musicians seize the day by simply playing to those who were interested and by facilitating other progressive political movements in the country. Because of their histories, many musicians did not measure their success in terms of how many people came to see them or how much money they made. Rather, the measure of their success was the content of their own conscience and their own judgments about the value and authenticity of their musical products and performances. Viktor said:

> You understand that, unfortunately, many groups and many people have gone down the path [of commercialism]. In other words, they understood the conjuncture of events (*kon'iunktura*), and they became fashionable. And they took flight from that which was in their soul. They became commercial groups, as in the West. This is bad. . . . When the circle of rock music became open and permissible, everyone began to come to the big stadiums. People came and paid a lot of money. And musicians began to get around one thousand rubles for a concert. And everyone became rich all of a sudden. People understood that they were coming to something that was forbidden, and it seemed to them that it was interesting, and everyone came. And then they understood that someone didn't like something, that it is uninteresting, and people stopped coming to such concerts, and only people who wanted to listen to that type of music began to come to the concerts.
>
> It's true that now musicians can't fill a stadium in order to get one thousand rubles. Now they're compelled to think about their music in order to find their own audience. This is a good situation. It is better than it was half a year ago. I'm real glad that it's so now. And with pleasure I'll appear now in an auditorium where five hundred people are sitting. Although earlier I could

appear in a stadium where ten thousand people were sitting. And, of course, I won't be getting such a large sum of money, *but this is O.K. too because money ultimately corrupts musicians* [emphasis added]. Everything is corrupted by money. . . .

Earlier, musicians really didn't get very much. We practically got nothing. We received ten rubles—and what the hell is ten rubles—just enough to go home by taxi from the auditorium where you played. And therefore, we were interested in music not for the sake of making money, but for the sake of developing ourselves. Then there was a period when it was possible to earn a living from music, and this was a bad period. And now this period is over, and musicians are again working more for art.

T. C.: Maybe musicians have to get used to the new situation because such a thing never existed before.

Viktor: Undoubtedly. Money problems will always exist. Even in rich groups in which musicians have bought themselves cars, they're now unhappy. They are dreaming about that time which was earlier because they simply have nothing to do now. They're ready to fall to pieces (*raspast'sia*).

Viktor found himself in the minority with his positive view of rock's important social function. Many musicians hewed to the idea of crisis and began to look at the situation in rather pessimistic terms. One musician, Ivan, noted that the situation of rock music relative to other emergent forms of culture was that rock was, in fact, disadvantaged. He felt that the development of a form of rock music which could capture the public mind and be meaningful to people in a situation of competition with other cultural forms was fundamentally dependent on good technologies, which were increasingly hard to find. In the previous era, the quality of performances often mattered little to audiences who valued rock primarily because of its secretness and because it was a beacon of difference in an otherwise desolate cultural environment. In a situation of competition, however, rock could be seen publicly by all, and its poor quality would be instantly recognizable in relation to, say, poetry, which relies on nothing more than a printed page to get its message across effectively. Ivan's pessimistic rendition of the pernicious effects of past attitudes and dispositions on the practice of rock in a new social context was a common view expressed by many Petersburg musicians. In some ways, many musicians began to understand that they simply were not ready to compete with other, less technologically dependent, forms of culture and were, thus, unable to make rock worthy of public attention:

There's a crisis of music which began sometime in the fall of 1988. Many people began to worry then, musicians, too. I don't share Viktor's view in this case [in reference to Viktor's more positive view noted above]. Look—the situation arose in such a way. All your life you were under prohibition: the KGB, the press, the radio, were like a joint venture against you, and you had to survive. And your whole life you spent in auditoriums of the worst sort, and you can't crawl out of them.

And suddenly one day you come to practice or to a concert in some kind of basement, and suddenly they come to you and say, "Hey, old buddy, collect your apparatus, all your stuff, and go off to the stadium. Everyone's already there." And you're not used to playing in a stadium. What you do isn't intended for such an enormous auditorium and at such a moment—an enormous twenty-thousand-seat auditorium which is designed for pop music—like you're just not ready for this. Your level of skill isn't up to this kind of large-scale, systematic concert activity. . . . People pay a lot of money to come and see these shows. Then they don't like what you do because you do it badly. And they say, "That's it. I won't come to this anymore." And this happens once, twice, a third time. When a person gets burned two or three times, he stops coming. He begins with great pleasure to go to see Alla Pugacheva because she always performs at a high level, even though it's pop.

One example, here at the festival last year. I won't say here who it was. But the musician said, "I don't have a string for the guitar. Give me a string." Well, someone gave him a string. What I'm saying is that people just aren't ready. And this is such a clear example of the Soviet psychology when you've got this devil-may-care attitude toward your work. We're all like this. I finished the institute. I work as an engineer, and I don't like my work because they don't pay me for it. And after work, I come to play at the club in the basement or somewhere else. Well I play, O.K. But when I come onto the stage, I've got implanted in my head this psychology of the Soviet man. And I also begin to do my own thing badly.

It was not only cultural competition which posed a threat to rock musicians' sense of their privileged status. Another major competitor was the general situation of economic privation which was a result of perestroika. We shall explore the effects of perestroika on the process of cultural production shortly. For now, it is important to stress the ways in which the changing economic situation in the Soviet Union began to affect the dynamic between musicians and their audiences. One of the most pronounced effects of economic restructuring in Soviet society was drastic shortages of goods. Such shortages were due to the restructuring of the basic processes of production and distribution. In an effort to salvage some of the benefits of the Soviet welfare state, the state refused to lift price controls. The prices of most products in state stores remained low, but this mattered little since very often such products were unavailable. Generally, in 1990, money was not a problem for most Russians; rather, the problem was finding something to spend one's money on. Petersburgians spent a great deal of time literally foraging for food every day, waiting in lines, and engaging in barter relations with one another. Between working and finding the basic necessities of life, people had little time for culture. This was, at least, the theory offered by musicians as one explanation of why concert attendance dropped off increasingly as the negative effects of perestroika increased. Said one musician, "People have too many everyday problems, and, to put it bluntly, they don't look up, like pigs at the trough." Stated in terms of a sociological proposition, it might be said that when economic times are tough, people engage less in cultural pursuits. This concern with material existence in a shortage economy no doubt was a major factor in diverting attention away from rock music as well as other forms of cultural expression.

Cultural Perestroika

The Transformation of Cultural Production and the Commercialization of Rock Music

In addition to the changes outlined above, the process of economic restructuring was a central driving force of the overall process of social and cultural reform. The key objectives of economic reform, as summarized by David Lane (1990, p. 38), included the growth of market transactions, the promotion of private and cooperative trade, the granting of greater authority to production units, and the adoption of an accounting principle for the management of financial affairs known as *khozraschet*, or the balancing of income and expenditures. The economic restructuring process included cultural organizations as well, and in this sense it is important to distinguish between the policies of cultural glasnost, which represented an ideological commitment to tolerance of competing cultural discourses, and cultural perestroika, which involved the actual restructuring of organizations involved in cultural production.

The most significant of these new practices for the production of rock culture was the policy of *khozraschet*. Under the policy of economic accountability, a movement began away from centralized state control of production toward a greater degree of autonomy and self-sufficiency of enterprises. The restructuring of Soviet society also took place at the individual level. Individuals were now free to choose their own social roles and occupations as long as they could support themselves financially in such occupations. This meant that formerly underground rock musicians could now choose to declare themselves as professional musicians without fear of reprisal on the part of the state. As with organizations and enterprises, however, these new professionals had to work according to the principle of self-sufficiency and earn enough money to support themselves and to finance the ongoing cultural activity of their groups. Perestroika thus changed the way institutions produced culture and, by way of that, changed the ways in which musicians thought of themselves. We will now explore the macrolevel changes in the production of culture and then turn to the ways in which such changes affected rock music, rock musicians, and the rock music community.

Reversal of Fortune: Melodiya Becomes the Master

One of the hallmarks of the Soviet economic system before perestroika was that production enterprises received money regardless of whether their products made a profit or not. In the case of culture-producing organizations such as Melodiya, the organization received money even if the cultural products that it produced were not actually bought by anyone. For years, in fact, Melodiya had produced cultural products which satisfied ideological criteria rather than any consumer demand for specific cultural products. To be sure, Melodiya produced recordings of Russian classical music which satisfied demand within the Soviet Union and even fetched hard currency in the West. Yet it also issued in huge quantities such products as the speeches of Brezhnev and other ideologically laden products which the Soviet taste public cared little for and certainly did not buy in any appreciable quantity. In the late 1980s, Melodiya itself underwent restructuring along the same lines as other enterprises in the Soviet system. No longer could the organization make money for producing albums which no one needed. One musical producer crystallized this transition succinctly in 1990:

Melodiya has changed to self-sufficiency (*khozraschet*). Before, the politicians were leaning on them. They restricted them quite a bit. But the benefit was that they got paid regardless of what they produced. There wasn't a market. It was all the same to them what they produced. Because all the same they got paid. They could issue a million copies of an album which no one would buy. They could make albums which no one needed. Yet they would still get their money for this. And now they've undergone *khozraschet*, which simply means that they only get paid in relation to the number of albums they sell.

Because of *khozraschet*, Melodiya had to find cultural products which would sell. The transformation of Melodiya is a case which illustrates how the terms of cultural production changed under the influence of cultural perestroika.[21] As with other enterprises, many of the previous party functionaries and bureaucrats were forced out of management positions and were replaced by those who just a short time before would have been considered criminal for their involvement in the production of underground rock music. Andrei, the underground producer of unofficial culture discussed earlier as the driving force behind the infrastructure for the production of unofficial music in the pre-glasnost period, was elected by the workers in the state division of Melodiya in Petersburg to be the new president of the organization. In complete contrast to his previous role, Andrei now had complete responsibility for overseeing the management of the newly restructured Melodiya and ensuring its economic profitability. This included, as in Western enterprises, the autonomy to choose the most profitable cultural objects to produce and distribute, the retention of profits by the enterprise, and the rechanneling of these profits back into the organization itself. The most immediate task for the newly restructured Melodiya was to find cultural products which would sell and allow the organization to operate independently.

As one might imagine, the previous sponsors and producers of unofficial popular culture, finding themselves in direct control of the official means of cultural production, allowed the unofficial musicians whom they had previously sponsored to have direct access to the mass production and distribution of their cultural products. Within months of his election, Andrei set about mass producing the tape-recorder albums which he had produced clandestinely in the late 1970s and early 1980s. Yet, whereas before Andrei was accountable only to the whims of his own taste and personality, he was now economically accountable to the organization of Melodiya and the principle of *khozraschet*. Melodiya was now obligated to be profitable. In return, it could produce any products which would make money for the organization. However, there was a direct cost for this control: if Melodiya was to be independent, it had to pay for the means of production. Upon granting the organization control over the means of cultural production, the state also presented it with a bill for the means of production. According to one source in Melodiya, the total bill for all of the equipment amounted to nearly 800,000 rubles, a massive amount of money at the time. In order to meet this financial obligation, the new leaders of Melodiya were forced to develop strategies for the maximization of profits. This brought on new tensions between musicians and the organization as each party struggled to maintain itself—musicians as autonomous culture producers who needed money to survive, and Melodiya as an autonomous culture-producing organization which needed profits in order to operate independently.

The first step of the restructured Melodiya toward increasing its profit was to repackage, mass produce, and distribute on a nationwide scale many of the most popular recordings of the unofficial groups of the 1970s and early 1980s. Andrei, the new president of Melodiya, simply took the recordings which he had made clandestinely, remastered them using superior technologies, repackaged them under the Melodiya label, and distributed them to state stores for sale to the general public. These tape-recorded albums, which had previously existed as a public good, had now become commodities to be sold for profit. The specific end of this process was to ensure the economic survival of Melodiya rather than a commitment to the production of independent music for its own sake. What is more important, the urgent need for profits by Melodiya meant that Petersburg musicians, as before, received virtually nothing for their products.

An example of this emerging tension between musicians and Melodiya can be seen in the nature of contractual agreements between the management and the musicians. One musician who aspired to make a recording was offered the following contractual terms: Melodiya would produce a recording and distribute approximately 100,000 copies nationwide at a selling price of three rubles per copy. Presuming that all copies were sold, the gross profit would be 300,000 rubles. According to the formula for the distribution of profits, however, Melodiya would give to the group only 1/100 kopeck for each album sold. In the terms of the official exchange rate of the time, one ruble was worth approximately sixty American cents. But by unofficial rates (the black market rates), one dollar was worth between fifteen and twenty rubles. Presuming that all 100,000 copies were sold, the group received as its share one hundred rubles, whereas Melodiya retained nearly all of the gross proceeds. If we figure the real exchange rate of the ruble at the time this was occurring at a conservative estimate of fifteen rubles per US $1.00 (a standard economic practice for determining the real value of the ruble), the group received about $6.00 as their share in producing the recording, whereas Melodiya received $19,994 for its role in the production. The Melodiya/musician profit-ratio, then, for an average production run was $3332:1.

Another well-known musician, Misha, was also offered such terms. He described the situation as absurd and recognized that such emergent contractual relations restricted his own creative processes by thwarting his ability to make money from his recordings:

> We just don't have the possibility of achieving financial independence. It's just an absurd situation. There's this group, First Aid, which did a single with Melodiya and which had a first run of 40,000 copies, but they only paid each of the band members two rubles and fifty kopecks. That's all. It's like they get a hundredth of a percent of the money from the copies which are produced. From 40,000 copies, they get 2.50 each. This is nonsense [he uses the Russified English word *nonsens*]. Such a thing never existed before.

Relations with Melodiya were not restricted to financial dealings, nor were they purely restricted to former members of the rock underground. Because so much depended on being profitable, the new management of Melodiya often exerted direct control over the groups themselves. In particular, the organization found itself in a bind because so many of the state-sponsored groups which played *popsa* were still quite popular and were therefore potential moneymakers. Yet since the new leaders had come from the underground, they found it difficult to restrain themselves from interfering in the affairs of groups who were formally state-sponsored musicians. The new "A and R man" (the person responsible for finding talent which he thought would be profitable) for Melodiya, himself a member of the Rock Club, offered the case of Igor R. (described at the end of chapter 2) as an example of how the new Melodiya treated former state-sponsored musicians. Igor had approached Melodiya with an album which he recorded himself and which he wished to issue under the name of his group, Soiuz: "They did not want to record the album of Igor R. because they didn't like the name of the name of his band, 'Soiuz.' You saw this album by 'The X group.' It wasn't called this at first. They told him: 'Change the name of the group, and we'll do the recording.' He told them no. And they didn't do it. And then he agreed to change the name, and then they did it." The new managers were frightened that a band by the name of Soiuz, a word meaning "Union" and a very common short form for the Soviet Union, would not sell. Such reticence is testament to how quickly the situation had changed and how complete the inversion between the past and the present had become. What is important is that the productive activities of the newly restructured Melodiya involved a complex logic of assessing demands for cultural products within the existing rock taste culture and finding appropriate products to meet such demands.

As before, Andrei was working with musicians and had an almost dictatorial degree of authority over them. If musicians wanted their recordings made by Melodiya, they would have to submit to the terms of contracts which Andrei himself made. For musicians, the profit was nominal in terms of satisfying their own requisites for economic self-sufficiency. Why, then, did they enter into such agreements? In the first case, as we have seen, a central attitude of musicians was an overt lack of concern with money. As an economic policy, perestroika was designed to move Soviet society toward a market economy, but it was also designed to preserve the basic identity of Soviet society as a welfare state. Even as late as 1990, many of the elements of the Soviet welfare state were still in place—a low cost of living, cheap housing and transportation, and free medical care, just to name a few. Even though perestroika had led to drastic shortages, Russians still enjoyed a certain degree of subsidized existence. Within such a subsidized existence, musicians could survive independently provided they could make money from their music or from some other source. Yet since money was still relatively unimportant—most people had money, but had little to buy with it—musicians could still consider that making money from music was not of primary concern to them. Indeed, one musician who received nothing from the production of one of his albums told me in 1990, "I'm a simple person. I don't drink, and I have my own room. I can survive if I can get three rubles a week."

There was another, more basic, reason why musicians accepted the terms of such contracts with Melodiya so unproblematically. As we have noted, existence as a musician and status within the musical community depended on acquiring a social identity as a musician. Such identity was predicated on the existence of objectified musical products. Musicians had submitted to Andrei's dictatorial pressure while in the underground in order to objectify their music and place themselves within the community of musicians. No one had profited from the underground production of culture, whereas now Melodiya was enjoying immense profit from the exploitation of independent rock music. Herein lay an essential defining characteristic which was to affect music-making in Petersburg at its very core: independent and autonomous music was now a commercial product. As a cultural object, it had been converted into something which was inimical to its very identity as a cultural form in the pre-glasnost era: a commodity.

Musicians had to submit to exploitative terms put forth by Melodiya because their status in the context of perestroika depended fundamentally on the objectification and the circulation of their music as a commodity. Lest we paint an excessively negative picture of the emerging scenario, however, it is important to point out that many musicians were quite euphoric about the possibility of seeing their music formally mass produced and distributed. Many were willing to tolerate such discrepancies in the distribution of profits in order to secure the advertisement (*reklama*) necessary to attract audiences at performances around the country. Musicians had never expected to receive profits from their work. In the past when they received money from their work, it had usually been a small amount made from quasi-public, basement (*podval*) performances. While Melodiya worked toward economic self-sufficiency by retaining almost all of the profits from record sales, musicians attempted to achieve their own self-sufficiency through performances which were enabled by the publicity provided by record sales. In other words, for musicians in Petersburg, the hope was that national distribution of their music would make a wider audience aware of their existence and of their music. Ideally, Melodiya would receive profits from record sales and musicians would receive profits from performances which would satisfy demand for live performances. This seemed like an equitable relationship, except that musicians were not guaranteed any profit from performances while Melodiya was guaranteed all the profit from recordings.

In spite of the relaxation of control on cultural expression, and in spite of the fact that musicians could now enjoy a virtually unlimited production and distribution of their products, yet another unequal symbiotic relationship emerged, this time between previously united forces in the Petersburg musical community. For concert tours (*gastroli*), as a source of individual financial self-sufficiency, were, in reality, much less lucrative than record sales. In a typical scenario, explained by Kolya, the president of a Rock Club in a major city in the Urals, we can see the limitations of performances as a means of achieving economic self-sufficiency for musicians. Kolya was happy to organize concerts for Petersburg musicians in his region. As he explained it, the problem for him was also financial. Operating with a budget of one thousand rubles (a sum derived from estimated ticket sales and existing club funds), he would invite a group from Petersburg to play in his city and surrounding cities. He would need one hundred to two hundred rubles to pay for support help and equipment for the concert, one hundred rubles for advertisements, and two hundred rubles to pay local party authorities for a place to play. He would offer the remainder of the money, approximately five hundred to six hundred rubles, to the band. From this sum, the band would have to pay for their train fares to the concert and for accommodations and expenses. The remaining rubles would then be distributed among the band members and channeled back into the group to cover its ongoing expenses. In the end, very little money would actually end up in the hands of band members. As a means of developing economic self-sufficiency, concert tours proved to be unprofitable. To make matters worse, concert organizers such as Kolya were often hesitant to organize concerts at all. For their own existence as organizers and promoters depended fundamentally on their ability to earn a living, and they usually got very little money from such ventures.

One might think that the musicians who were most prominent would have had little difficulty. But, in fact, even the most famous musicians got very little money for their concerts. As one musician, Vitya, a well-known musician put it, "Everyone involved in concerts—the people who produce them, the people who sell the tickets, the people who sell food here, and the cops—gets money except the musicians." Another wistfully noted, "Russia is the only country in the world where musicians don't get any money for their music." Indeed, to imagine this scenario in relation to the West is to illuminate its meaning. One would have only to imagine that at a concert featuring Bruce Springsteen the person selling beer at the concession stand would be assured of taking home more money from the concert than Springsteen himself. Yet this was exactly the situation which the most prominent Petersburg musicians faced as they attempted to realize the ideals of glasnost without the existence of an economic infrastructure which would allow them to do so. And herein lay what was perhaps the most fundamental crisis brought on by perestroika—the crisis brought on by the introduction of money into Russian society.

Making Music and Making Money

Independent musicians always made a sharp distinction between making music and making money. The most important consequence of perestroika, however, was the emergence of money as the fundamental basis for social roles and statuses in Russian society. People were now free to choose their own professions and occupations. Initially, as we have seen, this was not problematic for most musicians because the cost of living was still low and the burst of interest in rock brought on after glasnost made them more money than they had ever made before. Yet, as glasnost and perestroika progressed, people had more options to choose from. And, because of economic shortages, people had less energy to spare for consuming culture. Musicians could not make any money from recordings and found it increasingly difficult to make money from concerts. Ironically, musicians were now obligated to make money to survive as musicians, but the structural situation of Soviet society did not afford them the opportunity to do so.

Many musicians realized very early on that there was little opportunity to make money in Russia and looked to Western culture markets to make money. They were enabled in this activity by the fact that, as one musician put it, Westerners were infected with "glasnost fever." Yet because musicians had no money, they could not afford to go to the West to make money; there was interest in Russian rock music in the West, but Western promoters were usually not interested enough to pay the expensive costs of transporting Russian groups to Europe. Immediately after 1985, transportation out of the country was still affordable and cheap. The primary obstacles to traveling abroad were bureaucratic: such travel necessitated securing an invitation from the host and the issuing of a visa, both lengthy processes because of the difficulties of communication between East and West and inefficiencies of the state bureaucracy responsible for issuing travel documents. However, increasingly through the 1980s, transportation costs were rising, so that it became more and more difficult to leave the country in order to make enough money to live as a musician in the country. The leader of one prominent Petersburg group, Kolya, crystallized this crisis perhaps better than any other musician. Kolya saw the new money crisis simply as a form of constraint which replaced the earlier, political forms of constraint:

> Now all barriers are practically down. Now there is one barrier which is becoming worse than everything that has been before. This is the money barrier. Because when they raised air fares on January 1, we had to cancel our trip to England. We were supposed to have our sixth tour in England for two weeks, in February and March. There are fifteen of us, and it turned out that we have to spend $12,000 on the tickets only, to go to London and

back. So, if before there were some official, ideological reasons why this curtain was down, now it is going up again just because of money. It's just as simple as that.

In addition to the initiatives of independent culture producers, new cooperatives emerged which attempted to organize concerts. Initially, such cooperatives were successful, but they were increasingly heavily taxed by the state.[22] Igor, a musician who had turned to the cooperatives in an attempt to make money noted:

> A cooperative's an organization that takes on itself arranging concerts. They take us, sign an agreement. It's better to work in a cooperative because you can get your money more quickly. But cooperatives—you know what they can be like. They often don't plan properly, and that's the problem. We had one failure. Once I went with a cooperative, without any guarantee, to Sverdlovsk and they put only one poster in the city. Sverdlovsk didn't have any advertising, and we played and didn't get anything. Just made a trip, played a couple of concerts in half-empty houses. There is a risk here. There are also problems with taxes. It's become unprofitable for them to do it.

In addition to the heavy taxes on cooperatives, musicians themselves had to pay for licenses to go abroad and a tax of ten percent of their earnings—in hard currency—to the state upon their return. Because of the expenses of traveling and living abroad and buying instruments, this tax further eroded musicians' revenues from concerts abroad, revenue which was essential to them in order to live and work back home.

What was occurring in late socialist society was the intensification of patterns of free dissemination of cultural information which had begun during the glasnost era, with one major difference: the avowed end of such distribution on the part of both individual and organizational distributors was simply to make money. In the previous social context, the end of this system of informal distribution for the artists was not financial, but an increase in social status for the artists involved. In the nonmarket situation, informal social status was a major reward for independent musicianship. In such a situation, musicians could survive as musicians, protected by the cocoon of the Soviet welfare state and the relative lack of importance of money in Soviet society. With the transition to a market economy, however, the independence of musicians was severely compromised by the increasing importance of money. Like all Russians, musicians increasingly felt pressure to make money in order to survive autonomously in their new roles. Unfortunately, in the emerging system of production and distribution of musical products, musicians were left virtually unprotected by any legal enforcement of the payment of royalties. What emerged was a rather anarchic system of production and distribution in which, it seemed, everyone but musicians received money for their efforts.

Musicians were caught up in the webs of the new system which brought them in contact with new structures which were contradictory to the fundamental ideals of their culture, most notably the ideal of music's distance from economics and politics. The paradox can be simply stated: musicians had defined themselves and their musical products as lying outside of formal economic spheres, yet the transition to a market economy meant that, by necessity, musicians had to make money in order to survive as musicians. Such a situation was, at base, contradictory to the very meaning of rock music in the Soviet context. Glasnost allowed musicians, for the first time, to declare themselves publicly as musicians without fear of reprisal. Yet such cultural freedom was not without its costs. The terms of the social contract in the pre-glasnost era had been as follows: the state would provide its subjects with a decent standard of living and a number of social welfare benefits; in return, subjects would agree to curtail their critique of the state and its policies. Independent musicians had never abided by the terms of this contract. Nonetheless, they had benefited from the social welfare system. Their very ability to simply exist as musicians and "hang out" was enabled by the free time afforded to them by their subsidized existence. The new social contract which emerged during the glasnost era was roughly as follows: the state will grant its subjects freedom to say what they please and to play the roles which they wish to play, but the state will not subsidize such expression or roles, nor will it sanction them. Indeed, the state will actually profit because it will not waste resources on policing culture and will actually acquire resources by taxing independent economic activity, of which the production of culture is only one type.

One of the central failings of glasnost and perestroika as policies of social reform is that they attempted to retain a state-controlled welfare state while at the same time allowing full freedom of cultural expression. Within the context of Soviet history, such a policy could not work. Ironically, independent musicians could no longer be dependent on Soviet existence either as an object of critique or as a free space in which to live subsidized lives. Glasnost and perestroika eroded both the existential conditions which made music meaningful and the social conditions which enabled musicians to devote themselves to a simple life of making music for music's sake outside of politics and economics. Musicians and other culture producers could no longer survive simply by making music for music's sake: they now had to survive as musicians by making a living, to be transformed, in Marx's terms, into "productive laborers." Unfortunately, the biggest crisis for musicians was that there was no infrastructure which would enable them to do so. Ironically, glasnost had freed Russian musicians to say exactly what they pleased, but perestroika denied them the structural means of production and performance of culture necessary for them to do so.

Many musicians did not see a huge difference between the constraint of the state in the pre-glasnost era and the new constraints brought on by new economic practices. Given Petersburg musicians' tendencies to see all forces outside music as potentially troublesome, this is not surprising. The new progression of political, cultural, and economic forces combined to form an ongoing source of constraint on music-making. One musician, Zhenya, a guitarist in a fairly prominent band, crystallized the way this constraint was experienced by many musicians:

> First it was politics, then Andrei [the president of Melodiya] harmed us, then there were the lines, then something else still. No one could find molds to make the records. Molds could only be found in Moscow. Then there wasn't enough plastic. Then we got flooded with other Western albums, "symphony" music. We've got symphony music out the ass now, a boundless supply. Earlier, you could find an album with the speeches of Brezhnev which cost twenty kopecks. Now you can't even get that. I want to buy such an album in order to have it at home to get a laugh out of it. I can't find such an album anywhere.

The material situation had become so grave that even the raw stuff of satire was not available.

Copyrights and the Issue of Musical Ownership: Alienation from Music's Alienability

In addition to impediments to making money through new, formal channels of cultural production and performance, musicians also faced another problem: a legal one. The rapid change in the conditions of cultural production were not accompanied by the emergence of a functional legal culture which would guarantee musicians' rights of ownership over their own cultural products. Cultural products, like other products, are alienable. They can be taken away from those who produce them and used for a variety of purposes by others. Music is a particularly alienable product, especially in societies which have the technologies of mass reproduction. The alienability of music is, in part, the reason why it diffused so rapidly and effectively to Russia where it became the basis for an entire informal taste culture. In the Russian context, however, music was not alienated from its producers for the same reason that products are generally alienated from their producers in Western capitalist societies. In such societies, even though much music was produced and distributed privately, the entire infrastructure for the production of musical culture was based on the alienation of music from its producers for the purpose of profit by capitalist culture industries. In other words, even though music was available for a variety of "uses" in the West, its primary identity was as an economic commodity.

Prior to perestroika, music had very little economic value: its primary value was, rather, as a cultural object which allowed those who produced and consumed it to make commentary on existence and mark off some personal space for themselves within that existence. We have seen how Melodiya transformed rock music's identity from one of a code of opposition and difference to one of a commodity. But more generally in the city (and throughout the Soviet Union) music was also transformed into a commodity. Perestroika freed people to engage in all sorts of independent economic activity. One of these forms of economic activity was the selling of tape recordings of the music of Petersburg musicians by private individuals. Recall that there had always been a black market in the city which sold musical products at sometimes exorbitant prices. As a result of perestroika, musical products of every kind were now sold openly and at prices which the average person could afford. All around the city, kiosks sprung up which sold tape recordings; the tapes were sold, however, without any profit going to the musicians who had actually created the music. Once, a musician whom I was accompanying on the street walked up to a kiosk and showed me a list of his recordings on the "menu" outside and simply said, "You see, all of my recordings are being sold here, and I don't even get a kopeck." As in the West, music had become alienated from musicians for commercial ends. Unlike in the West, though, musicians received no money from the production and sale of their products. What was lacking in the Soviet Union was a functional system of copyright law which would protect the rights of ownership of musicians over their own music and the rights to receive payments (or royalties) for the sale or playing of their music.

This is not to say that there were no institutionalized laws which protected musicians. Traditionally, the Soviet constitution guaranteed copyright protection to "authors, inventors, innovators, and artists" (Boguslavskii 1979, p. 134). Prior to 1973, there were two organizations for the protection of copyright in the Soviet Union: the USSR Administration for Copyright Protection (known as VUOAP) which worked under the auspices of the Writers' Union, and a similar organization which worked under the auspices of the USSR Artists' Union. In 1973, a more encompassing organization, the Vsesoiuznoye Agenstvo Avtorskikh Prav (All-Union Copyright Agency), or VAAP, was founded (Boguslavskii 1979, pp. 142 ff). A set of corresponding articles of legislation concerning copyrights was passed in 1973. As one might expect, VAAP only worked to protect the rights of artists who were officially affiliated with artistic organizations and unions. Copyright protection was only offered to members of the Composers' Union; it was only those authors, inventors, innovators, and artists who were supported and sanctioned by the state whose cultural products were protected under the Soviet law. Only such musicians could realistically make legal claims if they felt that their copyrights had been infringed upon. Should any independent musician have made claim of copyright infringement, they would have found themselves subject to inquiries about their supposed illegal activity. The products of unofficial culture producers were not protected by law, and as a result, their musical products did not in any meaningful sense belong to them.

With the decreasing intrusion of the state into cultural affairs during perestroika, efforts were made to restructure the aims and function of VAAP. With the breakdown of the distinction between independent and state-sponsored musicians, VAAP became an agency which would, ideally, protect the creative rights of all culture producers, regardless of their status. Many of the former articles of Soviet copyright legislation were retained. This restructuring was aimed at enforcing these laws and protecting the rights of culture producers in the new context of openness. Yet there were two problems with the operation of VAAP which hindered the translation of the spirit of the copyright laws into practices which would protect the interests of musicians and guarantee them the financial resources which they needed to survive as professionals. The first was that the law was never enforced by any organ of state or local government. Technically, those who were selling tape-recorded albums were violating the law. But none of the musical kiosks were policed by local militia. In no case had any musician ever heard of owners of kiosks selling musical material being bothered by authorities. The second problem, according to musicians, was judicial. Even if musicians desired to press charges, there were numerous bureaucratic obstacles to getting one's case heard. One musician whose music made money for everyone but him felt that he would have to bribe judicial officials to get his case heard. Further, even if the court agreed to hear the case, bureaucratic torpor and inefficiency meant that it would take years for the case to be heard. The most general point is that copyright laws only work to protect musicians' interests when the structural means exist to enforce such laws and adjudicate claims of copyright infringement. Lacking any means of enforcement and lacking the resources and the political acumen to press claims, musicians developed a highly fatalistic orientation toward the legal system for the protection of copyrights. Indeed, when pressed to discuss the issue, most musicians simply laughed.

Andrei, an important independent rock producer, described the essence of the copyright problem in the new social context:

> We don't even have a notion of the performer's right. VAAP was created as an element of this Soviet ideological machine of control. From the point of view of this machine, a performer was nothing. Performers could be switched, shuffled in different ways, and they didn't mean anything to this machine. This organization was founded to protect the official Soviet cultural workers, in our case, composers. Composers, the members of the Union of Composers, were the caste of the chosen who had an exclusive right to control the whole musical market of the country. Accordingly, it was vitally important for them that their rights be protected, that they receive some income from every performance of their songs. Who and how would perform these songs was absolutely of no importance to them. It was another sphere. That is the reason I think we have never had any performers' rights.
>
> As for the Western artists, it is even more vague. Since here, behind the iron curtain, everything was half-prohibited, nobody ever really cared to protect the rights of Western musicians, composers, writers, artists, film directors. If we take an imaginary situation: I'm asked, "What will happen if your country signs the Bern Convention on Copyright Protection?" I answer, "Nothing will happen." Because it is not enough to have a law. One needs to have an instrument which obligates one to follow this law. One needs to have a powerful organization which would see to the observance and execution of these laws. An artist, for example, a musician, composes a song, registers it, pays money for the registration. And with this money you could fund an organization

which would have mechanisms for the protection of the rights of everyone together.

It is clear that nobody in this country pays for the registration of his rights. Consequently, there are no means to protect them. If we imagine a situation that today our state had to observe all these rights, we would have to close practically all the publishing houses, all the cinemas, all the recording kiosks—we have them on every corner.

T. C.: This is very interesting to me, because there is no such situation in the West. There was before, but now, of course, there are copyright laws.

Andrei: The thing is that we've never had such laws which worked, and in order to establish these legal norms one needs time, hard work, and the desire of the state to introduce these norms into everyday life. And now the state, I think, has neither time nor strength. Because there is a problem of the survival of our country as a whole. The problems of our [rock] culture appear to be in the second or third row. They are far less meaningful for our country. Unpleasant as it is to realize this, it's better to evaluate the situation seriously and honestly than to end up without a piece of bread.

A Western model of copyright protection, ideally, would have protected the rights of musicians by ensuring both mechanical and contractually determined royalties for such things as the sale of recordings, air play, or use of material by another artist. Such guarantees did exist at the formal level in law, and VAAP was technically responsible for ensuring the enforcement of these laws. Yet in practice, no one abided by such laws, and VAAP did little to ensure that copyright laws were upheld or that royalties were paid to those who had registered their cultural products. Since a market mechanism underlies the whole process, these costs are not—in most cases—borne by musicians themselves. Rather, they are built into the process of production and are negotiated by contract between the music industries and musicians themselves. However, Petersburg musicians had to pay for such production, and since they had no resources, they could not be guaranteed any copyright protection. The situation was summed up rather aptly by a young musician named Slava:

We have this VAAP company which is supposed to protect the rights, you know, but I've never heard of it working. Because you can do anything in this country, and no one can sue you. Anything. . . . I mean it didn't work with anyone. If you go to this company, and they register you or they do that kind of process—I don't know what they do exactly because not too many people seem to be interested in doing that because you can still steal from anyone and anyone can steal from you. You know this company will not work. It can't help you really, in practice. You've got the laws, you know, but no one cares about the laws. You know everyone wants to release an album here, so bootlegging is not a big problem. It's more like songs. You may steal from anyone any song. You can remake it to sound like your song or do whatever the hell you want with it.

The situation of Petersburg musicians which emerged in the late 1980s is directly comparable to the situation of musicians in the early twentieth century in the United States. The story of the difficulties surrounding the issue of musical ownership and the evolution of the rights of musicians to protect and receive royalties for their music has been told in great detail by John Ryan (1985). Originally, musicians had very little control over their own musical products and were virtually at the mercy of culture industries that could buy their products cheaply and pay no royalties. This situation changed, however, when musicians formed unions to protect their rights of ownership and entitlements to royalties. These unions, BMI and ASCAP, were extremely important for developing and enforcing laws which ensured that musicians would receive profits. Such laws were the fundamental bulwark upon which the profession of musician rested within capitalist societies. Indeed, without such laws, the situation of musicians in the early twentieth century in the United States was practically identical to the situation of Petersburg rock musicians in the late twentieth century. Without the evolution of laws comparable to those which emerged in the United States to protect the rights of exploited musicians, Petersburg musicians had little hope of becoming economically self-sufficient. Indeed, in a more general sense, the comparison between early-twentieth-century American musicians and contemporary Petersburg rock musicians suggests that there can be no category of self-sustaining professional musicians in any modern society as long as there is no legal culture which supports the rights of ownership and compensation for those who choose to make music.

The fundamental problem for Petersburg musicians at this time was that no concrete organizations or unions emerged which would work to institutionalize a legal culture to protect the rights and interests of musicians. Why was this the case? Again, the persistence of typifications about the nature of unions and organizations came into play within the rock community. Historically, in the Soviet context, the very idea of "trade unionism" had a decidedly negative and pejorative connotation (see, for instance, Hammond 1957). Trade unions were allowed in the Soviet context, but, like other organizations, they were mainly administrative organizations controlled by the Communist Party rather than independent organizations which would express grievances or press claims on behalf of workers (Kerblay 1983, pp. 184-85). In the consciousnesses of musicians, trade unions signified a complicity between workers and the state, and as such they were irrelevant to musicians. For a musician to declare that he was going to form a trade union for the protection of musical rights would have made him immediately suspect in the eyes of other musicians. Many musicians harbored resentment and disdain for those whom they derisively referred to as "rock bureaucrats." Even though the latter had helped them in the early 1980s, they were still considered to be outside the core of the musical community. The advent of glasnost brought many producers and others who were not actually musicians into the musical community. Musicians recognized that many of these new "producers" were motivated by their own self-interests. For such producers, to help musicians' interests would actually have been to hurt their own.

It was more immediately preferable to do like everyone else in the anarchic social context of the times: break the copyright laws and make money off the musicians' products. What was lacking in Petersburg and in the country as a whole was a distinct class of "organic intellectuals" who had the financial, legal, and cognitive resources to form an association such as ASCAP or BMI in the new Soviet social context. As a result, musicians were doomed to live in a state of constant alienation from their own cultural products. In the late 1980s there were no structures which could offer musicians any possibility to make a living from their music. This situation would not have been so bad if musicians could have continued to live outside of existing political and economic frameworks as they had earlier. Yet glasnost and perestroika forced them to live within a new system of economic structures and practices which were quite alien to the countercultural temperament. Musicians had all the freedom they could ever have hoped for, but such freedom meant little if they could not produce, perform, and make a living from their music.

A Crisis of Community

Emerging Tensions within the Rock Community

In the previous discussion, we focused primarily on musicians' emerging conflicts with new cultural forces and the logic of an emergent form of market capitalism. Central questions which emerge at this point are: How did these massive social and cultural changes in Soviet society affect the interactions between members of the Petersburg musical community? How did they affect musicians as a community and the cultural practices and products which were the cornerstones of that community? The most immediate result of glasnost was that it expanded the number of voices within the musical community. This expansion began to blur the previously well-defined boundaries of the Petersburg musical community. Glasnost cleared the way for a larger number of individuals to come forth and claim the status of professional musician. Such musicians had always been deeply committed to rock music but had never expressed that commitment publicly. They inhabited a space within Soviet society which lay between the formal and the informal worlds, a space which Czech sociologist Jirina Siklova (1990) has referred to as "the grey zone." Those musicians who inhabited the grey zone were dissenters, but did not translate such private feelings into visible, public forms of cultural practice. Within St. Petersburg, there was a rather large number of musicians who remained in the grey zone, with one foot in the world of formal Soviet institutions and culture and the other in the world of the counter-culture. These grey-zoners did not accept the formal world, yet the informal community did not totally accept them either because their participation in the official world was considered to be complicitous.

In the late 1980s, the Petersburg musical community expanded to include musicians from the grey zone. This expansion brought in new definitions of reality and ways of thinking about the meaning of rock music and the role of the musician in Soviet society. Recall that the Petersburg musical community was not only an elective community, but also an exclusive community. Individuals elected to become part of it, but their inclusion and status within the community was predicated on adherence to specific norms regarding music and the more general conduct of life. As a result, the expansion of the number of musicians laying claim to be "rock musicians" began to produce conflicts between the latter and the old guard of the community.[23] These changes forced new debates about the very meaning of rock practice and rock's identity in Russian society. The battle lines can be roughly drawn between those who argued that the central purpose of music was for entertainment and those who continued to see music-making as a serious form of art. The former's redefinition was fueled by a desire to expand the audiences for new forms of rock music and to increase the likelihood of making money from it. The latter hewed to the traditional norm of distancing themselves from politics and economics and were committed to the preservation of rock's identity as a code of opposition to existence.

Entertainment versus Primitive Protest:
The Emergence of Struggles over the Identity of Rock Music

In chapter 2, we examined the case of Vitya, the physician-musician, as an example of a musician who did not give up his official role. In the pre-glasnost era, his affinities for rock music were clear, yet he chose a path of secret music-making which was ultimately contained within his more normal life as husband, father, Komsomol member, and doctor. It was only when glasnost became a reality and musicians were allowed to play without threat of censure that Vitya took the step of moving away from his official role toward that of musician. As glasnost proceeded, Vitya increasingly distanced himself from his official occupation and moved more and more toward rock music as a profession. In 1989, he formed a band which claimed as its goal the task of "making music fun again."

Vitya is a representative of a new class of rock musicians who increasingly began to declare themselves to be rock musicians when it became clear that there would be nothing more than financial repercussions for such a decision. Vitya is a typical example of a musician from the grey zone, a musician who did not commit himself to musical activity until the social barometers indicated to him that it was safe to do so. More than that, Vitya was committed fundamentally to altering the definition of music in Russia. He believed strongly that Russian rock music had been held back by its emphasis on what he called "primitive protest." For Vitya, as for most musicians, the very image of associating all musical activity with politics was anathema. He was offended by Western iconography which played on official communist iconography by substituting things like electric guitars for hammers and sickles. Such an identification, he felt, destroyed the important separation between the sphere of culture and the sphere of politics.

Vitya agreed with the old guard of the rock community that music should be separated from politics, but he still felt that the existential critique which was embodied in so much Petersburg music was a form of primitive protest. For Vitya, primitive protest music robbed listeners of their right to be entertained and, instead, coerced them into listening to this or that philosophical position. Indeed, he felt so strongly about the pernicious effect of primitive protest that he defined the very *raison d'être* of the music as a battle against it. So primary was this battle in his mind that when I asked him a year after first interviewing him how he and his band were doing, he answered by saying, "We're doing well and continuing our fight against primitive protest music." He found the rhetoric of primitive protest obsolete within the context of a changing set of structural circumstances which had simultaneously made such forms of music both prosaic and inferior in comparison to his own music which he felt was more artistic and in touch with developments in world musical culture. As a backdrop to their own music, his group put forth a sustained critique of the underground music which was produced by the majority of musicians in the pre-glasnost era. In a press release explaining the new attitude of the group, we can see how this changing attitude toward earlier forms of rock music solidified this emerging division and, what is more important, set the stage for a new battle over music's identity:

> If you are an idiot, this music is not for you. This music is entirely different from typical Soviet rock. It is modern—built on energetic riffs which are unexpectedly harmonious and at times paradoxical. This music is intelligent. Listening to the cassette again and again, you will find completely new and interesting movements. It is physiological. Under its influence you will have an irresistible feeling to move, to dance. It entertains like a good book and tones you up like a cold shower. We don't put forth problems. Listeners themselves make their own problems, that is, if they aren't complete idiots.

In the rhetoric of the above passage, we see a renunciation of the previous communicative role of music as a form for elaborating and crystallizing philosophical sentiments in favor of a view which stresses the purely aesthetic and entertainment functions of music. From the point of view of the group's chief ideologist, Vitya, music should be fun again.

How was this rhetoric translated into the music itself? Curiously, the group made music fun again by poking fun at official Soviet cultural figures on the imagination of their youth:

Gagarin[24]

It was when I was born
At that very time, on that very day, in that very memorable year.
You seemed to say good-bye to us
And went off for the first rocket flight.

They shouted, "The rockets are leaving,"
And you left the Earth after lingering awhile.
And returned as a world hero
Having circled the planet in forty minutes.

And you were going to meet Nikita,
Without noticing your untied shoelace.
People were joyful like children,
As if each of them made a jump to the skies.

And nobody will ever know
Why your airplane crashed.
That day you said good-bye to nobody,
But you went off for your last flight.

I love you, Yuri Gagarin,
The first angel of the people's cosmic era.
And I am grateful to you for everything,
You helped me in a way, became one of my friends.

Valya Tereshkova[24]

The shadow of your smile
I'm recollecting at nights
Without any sadness,
And without any fuss.
I connect up an antenna to it,
Radiate waves into space,
Space responds
With your name:

Valya, Valya, Valya Tereshkova,
Valya, Valya, Valya Tereshkova.

In the morning I wake up
And look up at the sky,
I see you in a white dress
Waving your hand at me.
I'm pleased with this,
I take my guitar,
The strings respond
With your name:

Valya, Valya, Valya Tereshkova,
Valya, Valya, Valya Tereshkova.

Such lyrics were grafted onto a musical style which the group itself described as *tantseval'naia muzyka*, or "dance music." The purpose of the lyrics was, of course, to poke fun at these heroes and heroines of official Soviet culture, but for the purpose of enjoyment rather than serious social or cultural criticism. The very self-definition of this group revolved around a conscious and persistent distancing of its music from the earlier forms of rock poetry which were the fundamental bases of status within the musical community. The difference in the late 1980s, though, was that Vitya's band became a member of the Rock Club and, as such, was in a position to mount a challenge to the existing, traditional norms and values of the community. The result was that a new tension emerged between the old and the new. These tensions were based on competing definitions about what the new identity of rock music should be in an era of social change and reform. For the older members of the community, music as entertainment threatened rock's very identity as a serious art form. In some ways, the long-standing members of the rock underground were trapped by the definitions of music and musicianship which were at the core of the formation of their self-identity and social identity. Younger musicians presented the first intimations of a new definition of rock music in the glasnost era: in order for musicians to survive as musicians and to be financially self-sufficient, they would have to be popular. But to be popular meant that they would have to redefine the identity of music so it would be suitable for the new social context.

How did the members of the former underground deal with the threat posed by new musical groups such as Vitya's? We have seen before how political musicians such as Misha were sometimes sanctioned by members of the underground itself. Such sanctions could occur then because the community had been more closed and exclusive in the pre-glasnost era. But in an era of increasing openness, it would have been difficult to carry out any program of overt censorship of musicians without being accused of authoritarianism or repression. Instead, a new critique of such groups began to emerge from within the musical community. The chief ideologists of this critique were the older members of the rock community who had been thoroughly socialized within the old, exclusive, countercultural way of life. A key component of their critique featured the development of a reactionary rhetoric of a crisis in rock music that had been brought on by the new market situation. This critique focused on the decline of more organic forms of protest music in the face of emergent forms of music which stressed music as simple fun. In their view, fun music could not be serious, only mediocre. One prominent rock critic and a former organizer of the Rock Club (who, interestingly enough, wrote under the pseudonym of *staryi roker*, or "old rocker") wrote:

> Rock has become flat in the commercial and market situations. There are no fresh ideas. Today, an intensification of rock insuffi-

ciency, tomorrow a coma, and after that even a lethal end? Such a picture can be carefully drawn and is based on concrete empirical research. These prophecies are not far from the truth. It is stupid to argue with the thesis that we are observing the disintegration of the old music which was composed over many years through the system of the rock underground. That the idols of the past years are coming down off the stage and their places being filled by a large crowd of "mediocrities" (*seredniachki*). It is stupid to raise an objection against the assertion that yesterday's rules of the game are nothing more than sentimental recollections for today's pragmatic epoch. In the customary sense, the rock movement doesn't exist, it is dead. Would it be terrible to try to reanimate its power? . . . There is only one chance for rock to be preserved—it has to occupy an enduring and worthy place in the general flow of culture. Its own place. To become an equal part of the whole. (*Roksi Ekspress* 1990, 1)

There are a number of interesting aspects to this critique. We see an awareness and an anticipation of the effects of the process of the economic restructuring both on the role of musicians and on their cultural products. The general character of the lament is a reaction against what is perceived as the transmutation of the dominant identity of rock music into a new form of what critics themselves derisively refer to as "commercial music," or *popsa* (pop). By definition, *popsa* and those who produced it were mediocre in relation to authentic rock musicians ("idols," in the old rocker's terms) and their authentic music. Curiously, the lament embodied in the above quote represents an almost conservative critique by a member of the rock generation who is now old enough to remember the heady days of the pre-glasnost era when rock was first of all an existentially meaningful art rather than a simple form of entertainment.

In its rhetoric, this conservative critique is highly reminiscent of the tone of early Bolshevik political pronouncements; phrases such as "It is impossible to argue with the thesis" or "It is stupid to raise an objection to the argument" were mainstays of the Bolshevik arsenal of rhetorical strategies which featured combative and dualistic flourishes. The critique is also reminiscent of Theodor Adorno and Max Horkheimer's (1988) vitriolic critique of the effects of the culture industries on authentic art. While the latter would most likely not see rock music as art, the above "old rocker" emphatically does. The effects of the new culture industries and the ways in which the commercialization of art affected his art were the same as those which Adorno and

Horkheimer described in their discussion of high art: mediocrity, leveling, and the paralysis of music's ability to crystallize higher truth. Musicians' own theories of the relationship between art and economics mirror the high theory of analysts of culture. Like the latter, they reflect a sense that musical efflorescence led, ironically, to the obsolescence of rock music's status as a sacred cultural object.

This rhetorical critique was mirrored in the actual words of many musicians. When asked about bands such as Vitya's, they reacted almost viscerally. When I described it as "rock music" to one musician, he shot back with the retort: "That isn't rock music." When asked to define exactly what it was, he could not say, but explained that his feeling was that there was something about the music that was somehow inauthentic:

> About that band, since they are saying, "O.K., music is all fun," they try to—you know imitate those Manchester bands. It happened like six years ago. They started to combine rap rhythms with rock, so it was like a new movement, and what this band is trying to do—and I am totally sure about this—they are just trying to imitate that Manchester sound. But it just doesn't work, because maybe they got wrong somehow. I am not sure what their problem is. . . . I mean I just don't believe them when they sing, if you know what I mean. I just don't trust what they're doing, since it's all about fun. I don't know, I just don't believe it somehow. . . . I don't trust what they are saying.

The Commercial Underground

The above case points to the emergence of a contradiction within the rock community. Money became the most important concern for musicians, and the transmutation of rock's identity from a form of existential protest into a form of entertainment was seen by many as the surest way to achieve economic success. Yet the core members of the rock community retained a commitment to rock's authenticity as a noncommercial cultural object and remained deeply critical of music which did not claim the status of art. How did musicians justify such a contradiction? In order to resolve the tension between making rock and making money and to avoid falling off the slippery slope from rock to pop, rock musicians developed a new category to describe what they do. This category they described, in their own words, as the "commercial underground." When linked together, *commercial* and *underground* represent a contradiction. Rock musicians resolved this contradiction rhetorically by claiming a special ability to preserve the integrity and authenticity of their music in the face of rampant forces that sought to commercialize music. They unabashedly acknowledged the necessity to convert their cultural products into marketable commodities and thus confer upon them some exchange value. At the same time, they continued to claim that the wellspring of their creative activity lay within the realm of the soul and in experience. Only after music had been articulated "from the soul" could it be taken "to the market." And only after taking it to the market did musicians worry about the potential effects of commercialization.

On the one hand, the emergence of a market economy and the necessity of making money meant that musicians had to work within culture markets if they wished to survive as musicians. On the other hand, the very identities which were the product of participation in the countercultural community demanded that rock music emanate from within the individual rather than be constrained by external economic forces. The construction of a belief that one could pursue rock as a vocation and make money from music without "contaminating" it was vitally important for the preservation of rock musicians' identities as musicians within the new social context. This belief was a rationalization which was brought on by the intersection of new, proto-capitalist social forces and the persistence of countercultural habits and ways of thinking carried from the past into the present. The belief in something called "commercial underground rock music" sought to rationalize and justify competing demands—the demands of individual conscience and the demands of new culture markets—which the new social context brought on. However, the belief that rock could survive commercialization without any threat to its authenticity was somewhat chimerical, for the belief was seldom squared with a reflexive appraisal on the part of musicians as to the extent to which their cultural products were actually affected by the process of the capitalist rationalization of culture. In short, musicians believed that they could be autonomous, but the question remains as to whether they were actually autonomous within the emergent capitalist social context. In the final chapter, we will return to explore the difficult question of artistic autonomy and cultural freedom. In the next chapter, we examine the acceleration of the process of capitalist rationalization of Russian society and the effects of this acceleration on the practice of rock music in the post-Soviet context.

6

The *Tusovka* Is Over:
The Acceleration of Capitalism
and the St. Petersburg
Rock Music Counterculture

Into the great wide open, a rebel without a clue.

—Tom Petty

After the Fall: The Circulation of Constraints

I n the fall of 1991, the Soviet Union as a formal nation-state was dissolved. In the wake of this dissolution, the process of the capitalist rationalization of Russian society which had begun during the era of glasnost and perestroika intensified. Attempts at reforming the Soviet system were replaced by a program of economic reform often referred to as capitalist "shock therapy."[1] Shock therapy—or the rapid capitalist rationalization of Russian society—has resulted in the emergence of a system of what might be called "anarchic capitalism" (Burawoy and Krotov 1992) which is characterized by anarchy and unpredictability in relations of production and distribution, a tendency toward monopoly of industry, and autocratic patterns of control over production and distribution process.

Whatever we wish to call the change in contemporary Russia—"shock therapy," "capitalist rationalization," "anarchic capitalism," "McDonaldization" (Ritzer 1993), or even "the McGulag" (Luke 1990)—it is clear that the Soviet bureaucratic state is being replaced by a new form of capitalist social organization. The effects of the latter are being felt at the level of culture and consciousness. They have produced a situation of what Anthony Giddens (1990) has called "ontological insecurity." Giddens (1990, p. 90) defines ontological *security* as "the confidence that most human beings have in the continuity of their self-identity and in the constancy of the surrounding social and material environments of action." By contrast, ontological *insecurity* is simply a generalized, psychic state of anxiety, fear, and lack of confidence in the permanence and surety of one's existence which is brought on by rapid social change or breakdown of social structures which people have traditionally used to frame their existence and anchor their identities. While the dissolution of the Soviet Union was greeted with acclaim by those of liberal imagination both inside and outside the Soviet Union, it also threw many Russians into a psychic turmoil. For as problematic as Soviet existence was, it did offer a stable framework for individual and collective identity. With the progressive erosion of the Soviet social and material environments of action, the social transformation of Russian society began to erode the structural frameworks of existence against which many Russians defined their self-identities.[2] Ironically, this was no less the case with Petersburg counterculturalists. Even their counter-identities were defined in relation to and depended to a great extent on the constancy and continuity of Soviet existence.

The acceleration of the process of capitalist rationalization of Russian society and its effects on the Petersburg musical counterculture are the subjects of this chapter. In this chapter we see most clearly the dilemmas facing Petersburg musicians that have resulted from the capitalist rationalization of Russian society. We focus on three main effects of the accelerated capitalist rationalization of post-Soviet Russian society:

1. the more complete transformation of music from a code of opposition into an economic commodity subject to the control of outside, extra-musical economic forces and individuals;
2. the transformation of musicians from counterculturalists outside the social system into productive laborers inside the system, dependent on new culture industries and the accumulation of capital for their very survival; and
3. the exacerbation of conflicts between musicians who had formed the previous core of the musical community and the new types of musicians and music enabled by the intersection of East and West brought on by capitalist shock therapy. In place of trust, solidarity, and a common commitment to music as a special form of communication, the ethos of commercialism increasingly became the basis for social relations within the Petersburg rock community and for relations between the latter and members of Western musical communities.

Social Differentiation and Petersburg Rock Culture

Structural Changes in the Recording Industry

In the immediate post-Soviet period, there was no clear idea of who owned the cultural means of production in Petersburg. Technically, the managers and workers in enterprises such as Melodiya were obligated to buy the means of production from the state. The situation was one of rampant uncertainty: the state, by decree, did not own the means of production. They had been taken away from the Communist Party (at least *de jure*), although former party elites were in a good position to both make and benefit from new laws on property ownership. Yet the means of cultural production still did not belong to any one organization or to specific individuals. Andrei, an important figure in the former counterculture who had become an important facilitator of musical production in the post-Soviet context, described some of the most important changes in ownership and control of the cultural means of production:

T. C.: Who now owns the means of [cultural] production?

Andrei: The means of production? Yes, I see. Now this is very unclear. Nominally, many things don't belong to the state anymore, but they do not yet belong to any particular organization or person either. Right now they are speaking of this privatization, that is, this process which will result in the appearance of real owners. I think that in the majority of cases those who are working at these enterprises will try to buy them or do something of the kind. It's difficult to say. It may be some organization or joint-stock companies. Difficult to say. The situation is very delicate so far.

Now formally they [the means of cultural production] belong to nobody. There is a theory that former communists now own these organizations. There is such a theory, and it seems plausible, that what's going on now is a deliberate process of squeezing the plants and factories in order to drive them to bankruptcy, and then, with the help of some secret funds of the Communist Party to salvage them, that is, buy them and make communists the owners again, but this time without any ideological slogans. But truly speaking, I have my doubts about this. It is more likely that the so-called shadow economy, our mafia, controls everything now. Though I wouldn't be surprised if it turned out that some representatives of the former communist establishment are connected with the mafia. It's very probable. I think, in this case, the political party affiliation is not important. Mafia or not—I don't know what to call it—but there is a certain industrial clique, a group of people, part of the military-industrial complex, part of some large banks, which I guess are striving to control as much of our industry as possible. This is evident.

During the late 1980s, a restructured, market-oriented Melodiya enjoyed a distinct monopoly over cultural production. Up until 1991, the laws of the Soviet Union made it difficult for independent entrepreneurs and cooperatives to enter into the process of cultural production. Yet, by 1991, the pace of the transition had accelerated and a series of laws were passed which made it possible for individuals to start their own enterprises and, more important, to gain ownership of the formerly state-controlled means of production (see Nelson, Babaeva, and Babaev 1992). Previously, Melodiya had served as an umbrella organization which coordinated several different aspects of the cultural production process in both St. Petersburg and Moscow. Under new rules concerning privatization, however, it ceased to control the different organizations involved in cultural production. Because it no longer had anything to control, Melodiya ceased to exist. Studios, plants, and other organizations involved in the production process became independent entities which were connected by common economic interests and concerns, but these entities were not obligated by any law or political pressure from above to work together. As a result of the dispersal of Melodiya, there was no longer an organization in Petersburg to which musicians could turn to produce their music. In Moscow, a number of independent production organizations emerged which constituted a new oligopoly over the process of cultural production. As with the now-defunct Melodiya, these organizations had financial difficulties and, according to musicians, offered only the chance to make recordings without any guarantee of income. But the Moscow organizations posed an even greater impediment to the Petersburg musical community: Petersburg musicians now had to go to Moscow where they found themselves in competition with Moscow musicians.

How did the process of differentiation of the recording industry affect the process of making recordings for musicians? Andrei explained the process with an emphasis on the special role of money in producing a crisis of cultural production:

T. C.: Maybe you can explain the process of making a record. From the beginning to the end.

Andrei: O.K., it's very simple. Let's assume that there is a certain financial source from which I can draw money to pay for all the elements of this process. At first, after having found a group, I make a recording for it. We are recording, say, at the same studio, our Petersburg recording studio, pay for studio time and get a master tape as a result. A mix. After that or at the same time I find an artist. As a rule, I coordinate this with the group. Sometimes the group suggests its own variants. Sometimes I myself find an artist who makes a cover. Then we send a cover sketch, made according to certain technical specifications, to Moscow. There is an organization there which is engaged in manufacturing covers. It's called "bleaching" (*beleniye*). They produce master copies from which further covers are printed. The tape is then sent to different places. There are variants: one disk I made in Czechoslovakia, another in Bulgaria, another in Finland, another in Moscow. There are different variants. The most important stage is the manufacturing of a metal disk, from which the record is made. Now in Moscow the manufacture of the nickel original costs 120,000 rubles.[3] Polygraphic preparation of the cover costs from 10,000 to 20,000 rubles. Quite a lot of money.

T. C.: And where do you get the money from?

Andrei: I've said at the very beginning, there is some source. I can't begin all this work without some primary source, which I have to find myself, or the musicians have to find. Well, then I go to a record plant, to a certain plant near Moscow, or to the Petersburg plant here, or to the Riga plant in Latvia. I bring and sign a contract with them, bring the metal disk, tapes, polygraphy, and then I bring back the disks from the plant, pay the plant for [printing] the records. Now the manufacturing of one record by a plant costs 37 rubles. In total, with 10,000 copies it turns out to cost about 50 rubles per album [approximately US $0.50 in July 1992]. Then I try to sell the record. This is when it gets interesting. Or it's not interesting to you?

T. C.: It's interesting. Everything's interesting to me.

Andrei: You go with this record to shops and ask, "Would you like to take this record for sale?" "For sale" means that you leave the record. If it is sold, the shop pays you, if not, you take your records back. So getting back the money you've already invested is not all that easy. Also, now there are some independent salesmen, small shops, small firms. It's quite difficult to invest big sums of money in this whole process now, since the prices are growing all the time, money is being devaluated quickly, and you need to invest more and more, and they simply don't have such an opportunity. They don't have a large money turnover. That's why, for such small firms and small shops it's a very painful and complex process. These are, basically, the most important elements.

Andrei had the cognitive and technical capabilities to produce fine recordings, yet even as an extremely high-status figure in the musical community, he could not find the financial resources to sponsor his own autonomous productive activity. Says Andrei:

> Now the situation has changed. When a recording studio, say, Petersburg recording studio, lost connections with its head organization, Melodiya, it also lost access to its financial sources. Therefore, now a studio cannot release practically any recordings. It can record something for money, but it can't actually release anything. Now there is a need for an independent producer, with some money, with a large amount of money. Someone who can not only order a recording, but also, roughly speaking, pay for the whole production process. Today, there are no large organizations, at least in our city, which could pay for the process of manufacturing a disk from the beginning to the end. *This is the biggest problem, in my opinion. I myself can organize this process, but I cannot pay for it* [emphasis added].

Both in his previous existence and in his current one, Andrei made little or no money from his activities as a music producer. He was involved with the musical community purely because he saw music-making as a vocation. His testimony shores up the idea that money problems continue to be the central impediment to the production of musical culture in post-Soviet St. Petersburg. Yet there are at least three more developments which decisively affected the traditional practice of music-making in post-Soviet Russia: the rise of rampant inflation, the intrusion of the musical mafia into the affairs of musicians, and the intensification of illegal cultural production for profit, or cultural piracy. We consider each of these important developments in turn.

Inflation and Culture

After January 1991, as part of the program of capitalist shock therapy, the Russian government decreed an end to state price controls. The latter had been in place all through the perestroika era and, according to some analysts, this was a major reason why perestroika actually failed (see, for instance, Goldman 1991). For the first time in over forty years, Russians found themselves facing price increases which were a result of the normal laws of supply and demand within a capitalist market economy. The result of this was hyper-inflation. In 1992 inflation increased, on average, at a rate of about fifteen percent per month. In the era of perestroika, people had money, but very little to buy with it. In the post-Soviet context, there was an increased availability of goods, but because of the higher costs of such goods, people had less money to spend.

This was the case for musical products as well. For years, the price of an album had been three rubles, the price of a concert ticket about the same. With increasing inflation, however, the prices of both musical products and performances began to skyrocket. A vicious cycle of rising prices began: producers of music had to buy the raw stuff for production at higher costs, so they had to sell their recordings to stores at higher prices. The stores, in turn, sold albums at higher retail prices. By 1992, the average album cost around one hundred rubles. In dollar terms, this was not much more than the earlier prices, but people had less money available to buy goods in general, so they bought fewer albums. As a result, new recording firms were hesitant to issue new recordings because they felt that inflation would erode their profits even before they could finish the process of production. For instance, a production firm could make an album and send it to state stores with a bill. By the time the albums were sold and the bills were paid—approximately three to four months—the money from the bill would have depreciated in value about forty to sixty percent. With such a depreciation of the value of their invoices, production firms could not operate profitably. According to one producer, attempts to send bills which were adjusted for inflation were made, but stores refused to pay such adjustments because they felt they would have to increase record prices and would not be able to sell any albums at all. Their reasoning was that consumers, who were experiencing increasing financial difficulties, were already having enough trouble buying albums at noninflated prices.

Spiraling inflation, then, exacerbated and intensified the money crisis which musicians began to feel in the era of perestroika. Musicians needed more and more money to sustain themselves, yet less money was actually available because consumers were hesitant to spend their scarce resources on cultural products or performances. The situation of economic uncertainty in Russia following the dissolution of the Soviet Union made it almost impossible for the normalization of the process of cultural production. Virtually no member of the former rock underground could make enough money to support himself. The result of this was that musicians were forced to turn to outside, extra-musical social forces in the hope of finding financial support for their activity. In the previous social context, external sources of support from the state were the very antithesis of the spirit of the counterculture. New sources of external support were the functional equivalents of the Soviet state, but operated under a different logic: the logic of capitalism. The whirlwind of economic change had swept musicians into contact with this new force, and it grated at the very core of the countercultural cosmology and way of life.

The Musical Mafia and the Banalizing of Rock Music

In a situation where money was scarce but absolutely necessary for survival, musicians began increasingly to talk of the existence and the influence of what they referred to as the "musical mafia" (*muzykal'naia mafiia*), which consisted of individuals and groups who controlled vast amounts of financial and material resources. Such groups and individuals formed an interlocking directorate which aimed at controlling and monopolizing cultural production and performance in post-Soviet Russia. There were numerous stories circulating within the folklore of the Petersburg musical community about the activities of the musical mafia and the effects of these activities on music-making. According to one musician, the entire process of cultural production and performance had become centralized in Moscow under three organizations which constituted the core of the musical mafia. Without the support of these organizations, musicians felt they could not successfully produce albums or get performances in large venues. In order to be supported, musicians had to allow such organizations to dictate the terms of musical production. Because of their strong views against outside interference in music, this was a price which most musicians were unwilling to pay. Most musicians viewed the new musical mafia as being no different from the state-sponsored culture industries which had attempted to buy out musicians during the Soviet period. Many felt that mafiosi were former communists who sought to preserve the positions and interests which they had held in the old system. Whether communist culture managers or capitalist culture profiteers, such individuals were seen as sources of intrusion into the process of artistic autonomy.

It is virtually impossible (and perhaps unsafe) to find information about secret organizations such as the new Russian mafia (but see

Coulloudon 1990; and Vaksberg 1991). The information presented here comes from the stated experiences of musicians themselves. Again, as with other "realities" of the former Soviet world, the mafia is best seen in terms of its perceived effects on musicians' actual conduct. Musicians perceived that there was a musical mafia, and their actions were guided by this perception. One former underground rock producer who was trying to start an independent radio station informed me that he was approached by the mafia and told that his organization had "a better hope of surviving" if he gave them a share of the profits. Ironically, this radio entrepreneur turned to the local KGB for protection against the musical mafia; in the new context, the KGB, like the American FBI, had become the protector of legitimate business interests in the face of organized crime.

Mafiosi who chose to make money from culture were guided by the profit motive and were little concerned with artistic autonomy or the preservation of the special qualities of rock music's identity. Their express goal was to make as much money as possible from culture and they cared little for the interests and concerns of musicians. Because such powerful figures were increasingly in control of the means of production and performance, musicians who wanted to survive as musicians were forced to put their affairs in their hands. Conflicts between mafiosi and musicians were inevitable and quite pronounced. To those who remained most true to the traditional values of the musical counterculture and the idea of rock music as a noncommercial endeavor, mafiosi were considered "dirty people" (*nechistye liudi*) and "sharks" (*akuly*), the functional equivalents of communist culture managers of the previous era (and who, in some cases, were). As in the previous context, the new culture moguls turned away from formerly underground rock and, instead, focused on developing new forms of pop music which they felt would be more marketable. One former underground producer outlined the relationship between the musical mafia and rock musicians:

> *T. C.*: I've been told there are organizations in Moscow which control the situation there and want to control the situation here. . . . It's interesting to me why they don't want to work with Yuri [a very famous Petersburg musician for whom Andrei serves as producer]. He is very famous. Everybody knows who he is. Everybody listened to his music. Why don't they want to work with you and him?

> *Andrei*: With us? Our music is not interesting to them, and their rules of the game are not interesting to us. I think it is so. They

have this new cassette-recorder music (*magnitofonnaia muzyka*), all these monotonous songs that sound on every corner, in any recording kiosk, with a very simple computer accompaniment. I don't know their names, but there is a number of these very monotonous songs which are worse than American music of the same kind. It's like background music. Even still, in America, you have the higher cultural standard, musical professionalism, therefore the audience is more demanding. And this music is of a very low standard, very bad, very poorly made. Maybe again, it's because of the low level of information. This music is very easily understood, and that's why our people, who are undeveloped in the cultural sense, are oriented to this easy music, to the simplest variety of it, with hackneyed rhymes, with the simplest images and symbols, with the monotonous refrains.

And these musicians are very easy to control. They are as replaceable, interchangeable (*vzaimozameniaemye*), as in the past years. There is this *estradnaia* group, Laskovyi Mai (Tender May). And there were several other groups at the same time which were using one and the same recording, touring around the country and saying that they were Laskovyi Mai. You see? I mean, nobody knew them by sight at first, and different people, using one and the same tape, made heaps of money on this. And now this is going on all over the place.

When musicians approached the new culture industries, they had to accede to the demands of the latter rather than the demands of their artistic conscience. The case of one Petersburg band illustrates the often dictatorial and arbitrary control of the mafia over musical autonomy. Viktor, the leader of a Petersburg group, had succeeded in getting an audition with a major Moscow producer whom he considered to be part of the musical mafia. After the audition, the producer expressed interest in the group and agreed to produce them on two conditions: that they change the name of their group and that they replace the guitarist with someone else of the producer's own choosing. The latter demand had nothing to do with the guitarist's capability—he was one of the pre-eminent guitarists in the Petersburg music community. Rather, according to Viktor, the producer simply "did not like the looks of Andrei [the guitarist] and especially did not like the fact that he was bald." In the new context, musicians were again faced with arbitrary, external demands which compromised their artistic integrity. In a flash of conscience, Viktor decided not to accede to such demands and told the producer that his group would go elsewhere. Elsewhere, however,

Viktor found the same situation: producers demanded that they play certain pop songs which had been popular during the 1970s, and one producer even insisted that they begin to write and perform songs in English. This producer, according to Viktor, felt that English was "the only language of rock-and-roll" and that all of the possible permutations of rock music had already occurred. For him, the task of the Russian musician was to learn the formulas of rock and to make music using these formulas. He would only sponsor groups who acceded to and accepted his vision of rock music as a standardized cultural product. As one can imagine, he did not work with many members of the Petersburg rock community. The demands of such producers would force musicians to compromise on issues which were fundamental to the identity of their music and to their own identity as autonomous artists.

In light of the lack of resources, the inability to make appreciable amounts of money, and the tyranny of the musical mafia, Petersburg musicians increasingly sought to find sponsors who would aid them financially but not interfere in their music-making. These sponsors were usually individuals or organizations outside of the musical community who would agree to sponsor a band in exchange for a return on the profits. Most of these sponsors were entrepreneurs who had become rich by trading Russian goods with Western companies for hard currency. Others had become rich by engaging in local speculation. One sponsor of a Petersburg group whom I interviewed unabashedly offered the information that he received his money from two sources: from narcotics and from buying the apartments of alcoholics for extremely low prices and selling them to Westerners for huge amounts of hard currency. Many musicians have been forced to turn to such sponsors simply because they have no other means of support.

Corporate sponsors were often hesitant to offer direct financing of musicians, preferring instead to pay them in product. One musician wistfully reminisced about being sponsored by a large Western soft-drink firm. At a festival, he spoke with a representative of the firm and told him that his group was having a hard time and needed more support from the organization. The next day, during the rehearsal, five cases of soft drinks were delivered to the group. Because of such occurrences, musicians turned more often to individual sponsors, with little concern for the origins of the latter's money. According to musicians, the motivations of many sponsors appeared to be oriented toward gaining some name recognition for themselves as a cultural basis for further economic ventures.

The Entrenchment of Piracy

In the preceding chapter, we mentioned bootlegging as a serious challenge to the rights of musicians over their cultural productions. After 1991, this process intensified; at its core was none other than Andrei, the former underground record producer and president of Melodiya, whom we discussed in chapter 5. Andrei's principle role in the new context was recording pirate, a producer of bootleg (*butleg*) recordings. In his new role, Andrei successfully produced and distributed hundreds of Western albums without any observation of international copyright laws. Within an anarchic system where even Russian laws were not working, Andrei faced little threat from such violations of international law. As I mentioned earlier, Andrei would not be interviewed, but the process of bootlegging was described by a close associate.

Here is how the process worked: Andrei would choose an album (again based on his own personal tastes) and issue it in quantities of about 500,000 copies. The album covers were almost identical to those of the Western albums with two exceptions: the songs and credits were translated into Russian and slight alterations in the graphics were made. These alterations were often quite interesting and included the substitution of famous Russian musicians and countercultural figures for those who had originally appeared on the Western covers. Such large-scale piracy was a gross violation of international copyright law, but again there were no civil or judicial structures in Russia which protected the interests of Russian artists in Russia, much less the interests of foreign artists and corporations. Such bootlegging was primarily of recordings by Western groups which had been the object of the cultural fixation which I described in the second chapter. Some of this bootlegging created considerable animosity toward Russia on the part of Western musicians. For instance, ex-Beatle Paul McCartney had made a special album for release only in Russia. The album was immediately bootlegged by Andrei. Upon finding this out, McCartney vowed never to visit Russia again. Musicians could not understand this attitude. Bootlegging was simply a continuation of the informal process of tape-recorder culture on a larger and more formal scale. Even within an emergent capitalist setting in which the idea of private property was becoming increasingly central, the predominant idea was still that music was not owned by anyone, but was part of the public domain. More practically, many musicians and producers could not imagine why poverty-stricken Russians should have to pay royalties to a musician as rich as Paul McCartney. Said one musician:

You see, Paul McCartney does not refuse to perform in England, right? Though there are more bootlegs being released in England up until now than Andrei has made in his whole life. A pal of mine, a true fan of the Beatles (*bitloman*), has a book published in England, a catalogue of the bootlegs, only the bootlegs of the Beatles. It has hundreds or thousands of titles, you see? So, you also have a great number of bootlegs, but the musicians do not refuse to perform either in England or in the US.

Resentment and the Defense of Piracy

While it might seem that record piracy would be seen by many as a dirty business, many musicians felt that pirates were actually doing a service to the development of a more sophisticated Russian rock taste culture. They knew that the latter was decidedly backward and fixated on older cultural forms because of the isolation of the Soviet Union. Furthermore, many musicians began to express hostility and skepticism toward Westerners in general and Western rock musicians in particular. During the glasnost era, many Western artists—some of them quite famous—had come to Petersburg with good intentions to plan joint festivals and offer aid to musicians in the city. Yet, generally, such gestures of goodwill were not translated into practice. Western musicians sometimes played huge concerts in Russia, but seldom were any Petersburg musicians invited to play with them. Such concerts were planned by large Western organizations in conjunction with the local Petersburg musical mafia, and local Petersburg musicians were excluded not only from playing in them, but, because of the often high price of concert tickets, from even going to them.

After the dissolution of the Soviet Union lifted all formal political barriers to intercultural communication, Petersburg musicians wished to "make communion" with the Western rock stars who were the very source of their own identities as stars in the Russian context. Such communion was not forthcoming; very often Western musicians were invited to play in Russia and upon arriving would be hidden from indigenous musicians. This led to a great deal of resentment on the part of many Petersburg musicians, especially those who were the most famous, and such resentment led to a defense of record piracy. Indeed, piracy could be seen in a sociological sense as a form of social control of Western musicians: "You won't recognize us, so we'll steal your music." Some members of the rock community felt that piracy would only serve to anger Western musicians and alienate them further from Russian music, and they made emphatic pleas to stop it. One music producer clarified the nature of the debates between critics and defenders of piracy by reflecting on an emerging public debate between Andrei, the pirate, and Artem, a prominent Moscow rock critic:

A. B.: There were several articles about piracy of all kinds against Andrei, but this is all a private matter because it all turned into squaring accounts between Andrei and Artem. Since I'm involved in the process, I know that Artem is the person who was going to do the same [piracy], but Andrei left him behind, and so Artem is kind of appealing to world opinion in order to destroy Andrei. Actually, it's funny. I agree that Andrei is engaging in illegal business, but our state engaged in the same business for many years. The state in fact encourages this kind of business, like all these video salons, sound-recording kiosks, video-recording kiosks, like our cinemas which run the films bought without observance of the licensed rights, like our television which shows whatever it wishes without any permission. Now we have cable TV, right? And they show any Western films without observance of any copyrights, naturally. They show everything they want to. They can just record, copy concerts, musical shows somewhere in the West, or catch them with the help of the satellite television, and they use them without any permission. Because there is no state mechanism of control. There is no person who would sit and watch, "Aha, what is it that they're showing? Let's send them a bill, make them pay money."

There's another, more important, point here. Though Andrei is acting against the law, he's filling the huge gap in our culture, in our education. It's very difficult to advertise and sell here groups like Chaif or DDT to people who have never heard the Rolling Stones or the Beatles or Procol Harum or T. Rex, and so on. In the West every new group, every new generation of musicians rests on the experience of the previous generations, and the new audience also rests on this experience. I mean, [in the West] people have a tremendous bulk of musical information in their heads which they have acquired since childhood. In this country the majority of population has never even heard the Beatles. Never heard Elvis Presley. Those you are communicating with are a tiny percentage of the whole population of the country [a reference to the elite of the rock counterculture, whom A. B. knows to be the focus of my study]. Even people who are interested in this music, who are involved in the process of its consumption, very often are practically ignorant, having heard some fragments of this music—one or two records by Beatles some time on the radio, some songs of Deep Purple, some songs of Led Zeppelin. And thousands of other rock groups which are included in any [Western] rock encyclopedia are just mere names for them. Do you see what I mean?

That's why in order to be ready to perceive our [Russian] models of this culture, it is quite necessary that as many people as possible learn the elements of this culture. And Andrei gives an opportunity to huge numbers of people to buy cheap (six to ten rubles per disk) records of Beatles, *Jesus Christ Superstar*, Rolling Stones, T. Rex.

From my point of view, the fact that they [records] are being published without observing the copyright is bad, but the fact that they are published at all is good, in our situation. I would of course prefer to pay money for the registration of my rights as a journalist, as a writer, producer, and receive money for my work. But the situation is such that I don't receive money which I should receive for my books, magazine articles, records. I receive laughable sums. For my last record of Band X [one of the most famous bands in the country, from St. Petersburg], I got three hundred rubles.

T. C.: And that's all? How long did you work on it?

A. B.: Half a year.

T. C.: Six months. And you received three hundred rubles.

A. B.: Do you see? That's how it is.

T. C.: Why do you do it?

A. B.: For love.

Social Differentiation and Social Relations in the Rock Community

Emerging Conflicts between Producers and Musicians

In the previous Soviet social context, producers and musicians had been united by a common concern for making music. While certainly a pragmatic relationship, relations among musicians were also characterized by a high degree of trust and solidarity which served as a cultural integument which bound the musical community together against formal modes of existence and structures of authority. Yet as money increasingly became the precondition for the maintenance of autonomous social roles within the musical community, producers and musicians began to come into conflict with each other. Some of this conflict was due to the fact that producers had no options to make money outside of the country. Said Andrei:

> The people who are the necessary elements of this musical process but who are not musicians, say, the sound producer, the person who is engaged in the promotion, they are in a more complicated situation than the musicians. After all, the musicians who play can make money at the concerts, and sometimes it turns out to be big money. They can go to the West and make some money there too. We—the people who are producing stuff here—we're in a more difficult situation. I can't play the concerts. I can't organize a tour for myself in the West. Therefore, we're more limited as to the ways of making our living . . . and the musicians very often do not understand this. They think that they can do everything themselves, without mediation of some people. They think that they are the ones who should get all the money. For example, a record is released, so [they think that] only the musicians should receive money, but not the person who made this process possible. What we've got here is simply a moral problem.

In the face of such economic difficulties, an important new dynamic emerged in the relations between members of the rock community. Earlier, Andrei's role in the musical community had been to facilitate communication among musicians, to inform them about developments in Western rock, and to work with them as a critical adviser on musical quality. In the present context, Andrei is forced to assume a new role and play it within a new social context in which musicians cannot survive unless they actively try to achieve some measure of commercial success. If there is any member of the Petersburg counterculture who is steering a perilous course between the past and the present, it is surely Andrei. Andrei recognizes what sells and what does not sell, but musicians feel more inclined toward doing what they did in an earlier epoch: making music the way they wanted to with little concern and even disdain for pragmatic affairs. Musicians have found the logic of the division of labor in cultural production foreign; they are used to controlling their own culture products and the conditions of their own performance. Even though producers are allies, they still represent a potential source of constraint on the creative autonomy which is central to rock music's identity. Andrei noted that this relation did not exist before:

> *T. C.:* It [cooperation between musicians and producers] was not important before?
>
> *Andrei:* Before—no.
>
> *T. C.:* They simply played as they wished?
>
> *Andrei:* They didn't get anything [material] from it. A record was purely a moral moment (*moral'nyi moment*), it was simply a moment of moral satisfaction. That's why, if they wanted it to be this way, they could do everything as they wished. Because in principle nobody cared. Nowadays the situation is different. Today for me it's a very fundamental issue, the opportunity for developing musicians' ability for constructive cooperation. The opposite of rock is *estrada* which has its own norms and values. In *estrada* everything is a little bit different, and there the laws of show business are in operation. That, strictly speaking, is an absolutely different world.

Andrei sees the necessity for musicians to make one of two choices: either engage in constructive cooperation with producers like himself who are concerned with preserving the integrity of rock music, or work with those in the world of *estrada*, the dirty, commercially motivated producers of music who care nothing about the artistic integrity of musical products and only about money. For Andrei, it is a tough choice, but one which is absolutely necessary within the post-Soviet context of rampant commercialism. Andrei has a profound and empathetic understanding of the cognitive dissonance of rockers, especially those who were veterans of culture wars of days gone by. At the same time, he recognizes that musicians cannot continue to live on their status alone; the transition to a market economy has fundamentally altered the idea that status as a musician can be based, as it was before, solely on nonmaterial cultural factors:

> *Andrei:* It's very difficult for them [musicians] to adjust nowadays. On the one hand they would like such an atmosphere of an absence of obligations to be preserved, but on the other hand, they want to lead a life, to have certain rights, but absolutely no responsibilities. That's how it seems to me. If you would suggest

to them that they return and work as watchmen—for God's sake, who's stopping them? There's now probably still a lack of watchmen, and one can go to work in a boiler room as before. But I cannot imagine, say, Yuri or Kostya [two famous musicians] working in a boiler room now, truly speaking. I think they would not want to . . . I think that none of the musicians that feel a nostalgia for the past would want to return to the life they had lived in reality. . . . It is a nostalgia, first and foremost, for an absence of responsibilities.

T. C.: Yes, I see. Of course, nobody wants the situation to be as it was before. In my mind, that's a paradox. The reason these questions interest me is that it seems to me a very rare situation. We never saw what would happen with culture in this transition to a new situation.

Andrei: Yes, the most important thing now is to maintain the continuity of the artistic process. That is, if we now, at some point, just give everything up and say, "Ah, I don't care. Everything else can go to hell. Let there be no disks, no recordings, no concerts until life gets better." Then everything will die. All culture, at least our part of the culture, will definitely die, because an artistic process must be continuous. It can't be interrupted at any point with the words, "We've stopped here. Next year we will start again at this point." That's why for me—I could have found perhaps another, more profitable job, could have lived better than I do now, but I feel responsible for this work, responsible for this sphere of our common spiritual life which I can somehow influence. And only for that reason I'm trying to work in this sphere and do something. For me, it's a very important moment. Though, in fact, I'm not at all sure that if everything keeps going, the difficulties, I still will be able to do anything. . . . I've told you already that I would be glad to work hard, and I can work and do something well, but in practice it turns out that there is no place to do this work. There is no organization, no structures in which I could participate as an element, as a part of an executive mechanism. And this causes a kind of uncertainty, instability. I simply don't know whether I will have a job tomorrow which will allow me to drink tea and buy bread. All this is very unsteady. For example, in the last four months I've released two disks . . . and the other one is due in a couple of days. I don't think I will get any considerable money from it, that is, enough money to support a family. Therefore I have to look for some other means of subsistence. And the flow of records can run out. Because everything is getting harder and harder.

The Habitus of Dependency

For many music producers, one of the most important impediments to successful musical production lay in the historically conditioned dependency of musicians and the expectation of reward for little or no work. Andrei crystallizes his experience with musicians in terms of this crisis of dependency:

> Let's suppose that on the one hand making music is a kind of self-sacrifice and on the other hand there is a kind of dependency, a kind of parasitism going on as well. Like when musicians feel that someone has to do everything for them, that someone should find a club where they can rehearse, that someone should find a place for them to play, that someone should do everything for them all the time. In the West, you understand, that everything you get, you get yourself, let's say through their instruments, or, let's say through a manager, to whom, though, musicians pay a large part of their earnings. Here musicians aren't ready to pay for anything. They want only to receive. This is a big problem, and I'd say that a movement toward a reconstruction of consciousness in this direction is very complicated. Musicians think that, for example, the recording firm should pay them some kind of astronomical royalties, independently of whether or not their album is popular. When I explain and tell them how the system works in the West, they simply can't make any sense out of what I tell them because they simply don't believe what I tell them. They are brought up on Western journals with such beautiful covers and develop illusions about [how] Western show business works: a huge amount of money and a very small amount of work. When as a matter of fact everything is exactly the opposite.

Andrei's experience with complacent and dependent musicians shores up a central crisis in musical culture which is rooted in the historically conditioned consciousnesses of musicians. He observes that musicians do not yet have a consciousness about the necessity of self-survival or the idea that remuneration for cultural activity is dependent on the success or failure of these culture products in the marketplace. Andrei speaks of a "parasitic mentality" among musicians. The major component of this parasitic mentality is the idea that cultural activity should be supported from the outside or from above, regardless of the viability of such activity in the cultural marketplace. Many members of the musical community simply expected that they should be paid for making music regardless of its potential for making profit.

They expected that the new society and its new industries should support them in their new social roles regardless of whether or not they were economically self-sufficient. Because they were socialized in a welfare-state system which provided for their most basic needs, they expected to be able to pursue any vocation they wanted without having to worry about supporting themselves.

This attitude was evident especially among younger musicians who had come of age after the social reforms of the late 1980s and who had experienced both the subsidized existence of the Soviet welfare system and the openness in cultural expression. Some older Petersburg producers felt that young groups did not have the sense of dedication and sacrifice necessary to preserve the spirit of the counterculture in the face of the spirit of capitalism. Says one music promoter:

> If we turn to the musicians again, we say, "If the old leaders cannot reflect, maybe the young, more flexible ones can?" But the problem is that young groups—and I'm looking for many young groups, I'm touring around the country for half a year from festival to festival trying to catch something new, to see some new processes—and I see that there are not many young groups. I'm asking, why? They must reflect this process. But the young guys have another disease: they are not accustomed to work. That is the most frightening thing. They want to become stars, to be a success, but they don't want to work. Well it's not so much that they don't want to work as it is that they don't know how to work. There are many talented among them, but they cannot work every day, and this is a problem of motivation, of an attitude towards work. This is very important.
>
> Why don't they want to work? Because especially in the last years before perestroika there was such an atrophy (*marazmus*) in the society, that many people just fell out of the habit of working. And they're brought up on an attitude of unwillingness to work. They don't have this attitude towards work as a necessary element of achieving success. And you see not-bad, talented guys who don't realize their potential because they cannot work day after day to create a really artistic thing. . . . They cannot create anything artistically valuable because they must work hard, and they can't, or don't want to.

Fathers and Sons: The Conflict of Generations in the Petersburg Musical Community

In addition to conflicts among musicians due to the competing demands of their roles, new conflicts began to emerge in the rock community due to differences in age among musicians. The changing age structure of the musical community had little to do with the effects of economic shock therapy even though the changes brought on by this process opened up the community to a variety of new forms of culture. The latter pulled many younger musicians away from the old traditions of the counterculture. We shall explore this process shortly. First, we discuss the changing generational structure of the Petersburg rock community and its role in producing conflicts among musicians.

Conflicts between generations are an inevitable aspect of any society (Mannheim 1956; Feuer 1969; Eisenstadt 1956). Generally, we do not think that such conflicts could express themselves in groups such as the Petersburg rock community, since rock culture is usually thought of as the practice of the young. Rock music—both in the West and in Russia—is traditionally seen as a form of youth culture. As time progresses, however, those who produce and consume rock music become members of different generations. This is true also in the Petersburg musical community. Within what was a generationally homogeneous community there are now at least three generations of musicians who range in age from eighteen to sixty. Each of these generations has had a different set of life experiences which have affected their world views and their ways of making music and, as a consequence, have brought them into conflict with one another.

Such conflicts were exacerbated by the increasing penetration of money and the logic of capitalism into the rock community. In particular, many younger musicians began to be attracted to Western rock music not as a template for developing a code of opposition or a common symbolic integument of an alternative community. Rather, they were drawn to it as a way of making money in order to secure the material means of transcending their own existences in Russia. To be sure, there were conflicts between generations even before glasnost. Older members of the first generation of musicians forged a specific identity for rock music and for themselves in the 1960s and 1970s. In the 1980s, a second generation of musicians emerged which challenged the almost canonical definitions of rock music and the rock way of life. Second-generation musicians often attempted to transcend the boundaries set by first-generation musicians, most notably by being more overtly political in their music or by attempting to hasten the pace of the development of rock in Petersburg. Nonetheless, they never went so far as to cross the extremely important boundary between music-making and money-making. Those who did so were excluded from full participation in the rock community and the status which such participation conferred.

In the post-Soviet context, a new generation of musicians has emerged which consists primarily of individuals who came of age during the era of glasnost. Members of this generation are beginning to rebel not only against their elders in formal society, but also against the music and way of life of the elders in the informal rock community. Throughout the 1980s, young Russians had far more exposure to a wider variety of cultural experience from the West, not only through the increasing number of Westerners coming to Petersburg, but through the expansion of avenues of mass communication and the increasing importation of Western cultural texts into their environment. In light of the freedom of cultural expression and the plethora of information from the West, the highly cryptic and encoded rock music of the core of the Petersburg community was bound to appear obsolete and prosaic to young musicians.

The most important expression of this gap between young and old rock musicians is the increasing tendency of young musicians to write and sing their songs in English. There is ample evidence for this tendency not only in Petersburg, but in the country as a whole. In Petersburg, in the summer of 1992, a concert took place in a small park near a popular lake in the city. It was a kind of amateur hour, hosted by a self-described *staryi roker* (whose lament was discussed in the preceding chapter), that consisted of about ten young bands from the city. Also present were two famous Petersburg musicians. The idea behind the concert, according to the old rocker, was not only to offer young groups a chance to play and compete with one another, but also to have a chance to meet and see old veterans of the city's counterculture and perhaps be influenced by them. Out of ten bands who appeared at the festival, seven sang English lyrics. As is the custom at Russian rock concerts, musicians would say a few words about their music and their songs before they played. In one case, a young musician said, in Russian, "I know that some of you [in the audience] will think that it is bad that we sing in English, but it's part of our image." Viktor, a famous bass player, was at the concert. As the concert progressed, Viktor offered judgments of the performances. After the performances of the groups who sang in English, Viktor would simply say, "Center Aleksandr K.," a reference to a new cultural organization founded by the very same Comrade K. discussed at the end of chapter 2. Comrade K., a former doyen of state-sponsored rock, was now "Capitalist Entrepreneur K." His self-professed ideology was that the best forms of music were Western, English-language forms, and he would only promote those groups who would work within that idiom. Viktor's comments were sardonic; they called attention to the Center's sponsorship of events which were highly imitative, and in conflict with the indigenous forms of sophisticated, Russian-language music which he had worked his whole life to develop. These English acts were seen by this veteran of the rock scene as attempts at commercial success.

There is evidence that this linguistic turn is actually quite widespread in the country as a whole. One former president of a rock club in Siberia, Kolya, noted that he had solicited new music from new groups all over the country through an advertisement on the national media. He received over five hundred tapes, at least three hundred of which were young people singing in English and, according to Kolya, "in very bad English." At one concert that Kolya organized, he noted that one group not only sang in English, but introduced and explained their songs to the audience in English as well. Kolya asked them why they did this since no one in the audience could understand English. They replied that it was "part of their image." Kolya sarcastically replied that perhaps they ought to get a translator so that the audience—all Russians—would be able to understand them.

The above are rather graphic examples of a current situation which young people find entirely normal, and even preferable, but which older musicians find absurd and tragic. This linguistic turn in Russian rock music represents one of the most important developments in contemporary Russian rock culture. It is a profound source of conflict between members of the older and the younger generations of musicians. It represents a return to an earlier time in Soviet history when English was the language of rock even in the Soviet Union. In the present, though, there is a difference: the turn toward English is a result of Russia's entrance into the world-system and is part of a specific strategy of younger musicians to orient their activities primarily to the West in order to escape what they see as a hopeless situation in Russia. Increasingly, young people have come to see the practice of rock music as something which will allow them to escape from Russia and to go to live in the Western lands of their dreams.

We turn now to examine a case of a young musician, Slava, who sings only in English and whose attitudes are highly representative of Petersburg's younger generation of musicians. Slava's case illustrates in great detail not only the changing character of the *Weltänschauung* of the younger generation of Petersburg musicians, but also the relation between specific elements of that world view and new forms of music that are emerging in the city.

Slava: An Anglophile Russophobe Rocker

Slava is twenty-one years old and speaks fluent, idiomatic English. His language, like that of his counterparts in the United States, is peppered with superfluous "likes," "you knows," and dropped "g"s from words ending in "ing." A small, makeshift bookshelf near his bed contains English-Russian dictionaries of every conceivable variety. In a world where large apartments are scarce and expensive, Slava occupies a large room with carved wood trim and large bay windows. He has hundreds of cassettes and video tapes around the room, a color TV, and a video player. There is little to identify him as Russian except an occasional slip in his otherwise perfect accent.

Slava's genesis as a rock musician had very little to do with politics per se. While he thinks that all music is political at one level, he eschews involvement with Russian politics at a formal level and, indeed, cares little about the fate of Russia. Slava's decision to become a musician, in his own view, is due to family influences. His mother was a famous pop singer who was a major figure in the world of Soviet *estrada* in the 1970s. The only condition of my interview with Slava is a promise not to spread around the city the fact that he is the son of this woman. He fears that if people in the rock community discover this, then he will be the subject of merciless mockery and be excluded from the community of serious rock musicians (later, he laughingly retracted my obligation to keep this secret). His stepfather, now divorced from his mother but on good terms with the family, is the son of a former member of the Politburo and the Central Committee of the Communist Party. He was a leader in the production of hard rock within official circles in the 1970s and remains active in the production of hard rock in Moscow in a studio which bears his name. There is very little of the voice of working-class protest in Slava's music. Like many other Petersburg musicians, Slava is enabled by a comfortable upper-class existence and deep and lengthy exposure to Western culture. Money, travel, connections, and access to the means of musical production are of no concern to Slava; by virtue of his social background he is free to do as he pleases, and this is precisely what he does:

T. C.: So. Why are you a rock musician? That's what I want to know.

Slava: I don't know. It was like—'cause I was born in a family where there were musicians around all the time. And my mother is a singer, and my stepfather is involved with the business itself, and, I don't know, it was everywhere around, so I grew up listening to it all the time. . . .

T. C.: And your father influenced you a lot in your musical career?

Slava: Yeah, in a way. 'Cause he just told me lots of things, and it's the first time I saw a VCR and you know lots of music on video, not just listening to it, so. So he educated me. . . . I had this idea of starting a band and doing all that stuff since I was probably thirteen or something, so it was more like a dream. And there were all those rebellions going on in music at that time.

T. C.: That was probably about six years ago, so that was about 1986 or so?

Slava: Maybe a bit later, like 1987. There was Akvarium and all those guys. So they kind of symbolized the struggle against the government or something. I mean, I thought that it was real, and I trusted it, so I kinda got involved with it, but it did not have that much of an influence musically, it was more like a social thing, you know.

T. C.: So it was like music was used in some way to socialize with people. It was kind of a way of interacting with people maybe?

Slava: Maybe. Because at first I thought you just don't have to be able to play anything. It's just a social thing to do. That was just about it because not many bands could play at that time, it was just the lyrics of their songs that mattered, so people were kinda involved with the lyrics.

As the interview progresses, Slava intimates his real feelings about his relationship to Russian rock:

T. C.: What is your relationship to Russian rock? This is something that I'm interested in, this distinctive nature of Russian rock in Russian society. And then there's Western rock, which is also important. But it seems to me that they are different.

Slava: You know I've never thought of it as Russian rock or any kind of movement. I don't know, because I had like four or five albums of Russian music I was listening to 'cause it was fresh at that time, and it was a kinda new thing. Like I listened to Kino and Boris Grebenshchikov and a couple of Moscow bands, but you know what happened was that Gorbachev said, "You just go ahead and do what you want," and it happened so that ninety-nine percent of the bands could not go any further. They just stopped in their development, so I mean Boris Grebenshchikov— he is like doing small clubs now, and he is just doing acoustic music, with only a guitar and a violin or something. So it's pretty interesting, but you're not going to buy any of his albums. He is an old fart (*staryi perdun*), anyway [laughs].

Slava rejects a member of the older generation of rock musicians with the epithet *staryi perdun*. He sees them as anachronistic, unable to rise to and adapt to the central challenge of post-Soviet Russia: "Do what you want." Their primitive protest and low level of quality make him, Slava, look bad in the eyes of those to whom he would most like to look good, namely, a Western audience of similarly "postmodern" young people. Indeed, Slava's entire identity is guided by a meticulous and conscious mimesis of Western cultural values and norms, both behavioral and aesthetic. He feels that the older generation of rock musicians was mimetic. In his view, the great figures of the 1970s and 1980s merely took the major rhythms from Western rock and imitated them:

T. C.: But you think that Viktor [the dead musician discussed in chapter 3] was imitating?

Slava: Well, he definitely had his own voice and, you know, his own music, but I mean he did that with some of the songs, it was not just albums by Cure with Russian lyrics, definitely not like that, but I mean that particular band—they were into this primitivism, this kind of music.

T. C.: What do you mean by primitivism in that sense?

Slava: It's just a musical term that deals with playing very little. It's just vocal. They just kinda played this really simple thing, so maybe that really appealed to people.

T. C.: Do you sing in Russian, too? Do you have songs that you sing in Russian?

Slava: I never did. Never in my life.

T. C.: So you never sang—you always consciously kind of intended to sing in English?

Slava: Mm-hm.

T. C.: So you always had in your mind that you maybe thought it would be best to sing in English? Why is that? Can you explain?

Slava: Yeah. I can explain. First of all, 'cause I grew up listening to music that was all in English, ninety-nine percent of it. So I kind of had this idea in the back of my mind, you know. It was like, you know, I thought of it maybe subconsciously as a standard to follow, so I listened to a lot of these Russian bands, and I was just thinking, "Why doesn't it sound right to me?" I don't know. Maybe just because they sing in Russian. It doesn't make any sense. And I bet that lots of people who listen to the music, album buyers, that do not get involved with the process of making music. . . . So those people that do not really care about how it's made, they think, "O.K., it doesn't sound right 'cause it's in Russian. If it were in English, it would be much better." Or something like that. Because they also have maybe a stereotype that music has to be in English. You know. There is no other way to that. If the Beatles sang in Chinese, what would we do? . . .

And if you sing in Russian, you have to find something new, like bring that real folk music up, try to involve Russian folk music, or I don't know, whatever. And be a sort of alternative, I don't know . . . my attitude is maybe kind of too pretentious, but I don't think that such bands have any future doing that. I mean the band will just break up in the end. Nothing happens. I am not interested in playing in this country only. What I want to do is, since we sing in English, from the point of view of managers, there are several ways for us to go here in this country, but you take your chances, and it's a game, a very risky thing to do. I don't have any ambitions of becoming a popular singer here, in this country, 'cause it's like, I don't know, impossible.

T. C.: Why is that? Why is it so impossible? Maybe you have some theory about this?

Slava: Maybe bands that appeared in the last, I don't know, five or six years, they can gather a very small audience, maybe fifty people, not more than that. Ten bands playing at a big show can gather twice as many, but not more than that. So it's not only about actually playing, 'cause it's not the only problem. You can team up with a band and tour the country, but it's no longer interesting because there are very few people who can relate to this music anyway 'cause there is always pop going on, and people just don't have any information. They grew up listening to a totally different music that was official in this country. . . . So very few people in this town and in Moscow can relate to this music, but if you go deep into the country and tour just Russia, there's not gonna be too many people who would relate to this music. I mean if you do a stadium, there's gonna be like five people who would understand what it's all about, this music, what style it is. You know what I mean?

T. C.: Yeah.

Slava: And the rest of them will be just sitting and staring at it. Not more than that. They just can't relate to it. . . . So it's no longer—it's not interesting for me just to be playing in this country. I don't know. It's really not about becoming a second Jim Morrison and being a god.

T. C.: What is it about it that drives you?

Slava: I don't know. I am not sure. But it's just—I don't know. 'Cause it's strange for me. Why the hell I should sing in English since I live in this country, you know, but I think that's the only way to do it now for us.

T. C.: It's the only way to survive?

Slava: Right. Maybe. And another thing is that the type of lyrics that I want to write, they would not sound right in Russian at all. It's just impossible. So to write lyrics in Russian, you have to be— I don't know, you have to sit around—I mean it would take up a year to write what I want to sing about in Russian. I know that what I sing about in English people can relate to in America, 'cause I listen to American music, and I hear what they sing about. And if you just translate those lyrics, they would just not sound right in Russian at all. People would think that it's pop. They'd get confused, you know what I mean?

T. C.: Mm-hm, mm-hm.

Slava: So in Russian it's a different kind of balance between words and music, so for the music we play, for that kind of music, we will be doomed to play, to sing about this social protest stuff, like lots of swear words and stuff, so I mean, I don't know, it's not interesting. 'Cause I want to do more.

T. C.: Perhaps you want to maybe expand your horizons a little bit, not to be locked up in this?

Slava: Right. Exactly. I really want to penetrate the Western market of music. I don't know if that's possible, but that's what I'm gonna fight for.

T. C.: So you are just trying to become more international. It's as simple as that?

Slava: Me, personally, I don't feel like any kind of citizen of any country. I am more like, I don't know, citizen of the world inside, so I'm thinking about being more like an international band. And this lady from Moscow who is—she herself is a manager that deals with musical videos—we had a talk about how we could start here. You have to be at least a little bit famous in your own country to start out, so there are like several ways for us to start like saying, it's not a Russian band, forget about this. We're more like an international band. If you just say that you are a Russian band singing in English, and not more than that, nobody is gonna relate to that. . . . I mean if, for instance—I mean if we ever become like popular or something, like you know, you can give interviews: "Yes, there are some people in this band who are Russian," but that would not matter at that stage 'cause people would trust you. Russian would not mean, you know, shitty.

T. C.: But do you think that people won't listen to you here if you sing in English?

Slava: People in this country cannot relate to that kind of music. That's, you know, one of the reasons why I don't want our band to be any part of this Russian music structure. That's why I want to get more involved with the Western market or whatever you call it. . . . God damn it! I mean playing in small clubs in the United States would be definitely more interesting for me than being a superstar here. . . . That's for sure.

T. C.: Really? Why is it? Your goal is not to be a star?

Slava: Well, I don't know. I mean, I think the goal for our band is to be famous enough to have its own audience so that we can be more like an international band and travel. . . . So I mean that because if we start playing clubs in the United States, start at a low level, there is at least some hope that we can develop both musically, 'cause there is gonna be all that music around. You can go to a shop and buy any album you want, 'cause you can't do that here. . . . So if you start playing clubs in the United States, you have some hope. Because there's no hope here. 'Cause I mean everywhere you go in this country—business, music, everything, it's all, you know, fucked up. There's nothing right about it. Everything seems to be just, you know, be the opposite of what you may want to get. You know what I mean? And besides that I don't see any way of changing it, you know. If I could be a part of this change, I mean that's fine, but there's no—I mean I would join any movement if there was one actually. But there is nothing happening. There have been actually lots of people who have tried to convince me to start singing in Russian, but I don't know.

T. C.: Well, maybe one or two songs, right?

Slava: Right, exactly. [They're] not really pushing it, but they are trying to say, "O.K., English is not gonna sell here, and nobody is really interested in that." But I mean I am not interested in this country at all. Not really at all.

Slava is a representative of a new generation of young musicians who look increasingly to the West for their artistic inspiration. But what is most important, the pull of the West has occurred simultaneously with the development of a strongly negative view of his own country and the local traditions of Russian rock-and-roll. Slava wants nothing to do with that tradition and certainly does not see it as an important influence on his own artistic activity. The conflict of generations is partially fueled by the fact that younger generations have started to come of age in an era characterized by a new relation of the Soviet Union to the rest of the world. Contrary to conventional wisdom, it is not Russia's younger generation which is the "lost" generation, but rather the old generation. According to the eminent sociologist Igor Kon (forthcoming), with the loss of the Soviet Union, older Russians—perhaps even older musicians—face an identity crisis as a result of the evaporation of the structural conditions within which their identities were formed. Younger Russians, on the other hand, see the new context as one which offers hope, but not within Russian society. Rather, the new context pushes them toward the West to find models for their own thoughts, behaviors, and identity. As we have seen in the case of Slava, there is an almost contemptuous attitude displayed for all things Russian: Russia becomes the land of no opportunity, Russian language is seen as useless in the world-system, and Russian rockers are relegated to the status of "old farts" who no one in the West cares about.

There are bound to be generational conflicts in cultural communities—even in countercultural ones—over time. In the case of the Petersburg musical community, however, such conflicts appear to be intensified by both the increase of cultural information available in Russian society and by the acceleration of the capitalist rationalization of Russian society. The former process has led to a greater competition among cultural goods, a competition in which Russian culture products are bound to be judged negatively in relation to the more sophisticated and highly evolved Western forms of music which are the products of superior technologies and an infrastructure that is designed at its very core to expand the varieties and enhance the aesthetic qualities of music. The capitalist rationalization of Russian society has pushed younger musicians toward the West and away from the Petersburg musical community, away from its traditional norms regarding the proper identity of music and the social role of the musician, and away from the more general cultural values, norms, and mores which bound musicians together as an elective, countercultural community in an earlier age.

Kul't Deneg: The Cult of Money

Older members of the rock community offered theories as to why young musicians were turning toward the West and away from Russia. The most detailed and pronounced critique of the younger generation of musicians and their trajectory of musical development came from Misha, a self-professed member of the second generation of Petersburg musicians. Misha sees himself as different from the old rockers, but he remains anchored to them by a commitment to sing only in Russian. In the current context, music-making remains a vocation for him: he has mastered computers in order to write music, no longer drinks, is strictly monogamous, and never uses drugs. He lives for his music and, in the present day, he has some interesting things to say about the contemporary musical situation. Upon meeting him on the street, I asked him what he had been up to. "New Wave lifestyle, no drinking," he replied with a smile.

How does Misha relate to the changes which have occurred? His response is rather typical of the older, core members of the counterculture. It crystallizes many musicians' sentiments about the pernicious effects of money on Russian rock culture, but it also offers an indictment of the blind mimesis of Western culture on the part of the younger generation of musicians and the effects of this mimesis on Russian rock music. While he was a bona fide rebel in the 1980s (and still considers himself to be in the present) Misha's present state of mind is almost conservative; he offers a pronounced sense of nostalgia for the way of life of the old Petersburg rock counterculture as an ideal, even though he sometimes had difficulties with other musicians in earlier times. He offers a stinging critique of the effects of capitalist shock therapy on music and musicians in contemporary Russian society. His story hinges on what he sees as the pernicious effects of the entrance of money into the world of music-making:

It's a general tendency—this cult of money (*kul't deneg*). Yeah, a money cult.[4] It's like people simply forget about the fact that they're musicians, and they rush to scrounge and grab as much as possible, to grab more and to make off as quickly as they can. No one even thinks about the future. In the studio which I created, for instance, there was the hope of making some kind of independent studio where we would record some interesting young talent, and then maybe to produce them, to offer them some work, some vision for the future, to develop a genre. In the end, it got so . . . well the young talent didn't have any money, or they could pay [us] only very little [to produce their albums]. And my musicians wanted to get a lot right away, therefore the whole thing broke up. We didn't agree about it. It was like a war between me and the rest of the musicians because . . . well, I offered twenty-five rubles per hour, and I organized the work of the studio, and it was already in operation then, and they had the idea that they wanted to get paid twice that amount. Well, in general, it was all finished, and they're all in basically commercial and very unpleasant groups, well at least uninteresting, but in which there's money to be made. But I don't usually have anything to do with such bad music. . . .

Well it's just general insanity here now, a kind of mass insanity. Musicians are going into nonmusical businesses—and it really is only business—all the same they go into it. They buy some little thing here and then bring it there and then sell it for three rubles higher. Such petty, dirty work. Or they lose heart and drink vodka and get bombed. There aren't any alternatives. Well, there are two alternatives. They can go to the West. But they can't be musicians there either because they go there in order to wash dishes in a restaurant in order to get their own money, and that's enough for them. In my opinion, its like they're not even musicians. I had a guitarist, a former guitarist, and he wanted to emigrate to Germany. I asked him, "Do you agree that you'll go to Germany and you won't play the guitar anymore, like you'll stop being a musician? You're going to wash dishes in a restaurant somewhere?" He says, "I agree with you completely." Then I say, "Why should we collaborate then?" We simply separated then. We just brushed each other off. *Well it was as if he already stopped being a musician. He became simply a man who needed money. Another type of man, not a musician* [emphasis added].

T. C.: Maybe it's a problem for musicians now because they need money to live. It's a paradox.

Misha: Yeah earlier, perhaps. Earlier the cost of living was very low, a minimum amount of money was necessary in order to live. But now, the situation is approaching that of the West, like in principle it is even worse here because our cost of living is higher than yours. And our pay is much lower. And therefore, we don't have enough to eat, simply to eat. But let's talk about something else. Why do I like the first generation of musicians, well, not the first, but the generation of musicians from 1984 and 1985? *Because we came to rock-and-roll with something to say, first and foremost to express ourselves, and, naturally, nobody thought about money then* [emphasis added]. But on the other hand, it was worse. Everyone said that you couldn't ever earn any money doing it, that you could even end up in jail. And there was some kind of "hardening" (*zakalka*). Like I still can afford not to work, even if I don't have money. I simply get my act together, I don't drink, I buy fewer things, and I can survive. But the very latest generation of musicians, they have a little bit different relationship to music. Many groups are out to earn money. And where can they earn money? In the West. And such an orientation [toward the West] is developing now. They call themselves by English names. They sing songs in English. And in the majority of cases, this is so badly done, and so uninteresting. There's a kind of primordial degradation in all of this, the hope of pleasing an audience which they don't know, they haven't seen, but which they suppose will like them. They write songs which they feel would please a Western audience. And it's funny when eighteen-year-old kids sing in broken English. They completely don't know how to play, but they think that here no one understands them, because they play such music which is understood only in the West. It's all very funny.

T. C.: The groups I saw at the [youth] concert yesterday—the majority of them sang in English.

Misha: That's the whole generation. That's how it's degenerated.

T. C.: I met a young musician. His name is Slava. He sings only in English. He's interesting to me because he decided to sing only in English.

Misha: Well, there you have it. This is simply a mass illness.

T. C.: What do you think of this as a member of the older generation [of musicians]?

Misha: I think that this is definitely the attitude of this cult [of money] and of the Western way of thought. Mass information. Now they show MTV. And here there are monkeys. How funny. They take someone else's chunks of music—it's like another type of creation. These people haven't come up with something of their own to say. They only need to make an image (*vid*) instead of thinking a little bit about things or about what they want to say. It's kind of like self-deception. Well not even self-deception, but an attempt to deceive the audience. And this is accepted because there exists a format of middle-level stage musicians, pop musicians, people who specialize in the production of formatted music, music within a certain framework. They speak about this openly: "We make music for our people." But what do the people need? Anything which is a little simpler so that the melody is quickly recognized. And they're specialists in making such productions. The entire productive apparatus is interested in this. In Moscow, there's a group of composers, fifty people, who all know each other. They write songs, and all is done in such a fashion: the arrangement is roughly the same, all alike. And the people themselves are accustomed to such music. This is such brainwashing. The people are no longer able to listen to something different. A powerful siege on the head is occurring, and it's a very cynical one. Like, you know, they understand that what they're producing is shit . . . the producers and the composers understand that this is shit, but they know that the public will eat it.

Well this effect is simply everywhere here. I agree that some things can be taken, that there are such exchanges of creative methods, but when you take a piece of a song by M. C. Hammer and the man's very movements and manner of dress, here's what we have here. You've seen it, yes? They show it often on television here. Russian rap. *I think that this is typical, whatever is popular here* [in Russia] *needs to be born there* [in the West] [emphasis added] . . . it's funny that they show that [rap music] here, you know. We have a similar kind of music: bandit, prison music, worker music. We have "criminal song" (*blatnaia pesnia*). How can you simply take rap music and transport it onto our Russian soil? Rap—it's American criminal music.

T. C.: You don't like it?

Misha: I can't listen to it for a long time. As a musician I'm simply not interested in it. As a social phenomenon, that's different, I agree. But when a Russian person uses it, it's funny, because he lives here, and here it's a totally different milieu. Some stylistic borrowings can be done, I think, well, for instance rhythms. The rhythmic structure can be taken. It can be done well. . . . But people simply copy. And they try to introduce this into mass culture, to make it popular, and it slowly becomes popular. In connection with this, this can constantly be found on the television screen. But it's very funny. Here there's a guy under the influence of M. C. Hammer. Here's another guy under the influence of Prince. Under the influence of rap groups. They simply look at video clips, and they act like monkeys, and this is so funny. And this is completely unsuitable. It simply kills my ears, as a Russian man. And they try to carry this off. Even though these people are from another society, in a sense from another class. At base, these adolescents, these young people are well-cared-for adolescents, young people, whose parents have been abroad, who've brought them nice things, and brought them music. These are not poor black people from the Bronx. They are completely different. And therein lies the contradiction. When [a young musician] starts to sing about what's going on over there, this music about American working-class regions, in Russian, I don't believe him because workers here don't dress like that. No one carries themselves like that. It's so funny. It's just a kind of watering down of the brains which is going on now.

T. C.: I understand some of the words to rap songs in the States. They're impossible to translate.

Misha: This is not our criminal music. Ours is rather dark and gloomy. All our criminal music lyrics are, and there's something real primitive which goes with the Russian language. And rap clearly does not lay well on Russian language. Especially when the philosophy of the black minority of America is brought here. There's simply no way it can graft well. It's funny to me. And I say that kids here are also trying to speak using American expressions which are translated into Russian. This process, it seems to me, has no relation at all to music. It's a separate process. *The whole country is trying to be America, not understanding that we have different cultural roots* [emphasis added].

Russian Rock Music
"Beyond the Borders" (*Za Granitsei*)

The opening up of Russia to the West caused many musicians—not just young ones—to look to the West in ways which were fundamentally different than before. Ironically, the changes we have outlined up to this point created a situation in which the survival of Russian rock music within Russia depended increasingly on its success outside of Russia in the culture markets of the West. The lack of dependable means of cultural reproduction and distribution in the post-Soviet context, the lack of legal protections for musicians' copyrights, and the monopolization of existing technologies by producers who cared little about musical authenticity constituted a colossal matrix of forces which "pushed" musicians to seek opportunities abroad, *za granitsei*. In light of the crisis of cultural production and performance in Russia, it is understandable that musicians would seek out opportunities abroad.

The story of Russian rock musicians' experiences abroad represents a fascinating case history which illustrates a vitally important issue in the sociology of culture: the fate of Russian culture in Western contexts. Born in the West, rock music traveled to Russia and became the basis for an entire taste culture and regional countercultures based on that taste culture. In the wake of the dissolution of the Soviet Union, the forces of commercialism obligated Russian rock music to return home, to travel back to the West from whence it had come. But would its identity in the Russian context be recognized and valued for what it was? Which aspects of its unique history would be valued by Western compatriots, the long-lost cousins of Russian rock musicians? In what follows, we trace briefly the history of Russian rock's travels in Western contexts in order to shed light on some issues which were decisive for the rock community.

Encounters with the West

In the mid-1980s, a collection of Russian rock music was brought out of the Soviet Union by a young female rock singer from California. The album was marketed in the West as *Red Wave*, a title with decisive political overtones. The album brought some Western attention to the Petersburg musical community, but again, primarily as a political phenomenon rather than as a cultural phenomenon which was part of the world music scene. Andrei, the underground producer from the preceding chapter, dismissed the album: "This [*Red Wave*] is politics. In the pure technical aspect the disk is made awfully, and on the whole, we don't need [such] collections. An album should be a book, not a stitched selection of articles on different topics."

Musicians deeply resented the elision of two discrete phenomena: rock and politics. They wanted more than anything else to have their music be seen as culture. Unfortunately, as long as rock music was seen in the West as a battle with the Soviet state instead of a more general commentary on Soviet existence, Western attention to Russian rock depended on the existence of the Soviet state and, more particularly, on a state which had been demonized in the consciousness of the Western public. The disappearance of the Soviet state produced a crisis for Russian rock musicians, for without a state which supposedly thwarted musicians at every juncture, the battles of musicians themselves would be seen as superfluous. Of what use could rockers be if they no longer had a state to fight against? Since most Westerners had little or no knowledge of the local meanings of rock music (and were aided and abetted in this ignorance by Western scholars and journalists who persisted in reproducing the metaphor of art as politics rather than art as art, or at least art as existential commentary and critique), their attention waned almost as soon as the Soviet state dissolved. Many members of the Petersburg musical community were deeply aware and resentful of the superficiality and even banality of the Western perception of Soviet rock.

Even though most musicians expressed ambivalence about the West, they clearly saw opportunities to play there as important from a financial standpoint. Many of them even sought to forge connections and normalize relations between themselves and their Western counterparts. Generally, the idea of making tours to the United States was seen as impossible. Only two of the most famous Petersburg groups had ever been there. The leader of one group went to make a recording with a major American record company. Upon arriving, he was told by the managers of the venture that they did not want his group to make the recording. They wanted him to sing with a band of more accomplished American musicians. The leader accepted these terms and made an album which enjoyed little commercial success. Back home his decision was greeted with derision by the other band members who left the group because of it. According to one member, they simply could not understand why their leader would betray them in such a way. This case rather poignantly illustrates the alien quality of the capitalist logic of cultural production in the Petersburg scene. Musical decisions were never made based on financial considerations of those external to the world of music. Rather, such decisions were based on close affective ties of friendship and loyalty to one's fellow *tusovshchiki*.

Another group traveled to the United States and had both good and bad experiences. The group had failed to read the small print of their contract, which stated that they would have to pay for their own return trip home. A series of concerts got them as far as Los Angeles, where they actually played a concert in the Palladium, but then they ran out of money. The concert organizer refused to render them assistance to get back home, a fact which the musicians simply could not understand. In their local Petersburg culture, an invitation meant that a host was responsible for his or her guests. They began to see that music-making in the United States was not considered an affective activity, but rather was oriented toward making profit. After getting home, the leader of the group, Yuri, was extremely hostile toward Americans and actually began to express anti-American attitudes. When I asked to interview him in 1992 (through a local intermediary), he responded negatively by simply saying, "We don't need any Americans around."

In general, musicians hoped to make connections with Western (mostly European) musicians but realized that such connections were becoming increasingly difficult. Said one musician, reminiscing about the opportunities for cultural collaboration which were lost with the dissolution of the Soviet Union and the concomitant loss of Western interest in Russian culture:

> We need communication between very different musicians, more meetings of musicians with different experiences. We need some new forms of art. It would be great if our musicians could normally go abroad, make contact with Western musicians, if they could go there not in order to earn money to support their families, but just to meet people. If the Western musicians came here not to look at us as something exotic, but as a colossal cultural source, it would serve as a powerful spur to music as a whole.
>
> How revolutionary was the moment when white America discovered for itself black music. Jazz, and then rock-n-roll, were two major turning points in the history of American culture, in my opinion. How important in the early '70s was the discovery of reggae music and Jamaican folklore. Now the process of adapting some African-root music is going on. It changes things profoundly and influences the work of musicians, for example the work of Paul Simon with the African *makang*. This is kind of interesting. A lot could be learned from Russian culture and music too.

Almost since the beginning of the glasnost era, some prominent Western musicians made trips to Russia and paid visits to the Petersburg Rock Club. A major part of the folklore of the community concerns these visits. For the most part, these stories echo a bitterness about broken promises of collaboration between Western musicians and

Petersburg musicians. Many musicians simply could not understand why important and very rich Western musicians would not help them. After all, they felt, given the low cost of living in Russia, an important Western rock musician could support the development of an infrastructure for musical production and performance with only a minimal investment. It is vital to underscore the fact that many musicians felt increasing resentment and hostility about what they perceived as an act of abandonment by their Western musical comrades. Petersburg musicians had always imagined themselves to be part of the world rock community. Yet, in the context of a shifting world order, they discovered that while they had been famous in their own social context, their music was simply ignored, considered inferior, or seen as unintelligible in the West.

Much of the neglect of and even disdain for Russian music in the West had to do with the elemental process of cultural fixation described in the second chapter. Russian rock music was extremely mimetic: with the exception of its Russian language aspect, Western audiences saw nothing new in it as music and nothing which they could understand in its lyrics. Even those musicians who tried to bring Russian folk rhythms into their music found themselves restricted by a general sense of alterity toward Russian culture which had long existed in the West. In the new competitive arena of the world music scene, Russian musicians were forced to rethink their identities as well as the identity of their cultural idiom. Kolya, a producer who worked extensively with rock musicians and understood the challenges posed by a more sophisticated Western taste public, crystallized the essence of the crisis which Russian rock musicians faced as they were forced to confront the West which actually existed outside of their imaginations:

> At the current moment there is a discernible crisis of consciousness that has to be taken into account. There are these trips that are starting. In a closed society there was one idea of what is going on "there" (*tam*),[5] of the values and so on, and now that people can travel and see, it turns out that the values are changing, I mean the social, cultural, and other values in relation to the world of rock music. People are asking the questions: What is my role in this world process? Are my values needed only here, or are they values that are needed there also? Now it's very important to discover in which ways you are different, original in the world, not just on a local scale. If you, for example, played in the style of Deep Purple and it was different here because nobody here played like this, when you go there it turns out that there are thousands,

millions of groups playing in the same style, and you are not original any more. What then? This knocks you for a loop (*b"et' po mozgam*).

Many musicians recognized that Russian rock music—that is, music which was sung in Russian and conformed to local norms of what was considered good in music—faced a difficult future in the West. Nonetheless, they continued to try to find some space for their highly localized forms of music within a more general world rock community. The following case documents one of the more poignant efforts of Russian musicians to bring their culture to Western audiences. It illustrates dramatically the meeting of Russian musical counterculture with the infrastructure of capitalist modernity and its commercialized rock culture.

Za Granitsei: A Petersburg Rock Music Festival at the Palace of Tears

In late June and early July, a rock festival took place in Berlin. The festival was called "The Berlin-Petersburg White Nights Rock Music Festival." It featured a number of the musicians and groups whose lives and experiences comprise the core of this book. I traveled to Berlin to see exactly how Russian musicians and their music would be greeted in a major Western city. The rock festival took place near the Friedrichstrasse Bahnhof in East Berlin in a building referred to by Berliners as the "Tränenpalast," or "Palace of Tears." The Tränenpalast was a central conduit between East and West and a site at which East and West Berliners often said sad farewells to each other after visits, ergo the name Palace of Tears. After the wall was removed and the city was reunited, the Tränenpalast was vacated. It is now rented by a culture organizer, Marco, who stages events there. It is extremely ironic, for reasons which shall become obvious, that the Tränenpalast is in sight of the theater where Bertolt Brecht retreated to develop his own brand of authentic art which would be safe from the forces of commercialization which he felt were a major factor in the erosion of authenticity in art. For within sight of Brecht's theater, the very forces which were at work in the erosion of deeply held ideas of musical authenticity in Russian society were to make themselves painfully clear in the course of the week.

In the spring of 1993, Igor, a young culture organizer from Petersburg traveled to Berlin and proposed a festival of Petersburg music in Berlin to be called "The Berlin-Petersburg White Nights Rock Music Festival." The proposal was that six or seven groups consisting of a total of about forty-five musicians and their technical support personnel would play a festival for four days in early July at the Tränenpalast. The groups consisted of some older bands (veterans of Petersburg music), and some newer groups. The musicians would be responsible for their own transportation and other expenses such as food. On the German side, money would come from the Berlin city government, or Senat, and from corporate sponsors who would provide lodging for the musicians. It was impossible to discover exactly how much money was given by various sources for the concert. Marco claimed that it was a small amount, only about six thousand marks. Musicians later told me that they believed Marco had actually received fifty thousand marks.

Prior to any difficulties in Berlin itself, the first problem involved transportation of forty-five musicians and their equipment from Russia. Because of local financial difficulties, normal modes of transportation such as trains and the Russian national airline, Aeroflot, were out of the question. A solution was found, though, which involved paying Russian military officers ten thousand rubles (about eight dollars) per musician to arrange charter of a Russian military airplane to fly the entire Petersburg contingent to Berlin. Immediately upon arriving in Berlin, the musicians were told that they were not to be paid until they had played their concerts. Most of the musicians did not understand the principle of "pay for play" which is quite standard in Western contexts. Under the arrangement in Berlin, musicians would receive a percentage of ticket sales. Their payment would, therefore, depend on how many people would actually come to the concert. Some of the confusion was the result of the fact that Igor, the manager on the Russian side, had made promises of remuneration which he could not fulfill until he had been paid by Marco, the manager on the German side.

The result was that the contingent of Petersburg musicians found themselves in Berlin with little or no money. They stayed in a former hotel for Soviet diplomats which was paid for, according to Marco, with funds from the Berlin Senat and by sponsors. Since Marco, however, refused to give any money to the musicians until the concerts were actually played and the profits from the tickets were received, the musicians went for at least two days with nothing, or very little, to eat. As the beginning of the festival approached, it became clear that the festival would not be a success. A press conference was held at the Tränenpalast, but none of the major Berlin journalists attended. The Russians, as part of their end of the bargain, brought thousands of posters advertising the event. On all the posters, however, there was a misprint of the date of the festival: they all read 6.1.93-6.4.93 instead of 7.1.93-7.4.93. Marco recognized that in the hurly-burly cultural scene of Berlin this would be a fatal mistake. To compound matters even further, only a week before, another Petersburg rock festival called "White Nights of St. Petersburg" had occurred in the city. This festival consisted of less famous musicians and was organized independently of the White Nights of St. Petersburg festival at the Tränenpalast. The previously small world of Petersburg rock was now characterized by a new spirit of economic competition in which musicians engaged in all kinds of secret activities. Such blunders only strengthened Marco's resolve not to give any money to the Russians until he had actually taken in some money from ticket sales. According to him, he had already "lost his shirt" on the venture.

On a number of occasions, some of which I witnessed, musicians angrily approached Marco demanding at least enough money to live on while in Berlin. Marco continued to claim that he could not give them any money and that at least part of their payment was the opportunity for Berlin to get to know a little bit about Russian rock music and to lay the groundwork for future concerts and festivals. Much of the confusion had to do with the fact that musicians simply failed to understand that their failure to be paid was a result of a stand-off between the two organizers. Again, this illustrates some very basic conflicts between Russian musicians and their managers discussed earlier in this chapter. The misunderstanding also had to do with Russian musicians' conceptions of the definition of the word *festival*. As one musician explained it, festivals in Russia—as opposed to concerts—were usually paid on a flat-fee basis. That is, the organizers would agree on a price for participation, and the musicians would be paid either before arriving or, more usually, upon arriving at the festival to play. Usually payment for festivals was expected to be quite small since no one could anticipate audience attendance, especially in such tenuous culture markets which existed then in Russia. Musicians participated in festivals both because they felt it was an honor and because they thought it would be good advertisement (*reklama*). The fact that the event in Berlin was called a "festival" meant for the musicians—regardless of the actual specifications of the contract between managers—that each of them should receive a flat fee of one hundred marks for their participation regardless of ticket sales.

According to Marco, the first night of the festival, at which two groups played, approximately forty tickets were sold at 21 marks, or about $12.60 each, a bit steep by Berlin standards for unknown bands. The second night of the festival featured no Russian bands at all, but a self-described "fusion–hip-hop–funk" band from New York City which had been invited by Marco to hedge his bets against losses from the festival. The third night of the festival featured Yuri's band, one of the most famous in Russia. It was attended by somewhere between three hundred and four hundred people, most of whom were Russian guest workers living in Berlin. Yuri and his bands received a decent sum of money for their activity. Yet the musicians who had played earlier in the week, those who played to only forty people, felt that they had played well. This fact only strengthened their resolve that they should get their 100 marks (about US $60.00), not from Igor but from Marco.

Humiliation (*Unizhenie*)

On the final day of the festival, two groups were scheduled to play. One of the groups was Misha's, the musician whose critique of the younger generation we addressed earlier in the chapter. Misha had arrived in Berlin a full week before and, like the other musicians, had survived the week with little money or food. His "New Wave" ascetic lifestyle made this task a bit easier for him. The problems for Misha's group were compounded by the fact that his keyboard player, a Ukrainian, had failed to secure a travel visa due to bureaucratic torpor back in Ukraine. (This illustrates a further problem for groups consisting of different nationalities who lived and played in various cities of the Soviet Union: musicians of different nationalities who lived as "Soviet" citizens in St. Petersburg were now under the jurisdiction of new national entities, each of which was developing new policies for the administration of foreign travel. This reality has caused problems as musicians with little resources seek to coordinate cultural activities both at home and abroad.) On the eve of his concert, Misha refused to play until he got a promise from Marco that he and his band would get paid. Marco agreed to pay twenty marks to each band member. Misha refused to play for this amount. For once, Misha was without words to describe his feelings. When I asked him why he was not going to play, he simply said one word in Russian which captured the essence of the entire festival: *unizhenie,* or "humiliation."

It is not surprising that difficulties were encountered with a festival of Petersburg musicians in Berlin. The city is one of the cultural capitals of the world. It is rumored to have over one thousand rock groups—the most of any city in Europe. Moreover, West Berliners have a tradition of ignoring and even disdaining the culture of the East from within their own safe haven of capitalist modernity. East Berliners regarded the culture of Russia negatively as a reminder of Russian cultural imperialism. It stands to reason that Berliners would not be cognizant of the history of Petersburg rock music or the specific meanings of the terms which musicians used to describe their music in radio shows (which were organized hurriedly by Marco the day after the failed press conference).

In one interview with Yuri (for which I served as translator), the "Russian Bruce Springsteen" whose life history was presented in chapter 2, the interviewer asked Yuri how he thought he would play in Berlin. Yuri simply responded with the word *moshchnost'*, or "power." The interviewer responded by asking, "You mean, like heavy metal?" Yuri walked away from the interview. In such a way we can see how the most important local ideas which lie behind the Russian rock music vocation, the ideas of power (*moshchnost'*), drive (*draiv*), and energy (*energiia*), were simply misinterpreted outside of the Russian social contexts which gave them meaning. In this interaction lies a powerful metaphor for understanding the barriers to cultural understanding which are central impediments to the flow of Russian culture into Europe and its efforts to find a space, however small, within the sea of Western popular culture.

What is most striking, though, is that this most famous of Russian rock musicians could draw no more than three hundred people to his concert and that he would only be paid one hundred marks for his efforts. Certainly, some musicians cared deeply about this. Yet, in their own words, as we have seen throughout this book, they cared little about making a lot of money. They simply wanted to make enough to be able to survive as musicians back in Russia. They were aware of the limitations on creative activity in the West and of the irony of their own situation. Yuri, the most famous of the musicians to play in Berlin, captured the spirit in which the Petersburg rock musician, guided by a temperament of inner distance, met the forces of a humiliating commercialism:

> *T. C.:* It's interesting what you said that many people compare Bruce Springsteen and you.
>
> *Yuri:* Yeah, especially Western people, journalists—all the time.
>
> *T. C.:* It's interesting because if Bruce Springsteen came to Berlin, he would have made a lot of money, you know?
>
> *Yuri* [laughing]: Yes, I see.
>
> *T. C.:* It's just a horror for me. I cannot imagine such a situation [the situation which I had seen as a participant-observer at the Tränenpalast].[6]

Yuri: This is a usual situation for us. Of course, all the guys should have made a normal amount of money. They play well. You know it yourself. *But this is our cross to bear in life, and I regard it philosophically* [emphasis added]. Of course, if I were born in America, and sang there with the same *draiv,* I would be driving Cadillac— I understood this also. I would have been singing in English, would have been as popular as in Russia. Everything would have been all right. I would have bought a small island [laughing], a spaceship. But this is absolutely not the main thing for me.

Summary: The Clash of Typifications

The events at the Tränenpalast, together with the other issues which we have discussed in this chapter, illustrate the existence of a fundamental clash of cultures. Much of the discord in cultural relations between Russian musicians and the West have to do with phenomena discussed earlier such as the linguistic barriers, the lack of a taste public for Russian rock music, and the inability of Russian promoters to organize cultural ventures from within Russia itself. But, more fundamentally, what can only be described as a disappointing failure of cultural communication and articulation between Russian rock musicians and the West has much to do with the persistence of deeply held ideas about social reality held by each side. Understanding these differing ideas between "Easterners" and "Westerners" is the key to understanding the present state of cultural relations between Eastern and Western culture producers. Different definitions of reality—ideas about the meaning of rock music, the purpose of its performance, the role of music in society, what musicians are entitled to, the nature of audiences, and many others—are decisive for understanding the current situation of Russian rock musicians both at home and *za granitsei.*

Petersburg musicians became experts at accomplishing culture in their own local environment in the Soviet era and even in the difficult times of troubles during glasnost and beyond. The problem is that the techniques or recipes, or what I have called "typifications," regarding the practice of rock and the more general lifestyle of the counterculture had little utility either at home or in Western, capitalist social contexts. The ironic result is that musicians are relegated to live within a new capitalist system which is perhaps harsher on musicians than the Soviet state which came before it. In the final chapter, we summarize the central dilemmas of Petersburg musicians within the new infrastructure of capitalist modernity and draw on their experiences to illustrate the more general problems of individual and cultural freedom in post-communist societies.

7

Conclusion: Capitalism, Cultural Freedom, and Democracy in Post-Soviet Russia

> Only when the past ceases to trouble and anticipations of the future are not perturbing is a being united with his environment and therefore fully alive.
>
> —John Dewey, *Art as Experience*

> There is neither freedom nor discipline in the abstract, but only in the concrete forms that depend on the cultural context.
>
> —Karl Mannheim
> *Freedom, Power, and Democratic Planning*

Capitalism and the Aporias of the Rock Community

In the summer of 1992, on St. Petersburg's major thoroughfare, Nevskii Prospekt, in Ploshchad' Vosstaniya (The Square of the Uprising) a new electronic billboard of the sort found in New York City's Times Square was installed. Its simple message declared: *"Biznes—Eto Iskusstvo,"* or "Business Is Art." In terms of describing the situation of artists in Petersburg, the billboard might have proclaimed the opposite: *"Iskusstvo—Eto Biznes,"* or "Art Is Business." The central reality of artistic life in St. Petersburg after the dissolution of the Soviet Union is that art has become a business. In the West, this fact is not particularly extraordinary. Indeed, for Western artists, the fact that art is a business is something of a given, and they ignore this fact at their peril. For the most committed core of Petersburg musicians, however, the notion that music could be a business was an alien one. Yet, regardless of how they feel about it, the market has come to Russia. And to survive, Russian musicians must bring their aesthetic culture to the market. Herein lies the most essential paradox facing rock music in contemporary Russia: How will the freedom to make music according to the dictates of conscience fare in a context characterized by the swift and uncompromising infusion of the logic of capitalism into the process of cultural production and, indeed, into all areas of Russian social life? Members of the Petersburg musical community, like many other Russians, experience the emerging infrastructure of capitalist modernity both as a situation which enables their cultural freedom and as a quandary.

In previous chapters, we have presented a detailed story about the efforts of individuals to preserve a sense of autonomy and independence within two very different social contexts. Rock music and rock musical counterculture stood as a cultural contradiction to the world of socialist industrial modernity. Yet the rapid capitalist development of Russian society has, in a sense, contradicted this cultural contradiction. The rise of capitalism in Russia begins a new chapter in Russian history. And, therefore, at the end of our story, we are led back to Marx's famous dictum as a central guide for understanding the ongoing problem of human expressivity in post-communist societies: "Men make history, but not in circumstances of their own choosing." Petersburg musicians made autonomous culture, selves, and a community within a history that was not of their own making. Yet, as Hegel noted, history is cunning. The dissolution of the Soviet Union and of communism more generally does not signify the end of history, at least for those who live within the space of post-communist societies.[1] Rather, it signifies the beginning of a new history which is constituted by new structures, practices, and the cultural logic of capitalism, all of which intersect with the subjective states of mind and culture of the socialist period.

In this final chapter, we consider the theoretical implications of the fate of the Petersburg musical community, both in terms of what this fate tells us about the relationship between capitalism and aesthetic culture, and between capitalism, cultural freedom, and democracy more generally.

Capitalism as an Enabling and a Disabling Force

For those who profit from or find ways to satisfy their material desires within a capitalist order, capitalism is certainly liberating. But artists, poets, musicians, and the like are seldom comfortable with defining freedom and liberation purely in terms of financial or material satisfaction. For the ideal-typical artist, freedom and liberation are quite unrelated to the satisfaction of material desire. Ideally, as Herbert Marcuse (1993, pp. 181-82) noted: "Art, as an instrument of opposition, depends on the alienating force of the aesthetic creation: on its power to remain strange, antagonistic, transcendent to normalcy and, at the same time, being the reservoir of man's suppressed needs, faculties and desires, to remain more real than the reality of normalcy." The crisis of art in contemporary Russia subsists in the difficulty of maintaining inner distance and remaining "transcendent to normalcy" in a situation where all forms of action—including art itself—are being normalized according to the logic of capital.

The process of capitalist rationalization compels all forms of consciousness—even the most transcendent and oppositional—to become more involved in and complicitous with the world of external reality. What is clear from the previous pages is that the advent of a money economy in Russia has made it difficult for musicians to maintain a commitment to the values of musical authenticity, to the idea of music as a vocation, and to the more general way of life which defined the counterculture in an earlier era. Musicians are compelled to be commercially successful, but at the same time they must maintain the identity of music as an autonomous cultural form in the face of the forces of commercialization which work to transform the primary identity of music from art into commodity. Even so, a committed core of Petersburg musicians has tried to preserve the norms and values which define artistic integrity and autonomy in their local context. While many in the West choose to cast the capitalist rationalization of post-Soviet Russian society as a process which will bring about freedom and liberation, many Petersburg musicians have experienced the actual outcomes of rationalization as constraining and troublesome quandaries. The present situation in which they find themselves has compelled Petersburg musicians to learn how to "play the market" just like their Western counterparts. Yet, for them, playing the market cannot be a measure of success, for the very essence of the identity of their music and their own self-identities as rock musicians is the recognition that commercial success erodes artistic autonomy and autonomous selfhood. To put it simply: many Petersburg musicians remain dissidents within a new, emergent infrastructure of modernity.

This is not to say that the transition to capitalism and the rise of money as the new basis for sociation and cultural production has had only negative effects on individual consciousness or cultural expression in modern Russia. Most sophisticated sociological theorists of modernity hold the view that there is a two-sided character to capitalist modernity.[2] On the one hand, capitalist modernity enables individuals to think reflexively about their existence (Giddens 1990; 1991). Relative to both traditional society and socialist industrial modernity, capitalist modernity allows individuals a greater sense of freedom of choice and a greater degree of autonomy in choosing those roles which they wish to play (Coser 1991). In his classic work, *The Philosophy of Money* ([1907] 1990), Georg Simmel argued, *contra* Marx, that money was not purely an instrument of oppression. Rather, Simmel argued that money was a means by which actors could transcend and escape from the ascribed roles of traditional society. It is this sense of modernity which might be described as the positive, or enabling, dimension of modernity. It is this side of modernity which has caused many theorists to equate modernity with ideas such as freedom and individuality, or to see individuality as conterminous with modernity. On the other hand, most theorists of modernity recognize that it is a condition which actually and potentially disables cultural expression and autonomous projects of the self.[3] Ironically, modernity provides immense possibilities for autonomy and expressions of individuality. Yet it also contains forces which constrain human agency. Simmel himself recognized that a market economy freed the individual from the bonds of traditional society. He also recognized that it produced an existence which could lead to alienation, or at least to a sense of distance from the world (see, in particular, Simmel [1907] 1990). Capitalist modernity is both enabling and disabling.

The identities of Petersburg musicians were constructed out of the cultural stuff produced in Western capitalist societies. In the Russian environment, these identities became potent oppositional forces because one important force which served to make art conventional in the West was lacking in the Soviet social context—money. Rock music in the context of socialist industrial modernity was unique because it was one of the few contexts in which capital did not have any influence over the dynamics of cultural production. Simmel makes a convincing case for money as an instrument of freedom: money drives innovation in cultural expression even if it does sometimes determine the content of such innovation. Yet Simmel focuses on money's role in societies where there is an infrastructure which can provide individuals with the possibility of making money. Money may be a source of autonomy, but it becomes a source of constraint if those who need it cannot secure it in order to use it as a resource to enable their cultural projects.

In capitalist societies, markets and artists have always existed in a tense relationship. In an earlier time, Petersburg musicians did not experience that tension precisely because a market for their culture products did not exist. The normal position of the Petersburg musician was to reject money as the basis for cultural production (and as a basis for inclusion within the community of musicians); since Petersburg musicians had no possibility of entering directly into capitalist relations of production, the latter could not affect them or the autonomy of their culture. Ironically, it is the process of capitalist rationalization which is now eroding autonomous cultural practices and the autonomous identities based on those practices. In the Soviet context, rock music was instrumental in forming a community of critical discourse within the context of socialist industrial modernity. It is no longer possible for rock music's identity to remain a pure form of aesthetic expression which embodies a critical existential discourse. The experiences of Petersburg musicians within the new capitalist context are a stark corroboration of the power of capitalism to transform artists into productive laborers and their products into commodities. Indeed, it might be said that capitalism, especially in the anarchic forms in which it has manifested itself in contemporary Russia, possesses the ability to alienate alienation. Yet does this mean that rock music's existence as an art form has been extinguished in the post-Soviet Russian context? The central problem facing Petersburg musicians now—a situation which musicians face in all capitalist countries—is that of maintaining the authenticity of their culture products and their identities as artists in the face of the process of capitalist rationalization.

Lying behind Western capitalist shock therapy is a *telos* which assumes that, sooner or later, the same economic situation which exists in the West will unfold in Russia. Ideally, the process of capitalist rationalization will lead to differentiated culture markets which will provide a space for the expression of all types of music. Given time, the stabilization of the Russian economy and the institutionalization of political and legal guarantees will serve to protect musicians' rights and lead to a situation of cultural freedom in Russia. All culture must be produced, and we know that more of it is produced in capitalist contexts than in socialist ones. Western culture markets are highly differentiated, which allows a greater variety of cultural forms to find audiences and support. Artists can remain autonomous from large-scale culture industries by creating their products for smaller, more specialized markets which allow them more freedom to create what they want to create.

The telos presented above does not take into account the particulars of Russian cultural history and the effects of the latter on present and future cultural outcomes. There is simply no way to know that

even if the same structural arrangements which have led to a varie-
gated culture market in the West are imported into the Russian context that the results will be the same. Ultimately, the idea that Russia
will develop like the West politically and economically if it simply
adopts formal economic practices and institutions is a theory rather
than cold, hard, social-scientific fact. There are simply too many variables—personal, social-structural, and cultural—which might alter the
specific course of post-Soviet social development. We cannot say for
sure what might happen. The only thing we know for sure is what has
happened, and what has happened is that culture producers are increasingly at the mercy of those who control the cultural means of production, that is, the new owners of the new capitalist culture industries in
Russia. There are few, if any, structural niches in Russian society in
which autonomous and independent cultural activity can find
widespread expression. As a result, forms of art such as rock music are
destined to remain in a state of conflict with the dominant political and
economic structures and practices of the society.

Certainly in the West, the market has provided a huge marketplace for cultural goods from which culture producers can support
themselves in their roles and from which consumers can draw for a
variety of uses. In the West, artists are familiar with the logic of the
market; indeed, they are enmeshed in this logic from birth, and it is
deeply ingrained in their cognitive structures. The result is that they
know how to play the market, how to play the capitalist game, how to
find markets for their products, how to adapt their products to meet the
demands of different culture markets, and how to be active participants
in a social system which allows for cultural pluralism, although in many
cases artists have to be quite industrious to be authentically
autonomous and pluralistic. Conventional wisdom assumes that artists
in the "democratizing East" will learn how to play the market just as
artists in the West have (see, for instance, Goldfarb 1992). This may
take the sacrifice of one generation or even two generations of artists,
but sooner or later, so the argument goes, the relationship between
artists and the market will stabilize and the market will drive rather
than inhibit freedom of cultural expression.

The problem with such arguments is that they presume that it is
the market which is primary to culture and toward which the latter
must adjust if it is to have any hope of surviving. Such a view is certainly problematic if one sees culture as an autonomous sphere of communication which is independent of material and political forces and,
perhaps, exerts an influence on the latter. Indeed, Petersburg musicians
have a difficult time understanding why their culture has to articulate

itself to any external social forces, whether they are the product of capitalism or of socialism. Like artists in many contexts, they believe that their art has a value and utility of its own which ought to function independently of its ability to be commercially successful. They are deeply afraid that the value of their culture will be conflated with its value in the cultural marketplace. Their fear is not simply a rhetorical strategy for rationalizing their lack of success in the new marketplace of culture. They really cannot succeed because there is no infrastructure in place which will allow them to do so and they refuse to make the sacrifices which the existing anarchic infrastructure of cultural production demands of them. To do so would be to give up what is most valuable to their identities: artistic autonomy. They find themselves, ironically, in the same situation as they were in the socialist era—without means of support for their independent social roles and with a tendency to define freedom in a highly individualized, personalistic, and existential way. They are obligated to live in a world not of their own making and, because of that, they continue to make a world for themselves.

What kinds of things are Petersburg musicians doing to resist the forces of capitalist rationalization? In the West, the commercialization of music is often seen as the first step in the transformation of rock into pop (see, for example, Frith and Horne 1987). Rock musicians in St. Petersburg recognize this theoretical idea in their own vernacular ways. Sociologist of music Simon Frith (1990, p. 100) has noted that rock musicians in the West sought to distinguish their practices from commercial pop music by drawing on both folk and art values. A similar process seems to be at work in the current Russian environment: a number of Petersburg musicians have sought to preserve their artistic autonomy and integrity by bringing in a national *melos*, an indigenous Russian tradition, into their music.[4] There is an emergent sense of nationalistic pride among many Petersburg rock musicians who believe that, when it comes to folk music, Russians have a special capability. Traditionally, Petersburg musicians consciously kept their musical syntax imitative of Western rock. Increasingly in the post-Soviet context, however, many realize that if their music is to be taken seriously in the West, it has to exhibit something other than a Russian poetic. Some groups have begun to experiment with traditional Russian musical themes and instruments such as the *balalaika* and the *baian* from within the idiom of rock-and-roll. In this effort, producers have often aided them. As Andrei, the underground producer whose thoughts were presented at length in earlier chapters, notes:

> [Traditionally] attempts to introduce the elements of native folklore yielded, as a rule, terrifying results. Yet I spent much time, a

whole year, with the group Nol' (Zero). In my mind, this is one of
the best groups in the country which uses the national melos. . . .
Nol' is an amazing band consisting of a drummer, bass guitarist,
and an accordion player. The vocalist–accordion player sings in a
heart-rending voice and bangs out the rock-n-roll on an accordion
so dashingly that you get lost in admiration. Maybe, Stas Namin
was right when he tried to persuade the correspondents in an
American film *Rock around the Kremlin* that rock stemmed from
Russian *chastushki*. In the West they experimented with accor-
dions, but it is laughable compared to Nol'.

Interestingly, a new view that the traditional folk song known as
the *chastushka* is seen as the real source of all rock-and-roll music exists
among some members of the rock community. Another musician
expressed the opinion, quite seriously, that the Russian language would
soon be a major, worldwide language of rock music. Such nationalistic
pride is understandable within a social context in which Western taste
publics have virtually ceased to be interested in Russian culture and
have turned their backs on that culture and its producers.

Inner Distance, Musical Identity, and the Capitalist Present

In light of the dilemmas of capitalist modernity outlined in this book, it
would be understandable if Petersburg rock musicians expressed a nostalgia for the past and perhaps even a desire to return to an era and a
social system which had, ironically, offered them the opportunity to
find a degree of authentic meaning in existence. Yuri, whose life we
have discussed often in previous chapters, has emerged as probably
the most famous rock musician in Russia. The social organization of
Russian society has presented him with many difficulties, and he barely
survives in spite of his fame. But he clearly admonishes anyone who
expresses a nostalgia for a return to the past. During a collective discussion in 1993 about how much easier music-making was in the 1980s,
Zhenya, a young guitarist, began to wax nostalgic about the old days.
Yuri, Zhenya's elder, sternly admonished him: "Zhenya, we don't need
such nostalgia." Yuri recognizes that the rock *tusovka* was a moment
which should be cherished, but warns that it is not a moment which
those who are disillusioned with the present should seek to reclaim.
What is more important, he recognizes that the new context allows him
to express his individuality for perhaps the first time in his life. Yuri
anticipates what is an essential characteristic of capitalist modernity:
the rise of conditions that enable individuality. Yuri's own words cap-

ture this sense of lament about the loss of the collective feeling of the *tusovka*. He understands the persistently troublesome quality of the new capitalism in Russia. Yet at the same time, he conveys a sense of optimism about the creative possibilities of a new spirit of individualism in musical life. He expresses how the best musicians of the former rock underground meet the challenges of the present and the future:

> *Yuri:* All of those in the underground were just monumental people. Now it's not like this anymore, of course. Now painting, theater, everything is permitted. Then there was only rock-and-roll. But then all the best forces, all the best people I saw in rock-and-roll only, in these *tusovki*. That was a real rock-and-roll, it was just a safety valve. We found it, and the communists could do nothing about it. It was our language. We would gather at night, at somebody's flat. . . . And I'm singing, you know. Those were like last suppers. A bottle of port wine being passed around from person to person—what rock-and-roll it was then! . . . those were the finest (*krutye*) moments in my life. It was ten years ago. And all of us are raised on this, you see.

> *T. C.:* When I returned last year [1992] I felt that the situation has changed a little bit.

> *Yuri:* Yes, now it's changed again.

> *T. C.:* How can I say it—it's like anarchic capitalism.

> *Yuri* [laughing]: Do you know how I call it? Now there is an epoch of mystical capitalism in Russia. I made it up [laughing]. Now things have changed immensely again. But I don't have any nostalgia for the past. I don't know, of course. I remember. But I'm just trying to accept the world as a given. We have a lot to learn from our children. Many people don't understand that. The old people are crying now, "Before, under Brezhnev, it was good. There was everything, salary, money." Nowadays—a young man who is entering the world right now, for him all the problems in today's Russia are a given. And, maybe, he is happy in this world, and he knows how to live here, how to hustle, how to make money, you see. And the world has changed completely. This freedom of expression—you are welcome to do what you want, work in this way, in that way. And I consider this absolutely normal. . . . And this is a colossal problem. The world is changing, and a person is interesting for me, and has been before, and will be in the future. That's why I don't have this dead end of creativity that

everyone's talking about. For me it's just laughable to think about it. If you have an interest in life, in people, who are, in fact, an adornment of life, it's still interesting.

T. C.: That is, one has just to get used to—

Yuri [urgently]: Yes, yes. To seek, to feel. And to make new music, to work, go further, make new programs. So, in this respect I'm an optimist. Of course, rock-and-roll has changed completely. . . . Before, you see, we—all these groups—were being oppressed in the same way. We all were in the same position. We had the same press and were more together. Because all of us were under political press, and this united us somehow. But when the press was gone, very many of us realized that we were all different. And very many have broken away, have got upset, and they're saying that the rock movement is gone in Russia. But I'm glad it happened, because everybody has become an individual. We became free from this engagement with those who are walking beside you.

And I want to feel free. I don't want these collective relations. Of course, everything should be proper, like here, for example [referring to the concert in Berlin where the interview is taking place], but on the other hand, we are so utterly different. But many people felt like they were cut off. They didn't understand that was just another life, another time, that in fact you are solitary. We got so used to this sense of collectivism, we were oppressed together and were kind of brothers, and now—boom!—this one has his own problems, that one has his. And many are complaining. But some freedom of personality is inherent in this. All of us, they say, will die alone. All of us are artists, and an artist is in the first place solitary. And the way to the truth is through silence. It's natural. Therefore I don't like to hang out (*tusovatsia*) now. I don't like the company. I like to be alone, to sit and think, work, and talk to my friends, the artists. Truly speaking, I don't like present rock happenings (*tusovki*). It's all false now. The old spirit is gone, and it all became boring to me. It's all superficial.

I like solitude. That's why after Berlin I'll go to the forest alone, and I'll write. I'll be listening to the music in the forest, and trying to make sense of it. Because as a matter of fact we have to work hard. We lack a lot in relation to the West. But everything is O.K.

Capitalism has come to Russia and has profoundly altered the practice of music-making. Yet it has not extinguished the very spirit which was at the center of the rock vocation: the practice of making music for its own sake as a means of crystallizing and communicating existential truths both to oneself and to others. The question we turn to now concerns the importance of such forms for the construction of a democratic social order in post-Soviet Russia. In what follows we explore the theoretical relationships between capitalism, cultural freedom, and democracy.

Capitalism, Cultural Freedom, and Democracy in Post-Soviet Russia

The case study presented in this book raises a host of questions which are relevant to understanding the prospects for the democratization of Russian society: What is the relationship between capitalist development and cultural expression? Can there be such a thing as autonomous cultural expression which is not influenced and conditioned by outside structures? If aesthetic culture must be produced within formal political or economic structures of authority, what are the consequences for the forms of culture which are produced and for those who produce them? What do we mean when we speak of cultural freedom in a sociological sense? What kinds of social structures enable or disable freedom of cultural expression? What is the relationship between cultural freedom and democracy?

These are lofty and difficult questions, yet they are vitally important to the tasks of a critical-interpretive sociology of post-Soviet culture which seeks to invest its knowledge in the service of constructive and progressive social change. In the face of the more general trials and tribulations facing Russian society, one might ask: How can an understanding of the experience and fate of a small community of musicians in just one Russian city help us to answer these questions? Given the recent turmoil in Russia, the events described in this book might seem irrelevant. Yet the case of the origins and fate of the Petersburg musical community under changing social conditions illustrates the existence of a general tension between freedom of cultural expression and capitalist development in the Russian context. This tension has more to do with the prospects for the democratization of Russian society than initially meets the eye. For a sociological view of democracy focuses not only on formal political processes, but on more fundamental communicative processes which allow actors to develop and share their experiences in the form of a common culture. Democracy depends on cultural freedom; the latter is the very bulwark of a democratic social order. Yet capitalism, as we have seen, intrudes on the process of cultural communication and therefore restricts cultural freedom. An exploration of the prospects for democracy in Russia, then, depends on understanding the complex relations between capitalism, cultural freedom, and democracy. We begin with the idea of cultural freedom.

The Sociological Meaning of Cultural Freedom

The lives we have examined in this book offer us a glimpse of a more fundamental sense of freedom—a highly individuated and existential sense of freedom rooted and forged in historical experience—than the other senses of economic and political freedom which serve as the usual measures of freedom in the Russian context. The freedom of the marketplace or the freedom to vote for the candidate of one's own choosing are the usual standards used to measure the extent of freedom in society. Such senses of freedom seem to have more discursive and rhetorical power in emergent discourse on post-Soviet society, yet they have offered the musicians of St. Petersburg very little. In fact, economic freedom in Russia is now supported by the strong arm of an increasingly authoritarian state. The forces of capitalist rationalization described in the previous pages are likely to accelerate even more, enforced, if necessary, by military power. As a result, the process is likely to threaten the core values and beliefs of the Petersburg musical community—to say nothing of Russian culture more generally—in some ways even more so than the previous political-economic infrastructure which tolerated rock music and counterculture and even provided the free time and space which enabled countercultural practice.

While the breakdown of the Soviet Union and the erosion of the infrastructure of Soviet modernity have been perceived almost inherently as a movement toward freedom, we have seen that there are different senses of freedom in the post-Soviet context. We have excavated powerful senses of existential freedom which had their origins in the condition of Soviet industrial modernity. What is remarkable about all of the life stories of Petersburg musicians is the profound sense of personal freedom which they felt in their own private lives. They constantly sought to translate that individual sense of freedom into cultural practices which would stand as metaphors of cultural freedom. Yet is cultural freedom really possible? The idea of cultural freedom is a relative one. As the epigraph by Karl Mannheim (1950, p. 311) at the beginning of this chapter states: "There is neither freedom nor discipline in the abstract, but only in the concrete forms that depend on the

cultural context." In an important sociological study of cultural freedom in socialist industrial society, Jeffrey Goldfarb (1982, p. 40) defines
cultural freedom as

> . . . the free activity in cultural institutions differentiated and rela-
> tively autonomous from societal power centers in which artists
> react to the contemporary world and are supported in doing
> so. . . . The cultural creator's reaction to the contemporary world in
> the freest work involves a symbolic critique of societal and insti-
> tutional mechanisms of social control and domination. Such free
> work is possible when the creator (either collective or individual)
> avoids being overly influenced in his work by the economic, polit-
> ical, and bureaucratic operations of a cultural institution, and the
> cultural institution as a whole maintains a semblance of auton-
> omy in the face of control by those who benefit from the existing
> order of domination.

Although he does not posit it as such, Goldfarb's conception of
cultural freedom is an ideal-type construct in the sense that it is unimaginable that "pure" conditions for the expression of cultural freedom
could ever be realized in any society. There are only degrees of cultural freedom, and the extent to which cultural freedom exists is dependent on both the presence and the extent of the influence of constraining
social forces on the process of cultural production. To the extent that
social forces impinge on the process of culture production, cultural freedom is limited in the sense that culture products assume forms which
are not solely the products of the intentional creative power of culture
producers.

As much of the sociological work on the production of culture
has demonstrated, the process of cultural expression is inherently limited by the collective nature of cultural production (see, for instance,
Fine 1977, p. 454; and Becker 1982). And while such collective endeavors
are often extremely successful in expanding the boundaries of cultural
expression, such undertakings are themselves subject to the direct and
indirect cultural constraints outside the sphere of culture production. As
Krishan Kumar (1992, pp. 332-33) has noted, forms of consciousness
which reject the outside world and locate reality within the lifeworld
itself are bound to have difficulty in a new social context which
demands participation in the outside world. The cultural logic of capitalism is not a passive force which can be avoided by musicians or other
artists, any more than they could avoid the cultural logic of socialism in
the previous era. Capitalism demands the participation of individuals,

but not always on their own terms. The emergence of a new economic mechanism in the process of cultural production has brought on new types of limitations on the possibilities for autonomous cultural expression and cultural freedom in contemporary Russian society.

Cultural Freedom, the Public Sphere, and Democracy

Proponents of the rapid capitalist rationalization of Russian society believe, almost intuitively, that the application of economic principles will lead to the construction of a democratic social order. In the ideologies of those who guide the process of social reconstruction, capitalism is almost always seen as a positive force which will bring about freedom and democracy. This ideology is not restricted to the Western advocates of rapid economic reform. It now infuses the very core of political power in Russia and has been used already—in the crushing of the Russian Parliament, for instance—to justify the most undemocratic of actions on the part of Russian politicians in the name of democracy and freedom. Seldom in any of the policies or theories which are the driving force behind the capitalist rationalization of Russian society does one find any discussion of the negative or disabling qualities of capitalist modernity.[5] The defining characteristics of Western capitalist societies—money, the pursuit of private gain, private property—are seen as means toward the end of the transformation to a democratic society rather than as forces which actually obstruct the forms of communicative action and cultural expression which are the most important cultural bulwarks of a democratic society.

In these final pages, I would like to rethink the idea of democracy and the relationship between capitalism and democracy from the standpoint of social theory. My starting point in this task is Max Weber. Weber would have been appalled by the course of Soviet historical development, but he also would have cautioned against any euphoria about seeing the expansion of capitalist economic rationality as the mechanism for the advancement of freedom in the modern world. Indeed, while he avoided overt discussions of freedom, his entire life's work was concerned with understanding the relationship between sociohistorical development and freedom (see Levine 1981). A central question of concern for Weber was this: "How are freedom and democracy in the long run possible under the domination of highly developed capitalism?" (Gerth and Mills 1946, p. 71). Our question is: How are freedom and democracy possible under the domination of underdeveloped, anarchic capitalism which we have documented in this book? And beyond that, what are the prospects for freedom and democracy in the long term of Russian history?

Anthony Giddens (1992, p. 185) notes that democratic societies allow individuals to develop and express their "diverse qualities; they serve to protect citizens from arbitrary use of political authority and coercion"; they allow individuals to determine "the conditions of their own association"; and they expand the conditions for economic opportunity. Certainly, the Soviet system was not democratic, for it did not fulfill any of the conditions of Giddens's definition of a democratic society. Yet this is not to say that elements of a democratic culture were not present in the Soviet social context. The experiences and practices that I have described in this book are evidence that the spirit of democracy was alive in St. Petersburg, albeit hidden under the structures of domination of socialist industrial society. Indeed, none other than one of the most prominent Western propagandists, Francis Fukuyama (1993), has argued that such communities represented "proto-typical civil societies" which embodied the very cultural sentiments and values which are at the core of the more formalized civil societies of Western capitalist democracies. The Soviet Union remained undemocratic because the elements of a democratic order were not institutionalized or protected by the state apparatus. They nonetheless existed at an informal level in the culture of elective, moral communities who lived, to use Polish philosopher Adam Michnik's terminology, "as if" the outside world did not exist.[6]

The fate of cultural communities such as that of the St. Petersburg musical counterculture is important to ongoing discussions about democracy in Russia. What goes on in the sphere of culture—and in particular in the sphere of aesthetic culture—is vitally important for constructing and maintaining a democratic social order. According to Jürgen Habermas (1991), the cultural bulwark of a democratic social order is the existence of a vibrant "public sphere." The public sphere is constituted by the free marketplace of ideas in which the validity and utility of ideas is based purely on collective judgments of their utility and truth value. In the Soviet Union, a formal, institutionalized public sphere of culture did not exist; public culture was expressed underground and circulated privately, and because of this it was not really public at all, but quasi-public. What Petersburg musicians wanted more than anything else after they came up from underground was to have their critical discourse become a vibrant part of the Russian public sphere of cultural communication. What is more important, they wanted to contribute to the public sphere on their own terms rather than on the terms set by the sphere of economics or politics.

Yet, as we have seen, the new capitalist structures of Russian society determine, for the most part, which elements of culture will become part of the public sphere of cultural communication. Habermas (1991) has argued that the public sphere in Western societies has progressively eroded under the influence of the political and economic forces of advanced capitalist society. The forms of culture which constitute the public sphere of capitalist industrial society often find their way into that sphere based on financial or political considerations rather than on considerations of their truth value. We might say that the same process is beginning in Russia with the effect that the autonomous development of the Russian public sphere has been compromised before it has even had a chance to get started.

The construction of a democratic society in Russia is predicated on the existence of a public sphere of communication which is independent of the sphere of politics and economics. The freeing of the mass media and the means of cultural production and distribution from the control of the state has not necessarily facilitated the institutionalization of formal channels which guarantee the development of an open and vibrant public sphere in Russian society. The Russian public sphere is now controlled in large part by new culture managers who have monopolized the means of cultural production. The content of the Russian public sphere, a sphere to which the community of Petersburg musicians contributes only a small part, is now constituted by many cultural forms which have been profoundly affected by the logic of capitalist rationality. It is that logic which actually and potentially determines what forms of culture will be produced and distributed into the public sphere of cultural communication. It is in this sense that the cultural logic of capitalism and that of democracy might be said to be antagonistic forces in contemporary Russia.

Sociological Democracy

The ideas of democracy put forth above are a bit different than those which are normally assumed in discussions of democracy in general, and the democratization of Russian society in particular.[7] They are grounded in theoretical understandings of the process of communication and the social forces which enable and constrain that process. I would like to refer to this communicative sense of democracy as "sociological democracy."[8] A sociological democracy is predicated on the existence of a communicative infrastructure which guarantees the possibility of free and open cultural communication among individuals. Such a system of cultural communication contributes to the public sphere of ideas and information which is independent of the logic of the marketplace.[9]

In a world where capitalism is almost always elided with the idea of freedom, a sociological view holds that there are different senses of freedom—cultural, existential, economic, and political—and that freedom of cultural expression does not always follow from freedom in economic or political life. Indeed, as John Dewey (1939) notes, it is freedom of cultural expression which underlies all other types of freedom and, therefore democracy itself. Too often, as Dewey (1939, p. 9) noted, culture—in particular aesthetic expression—is seen as an adornment of democracy rather than an essential precondition for its establishment. Dewey notes (ibid.) that "Works of art once brought into existence are the most compelling of the means of communication by which emotions are stirred and opinions formed . . . emotions and imagination are more important in shaping public sentiment and opinion than information and reason." Dewey, like pragmatists past and present, sees communication as the underpinning of a just and democratic social order. Moreover, he sees vast potential in modernity to provide the communicative means upon which a democratic social order can be based. Habermas (1970), like Dewey, argues that authentic democracy is predicated on the ability of actors to realize a common identity, a "mutuality of understanding" of their similar existential circumstances through the process of communication. Ideally, then, a democratic social order is grounded in the existence of unimpeded channels of communication between members of a particular cultural community. These channels are the means by which actors can communicate their recognition of their common positions in society (their sense of "we-ness") and their relations to the structures of authority which impinge on them (their sense of "they-ness").[10]

A democratic social order is characterized by structural arrangements and institutions which guarantee free and open cultural communication between actors regardless of the content of that communication. Such institutions guarantee that democracy is grounded in (and adapted to, if necessary) the experiences of people who live in society. It is in this way—rooted in the "habits of the heart" of a people—that a democracy is stabilized. The promise of constructing a democratic social order depends not on the importation of Western political or economic structures, but on the protection of local forms of culture and cultural communication from the unbridled force of such structures. Dewey and contemporary critical theorists such as Habermas who have followed his line of thought have argued that capitalist modernity is not equatable with the term *democracy*. However, as Robert Antonio and Douglas Kellner (1992, p. 283) note, Dewey also recognized the dark side of capitalist modernity, in particular, its tendency to produce "rampant commodification, hyperspecialization, and demagoguery." Dewey's insights, transposed to the post-Soviet context, are illuminating: capitalism does not in and of itself make democracy, in fact, it can lead to social outcomes which violate the very spirit of a democratic social order. In one case—that of the Petersburg musical counterculture—we have seen how the process of anarchic capitalism has led to the erosion of the communicative and cultural foundations of a democratic social order.

The task of the social reconstruction of Russian society in a democratic direction, ideally, lies in the preservation of the indigenous culture of moral communities and the broader elaboration of the sentiments and values of that culture as the basis for a new order. Ideally, as Alexis de Tocqueville (1969) brilliantly showed, a viable democratic order rests on the values, norms, and dispositions of those who constitute the *demos* of a particular society. It is often said in the West that Russian culture, broadly conceived, does not contain the seed or the germ upon which an effective democratic order can grow. Yet Russian culture includes forms of counterculture such as the one upon which we have focused in this book. And it is such cultural communities that can contribute their own "habits of the heart" to the construction of a viable democratic order.[11] A viable democracy cannot emerge solely through the importation of political or economic structures: democracy is sustained by culture and, more important, by the communication of culture among the actors who constitute the *demos*. A democratic social order in the post-Soviet context would be one which would draw on the knowledge and experience—the culture—of the various moral communities which existed underground in Soviet society. This is another way of saying that the idea of democracy is an abstraction or a form which ought to be filled with the local knowledge of Russian cultural communities which embody democratic ideals. In this way, the radical, resistant actions of St. Petersburg musical counterculturalists—and indeed, those of all Russians who resisted the project of socialist industrial modernity—would mean something in the present. One thing is clear: the ideas of the West—whether cultural ideas such as democracy or economic ideals such as the free market—cannot be grafted onto Russian society without an active contribution from the culture of those who are destined to live according to those ideas.

We have seen through the rich accounts presented in the previous chapters that rock musicians are quintessential existentialists. They remain counterculturalists in the face of the capitalist juggernaut. They are, in Jean Paul Sartre's sense, *engagés*. As active and resourceful agents, Petersburg counterculturalists are veteran systemic warriors, and if we expect that Russia under capitalism is to become a more humane and democratic place, then we can be confident that Petersburg musical counterculturalists will be at least a small part of making that history. No one gives a society its public sphere, nor is the autonomy of that sphere guaranteed by any one individual, group, or social force. Rather, the public sphere is constructed and protected by those who wish to participate in it according to the dictates of their own consciences as opposed to the dictates of others. Democracy will find expression in Russia only when it is constituted by local forms of culture, by local senses of the sacred, and by the cultural practices which have been forged by Russians in the pursuit of authentic and meaningful vocations.

Appendix 1

Researching Russian Counterculture: Some Reflections on Method

Since I have offered this work as a first step toward a critical-interpretive sociology of Russian culture and society, it is important to offer a brief natural history of the study, some commentary on how it was carried out, some of the problems encountered in the research, and the relevance of the case-study method of social research for advancing knowledge of communist and post-communist societies and cultures. It is my hope that these observations and reflections will be of use to other qualitative and theoretically-minded researchers who wish to pursue any of the virtually infinite number of topics which the Russian past and present have laid before us.

Qualitative Sociological Research in the Russian Setting

The initial difficulty with carrying out this study was the lack of firm tradition of qualitative sociological research on Russian society and culture which could serve as a guideline for my own research. In the United States, sociologists have produced rich qualitative accounts of social life for nearly a century; indeed, the contributions of the Chicago School are at the core of American sociology. The lack of a viable qualitative tradition of sociological research in Russia can be explained, in the first instance, by Soviet politics. Soviet authorities were seldom sanguine about allowing qualitative sociologists to delve into the deeper realities of Soviet social and cultural life. Sociology in general has not enjoyed a happy fate in the Soviet Union (see Shlapentokh 1987; Shalin 1990; and Greenfeld 1988). Mainstream Soviet sociology was "a branch of social technology, a managerial science oriented towards the promotion of the goals and the increase of the ideological and administrative efficiency of the Soviet government" (Greenfeld 1988, p. 99). As such, independent sociological work in the Soviet Union—especially of the critical-interpretive type presented in this book—was always rigidly circumscribed in the Soviet Union. Yet, there were other impediments to carrying out interpretive social research in this context, some of which have their roots closer to home.

In 1990, when I began this study, the prospects for engaging in successful qualitative sociological research in the Soviet Union were still rather unclear. Until 1990, some Western anthropologists had been able to gain access to cultural communities, mostly to those of traditional peoples of the Soviet Far East (see, for instance, Humphrey 1983). Yet, in general, there was still some hesitancy and even pessimism within the Western Sovietological community about the possibility of doing qualitative and interpretive research in the Soviet context. In 1989, when I first proposed the idea for participant-observation research on aspects of Russian society to certain colleagues in Soviet studies, their responses seemed to fall into one of two categories. First, I was told that it would be impossible in this context because the authorities would not let me do the research, or if they did they would not let me take my data out of the country. Second, I was told that even if I did get to talk to Russians, they would not tell me the truth. Many Western researchers were reticent to accept the realities of cultural pluralism which were the result of glasnost (elsewhere, I have tried to explain this reticence partly as a function of deeply held myths about the "evil" nature of Soviet society which pervaded Western Sovietology [see Cushman 1995]). Even as late as 1989, these myths were still pervasive and served to keep many scholars from understanding that glasnost was a reality. Even more disturbing to me was the implication that Russian subjects were somehow more duplicitous than subjects in other contexts.

In contrast to what conventional wisdom predicted, the research situation in St. Petersburg in 1990 was extremely conducive to the use of interpretive methods of social research. In contrast to hesitant, lying subjects, I found people who were, at first, a bit suspicious of an American sociologist proclaiming that he was in town to write a book about Russian rock culture, but who later opened up in unimaginable ways to offer me glimpses into their lifeworlds. Most of the people whom I encountered plied me with more sociological information than I could possibly hope to assimilate. Some called me at home to tell me whom I should meet or to tell me that there was something important that they had forgotten to mention during the previous day's interview. One informant attached himself to me very early on with the promise that he was going to help me "make a very fat book," a promise that was fulfilled beyond either of our expectations. Also, not once in the course of any aspect of this research was I ever interrogated, harassed, or otherwise obstructed by any Soviet official agency or individual.

My sense of the discrepancy between what many felt could be done and what I was actually able to do caused me to rethink the limitations of working too closely within the dominant epistemological and ontological frameworks which guide Western research on the Soviet Union. This was more so the case as I became aware of the resistant and anti-establishment stance of the people whom I was studying. I came to see that studies of "outsiders," marginal figures, and groups must proceed at a certain distance from modes of social science which are fundamentally connected to official structures of administration and political domination (see, for instance, Becker 1963). This is especially the case when the researcher seeks to offer a critical interrogation of such structures.

The research presented here was carried out at some distance from conventional, establishment Russian sociology. My approach is critical of developments in Russian society as well as the dominant forms of social science which purport to offer us some absolute Truth about those developments. My perspective is greatly influenced by Horkheimer's (1972) classic statement of the aims of critical theory and his critique of the political proclivities of positivism. In this respect, this book offers an independent interpretation of independent cultural expression in the Soviet Union. It is the product of methods of research and theoretical perspectives which have not generally appeared in the discourse on the Soviet and Russian Other.

Moreover, my work self-consciously seeks to be independent of the methodological and theoretical perspectives from disciplines such as political science or history which predominate Western studies of Russia and the Soviet Union more generally. For reasons too complex to discuss here, sociologists have been quite marginal within the field of Soviet studies as that field has developed in the United States since World War II. In fact, the social scientific stock of knowledge about the Soviet Union has been produced almost exclusively by historians and political scientists. As such, the character of knowledge about the Soviet Union is decisively inflected with the epistemological and ontological orientations of history and political science. This is not to say that sociologists have had no place in the development of knowledge about the Soviet Union. Nor is it to say that historical knowledge or knowledge of politics is not important to sociology; indeed, the account which I present here depends on a fundamental understanding of the interrelations between Soviet history, politics, and culture. Yet sociologists working in this field have seldom had the chance to gather data using the rich methods of their discipline and, as such, they have not been able to inflect the dominant intellectual discourse on Russia and the Soviet Union with the rich data produced from qualitative research and the insights of sociological theory.

The Techniques of Interpretive Research:
Life-History Analysis, Open-Ended Interviewing,
and Thick Description

Through the course of the study, roughly from 1990 until 1993, I engaged in intensive participant-observation of the St. Petersburg musical community. My research consisted of two separate trips to Russia, one in 1990 before the dissolution of the Soviet Union, and one in 1992 after the breakup of the country. These trips allowed me to study musical practice *in situ*, and an additional trip to Berlin in 1993 allowed me to observe Petersburg musicians' experiences with capitalist culture markets abroad. My participant-observation of the musical community drew primarily on three methods of interpretive social research: life-history analysis, open-ended interviewing, and ethnographic thick description. The products of each of these methods can be seen at various points throughout the book.

While a good deal of time was spent simply hanging out with musicians, I formally interviewed a total of forty people who identified themselves as members of the Petersburg musical community. I also interviewed a number of individuals who were not directly involved in the musical community, but who shed light on its history or who affected in one way or another the practice of rock music in Russia. The sample of musicians was developed through the use of the technique of snowball sampling (to be discussed in detail below). Quite often, the novelty of my presence made musicians more comfortable with the idea of being interviewed in groups; even in 1990 many felt that there was safety in numbers. Interestingly, it was these group interviews which facilitated the telling of the stories which bound the members of the rock community together and provided them with the consciousness of their kind. In this respect, I am aware that my research efforts actually enabled and perhaps even altered the dynamics of sociation and community which it was my intention to study.

My research strategy after these group interviews was to select the individual or individuals whom I thought could best illuminate the experiences and attitudes of a variety of members of the musical community. Based on initial interviews, I selected ten members of the musical community as the focus of more intense and detailed investigation. These individuals were selected because they represented a broad range of ages, roles, and statuses within the musical community. In these ten cases, I asked individuals to elaborate the stories of their lives, what led them to choose rock music as a vocation, what music meant to them, how their music was related to the more general conduct of their lives, and their experiences with the social forces operating within their society. To as great an extent as possible, these life histories were elaborated in the words of members of the musical community themselves. Norman Denzin's (1989a, 1989b) work on life history, biography, and interpretation (what he labels broadly "interpretive interactionism") stresses the importance of letting subjects speak in their own words. He points out the dangers of "sociological glossing" which occurs when researchers inject too much interpretation into their interpretive research. Instead, Denzin argues that the researcher must let subjects speak as much as possible in their own words, and I was guided by this principle throughout my research.

The total number of life histories collected was rather small, but this number was more than counteracted by the detail which members of the musical community provided about their lives. This is in keeping with the method of life-history analysis which stresses the depth and quality of data rather than the quantity (Denzin 1989b). It was also necessary because of the small size of the rock community and the impossibility of locating all of its members and attempting some kind of systematic sampling strategy. Some of the life histories were more truncated than others; in some cases, the method simply did not work since many musicians felt that their music spoke for itself. In other cases, however, musicians' ruminations on their lives were quite prolonged, sometimes taking up the better part of a morning or an afternoon and, in some cases, days. It is important to stress that most of the people whose histories are presented in this book were expert storytellers, able to embody the central experiences and epiphanies of their lives with great eloquence. Indeed, I believe future research ought to explore the fascinating narrative conventions of this community and others in the Russian social environment.

These ten individuals provided the core life histories from which subsequent research questions were developed and articulated. The life histories collected in St. Petersburg represent the central starting point which grounded further open-ended questions about musical life and countercultural life more generally. Not all of these life histories appear in the text of the book; in some cases I have presented complete life histories exactly as they were told to me. In other cases, I have selected elements of those histories which illuminate the more general issues of the study which were then explored through additional open-ended interviewing. In chapter 1, as a way of orienting the reader to the scope of the study, I presented the central questions asked of members of the musical community. These questions were firmly grounded in the life histories of musicians as those histories were related to me in their own words and in their local settings. These life histories and answers to more pointed but open-ended questions were taped. All of my dialogues with members of the Petersburg musical community, except one, were carried out in Russian. These interviews were then transcribed and, in segments which appear in this book, translated into English.

In addition to life-history analysis and open-ended interviewing, I relied on the ethnographic technique of "thick description" (Geertz 1973) to frame the lives and activities of members of the Petersburg musical community. Thick description "attempts to rescue the meanings and experiences that have occurred in the field situation" (Denzin 1989a, p. 31). In cases where it was impossible to capture peoples' own experiences—as, for instance, in describing the "taking of the bridge" in chapter 4—I have provided my own descriptions and interpretations of various events which I encountered. The words of people themselves are at the core of an interpretive sociology, but often in the stories which are told the context which gives meaning to words and actions is not provided. I have been greatly influenced by Clifford Geertz's (1973) powerful analysis of a Balinese cockfight which provides a truly insightful interpretation into the meaning of this practice without much recourse to the thoughts and ideas of the participants. Certainly, the words of participants in the cockfight might have made Geertz's interpretation stronger (or perhaps weaker). Yet his structuralist reading of this practice did much to illuminate the deeper meanings of play which he observed in this social context. In various chapters, my approach belies a certain affinity for semiotic and structuralist approaches. I believe that such approaches are not inconsistent with one which stresses the presentation of the lives and thoughts in the words of those who are studied. The words of members of the musical community and the words which I use to describe and interpret their lives are meant to work in tandem to illuminate the world of the Petersburg musical counterculture. I shall leave it to postmodern social theorists to determine whether my ethnographic descriptions and theoretical interpretations are "glosses" or "acts of colonization." I see them as central to the tasks of interpretive sociology.

Finally, a word is in order as to the part which the analysis of rock lyrics and other texts played in this study. In choosing to emphasize musicians themselves as the unit of analysis for this study, I do not mean to infer that other methods of cultural analysis, such as textual analyses of songs or surveys of consumers of musical culture, are not important. Nor does this mean that secondary printed sources are not important. Many studies of rock music in communist societies have relied on an approach which stresses the exegesis of rock lyrics (see, for instance, Kataev 1987; Ramet and Zamascikov 1990; and Kurti 1991). Such approaches represent a literary or textual approach to culture rather than a sociological one. The examination of rock lyrics as the embodiment and reflection of resistant consciousness is an important part of the more general cultural analysis of rock musical counterculture. Yet the interpretation of rock lyrics must occur within a more general approach which gives primacy to the actual experiences of musicians themselves. I have used rock lyrics to illuminate particular states of mind educed from interviewing and life histories. I have also drawn on lyrics when it was impossible to gain access to the lifeworlds of key figures in the Petersburg rock community. Invariably, in a study of this kind, such access is not always possible, and in such cases, the analysis of rock lyrics serves to illustrate points about the meaning and significance of rock music within the Russian social context. Finally, at various points in the book, I have used documents from underground rock sources which illuminate some of the particulars of the history of the rock community and the meaning of rock music within that community.

On Naming Names of People and Places

In my elaboration of the story of the St. Petersburg musical counterculture, I have not engaged in the historian's habit of "naming names." Rather, following Georg Simmel, I have chosen instead to view members of the rock community as social types (1971, pp. 143 ff). What is most intriguing about viewing actors as social types is that it allows the reader to recognize the familiar in what is, at first glance, rather foreign or strange. Most readers of this book will know little about Russian rock music or musicians. Yet readers will come to recognize that, in a formal sociological sense, rock musicians in St. Petersburg are very similar to those in the West. There are, of course, fundamental differences, and these differences have a great deal to do with the local meanings which rock music has in Russia, meanings which are quite different than in the West. Simmel's notion of social types demonstrates both the universality of "typical" cultural responses to the world and the individuality which lies behind such responses. It is for this reason that the notion is useful for providing a sociological understanding of rock practice in St. Petersburg. There is something timeless about musicians and their relation to other elements of the social world. The personae and activities of Petersburg musicians reflect a more fundamental, formal relationship between musicians and society which exists across social time and space. The vignettes presented in this book illustrate the consciousness of the different types of individuals from the St. Petersburg musical community at different points in time. Readers who are unfamiliar with Russian rock culture, but more familiar with Western rock culture, will see how elements of Russian rock culture are similar to or different from those Western forms of rock music and counterculture with which they are more familiar.

As much as possible, I have tried to protect the anonymity of the people whose accounts and experiences are found in this book. In most research on the Soviet Union, especially that of historians, names and places are freely offered. In fact, the end of most historical analyses of Russia seems to be—consciously or unconsciously—the elaboration of a cartography of personalities and individual actions and motivations. The normal stance of the sociologist is to protect the identity of both the place of study and the people who are studied. Masking the identity of subjects might seem strange to the Soviet historian. Yet to the sociologist, it is an important strategy for offering an account of social and cultural processes and general experiences which are neither reducible nor unique to specific personalities. This is a book about practices and the types of people who produce them. In some cases, preserving anonymity has been rather easy. In other cases, however, it is difficult, because the identities of specific musicians will be readily discernible either from descriptions of their lives or of their music. Some of the musicians in this study are the most famous in the country, and it is neither desirable nor feasible to hide their identities. Indeed, what makes them so sociologically interesting is the fact that they were known by millions of people in spite of that fact that they were denied access to widespread means of production and dissemination of their cultural work.

While some sociologists have taken great pains to protect even the identity of the cities or organizations in which they work (see, for instance, Lynd and Lynd 1956; Warner 1963; and Caplow et al. 1982), I have found this impossible to do in the present study. The story in this book is based on life in the city of St. Petersburg, and the meaning of this story is entirely dependent on an understanding of the centrality and uniqueness of this city in Russian cultural life. It is impossible to hide the identities of various musical organizations within the city. It is hard for Westerners to understand just how small the world of Russian rock culture is. While this small world is becoming larger and more complex, in earlier days members of the rock subculture were a tightly knit group. Each participant in the rock counterculture was intimately aware of the others' cultural activities, individual feelings, and thoughts. During the socialist period, most of the activities of the rock community were centralized in the Leningrad Rock Club; indeed, it might be said that the Rock Club had a monopoly on the organization of countercultural life in the city. During the Soviet period, there was only one rock club of this stature in the city, and, as some musicians would argue, there was only one rock club like the Leningrad Rock Club in the entire Soviet Union. Its identity cannot be hidden.

This is not to say that I present information which might lead to the identity of some figures in the world of Russian rock without some trepidation. For those who study communist or post-communist societies, the weight of dead generations hangs heavily over our fieldwork, casting its shadow over what we do in the field and what we write after it. There is always the fear that the present situation in Russia may change radically and that things may fall apart. If that were to happen, this very text might jeopardize the safety of those whose identity can be gleaned from the pages. Rock musicians are favorite targets of conservatives, foreign and domestic. I am aware of this danger, but comforted by the fact that the people whose thoughts I present in these pages continually belayed my concerns about hiding their identities; most of my subjects would have none of it. This book is about people who have chosen to express themselves as they please through a highly public, expressive, and often confrontational idiom. Many of them are famous, and some of them have suffered trials and tribulations because of that fame. Yet in no case did any of the more famous musicians whose accounts appear here ever hide from the consequences of their activities.

During the second period of my fieldwork in Petersburg in 1992, the country was racked by rampant inflation, increasing crime, and high levels of social discontent. On the eve of my departure, I expressed fears about a possible right-wing coup by Russian nationalists (former communists I was, and still am, rather unconcerned about). Those whom I interviewed in these last days in the city were quintessential antipoliticians who took a definitive *que será será* attitude on the consequences of such a coup. When I expressed fear for what might happen to them, they simply said that if it happens again, "We'll simply go to the public square and start playing loudly just like we did last time." This attitude expresses the commitment to public expression on the part of Petersburg musicians and testifies to the undesirability of keeping them anonymous. Those whose stories are the richest and most interesting sociologically have never been afraid of the consequences of their expressive activity.

Encounters with the Russian Subject

While access to the field is of fundamental importance, access to the subjectivities within that field, as in all ethnographic studies, is also vitally important. Access to the Soviet subject is conditioned by two interacting and mutually reinforcing factors:

1. the historically conditioned social distance between the Soviet subject and outsiders, especially those from societies considered by official sources of authority to be enemies of the Soviet Union. This distance was reinforced by concrete laws emanating from the Communist Party which proscribed interactions of Soviet citizens with foreigners; and
2. the more general, universal problem of outsider status encountered by researchers in a variety of social contexts across time and space and especially in regard to approaching countercultural social types.

Since there were very few precedents to guide the process of qualitative research in the Soviet setting, my research design took into account both the traditional problems of interaction between researcher and subject and the particulars of the Soviet social context. One of the major problems with the method of snowball sampling is gaining entrance into the population under study. As most ethnographers know, the first contact is extremely important, since if this contact is spoiled, the success of the entire project is, in effect, spoiled as well. As underground musicians who had a history of confrontation with the Soviet state, most of the subjects who interested me were, either by their own account or by the accounts of others, considered to be members of the Petersburg musical counterculture.

Following normal ethnographic procedures for initial encounters between researchers and subjects, I reasoned that if I could get close to and build trust with one member of the community I could then branch out within that community to secure additional contacts. Yet my status as an outsider was a potentially serious impediment since the Petersburg musical community was characterized by a number of norms and procedures which made it difficult for outsiders to gain entrance. The difficulties which I expected were based on my own presuppositions about the perceptions of me which Petersburg musicians were likely to have. Among the perceptions which I felt would inhibit my ability to make initial contact were the following:

1. my status as a sociologist. Given sociology's close affiliation with official political structures, the word *sociologist* in the Soviet Union

conjured up many images of the official bureaucrat collecting information about the private attitudes and affairs of citizens which would be put into service by political officials. In this sense, it was reasonable to expect that the Petersburg musician would see the sociologist as a metaphor for the forces of social domination which were the very wellspring of countercultural sentiments and practices in the Soviet context;

2. my status as a nonmusician. Since the object of my research was to gain the trust and confidence of popular musicians in order to elicit their life histories, the fact that in my own social context I was not a practicing, professional musician might be an impediment to gaining the trust of those whose identities were tied to playing that role in the Soviet context. Moreover, my appearance as a professor did not indicate that I shared counterculturalists' particular semiotic tastes for alternative styles such as earrings, long hair, shabby clothes, and any other style or fashion which grated at what the official world would consider appropriate adornment of the body; and

3. my status as a foreigner. Much has been written about the supposed xenophobia of Russians. This xenophobia was held to be a product of survival under conditions of harsh totalitarian rule which impeded every aspect of social life, including interpersonal relations. Fieldworkers in most contexts can expect some resistance based on their alterity and the fact that in many cultures socializing with outsiders is considered an extraordinary and even deviant form of behavior in everyday life. In the Soviet Union there were laws restricting contact with foreigners. The sometimes harsh penalties for such contact no doubt had major ramifications for attempts to interact with Soviet citizens even at the most superficial level, never mind at the level of getting close enough to educe intimate life histories and carry out extended, open-ended interviews.

These three methodological assumptions guided my pre-field strategizing about the possibilities for effective contact and the ultimate success of my study. They created a feeling of anxiety, since as most field researchers understand, there is a critical moment at which a study can either be a tremendous success or a dismal failure, depending on the researcher's ability to offer an appropriate presentation of self. As William B. Shaffir (1991, p. 73) notes, "Successful entry to the research setting, and securing requisite cooperation to proceed with the study, depend less on the execution of any scientific canons of research than upon the researcher's ability to engage in sociable behavior that respects the cultural world of his or her hosts." In the Soviet context this respect entailed the construction of a "field identity" which would respect the cultural conventions of the community, which would not be overtly duplicitous, and which would lead to successful interpretive research in a difficult setting.

The problem of being a sociologist was easily solved. My initial contact involved simply showing up at the club and introducing myself to the first person whom I encountered as an American who was collecting information to write a book on the contemporary popular music scene in Leningrad. In my presentation, I was extremely concerned not to use the word *sociologist* and compensated for this duplicity by stressing the truthful statement that I was collecting information in order to write a book on recent developments in popular music in the Soviet Union. As the study proceeded and I increasingly gained the trust of the countercultural community, I slowly debriefed them by admitting that I was in fact a sociologist. In doing this, I took great pains to stress that I did not fit their stereotypical image of the Soviet sociologist as an accomplice of the Communist Party which had traditionally sought information in order to control and socialize the "wayward" and "antisocial" Soviet youth (see, for example, Arshavskii and Vilks 1991). Upon my initial introduction, I was quickly introduced to the president of the club and his staff and was informed that if there was anything he or his staff could do to help I should just ask. The president also invited me to come to a concert to be held in the courtyard of the Rock Club that evening. At the concert, I was introduced to the manager of foreign affairs of the Rock Club, who offered me any help possible in my endeavors and proved to be my most essential informant during my research stay. From that point on, the problem of access was solved, although throughout the course of the study I had to be very careful about stressing my identity as professor, sociologist, or representative of any other role considered to be part of an official institutional structure.

The second problem—that of being a nonmusician and not having the appearance of a counterculturalist—was solved rather simply by making sure that my demeanor was in keeping with how a member of the counterculture might be expected to behave. A similar strategy is followed by most field researchers and is an essential part of qualitative research. A recent example of the importance of identity management through style is provided by Mitchell (1991) who assumed the identity and style of mountain climbers in order to build trust within this community. In contrast to the detached scientific sociologist who, by his or her very demeanor attempts to distance himself or herself from the subject, the ethnographer must ultimately take on the appearance and demeanor of those whom he or she wishes to study. This was perhaps even more the case in the Soviet Union, where first impressions and encounters were so important to the success or failure of future interactions (Shlapentokh 1984, 1989). While the researcher's aim is to convince the subject of the researcher's sincere intent, this act is not simply a cynical Goffmanesque performance put on for the sake of carrying out a study. In fact, the construction of a new identity is extremely important in providing the conditions for "surrender" necessary for the researcher to "catch" the lived experiences of his subjects; without such an identity the researcher cannot possibly hope to catch the subjective experience of the other that is so central to interpretive sociology (Wolff 1976). Moreover, in the course of this process, the researcher often uncovers previously hidden aspects of his or her own identity and is thus transformed. I, myself, am more of a counterculturalist now than I was before I embarked on this study.

There are two other variables which proved to be of importance in the study of rock musicians in the Soviet context: age and gender. My relatively youthful appearance and male gender proved to be a great asset in the Soviet context. My experience shores up the vital importance of two variables related to the success of field researchers working on Russian counterculture: the youth and gender of the researcher. My age—which was 29 when I began the study—was important, since most members of countercultures (especially in the Soviet context) were characterized by an essential distrust of all members of the "older generation" (and not just officials). In fact, the very basis for the elective affiliation of members of a given subculture or counterculture is often a shared distrust of adults (see, for instance, Willis 1977). This was also the case with older members of the rock community, since even in their status as members of the older generation of counterculture, they retained a youthful sense of distrust for other, more conventional members of their generation.

Gender was also extremely important in the Soviet context. While most members of the countercultural community saw themselves as progressive sources for cultural and social change, their attitudes toward women were often decidedly conventional. These attitudes were explored in chapter 4. I feel it would have been exceedingly difficult for a female researcher to have been taken seriously in this male-dominated cultural community. By way of summarizing the important effects of age and gender on the research process, it might be said that it would be impossible for men of a certain age or women of any age to approach the Soviet countercultural subject with a great deal of success.

The final factor, the foreigner factor, is perhaps the most important since what I ultimately found to be the case dispels many of the conventional wisdoms and methodological assumptions which have guided Western scholars' approaches to the Soviet and Russian Other. As most sociological researchers approach elites, they assume, many times quite rightly, that the status differentials involved will preclude effective contact and the generation of valid and reliable data. I myself worked under the assumptions about fame which were conditioned by the meaning of fame in American society. My reasoning was that since the people with whom I wished to work were often quite famous, they would not be willing to speak freely with me even if I downplayed my status as a sociologist and showed awareness and respect for their countercultural lifestyle. What I discovered, however, is that my own local assumptions about how members of this community might behave toward me impeded my initial efforts at successful contact.

In Western contexts, famous musicians are generally rewarded with great wealth that serves to increase the social distance between them and the public that consumes their music. In the Soviet context, however, the situation was precisely the opposite: rock musicians were considered deviant in "normal" society and were often negatively sanctioned, both by representatives of officialdom and by members of older generations in the public at large. While there was great social distance between the more prominent musicians and their fans, the former were extremely accessible to their fans, much more so than their counterparts in the West who are shielded behind phalanxes of money and agents. This accessibility extended to me as well. My status as American proved to be of advantage in securing contact with members of the rock community. I discovered this when I approached a rather prominent young musician and simply asked him if I could talk to him about his life and music. Working within my ethnocentric assumptions as to how I would expect a young American musician to respond, I thought he would be reticent. On the contrary. He was flattered that I, an American writer, would want to talk to him, and he proceeded to offer me a detailed account of his life and his views on music.

American status, then, was a distinct advantage in facilitating effective research interactions in this setting. Yet such status is a two-edged sword. In a society which is currently undergoing a severe economic crisis, Americans—and Westerners in general—are symbols for affluence. As such, Americans run the risk of becoming prey for those who are desperately seeking a way out of their rather tortuous economic and political malaise. As in many research situations in which the people studied are relatively deprived, the participant-observer is subject to the possibility of becoming a means to some end(s) for members of the cultural community. This was apparent in the Soviet case and was magnified by the exceedingly difficult circumstances under which Russians lived during the era of perestroika and afterward. In the first case, during my research in Leningrad there were severe shortages of food, cigarettes, and alcohol. With my supply of hard currency and access to stores with ready supplies of cigarettes and alcohol sold for hard currency only, I had to be wary of the possibility that my contacts were interested in giving me the type of information that I wanted in exchange for the goods I could provide.

More important, the changes in Russian society after the dissolution of the Soviet Union have placed a new set of economic constraints on culture producers. In chapters 5 and 6, I outlined in detail the ways in which the process of capitalist rationalization produced conditions of stark economic privation among members of the former rock underground. The ability of Soviet musicians to maintain their principle identity as musicians was increasingly determined by their ability to secure the conditions of their own economic sustenance. A major strategy for self-survival was to travel to Europe to play concerts for hard currency which could then be brought back to the Soviet Union and exchanged for rubles on the black market. As a Westerner, I was often seen as a major potential link between Soviet musicians and opportunities to play concerts in the United States. Many musicians saw me as a rock fellow traveler and hoped that I would assume the status of concert promoter rather than sociologist. One prominent producer from the former rock underground commented sardonically: "I wonder why there is money in the West for sociological research on rock music, but no money to help support rock music." At one point, a frustrated musician simply urged me to forget about my research and concentrate instead on organizing a major festival of Russian rock music in the United States. At times, questions were raised as to whose side I was on. One frustrated musician told me that he and his group had trouble understanding whether I was "a sociologist or a 'rock-n-roll man' (*rok n rol'nyi chelovek*)." He had trouble understanding me when I told him that I felt I could be both. Such tensions were ironic since the trust which enabled my fieldwork came at the cost of having to guard continually against becoming something I was not, namely, a sponsor or manager of Petersburg rock groups.

While this experience is perhaps unique to the people with whom I worked, it is important to point out that researchers in present-day Russia are likely to find themselves preyed upon by actors who are living under extreme conditions of economic deprivation. As Mitchell

(1991, p. 102) points out, the researcher may feel that he or she has built an affective base with subjects which provides him or her with a source of reliable and authentic information: "Fieldworkers must remain aware that the apparent cooperativeness of subjects may be in fact intentional, self-serving efforts to warrant a continued supply of such goods and services as the researcher is able to provide." As such, in the Soviet context, the ethnographic researcher must continually be aware that while he or she is involved in the dreamy bliss of surrendering in order to catch experience, his or her subjects may be more concerned with a this-worldly, rational approach to solving the problems of their existence. Ironically, this was even the case among counterculturalists who had been forced by capitalist shock therapy to abandon their sometimes sheltered and ethereal existence.

The Virtues of a Case-Study Approach

The case-study approach used in this book has a number of advantages for the type of critical-interpretive sociology which I proposed as a model for the sociology of culture in the first chapter. Joe Feagin et al. (1991, pp. 6-7) outline four distinct benefits of a case-study approach in social science:

1. it allows the researcher to "ground" his or her concepts in a natural setting and ensures that these concepts reflect local meanings assigned to phenomena by actors themselves;
2. it permits a "more holistic study of complex social networks and of complexes of social action and social meanings" over time;
3. it enables the researcher to "examine continuity and change in lifeworld patterns" over time; and
4. it "encourages and facilitates, in practice, theoretical innovation and generalization."

The use of the case study in this book allowed me to delve deeply into the lifeworlds of a selected number of individuals and track their experiences over time in two different periods. Indeed, the longitudinal dimension of this study—to understand the changing experiences of musicians in two different periods of Russian history, one socialist and one capitalist—was greatly enabled by the use of the case-study method. Using this method, I was able to capture one sense of existence and the meaning of music as the latter unfolded within the epoch of socialist industrial modernity and then trace changes in the lifeworld experiences of those same members as a new epoch of capitalism unfolds in present-day Russia. Moreover, it was through the intense interaction with select individuals in this community that I was able to ground the theories and concepts which are elucidated here in the life-world experiences of musicians themselves. I went to the field armed with many ideas and concepts which were deduced from outside the lifeworlds of musicians themselves. After only a very short while, I came to understand that these concepts and ideas were foreign to the very same people whose lives I was attempting to study. As is evident throughout this book, the local meanings of rock music are a fundamental aspect of this study, and it was only through intensive interaction within the locale of St. Petersburg that I was able to extract these local meanings. Finally, what might be called the "closeness to subjects" which the case-study approach affords allows one to be theoretically innovative. As Feagin et al. (1991, p. 13) note, the case-study approach in sociology has been crucial for generating new ideas and concepts in social science. The theoretical framework presented in chapter 1 serves as a starting point for the development of the sociological analysis of Soviet and post-Soviet-type societies and cultures. This theoretical strategy and its application to the empirical findings of the book are subject to reworking, revision, and extension.

While questions of reliability and validity will always hedge about the use of the case-study method, it is my hope that other sociologists will study other sites for the production of culture and meaning both in Russia and in other post-communist societies and compare them with the findings presented here. Clearly, the biggest criticism of a case-study approach is the degree to which the findings can be generalized. It is my belief that the experiences of St. Petersburg musicians embody the basic experiences of other culture producers in Russia and in post-communist societies more generally. Time and time again, I was told by painters, photographers, writers, and other artists in Russia that they experienced exactly the same kinds of problems outlined in this book. Ultimately, more case studies will have to be carried out to see how different types of culture producers and cultural products are affected by the ongoing process of rapid capitalist rationalization. Such case-by-case efforts can contribute greatly to our understanding of the complex intersection between culture and social structure in post-communist societies and cultures.

Appendix 2

The Structure and the Intonation of Rock Songs and Songs by VIAs

Tables 1 and 2 present a summary and comparison of the musical intonation and lyrical content of the songs of independent rock musicians and those that were played by Soviet VIAs. These tables are presented in Kataev (1987, p. 79). Kataev analyzed 201 songs from independent rock groups and 100 songs from VIAs. The songs were from the following groups:

Rock Groups

1. Mashina Vremeni (Time Machine)
2. Dinamik
3. Karnaval (Carnival)
4. Alians (Alliance)
5. Akvarium (Aquarium)
6. DDT
7. Hulliver (Gulliver)
8. Zdorovie (Health)
9. Turneps
10. Alisa
11. Telefon (Telephone)
12. Strannye Igry (Strange Games)
13. Proba 1000 (Probe 1000)
14. Kruiz (Cruise)
15. Picnic
16. Dialog
17. Zoopark (Zoo)
18. Nochnoi Prospekt (Night Avenue)
19. Primus
20. Dilizhans (Stagecoach)

VIAs

1. Krasniye Maki (Red Poppies)
2. Samotsvety (Gems)
3. Verasy
4. Ariel
5. Zdravstvui, Pesnia (How Do You Do/Hello, Song)
6. Siniaia Ptitsa (Blue Bird)
7. Records by Composers:
   • A. Derbenev
   • V. Kharitonov
   • V. Dobrynin

TABLE 1
Intonational Structure of Youth Songs
(% of songs within each style)

Intonation	Rock	VIA
Effusive (fervent, ardent)	19	46
Lyrical	11	30
Ironical	28	2
• in the sense of:		
unmasking accusatory irony	12	0
irony with a positive, ideal image	7	2
Contemplative-analytical	16	4
Asthenic[1]	10	16
Serious-anxious	15	2
• in the sense of:		
with very pronounced pathos	7	2
prophetic-accusatory	4	0
edifying-preaching	4	0
Neutral-narrative	2	1

[1] This is a medical term (*astenicheskaia*) used to describe a person who is weak, enervated, or suffering from malaise.

TABLE 2
The Structure of the Contents of Youth Song
(% of songs in each category)

Themes of Songs	Rock	VIA
Social-moral themes	45	4
•including:		
moral choice, ethical values	17	1
ethical parables and preaching	20	3
Social-psychological themes	25	5
•including:		
problems of socialization	4	1
socio-psychological portraits,		
character of people	2	2
expression of mood, feelings	11	2
scenes from the life of young people	8	0
Social themes	10	4
•including:		
anti-war songs	5	1
ecological issues	4	2
Themes of love, relationship between		
man and woman	18	76
Themes of music and dance	6	5
Sports	2	2
Themes about children	0	4

Glossary

The following words are taken from the argot of Petersburg musicians. They are the words most commonly encountered in the course of my research and reflect a slang used more generally in Russia. This is by no means an exhaustive list. Entries marked with an asterisk include translations from a glossary of Russian slang which appears in Zapesotskii and Fain (1990).

bitloman; bitly; bitlovsky: a fan of the Beatles; the Beatles; anything related to the Beatles.

bliad': obscene interjection, particle. Used most often as an interjection but also as a noun which means literally, "slut." This word is considered extremely obscene, yet appears quite commonly in the everyday speech of musicians, especially when the speaker is angry or excited.

butleg: bootleg, illegal, pirate recording.

chukcha: a derogatory reference to the Chuchki, a people of northern Siberia. This term corresponds to the English expression "monkey see, monkey do." In Russian, used to convey the idea of a person who simplistically sees something and does exactly what he sees. Generally used to describe overt and unimaginative imitation in music.

clichka: nickname. Unlike in Western rock music, Russian musicians seldom have nicknames (with the exception of punks who almost always have them).

derymo: shit. Often applied either to social conditions or to popular, commercial music.

draiv: one of the most important evaluative criteria of authentic rock. It is that which makes rock good and which makes it, most important, a form of oppositional noise in the context of the dull static of Soviet modernity.

dushilovo: a neologism made up of a neuter, nominative form from the verb *dushit'*, to strangle or smother. Used in colloquial speech to describe the press of external affairs on the activities of musicians (see entry for *press* below).

figa; po figu: a term of derision, signifying noncompliance or severe disagreement.

gad; gadost': slimeball, reptile (of a person), sliminess.

gastrol'; gastroly: tour; tours.

govno: shit.

imadzh: image, or a group's definition of the way it wants to be perceived by the public and the way it actually is perceived by the public.

kaif; v kaif: excellent; well done.

khippak; khippar', khippi: hippie.

khui; poshel na khui: literally, "go to my dick," often simply expressed as *na khui.* Equivalent of "fuck off."

kommanda; gruppa; bend: group or band.

kruto; krutoi (adj.): literally, steep or drastic, but really means "very fine." Something which is successful on its own terms. Equivalent to "hot shit."

marazm: literally, a marasmus, or a term connoting a condition of social decay or atrophy. Used quite commonly by musicians to describe their social conditions.

oblom; oblomat'(sia): something which is a real failure.

pizdets: an obscene slang word derived from the slang *pizda,* or "cunt." Used as an exclamation to convey a sense that something or someone is really excellent or really awful. Used more in positive sense in Petersburg musical community than in the public at large, e.g., "If such and such happens, I will be in real trouble (*mne pizdets*)." Can also be used as an adverb, *pizdato,* in phrases such as *ia pizdato khodil,* which means "my trip was fucking great." An English equivalent might be "fuckin' a," which can be an exclamation of surpise, delight, or anger.

plastinka; plastinki (pl.); also *rekord:* a record album.

podvorotnia: literally, the space between a gate and the ground; a term applied to certain individuals who are marginal in one sense or another. A literal translation would be "a nowhere person" or a bum.

pops; popsa; estrada: popular culture; the realm of entertainment which lies outside of the realm of artistic, authentic rock-and-roll. True rock-

and-roll is, by definition, not popular, but cryptic and encoded. True rock-and-roll is also always in danger of being transmogrified into pop by outside economic and political forces.

popsovat': interfere, meddle, spoil.

press: a Russified English word signifying intrusion of external events or aspects of existence on the lives of musicians. Often used to describe state intrusion into their activities, but also used to describe general existential pressures, e.g., "society presses on me."

restorannaia muzyka: restaurant music, synonymous with *popsa* but even more derogatory in the sense that most restaurant performers aspire to pop status but have not succeeded. They are, therefore, bad pop artists, which is to say, from the point of view of true rockers, they are very bad indeed.

seishn: session, or live performance, usually in front of an audience and for some remuneration.

shou biznes: show business, the world of commercial, popular music, and *estrada*, a world which the authentic rock musicians attempt to avoid at all costs.

streng: string for a guitar.

Sovdep; Sovok: slang terms for the Soviet Union.

stebat'sia: mock, make fun, play jokes, laugh, or amuse oneself. Also *steb*, something funny, amusing, or the process of making fun, mocking.

stremnyi: an adjective meaning weird, with connotations of danger.

thresh: thrash, to play wildly; usually used to describe music of poor quality.

tirazh: the number of issues which constitute the circulation of a record album.

tusovka: (1) a company or group of people united informally on the basis of common interests (rock fans or fans of some groups in particular, football fans, hippies, etc.), e.g., *metalicheskaia tusovka* is *tusovka* of the heavy metal fans; (2) an undertaking, *seishn*, a gathering, e.g., "The *tusovka* is here today"; (3) any crowd in general; (4) any interesting, remarkable event.

tusovshchik (m.); *tusovchitsa** (f.): someone who participates in a *tusovka*. While *tusovka* is used a great deal in the senses above, this word is not usually used by musicians to describe each other. It is often used to describe a fan who hangs around a *tusovka* and tries to get close to those who are famous within it. Can also be used to signify a decline in one's creative capacities.

*tusovat'sia** (verb): (1) to belong to a certain group of people, or a *tusovka* (*tusovat'sia* with somebody); (2) to gather somewhere, e.g., *Oni tusuiutsia u Saigona*, "They usually gather at the Saigon" (a cafe near the Rock Club); (3) to move somewhere, e.g., *utusovat'sia v Saigon*; (4) to go out, or live with somebody. Variants (derivatives formed by means of prefixes):

utusovat'sia: to get/grow tired of *tusovki*.

stusovat'sia: to meet one another.

rastusovat'sia: to break up, split up, as of a group.

zdorovo: well done; great!

Notes

1. A Recovery of the Senses: Toward a Critical-Interpretive Sociology of Russian Culture

1. It is beyond the scope of this book to provide an in-depth exploration of the issue of where the Soviet Union fits into current discourse on modernity. The most general problem in the theoretical discourse on modernity is the conflation of the terms *capitalism* and *modernity* in contemporary social theory. Giddens (1990) argues that the terms are essentially coterminous, but also suggests that the Soviet Union represents a particularly rigid form of modernity in the twentieth century.

2. For a clear discussion and critique of the parameters of this debate, see Jowitt (1992, pp. 124-27).

3. It is important to add two codicils to the use of the term *modernity* to describe the outcome of Soviet modernization. First, its use is not to infer that there is a *telos* to the process of historical development. As Jowitt (1991) points out, the use of the term *modernization* in Sovietology often assumes that the end of all industrial development is characterized by an inexorable tendency toward capitalist rationality and rationalization. This is not necessarily the case, and I make no assumptions that a move toward capitalist rationalization was somehow an inevitable result of Soviet historical development. Second, the idea of modernity as it is used in social theory often conveys a sense of movement, flux, change, and individuality (see, for instance, Lash and Friedman 1992, p. 1). While it is clear that Soviet society was not "modern" in these senses, I do want to argue that alternative forms of cultural practice and identities did emerge within the infrastructure of modernity which was the result of the rationalization of Soviet society. Theorists of modernity since Simmel have recognized the dual character and often contradictory nature of modernity: it simultaneously expands and thwarts the process of individuation. Analysts of the Soviet Union (including Jowitt 1992; and Cushman 1988) have often stressed the collectivist nature of the Soviet Union. Certainly, a sense of collectivity, or *kollektivnost'*, is an important aspect of Soviet culture. Yet its existence as a guiding norm of both Soviet political culture and culture at large does not preclude the existence of forms of individual expression within the infrastructure of Soviet modernity. Indeed, the quest for *individualnost'*, or individuality, which is outlined in the following pages might be seen as an attempt to escape from the domination of the cultural logic of *kollektivnost'*.

4. It would be a mistake to simply draft Western theories of modernity into the task of interpreting the Soviet experience without taking into consideration the complex historical differences between socialist and capitalist modernity. Any discussion of modernization or modernity in Russia must proceed with a clear understanding of the particulars of Russian history (Jowitt 1992, p. 120). Ken Jowitt writes: "All too often, terms and phenomena that mean one thing in one setting mean something fundamentally different in another" (1991, pp. 38-39). Jowitt criticizes modernization theorists for foisting on Russia an ontology of historical development (see, for instance, Jowitt 1992, pp. 124 ff) which detracts from seeing the Soviet Union as a unique form of modern society. While theory can serve as an aid in the interpretation of culture within socialist industrial modernity, the latter can never be understood without delving into the history of institutions and cultural processes which are specific to Russia. Throughout this book, general theoretical understandings of cultural expression under conditions of industrial existence are balanced with an appreciation of the particulars of Russian history.

5. I prefer the term *counterculture* to *subculture* when referring to the community of rock musicians in St. Petersburg, although I believe that scholars often use the terms interchangeably (see, for instance, Becker 1963; Hebdige 1979). Yinger (1982, pp. 39-40) defines countercultures as "*situationally* created designs for living formed in contexts of high anomie and intrasocietal conflict, the designs being inversions of, in sharp opposition to, the historically created designs" (emphasis in original). Yinger (1982, p. 41) quite rightly notes that "as expressions of norms and values sharply at variance with those of society at large, countercultures tend to be defined, both by themselves and by others, as much as what they are set against as by their own normative system." The term *counterculture* as Yinger defines it captures a sense of the dialectical view which I have posited as central to the understanding of Russian culture. Moreover, as opposed to the term *subculture*, counterculture conveys a sense of purposeful resistance, of the choice of an alternative system of values, norms, and beliefs, to those which are dominant within Soviet society.

It is also important to stress here that the term *counterculture* is not used as a synonym of the term *youth culture*, which I believe can be traced back to Theodore Roszak's (1969) classic work on counterculture in which he viewed youth culture as "youthful opposition" to a "technocratic society." Yet as the technocratic society has progressed, a wider number of individuals from a variety of age groups have taken a critical, countercultural approach to conventional existence. The term *youth culture* is a favorite synonym used by Western analysts of Russia to describe a plethora of modern cultural practices which are neither produced nor consumed solely by young people (see, for instance, Easton 1989; and Stites 1992). While the majority of consumers of rock music may be young people, this study focuses on the makers of rock music. Many of them are not young at all; some are in their thirties, forties, fifties, and sometimes even older. Rock music is no longer the young form of culture it once was. Those who might have made rock when they were young have now grown old, but they have not abandoned their cultural idiom. Rather, they have inflected it with their experience and, in some cases, protected it from onslaughts by "young Turks" who would pervert rock as an art form by turning it into a marketable commodity. Russian rock is now in its second generation, and soon its producers and consumers will be (or perhaps already are) grandparents. It is already possible to speak of old and new generations of the rock community and to distinguish between the different forms of rock music which are associated with these generations. This interesting generational dimension of rock music will be discussed in chapter 6.

6. Habermas's treatment of state-socialist society is discussed at length in Arato (1993).

2. Stories from Underground:
The Origins of St. Petersburg
Rock Music Counterculture

1. This Sartrean, existentialist approach to the active use of culture is taken by Hebdige (1979) in his analysis of the rise of punk rock culture in Britain.

2. This is not to say, however, that rock was not a product of diverse ethnic experiences. Blues, the cornerstone of rock, has its origins in Africa and the African-American experience. But rock, as a widespread, global phenomenon, was fundamentally dependent on the capitalist mode of production and technologies of production and distribution in America and England.

3. This was a name for 1970s rock bands that received financial and material support in exchange for their agreements to temper the content of their lyrics. I refer later to the VIA as part of the invented tradition of Soviet rock music.

4. Mify and Rossiiane were two important state-sponsored groups of the 1970s.

5. Kino was the name of an important Petersburg "underground" band led by Viktor Tsoy, a Soviet-Korean who died in 1990.

6. Akvarium was an important Petersburg band led by Boris Grebenshchikov, one of the most famous rock musicians, not only in Petersburg, but in Russia generally. Akvarium was formed in the 1970s and dissolved in the late 1980s. Grebenshchikov was one of the few Russian rock musicians to make a recording (*Radio Silence*) with a major record label in the United States, CBS.

7. Mashina Vremeni was one of the first independent rock bands in Petersburg. It was led by Andrei Makarevich. Both he and his group enjoyed

wide fame throughout the Soviet Union. Mashina Vremeni remained an important influence on the development of Petersburg rock, but was not an integral part of the rock underground after 1980. In the words of one musician: "Andrei just became commercial after glasnost came around."

8. *Estradnaia muzyka*, or more often simply *estrada*, is an untranslatable word, which refers to music that is produced for commercial purposes and for mass distribution. It roughly corresponds to "pop" culture. Important distinctions between terms used to describe the identity of music are discussed in chapter 3.

9. A *tusovshchik* is one who participates in a *tusovka*, which is, roughly speaking, a "happening" or gathering among counterculturalists. A more complete sociological analysis of the idea of *tusovka* is offered in chapter 4.

10. Another important Petersburg band formed in the early 1980s and led by singer Yuri Shevchuk.

11. The first commercially produced album of independent Russian rock. The songs were taken from Russia by an American fellow traveler of the Russian rock community and produced commercially in the United States.

12. Very often, especially in the initial stages of the fieldwork, interviews were taken in the presence of others. In most cases, these observers were silent, but at times they would make a point related to the discussion which would facilitate further discussion of an issue. These interviews were key events in the lives of many of those present, for they allowed for the repetition of important stories in the folklore of the Petersburg community and, therefore, of its own oral history.

13. "Cranberry" is a Russian metaphor for something which is illusory or fraudulent.

14. *Samizdat* is the Russian word for printed sources which are produced independently and circulated underground. The etymology of the word is interesting, a combination of the Russian determinative pronoun *sam* and the verb *izdat'*, "to publish." Thus the word, quite literally, means "self-published."

15. In contrast, it is possible to argue that in many open societies where there is a plethora of public information not only about Freud, but about any topic, one might find groups of graduate students, say, in the social sciences who have a rather anemic grasp of Freud.

16. For background on the state's ideological position on music and song, see Gerald S. Smith (1984, pp. 9-32).

17. The word *muzhik* is an older word often used to describe a Russian peasant. It is also used to describe a bumpkin or a clod, but can also simply mean "a simple fellow" or just a "guy." It is a favorite term used to describe the protagonist in Russian jokes.

18. For a general discussion of *magnitizdat* and its importance to musical diffusion, see G. S. Smith (1984, pp. 95 ff). What follows here is not novel; rather, it is refracted through a sociological lens to offer new insight about the significance and meaning of *magnitizdat*.

19. One finds it difficult to understand why the technologies of musical reproduction were so prevalent while other technologies were so rigidly circumscribed. This certainly is an issue which demands further theoretical inquiry.

20. Indeed, as Smith (1984, p. 98) notes, a quantitative account of the numbers of people involved in the production and circulation of imported forms of culture cannot be determined.

21. Norman K. Denzin (1989*b*, pp. 70 ff) is one of the few interpretive sociologists who has argued eloquently for a focus in social research on epiphanies in individual lives. Denzin defines epiphanies as "interactional moments and experiences which leave marks on people's lives. In them, personal character is manifested. They are often moments of crisis."

22. The term "grey zone" is used by Czech sociologist Jirina Siklova (1990) to describe the existence which many people in Soviet-type societies led during the communist period. Inhabitants of the grey zone sympathized with dissidents and independent culture producers. Yet they did not take the risk of publicly identifying with the latter. I discuss the emergence of a cadre of rock musicians from the St. Petersburg grey zone in chapter 5.

23. Russian musicians often use the impersonal "they" to refer to state authorities.

24. Misha is referring to the practice of getting what was often called a "yellow card," which declared one mentally unfit for military service. It is similar to the American classification of "4F," except in this case it was a stigma which was stamped in one's internal passport. During the Soviet period, all citizens were required to carry internal passports which contained information about ethnicity, nationality, place of residence, work, and medical history.

25. Misha uses the Russian word *sotsium* to describe the collective social context which he finds alienating. The word is not directly translatable into English, but seems to be derived from the Latin *socius*, which can mean a "sharing," "joining," or "participation" with others. He uses the word to convey a Soviet sense of the collective community in which conformity to the collective will is valued above all and in which individual thought and action are proscribed. The *sotsium* might also be seen in a Durkheimian sense as a kind of collective conscience which is independent of the individual parts.

26. Yuri is referring to a common saying in the Soviet period: "The West is rotting, but it still smells sweet."

27. For further information on Vysotsky, see Smith (1984), Lazarskii (1992), and Stites (1992).

28. The idea of the "invention of tradition" is taken from Hobsbawm and Ranger (1983).

29. The VIA is discussed briefly by Stites (1992, p. 162) as a means of cultural co-optation.

30. Indeed, this could either be accepted as evidence of a pluralistic tendency or as evidence of a strategy of cultural containment (or in Gramscian terms, an attempt at forging "cultural hegemony") in Soviet society. There is, in fact, evidence of such a strategy in other cultural spheres deep in Soviet history, for instance in the early Soviet policy of *korenizatsiia* which divided those with common ethnic heritage into republics. This strategy was meant to divide those who had actual or potential "consciousness of kind" and can, in this sense, be seen as a strategy for the containment of culture. See Saroyan (1988) for a discussion of this policy.

31. These observations are based on Kataev's (1987) content analysis and comparison of the lyrics of rock groups and VIAs. A summary of Kataev's research relevant to the present discussion can be found in appendix 2.

32. The *baian* is a traditional Russian type of accordion.

33. The Russified English word for "session," *seishn*, is frequently used by musicians to describe a formal playing situation where money is made.

34. The word *bezvykhodnost'* is difficult to translate. It literally means "no-way-out-ness," but I have translated it as "hopelessness."

35. The word *kostiak* literally means "backbone."

36. The official bureau for the planning and promotion of concerts; it is controlled by the conservative Union of Composers and is, therefore, conservative in its cultural orientation.

37. *Sovok* is a common slang expression used to describe either the Soviet Union or a citizen of the Soviet Union. Its normal meaning is "shovel."

38. Theodor Adorno (1976) notes that one of the most important aspects of the success of commercially produced musical styles is the formation of what he calls "entertainment audiences" which are at once homogeneous in their cultural tastes and uncritical of their social surroundings.

3. Musical Identity and Authenticity: The Local Meanings of Rock Music in St. Petersburg

1. Similar themes were raised in the work of other Marxists, in particular, Gyorgy Lukacs (1971), Walter Benjamin (1968), and the Frankfurt School Marx-

ists, especially Marcuse (1964, 1978, 1993); Adorno (1970, 1976); and Adorno and Horkheimer (1988). For an in-depth discussion of Marxian theories of art, see Janet Wolff (1983).

2. Bürger (1992) provides an important overview of the problem of the autonomy of art.

3. In the case of literature on rock music in the Soviet Union, for instance, one finds articles and books with explicit references to rock's politicality in the Soviet context. Such references evoke categories of conventional politics and relate such categories to the world of Russian rock. The texts of such works follow a fairly predictable story line. Having labeled rock music as a deviant cultural practice, the repressive Soviet state developed a sophisticated set of practices to impede and thwart its expression. Rock musicians bravely found ways to evade such practices. The story line is one of a cat-and-mouse game, in which rock practice becomes a reflex of official, institutionalized political practices.

4. *Peredvizhniki* were members of the Russian school of realist painters in the second half of the nineteenth century.

5. This conception of art as a higher form of communication which stands above history is a central idea of Aristotle's *Poetics*.

6. Yuri is referring to an earlier conversation in Berlin in which he had told me that it made little difference to him what city he was in, since "everything was basically the same everywhere anyway."

7. A key aspect of Weber's historical sociology was the exploration of homologies or "elective affinities" among seemingly different idea systems and human interests. Originally, Weber developed the idea of elective affinities to explain the similarities between the cultural logic of Calvinism and that of the market. For a discussion of Weber's notion of elective affinities, see Gerth and Mill's discussion in Weber (1946, pp. 62-63).

8. Gerald Stanton Smith's (1984) pioneering research on the identity of Soviet mass song as a form of "guitar poetry" has done much to underscore the important idea of music's primary identity as poetry in Russia. Curiously, because he has inflected his own biases about what is and what is not poetry onto the study of Russian music, Smith has excluded the Russian rock tradition from the "guitar poetry" which he studies. His view of rock in relation to the great bards of the twentieth century is worth noting in detail: "There are no signs that a second generation of guitar poets is ready to carry on the work of the original masters. Instead, if anything, the next generation of dissident singers in the U.S.S.R. has turned from the forms and themes of guitar poetry and is looking instead to Western rock music as its source of inspiration" (Smith 1984, p. 233). Smith's idea not only reflects a failure to explore rock music as a legitimate form of poetry in the Russian context, but also represents a fairly typical refusal on the part of cultural elitists to grant rock music status as an authentic form of poetry.

9. A very important Petersburg group led by Konstantin Kinchev. Alisa is characterized by an inversion of the symbols of the Soviet order—torn flags, inverted and mutilated hammer and sickles—but the themes of Kinchev's songs resonate closely with those of Western industrial music.

10. *Sovdep* is a slang expression for the Soviet system.

11. Avia was a group known for its use of elements in the Russian tradition of modern art to construct parodies of official Soviet organizations and practices.

12. The root of the word *istina* appears to be *ist*. Its adjectival form is *istinnyi*, which is used to modify abstract concepts such as friendship, love, truth, or faith. It is interesting, though, that the normal definition of *istinnyi* is "genuine," "true," or "authentic." It would not make sense to say *istinnaia muzyka*, or "genuine music," although the definition of the essential identity of music as the crystallization of *istina* has strong connotations of music as a search for authentic truth.

13. On this notion of the gap between the realities and truths of public and private life in the Soviet Union, see Shlapentokh (1989).

14. Quoted from a *samizdat* issue of the underground rock periodical, *Roksi*.

15. Quoted from an interview in a *samizdat* issue of the underground rock publication, *Roksi*.

16. On the more general importance of credentials in modern society, see Collins (1979). On the idea of symbolic capital in status attainment, see Bourdieu and Passeron (1970).

17. About US $120 at official exchange rates for foreigners at that time. The average monthly wage for a Soviet worker in 1987 was between 150 and 200 rubles.

18. There are certainly communities of culture producers in Western societies who believe, like Petersburg musicians, that money can corrupt musical authenticity. Yet such communities always have the option to go commercial with their cultural products without necessarily having to alter them as much as a Petersburg musician would have to if he or she went commercial in the Soviet context. As such, this situation is unique to socialist industrial societies. Even in underdeveloped Third World societies, musical production is excessively concerned with profit making. The history of musical expropriation in Jamaica offers an example of the connection between capital and musical culture in peripheral nations of the capitalist world-system (see Cushman 1991).

19. Some analysts have lumped together all forms of Russian musical expression under the category of "entertainment." At base, though, rock

music—since it is primarily identified as art—is not seen as entertainment at all. To refer to it as such would be, in the minds of Petersburg musicians, tantamount to referring to the poetry of Pushkin or the paintings of Kandinsky as entertainment. Even though rock music entertains, this entertainment function has little to do with the ways in which musicians themselves define the primary aims of their musical activity. A conflation of rock music's entertainment functions and the views that musicians themselves have of their craft are tantamount to labeling academic philosophers who engage their students by making them laugh as "entertainers."

20. I do not take credit for discovering this definition of *popsovat'* in Dal's dictionary. Indeed, my sense of the idea of pop was that it was a term associated with the commercializing processes in the production of culture in modern industrial societies. As a result, I would never have sought its meanings in a dictionary of nineteenth-century colloquial Russian. In the course of an interview with an important Petersburg musician, the reference was pointed out to me by this musician in order to convey to me his sense of the true meaning of the word *popsa* and the idea of its unauthenticity in relation to rock music. Such philological depth on the part of rock musicians is further testament to their status as intellectuals, a status which very few intellectual historians (but see Kagarlitsky 1988) are willing to grant them.

21. This is from a second edition of Dal's dictionary. This suggests that popular usage of the verb *poposovat'* goes back even earlier in Russian cultural history.

22. Foremost in this regard is Richard Stites's (1992) analysis of Russian popular culture. Stites misleadingly subsumes virtually all forms of cultural expression—both commercial and noncommercial, official and unofficial—under the rubric of *popular culture*. This is a serious analytical mistake, for it fails to take into account any consideration of the ways which terms like *popular* are defined and articulated in local cultural contexts. The negative connotations of the adjective *popular* and the verb *to popularize* shared by most members of the Petersburg rock musical community should lead us to rethink how the term *popular* is deployed by Western analysts to study Russian culture. A start in this direction, as Kellner (1992) has noted, might be to dispense with the analytic category of popular culture entirely in favor of a more general idea of culture.

23. When I did so, I was immediately corrected and instructed instead to use the term *contr'kultura* or *subkul'tura* ("counterculture" or "subculture" respectively), to describe the identity of rock music.

24. Included within this category is the idea of *estrada*, yet with one important distinction: *estrada* is viewed as being even more inauthentic than *popsa*.

25. In one case, the Russian medical word *astenicheskii* was used to describe the lack of energy in pop music.

4. At Play in the Fields of the Soviets: Individual and Collective Identity in the St. Petersburg Rock Music Community

1. Durkheim notes that in some societies "even the *excreta* have a religious character" ([1915] 1965, p. 261n), thus making the important point that even objects which are considered profane can be defined as sacred.

2. It is interesting to note that such speciality appears to be reserved for musicians; artists and other producers of aesthetic culture seldom enjoy such immense status and prestige either in life or after death. This fact may have something to do with music's special status as a privileged form of communication. The question of why musicians seem to be conferred with sacred status more than other types of artists is an open one and worthy of further exploration.

3. While Milner's theory of the relationship between status and sacredness is an interpretive one, it ultimately sees sacredness as a cause of high social status. I reject such a mechanistic approach, for it downplays the idea that the relationship between status and sacredness is a processual one.

4. See David Owen (1990) for a valuable discussion of Weber's idea of "inner distance."

5. It might be argued that the very heart of the crisis of legitimacy which emerged in Soviet-type societies in the 1980s had much to do with extinguishing the possibility of politics as a vocation. The practice of politics as a vocation emerged in the form of "anti-politicians" such as Vaclav Havel and Gyorgy Konrad and in the form of artists and musicians such as the ones I am discussing here. As an example of the impossibility of politics as a vocation in the Soviet Union, the case of the career and fate of M. S. Gorbachev is instructive. Gorbachev's political crusade was based on an appeal to return to the fundamental ethical and moral values of communism which had been perverted by Stalin. In this sense, he was trying to bring some degree of authenticity and meaning into politics, to practice politics as a vocation. Yet the very institutional order which he presided over was so thoroughly infused with the ethos of instrumental rationality that it spewed out Gorbachev for his attempt to live *for* politics rather than to live *off* politics.

6. I was obligated to do so as well and, upon stopping momentarily to get my bearings, was struck in the back by a policeman who told me to "get my ass moving."

7. The reference is to the hills where the witches in Mikhail Bulgakov's novel *The Master and Margarita* met to hold their sabbath.

8. In the philosophies of more staid literary nihilists such as Chernyshevsky and Pisarev, such egoism was referred to as *razumnyi egoism*, or "rea-

sonable," or "intelligent," egoism. For a more complete discussion, see again Gubankov (1989, p. 120).

9. It is important to add an ethnographic note to this discussion. While I had intended to include Viktor's life history in this study, I never succeeded in interviewing him because he died in a car crash in early August 1990, during the first phase of my field research. His wife, however, had been a major source of information for me and I had been scheduled to meet with her. When I called in the morning to confirm the appointment, it was immediately after his wife received the news that Viktor had died, making me, a foreigner, one of the first persons in St. Petersburg to find out. The account of the aftermath of his death is based on my own observation of events in the city.

10. These letters are taken from Tsoy and Zhitinskii (1991), which provides a rich collection of materials related to Viktor's life and attitudes of other members of the rock community toward him.

11. Caillois was a French thinker who, together with a number of other thinkers, formed an informal "college" in Paris called the "College of Sociology." Like the great classical sociologists Marx, Weber, and Durkheim, the members of the College of Sociology recognized that the modern world had made the attainment of authentic experiences of the sacred increasingly problematic. Yet, they argued, following Durkheim, the sacred was such a fundamental aspect of human existence that people would always find ways to express and appreciate it. The College examined a wide variety of expressions of the sacred both at the macrolevel and at the microlevel of social existence. This enterprise they referred to as the "sociology of the sacred." For an extensive background on the College and articles by its members, see Hollier (1988) and Ambrosino, et al. (1988).

12. In addition to the following explanations in Soviet folklore, some believe that the etymology of the word derives from the verb *tusovat'*, "to shuffle."

13. Stites (1992, p. xvii) defines *tusovka* as a "hangout, crash pad, or happening among hippies and rock fans." This definition captures the essence of the *tusovka* as either a "happening" or a specific place where those engaged in a similar type of collective action "hang out." Yet the word is not only used to describe musical life or hippie lifestyles. It is used more generally by Petersburg musicians to describe collective and alternative experiences as musicians.

14. Although this is not what Silver argues. Rather, he criticizes the idea that commercial society "colonizes" friendship on the grounds that there is no empirical evidence for it. Chapters 5 and 6 should provide enough preliminary evidence to reject Silver's argument: the forces of commercialization in Russian society are a major factor in the erosion of traditional friendship ties within the Petersburg musical community.

15. Zhenya, the son of an Englishman, spoke quite passable English and was fond of developing his English vocabulary, particularly slang words. The word *puffous*, in his mind, was an English word used to describe an arrogant person.

16. The bridges have always been a site of struggle between authorities and urban dwellers, in particular, young people who attempted to put the bridges to alternative uses, mostly by crawling on them or diving from them into the Neva. Press reports in Leningrad papers throughout the 1980s report confrontations between youth and authorities at the bridges and, occasionally, deaths from drowning or falling to the pavement. In no case, though, have I read of any acts of artistic adornment of the bridge such as the one described here.

17. This idea is reflected in Hebdige's (1979) discussion of the ideology of capitalism which is reflected in the architecture of the capitalist urban environment. The idea that ideologies and belief systems are encoded in architecture is also central in the work of Panovsky (1957). The general idea that architecture speaks metaphorically is, of course, a mainstay of the field of semiotics.

18. See Stites (1992, p. 200) and Riordan (1988) for brief discussions of the activities of this group.

19. This observation shores up a central point which is addressed as well in appendix 1: the research presented here most likely could not have been accomplished by a woman since the norms and values of male culture were so strong in the Petersburg counterculture.

20. This is not to say that rock lyrics do not include critiques of the passive roles which, ironically, the male culture of musicians forces women to assume. One example from a prominent Moscow group comments on the difficulties of male-female relationships in situations of close proximity which were the norm of Soviet industrial existence. The song leers:

You never say anything, you just sit and keep your mouth shut
You never go out anywhere, you just sit and watch,
You're always around.

21. Bernstein studied the ways in which the use of Cockney dialect in England served as a linguistic code underlying group identification and solidarity formation among Cockneys.

22. The glossary presents a listing and explanation of all of the terms which I encountered in the course of this research. It is not a complete vocabulary of the argot of the musical community, but one which provides a general cartography of the language used by Petersburg musicians in the course of talking about their lives and music.

23. Galtung's conception of cosmology is the cornerstone of what he calls "civilizational analysis" which aims to mark fundamental differences among

modern cultures. In this respect, his orienting scheme might be useful for point-ing out differences and similarities between socialist and capitalist industrial civilizations.

5. Notes from Underground:
Glasnost, Perestroika, and the
St. Petersburg Rock Music Community

1. *Komsomol* is a Russian abbreviation for the Young Communist League, a political organization of the Communist Party designed for the socialization of youth. Komsomol activities were often centered in buildings known as "Palaces of Culture" or "Houses of Youth."

2. This process is outlined in early issues of the *samizdat* journal *Roksi*, a cornerstone of popular music counterculture in Leningrad. This particular pro-ducer has achieved a degree of fame within the folklore of the Petersburg coun-terculture and is considered the "savior" of Soviet rock-and-roll in the pre-glas-nost period. It is therefore impossible to hide his identity from those who know something about Petersburg rock music. Nonetheless, I use only Andrei's first name. This explanation of the process of underground musical production is part of the folklore of the Petersburg musical community, and details of it were provided to me by a high-level informant in the state recording company, Melodiya.

3. It must be stressed that even countercultural communities have their elites. Indeed, this book is really a study of what might be called "informal elites." The qualitative sociological study of elites poses a host of difficult methodological problems. For one reason or another, elites do not wish to engage researchers in speculation about their motivations and intentions. For an overview of issues related to problems in interviewing elites, see Hertz and Imber (1993, pp. 3-6). The problem of studying the Petersburg music community as an elite community is addressed in appendix 1.

4. As Jensen (1990) and Jones (1990) have argued, this is the general case for the production of music worldwide. This fact throws the relationship between oppositional popular music and the dominant society into a new light: the dominant society provides the means of production which enable certain individuals to create the cultural means of opposition.

5. The interview itself is humorously entitled "Anthropological Revela-tions" (*"Antropologicheskie Otkroveniia"*) which is a pun drawing on the name of Andrei's underground recording studio, "Antrop." The interview was taken from the Spring 1987 issue of *Roksi*, the bulletin of the Leningrad Rock Club, which was published and distributed by members of the rock community. This particular issue is part of the personal collection of the author.

6. Fyodorov was a Russian printer who is considered something of a Russian Gutenberg.

7. A common way to refer to Boris Grebenshchikov, a famous Petersburg musician.

8. The Russian word *marazm* is quite commonly used by musicians to describe a condition of social decay or atrophy. The prevalence of *marazm* in Soviet society is characterized by a play on weather forecasters' statement: "Last night, frost fell (*moroz krepchal*)", substituting *marazm* for *moroz* to yield *marazm krepchal*, "social decay is all around."

9. From *Roksi*, vol. 21, n.d.

10. From *Roksi*, vol. 21, n.d.

11. Indeed, the concrete organization of the Leningrad urban environment reflected a state concern with youth cultural activities: one of the largest Palaces of Youth, a building which features a youth hotel, restaurant, bar, and large auditorium, was conveniently located across the street from one of the largest headquarters of the city's militia.

12. This practice has many analogs in Russian history, most notably, in the Soviet state's creation and management of non-Russian nationalities. In the 1920s, the Bolsheviks created republics for the largest ethnic groups in the Union. This process, described with the social scientific neologism *korenizatsiia*, was designed to fix boundaries between states, submit them to Russian state practice and, thus, keep them under control and surveillance. For a discussion of this practice, see Saroyan (1988). I have discussed this theoretical issue further in another work on the politics of culture in Russia (see Cushman 1993).

13. But see my article (Cushman 1993) in which I explore the question of such strategies in a more detailed, theoretical way which is not possible in the present analysis.

14. The word *dushilovo* is one which was made up by a musician in the course of an interview to describe the idea of a "press." Over the course of three years, I heard this word used again to describe the same situation.

15. The words from this song were taken from a documentary entitled *Rock in Russia*, produced and directed by Ken Thurlbeck. The specific circumstances surrounding the performance were detailed by Yuri himself in a later discussion.

16. For an overview of relations between the elites and members of reform movements, see Staniszkis (1984).

17. In the summer of 1990, KGB General Major Oleg Kalugin defected from the ranks of the KGB and went on national television to describe and con-

demn the secret activities of the KGB during the Brezhnev era. Throughout the summer, Kalugin provided details on the KGB's involvement in a vast array of domestic and international arenas. At one point, he noted that the KGB had even been involved in the formation of the Rock Club, a fact which did not surprise most musicians, but still had the effect of publicly identifying those who were complicitous. For an interview with Kalugin, see Yelin (1990).

18. For the English translation of the text of this law, see *Current Digest of the Soviet Press* (1990). For a discussion of the significance of this law in relation to the more general policy of glasnost, see Orland (1989).

19. *Stiliagi* were jazz fans who adopted sartorial styles associated with jazz culture and who were often harassed on the streets by authorities. See Starr (1983) for background on the *stiliagi*.

20. The New Economic Policy (NEP), instituted by Lenin in 1918, involved the introduction of a modified market economy in the wake of the social turmoil of the post-revolutionary period. This policy was seen by many to be a concession to buy time for the Bolsheviks while they consolidated their tenuous hold on power.

21. This information on the changes at Melodiya was provided to me by a high-level informant within the organization who remains anonymous.

22. For a general background on the emergence of cooperatives and the legal, bureaucratic, and economic restrictions they faced, see Jones and Moskoff (1991). For a background on the specific laws related to the formation and operation of cooperatives, see Nelson, Babaeva, and Babaev (1992).

23. Murray Milner (1993) notes that social status is not an infinitely expandable resource. In other words, there is only so much status to go around within any given society or group, and conflicts within the latter are often an expression of conflicts over the limited resource of status.

24. Yuri Gagarin was the first Russian cosmonaut and the first human being to travel into outer space.

25. Valya Tereshkova was the first female cosmonaut to travel into outer space.

6. The *Tusovka* Is Over:
The Acceleration of Capitalism and the
St. Petersburg Rock Music Counterculture

1. For an overview of Western policies on the economic reformation of post-communist societies in general, and Russian society in particular, see Sachs (1990); Lipton and Sachs (1992); and Peck and Richardson (1991). For critical

sociological analysis of the social and cultural dimensions and outcomes of shock therapy, see Luke (1990); Nelson, Babaeva, and Babaev (1992); and Burawoy and Krotov (1992).

2. This point is stressed in a recent paper by Igor Kon (1993).

3. The exchange rate at the time of the interview (summer of 1992) was approximately 130 rubles per US dollar. Thus, the cost to Andrei for producing a mold for a recording—120,000 rubles plus another 20,000 for producing covers—was about US $1074.00. During this time, the average wage of workers was about 2,600 rubles per month, or US $20.00.

4. Misha uses the terms *denezhnyi kul't* and *kul't deneg* relatively interchangeably throughout the interview. The former literally translates as "money cult," the latter as "cult of money." Cult of money is a bit more dramatic and is used in my translation.

5. The West is often referred to in everyday discourse simply as "there," or *tam* in Russian. Increasingly, *tam* is being used to describe the pre-glasnost days of countercultural existence.

6. This interview occurred at the end of four years of ongoing observation of and interaction with Petersburg musicians. Based on all I had seen and heard and because of the situation that was unfolding at the Tränenpalast in my presence, I simply could not restrain such an overt demonstration of empathy. Indeed, empathy is a central aspect of all interpretive sociology.

7. Conclusion: Capitalism, Cultural Freedom, and Democracy in Post-Soviet Russia

1. The reference here is to a recent work by Francis Fukuyama (1992) in which he declares that the dissolution of communism signifies the victory of capitalism and the end of the historical confrontation between ideologies. Fukuyama's argument ignores the rise of such phenomena as nationalism as a challenge to the capitalist new world order. An extended sociological critique of Fukuyama's argument can be found in Mestrovic (1993a).

2. Peter Berger (1977, 1986), for instance, argues that capitalism offers a choice of not only goods, but also lifestyles and systems of meaning which were impossible within the confining contexts of traditional society. Rose Laub Coser (1991) argues that capitalist modernity has facilitated the growth of role complexity. Such role complexity, she argues, offers more opportunity for individual initiative, reflection, creativity, and the articulation of new types of roles. Even Habermas, a critical theorist in the tradition of the Frankfurt School, stresses the two-sided character of modernity by acknowledging, unlike the more negative proponents of this tradition, the positive aspects of modernity.

3. This is a central argument underlying Jürgen Habermas's critical theory of society. This theory is elaborated in two works (1984, 1989) but is also summarized very clearly in Arato and Cohen (1992).

4. Interestingly, this response of rock musicians in the late twentieth century is remarkably similar to the response of Russian classical musicians such as Glinka in the early nineteenth century. In each case, musicians—whether high or low—felt that there was a distinctive Russian musical idiom which had to be protected from outside forces. I am grateful to Tom Hodge for pointing out this comparison to me.

5. Indeed, the negative consequences of shock therapy—rising crime rates, unemployment, homelessness, poverty, and a host of other social ills—are described as "externalities" which are necessary before the positive aspects of capitalist modernity can be enjoyed.

6. For a discussion of Michnik's philosophy, see Goldfarb (1992).

7. Normally, it is difficult to tell what scholars who write about democratization in Russia actually mean by the term "democracy." A predominant sense of democracy is that it is a system in which there are formal, institutionalized structures which guarantee that those who have power are elected by the people (see, for instance, Schumpeter 1950). Conventional political analyses of Russia argue that the future of Russian democracy depends fundamentally on the institutionalization of large-scale, democratic structures which will ensure such things as freedom of speech. There is also a pervasive idea that somehow capitalist economic performance necessarily leads to or supports a democratic social order (see, for instance, Przeworksi 1991, p. 189; Lipset, Seong, and Torres 1993; and Lipset 1994).

8. The idea of sociological democracy is a derivative of Donald Black's (1989) idea of "sociological justice." Black argues that the administration of justice ought to be based on a firm understanding of the sociological realities underlying jurisprudence. I am making a similar argument, except that in this case it is sociological knowledge—especially empirical and theoretical knowledge about intersubjective, communicative processes—which ought to inform and guide the construction and practice of a democracy.

9. The idea of sociological democracy is another way of stating Habermas's view of democratization. This view is crystallized most cogently and succinctly by John B. Thompson (1993, p. 185): "The task today of a radical programme of democratization should be . . . to push back the colonizing intrusion of system imperatives into the lifeworld and to achieve thereby a new balance between forms of societal integration, so that the practically oriented demands of the lifeworld can prevail over the exercise of economic and administrative power."

10. In an argument which is strikingly similar to Habermas's and Dewey's and perhaps even more relevant to the present study which has focused a great

deal on the importance of the sacred in Soviet society, Martin Buber (1992) notes that it is the very process of intersubjective communication which guarantees individuals the possibility of creating a democratic society which is based on the apprehension of locally defined senses of the sacred. In a society without a clear sense of the sacred and a means of protecting the communication of the sacred, there can be no cultural buttress for a democratic order. S. N. Eisenstadt (in Buber 1992) crystallizes the essence of Buber's thought about the relation between creativity, intersubjectivity and social structures: "Communicative openness is maximized in situations which have certain structural attributes. The most important attribute is that the participants have a strong commitment both to direct interpersonal relations, transcending and cutting across more institutionalized and formalized frameworks, and to direct relations to the realm of the sacred, the transcendental, to the sphere of ultimate values."

11. This idea has also been explored by Stjepan Mestrovic (1993*b*) who argues that local cultural categories must infuse the categories of democracy imported by the West into post-communist societies if viable democracies are to be constructed in these societies.

Bibliography

Adorno, Theodor. 1970. *Aesthetic Theory*. London: Routledge & Kegan Paul.

———. 1976. *An Introduction to the Sociology of Music*. New York: Seabury Press.

Adorno, Theodor, and Max Horkheimer. 1988. "The Culture Industry: Enlightenment as Mass Deception." Pp. 120-67 in *Dialectic of Enlightenment*. New York: Continuum.

Alexander, Jeffrey. 1987. *Twenty Lectures: Sociological Theory Since World War II*. New York: Columbia University Press.

Althusser, Louis. 1969. *For Marx*. New York: Random House.

Ambrosino, Georges, Georges Bataille, Roger Caillois, Pierre Klossowski, Pierre Libra, and Jules Minerot. 1988. In Denis Hollier, ed., *The College of Sociology (1937-39)*. Minneapolis: University of Minnesota Press.

Antonio, Robert J., and Douglas Kellner. 1992. "Communication, Modernity, and Democracy in Habermas and Dewey." *Symbolic Interaction* 15:277-97.

Appadurai, Arjun. 1986. *The Social Life of Things: Commodities in Cultural Perspective*. Cambridge and New York: Cambridge University Press.

Arato, Andrew. 1993. *From Neo-Marxism to Democratic Theory: Essays on the Critical Theory of Soviet-Type Societies*. Armonk, NY: M.E. Sharpe.

Arato, Andrew, and Jean Cohen. 1992. "Civil Society and Social Theory." Pp. 199-219 in Peter Beilharz, Gillian Robinson, and John Rundell, eds., *Between Totalitarianism and Postmodernity: A Thesis Eleven Reader*. Cambridge, MA: MIT Press.

Arnason, Johann P. 1992. "The Theory of Modernity and the Problematic of Democracy." Pp. 32-53 in Peter Beilharz, Gillian Robinson, and John Rundell, eds., *Between Totalitarianism and Postmodernity*. Cambridge, MA: MIT Press.

———. 1993. *The Future That Failed: Origins and Destinies of the Soviet Model*. London and New York: Routledge.

Arshavskii, A. Iu., and A. Ia. Vilks. 1991. "Antisocial Manifestations in the Youth Environment: An Attempt at Regional Prognosis." *Soviet Sociology* 30:88-98.

Attali, Jacques. 1985. *Noise: The Political Economy of Music.* Minneapolis: University of Minnesota Press.

Bakhtin, Mikhail. 1973. "Laughter and Freedom." Pp. 295-300 in Maynard Solomon, ed., *Marxism and Art: Essays Classic and Contemporary.* Detroit: Wayne State University Press.

Batygin, G. S., et al. 1987. "Rok muzyka: muzyka? subkultura? stil' zhizni?" *Sotsiologicheskie Issledovaniya* 14:29-51.

Baumann, Zygmunt. 1992. *Intimations of Postmodernity.* London and New York: Routledge.

Becker, Howard S. 1963. *Outsiders: Studies in the Sociology of Deviance.* London: Free Press of Glencoe.

———. 1982. *Art Worlds.* Berkeley: University of California Press.

Bellah, Robert. 1967. "Civil Religion in America." *Daedalus* 96:1-21.

Benjamin, Walter. 1968. "The Work of Art in the Age of Mechanical Reproduction." Pp. 219-253 in *Illuminations.* New York: Harcourt, Brace, and World.

Berger, Peter. 1977. *Facing Up to Modernity: Excursions in Society, Politics, and Religion.* New York: Basic Books.

———. 1986. *The Capitalist Revolution: Fifty Propositions about Prosperity, Equality, and Liberty.* New York: Basic Books.

Berger, Peter L., and Thomas Luckmann. 1966. *The Social Construction of Reality: A Treatise in the Sociology of Knowledge.* Garden City, NY: Doubleday.

Bergesen, Albert. 1979. "Spirituals, Jazz, Blues and Soul Music: The Role of Elaborated and Restricted Codes in the Maintenance of Social Solidarity." Pp. 333-49 in Robert Wuthnow, ed., *New Directions in the Empirical Study of Religion.* New York: Academic Press.

Berman, Marshall. 1982. *All That Is Solid Melts Into Air: The Experience of Modernity.* New York: Simon and Schuster.

Bernstein, Basil. 1975. *Class, Codes, and Social Control: Theoretical Studies Towards a Sociology of Language.* New York: Shocken.

Black, Donald. 1989. *Sociological Justice.* New York: Oxford.

Bloom, Allan. 1987. *The Closing of the American Mind.* New York: Simon and Schuster.

Bogemskaya, Kseniia. 1991. "The Open-Air Market for Art: The Commercial Expression of Creativity." *Journal of Communication* 41:19-30.

Boguslavskii, Mark. 1979. *The U.S.S.R. and International Copyright Protection.* Moscow: Progress Publishers.

Bourdieu, Pierre. 1984. *Distinction: A Social Critique of the Judgement of Taste.* Cambridge, MA: Harvard University Press.

Bourdieu, Pierre, and Jean-Claude Passeron. 1970. *La reproduction: elements pour une theorie du systeme d'enseignement.* Paris: Editions de Minuit.

Buber, Martin. 1992. *On Intersubjectivity and Cultural Creativity.* Edited by S. N. Eisenstadt. Chicago and London: University of Chicago Press.

Burawoy, Michael, and Pavel Krotov. 1992. "The Soviet Transition from Socialism to Capitalism: Worker Control and Economic Bargaining in the Wood Industry." *American Sociological Review* 57:16-38.

Bürger, Peter. 1992. "On the Problem of the Autonomy of Art in Bourgeois Society." Pp. 51-63 in Francis Frascina and Jonathan Harris, eds., *Art in Modern Culture: An Anthology of Critical Texts.* New York: Harper Collins.

Bushnell, John. 1988. "A Popular Reading of Bulgakov: 'Explications des Graffiti.'" *Slavic Review* 47:502-11.

———. 1990. *Moscow Graffiti: Language and Subculture.* Boston: Unwin Hyman.

Caillois, Roger. 1988. "Brotherhoods, Orders, Secret Societies, Churches." Pp. 145-56 in Denis Hollier, ed., *The College of Sociology, 1937-1939.* Minneapolis: University of Minnesota Press.

Callinicos, Alex. 1988. *Making History: Agency, Structure, and Change in Social Theory.* Ithaca, NY: Cornell University Press.

Caplow, Theodore, and Howard M. Bahr, et al. 1982. *Middletown Families: Fifty Years of Change and Continuity.* Minneapolis: University of Minnesota Press.

Certeau, Michel de. 1984. *The Practice of Everyday Life.* Berkeley: University of California Press.

Clark, Katerina. 1981. *The Soviet Novel: History as Ritual.* Chicago: University of Chicago Press.

Collins, Randall. 1979. *The Credential Society: An Historical Sociology of Education and Stratification.* New York: Academic Press.

Connor, Walter. 1979. *Socialism, Politics, and Equality: Hierarchy and Change in Eastern Europe and the U.S.S.R.* New York: Columbia University Press.

Cooley, Charles Horton. [1902] 1956. *Human Nature and the Social Order.* New York: Free Press.

Coplan, David B. 1985. *In Township Tonight: South Africa's Black City Music and Theatre.* London and New York: Longman.

Coser, Rose Laub. 1991. *In Defense of Modernity: Role Complexity and Individual Autonomy.* Stanford, CA: Stanford University Press.

Coulloudon, Virginie. 1990. *La mafia en Union sovietique.* Paris: J. C. Lattes.

Crowley, Tony. 1988. "Language and Hegemony: Principles, Morals, and Pronunciation." *Textual Practice* 1:278-96.

Cuba, Lee. 1987. *Identity and Community on the Alaskan Frontier.* Philadelphia: Temple University Press.

Cuba, Lee, and David M. Hummon. 1993. "A Place to Call Home: Identification with Dwelling, Community, and Region." *The Sociological Quarterly* 34:111-32.

Current Digest of the Soviet Press. 1990. "Law Protecting President's Honor, Dignity." *Current Digest of the Soviet Press* 42(21):19.

Cushman, Thomas. 1988. "Ritual and Conformity in Soviet Society." *Journal of Communist Studies* 4:161-80.

———. 1991. "Rich Rastas and Communist Rockers: A Comparative Study of the Origin, Diffusion, and Defusion of Revolutionary Musical Codes." *Journal of Popular Culture* 25:17-62.

———. 1993 "*Glasnost*', *Perestroika*, and the Management of Oppositional Popular Culture in the Soviet Union, 1986-1990." *Current Perspectives in Social Theory* 13:25-67.

———. 1995. "Constructing the Soviet Other: Rhetorics of Reputation and Representation in Western Sovietology." In Richard Harvey Brown, ed., *Postmodern Representations: Truth, Power, and Mimesis in the Human Sciences and Public Culture.* Chicago and London: University of Illinois Press, forthcoming.

Dal', Vladimir. [1880] 1955. *Tolkovyi slovar' zhivogo velikorusskogo iazyka* (Explanatory Dictionary of the Living Russian Language). Moskva.

Denzin, Norman K. 1989a. *Interpretive Interactionism.* Newbury Park, CA: Sage Publications.

———. 1989b. *Interpretive Biography.* Newbury Park, CA: Sage Publications.

Dewey, John. [1934] 1959. *Art as Experience.* New York: Capricorn Books.

———. 1939. *Freedom and Culture.* New York: G. P. Putnam's Sons.

Dobson, Richard B. 1980. "Education and Opportunity." Pp. 115-37 in Jerry G. Pankhurst and Michael Paul Sacks, eds., *Contemporary Soviet Society: Sociological Perspectives.* New York: Praeger.

Douglas, Mary. 1985. *Purity and Danger: An Analysis of Concepts of Pollution and Taboo*. London: Ark Paperbacks Reprint.

Durkheim, Emile. 1933. *The Division of Labor in Society*. New York: Macmillan.

———. [1915] 1965. *The Elementary Forms of the Religious Life*. New York: Free Press.

Easton, Paul. 1989. "The Rock Music Community." Pp. 45-82 in Jim Riordan, ed., *Soviet Youth Culture*. Bloomington: Indiana University Press.

Eisenstadt, S. N. 1956. *From Generation to Generation: Age Groups and Social Structure*. Glencoe, IL: Free Press.

Eliade, Mircea. 1959. *The Sacred and the Profane: The Nature of Religion*. New York: Harcourt, Brace.

Erlmann, Veit. 1991. *African Stars: Studies in Black South African Performance*. Chicago and London: University of Chicago Press.

Feagin, Joe, Anthony Orum, and Gideon Sjoberg. 1991. "Introduction: The Nature of the Case Study." Pp. 1-26 in Joe Feagin, Anthony Orum, and Gideon Sjoberg, eds., *The Case for the Case Study*. Chapel Hill and London: University of North Carolina Press.

Feuer, Lewis S. 1969. *The Conflict of Generations: The Character and Significance of Student Movements*. New York: Basic Books.

Fine, Gary Alan. 1977. "Popular Culture and Social Interaction: Production, Consumption, and Usage." *Journal of Popular Culture* 11:453-56.

Fish, Stanley. 1980. *Is There a Text in This Class? The Authority of Interpretive Communities*. Cambridge: Harvard University Press.

Foucault, Michel. 1975. *The Birth of the Clinic: An Archaeology of Medical Perception*. Translated from the French by A. M. Sheridan Smith. New York: Vintage Books.

Freund, Peter E. S. 1982. *The Civilized Body: Social Domination, Control, and Health*. Philadelphia: Temple University Press.

Frith, Simon. 1984. *The Sociology of Youth*. Ormskirk, Lancashire: Causeway Books.

———. 1990. "What Is Good Music?" *Canadian University Music Review: Revue de Musique des Universites Canadiennes* 10:92-102.

Frith, Simon, and Howard Horne. 1987. *Art into Pop*. London and New York: Methuen.

Fromm, Erich. 1941. *Escape from Freedom*. New York: Farrar and Rinehart.

Fukuyama, Francis. 1992. *The End of History and the Last Man.* New York: Free Press.

————. 1993. "The Modernizing Imperative: The USSR as an Ordinary Country." *The National Interest* 31:10-18.

Galtung, Johan. 1981. "Western Civilization: Anatomy and Pathology." *Alternatives* 7:145-67.

Gans, Herbert. 1974. *Popular Culture and High Culture: An Analysis and Evaluation of Taste.* New York: Basic Books.

Geertz, Clifford. 1973. "Deep Play: Notes on the Balinese Cockfight." Pp. 412-53 in *The Interpretation of Cultures.* New York: Basic Books.

Gerth, H. H., and C. Wright Mills. 1946. "Introduction: The Man and His Work." Pp. 3-74 in H. H. Gerth and C. Wright Mills, eds., *From Max Weber: Essays in Sociology.* New York: Oxford University Press.

Giddens, Anthony. 1984. *The Constitution of Society.* Berkeley: University of California Press.

————. 1987. *Social Theory and Modern Sociology.* Stanford, CA: Stanford University Press.

————. 1990. *The Consequences of Modernity.* Stanford, CA: Stanford University Press.

————. 1991. *Modernity and Self-Identity: Self and Society in the Late Modern Age.* Stanford, CA: Stanford University Press.

————. 1992. *The Transformation of Intimacy: Sexuality, Love and Eroticism in Modern Societies.* Stanford: Stanford University Press.

Goffman, Erving. 1973. *The Presentation of Self in Everyday Life.* Woodstock, NY: Overlook Press.

Goldfarb, Jeffrey C. 1982. *On Cultural Freedom: An Exploration of Public Life in Poland and America.* Chicago: University of Chicago Press.

————. 1992. *After the Fall: The Pursuit of Democracy in Central Europe.* New York: Basic Books.

Goldman, Marshall I. 1991. *What Went Wrong with Perestroika.* New York: Norton.

Gramsci, Antonio. 1971. In Quintin Hoare and Geoffrey Nowell Smith, eds., *Selections from the Prison Notebooks.* New York: International Publishers.

Greenfeld, Liah. 1988. "Soviet Sociology and Sociology in the Soviet Union." *Annual Review of Sociology* 14:99-123.

Griswold, Wendy. 1986. *Renaissance Revivals: City Comedy and Revenge Tragedy in the London Theatre, 1576-1980.* Chicago: University of Chicago Press.

Gubankov, N. N. 1989. "Mesto russkogo revoliutsionnogo nigilizma v evolyutsii osvoboditel'nogo dvizheniia." Pp. 110-123 in Yu. A. Bezuglaya, ed., *Filosofiia i osvoboditel'noe dvizhenie v Rossii*. Leningrad: Leningrad University Press.

Habermas, Jürgen. 1970. "On Systematically Distorted Communication." *Inquiry* 13:205-18.

————. 1975. *Legitimation Crisis*. Boston: Beacon Press.

————. 1981. "Modernity vs. Post-Modernity." *New German Critique* 22:3-14.

————. 1984. *The Theory of Communicative Action*. Boston: Beacon Press.

————. 1989. *The Theory of Communicative Action*. Vol. 2. Boston: Beacon Press.

————. 1991. *The Structural Transformation of the Public Sphere: An Inquiry into a Category of Bourgeois Society*. Cambridge, MA: MIT Press.

Halliday, M. A. K. 1976. "Anti-Languages." *American Anthropologist* 78:570-584.

Hammond, Thomas Taylor. 1957. *Lenin on Trade Unions and Revolution, 1893-1917*. New York: Columbia University Press.

Hebdige, Dick. 1979. *Subculture: The Meaning of Style*. London and New York: Methuen.

————. 1987. *Cut'n'mix: Culture, Identity, and Caribbean Music*. London and New York: Methuen.

————. 1988. *Hiding in the Light: On Images and Things*. London and New York: Routledge, 1988.

Hertz, Rosanna, and Jonathan Imber. 1993. "Introduction: Fieldwork in Elite Settings." *Journal of Contemporary Ethnography* 22:3-6.

Hobsbawm, Eric, and Terence Ranger, eds. 1983. *The Invention of Tradition*. New York: Cambridge University Press.

Hollier, Denis. 1988. "Forward: Collage." In *The College of Sociology, 1937-1939*. Edited by Denis Hollier. Minneapolis: University of Minnesota Press.

Horkheimer, Max. 1972. "Traditional Theory and Critical Theory." Pp. 188-243 in *Critical Theory*. New York: Herder and Herder.

Hough, Jerry. 1977. *The Soviet Union and Social Science Theory*. Cambridge, MA: Harvard University Press.

Huizinga, Johan. 1950. *Homo Ludens: A Study of the Play Element in Culture*. Boston: Beacon Press.

Humphrey, Caroline. 1983. *Karl Marx Collective: Economy, Society, and Religion in a Siberian Collective Farm*. Cambridge: Cambridge University Press.

Hunter, James Davison. 1983. *American Evangelicalism: Conservative Religion and the Quandary of Modernity*. New Brunswick, NJ: Transaction Books.

Jensen, Joli. 1990. "Technology/Music: Understanding Processual Relations." *Popular Music and Society* 14:7-12.

Jones, Steven. 1990. "Technology and Popular Music Practice." *Popular Music and Society* 14:1-6.

Jones, Anthony, and William Moskoff. 1991. *Ko-ops: The Rebirth of Entrepeneurship in the Soviet Union*. Bloomington and Indianapolis: Indiana University Press.

Jowitt, Ken. 1991. "Weber, Trotsky, and Holmes on the Study of Leninist Regimes." *Journal of International Affairs* 45:31-49.

———. 1992. *New World Disorder: The Leninist Extinction*. Berkeley: University of California Press.

Kagarlitsky, Boris. 1988. *The Thinking Reed: Intellectuals and the Soviet State, 1917 to the Present*. London and New York: Verso.

Kataev, S. L. 1987. "Soderzhanie i intonatsia molodezhnoi pesni." *Sotsiologicheskie Issledovania* 14:77-80.

Kellner, Douglas. 1992. "Toward a Multiperspectival Cultural Studies." *Centennial Review* 36:5-42.

Kerblay, Basil. 1983. *Modern Soviet Society*. New York: Pantheon.

Kniazeva, Marina L. 1991. "Theater on the Market." *Journal of Communication* 41:31-38.

Kon, Igor. 1987. *Druzhba: etiko-psikhologicheskii ocherk*. Moskva: Polit-Lit Izdat.

———. 1988. *Rebenok i obshchestvo: istoriko-etnograficheskaia perspektiva*. Moskva: Izdatel'stvo "Nauka."

———. 1993. "Identity Crisis and Postcommunist Psychology." *Symbolic Interaction* 16:395-410.

———. Forthcoming. *Sexual Revolution in Russia*. New York: Free Press.

Kumar, Krishan. 1992. "The Revolutions of 1989: Socialism, Capitalism, and Democracy." *Theory and Society* 21:309-56.

Kurti, Laszlo. 1991. "Rocking the State: Youth and Rock Music Culture in Hungary." *Eastern European Politics and Societies* 5:483.

Lamont, Michele. 1992. *Money, Morals, and Manners: The Culture of the French and the American Upper-Middle Class*. Chicago and London: University of Chicago Press.

Lane, Christel. 1981. *The Rites of Rulers: Ritual in Industrial Society: The Soviet Case*. Cambridge, U.K. and New York: Cambridge University Press.

Lane, David. 1990. *Soviet Society under Perestroika*. Boston: Unwin Hyman.

Lasch, Christopher. 1977. *Haven in a Heartless World: The Family Besieged*. New York: Basic Books.

Lash, Scott, and Jonathan Friedman. 1992. "Introduction: Subjectivity and Modernity's Other." Pp. 1-30 in Scott Lash and Jonathan Friedman, eds., *Modernity and Identity*. Oxford, U.K. and Cambridge, MA: Basil Blackwell.

Lazarskii, Christopher. 1992. "Vladimir Vysotsky and His Cult." *The Russian Review* 51:58-71.

Levine, Donald A. 1981. "Rationality and Freedom: Weber and Beyond." *Sociological Inquiry* 51:5-25.

Lewin, Moshe. 1989. "Perestroika: A New Historical Stage." *Journal of International Affairs* 42:299-316.

————. 1991. "Russia/USSR in Historical Motion: An Essay in Interpretation." *The Russian Review* 50:249-66.

Lieberman, Robbie. 1989. *My Song Is My Weapon: People's Songs, American Communism, and the Politics of Culture, 1930-1950*. Urbana: University of Illinois Press.

Lipset, Seymour Martin. 1994. "The Social Requisites of Democracy Revisited." *American Sociological Review* 59:1-22.

Lipset, Seymour Martin, Kyount-Ryung Seong, and John Charles Torres. 1993. "A Comparative Analysis of the Social Requisites of Democracy." *International Social Science Journal* 45:155-176.

Lipton, David, and Jeffrey D. Sachs. 1992. "Prospects for Russia's Economic Reforms." *Brookings Papers on Economic Activity* 2:213-84.

Lowenthal, Richard. 1974. "On 'Established' Communist Party Regimes." *Studies in Comparative Communism* 7:335-58.

Lukacs, Gyorgy. 1971. *The Theory of the Novel: A Historico-Philosophical Essay on the Forms of Great Epic Literature*. Translated from the German by Anna Bostock. Cambridge, MA: MIT Press.

Luke, Timothy. 1983. "The Proletarian Ethic and Soviet Industrialization." *American Political Science Review* 77:588-601.

————. 1987. "Civil Religion and Secularization: Ideological Revitalization in Post-Revolutionary Communist Systems." *Sociological Forum* 2:108-34.

———. 1990. "Postcommunism in the U.S.S.R.: The McGulag Archipelago." *Telos* 84:33-42.

Lull, James. 1985. "On the Communicative Properties of Music." *Communication Research* 12:363-72.

———. 1987. "Popular Music and Communication: An Introduction." Pp. 10-35 in James Lull, ed., *Popular Music and Communication*. Newbury Park, CA: Sage.

Lynd, Robert, and Helen Lynd. 1956. *Middletown: A Study in Contemporary American Culture*. New York: Harcourt, Brace, and Company.

McDowell, Jennifer. 1974. "Soviet Civil Ceremonies." *Journal for the Scientific Study of Religion* 13:265-79.

McLaren, Peter. 1986. *Schooling as a Ritual Performance: Towards a Political Economy of Educational Symbols and Gestures*. London and Boston: Routledge and Kegan Paul.

Mannheim, Karl. 1950. *Freedom, Power, and Democratic Planning*. New York: Oxford University Press.

———. 1956. *Essays on the Sociology of Culture*. London and Boston: Routledge and Kegan Paul.

———. 1993. "The Sociology of Intellectuals." *Theory, Culture, and Society* 10:69-80.

Manuel, Peter. 1988. *Popular Musics of the Non-Western World*. New York and Oxford, U.K.: Oxford University Press.

Marcus, Greil. 1991. *Dead Elvis: A Chronicle of a Cultural Obsession*. New York: Doubleday.

Marcuse, Herbert. 1958. *Soviet Marxism: A Critical Analysis*. New York: Columbia University Press.

———. 1964. *One-Dimensional Man*. Boston: Beacon Press.

———. 1965. "Repressive Tolerance." Pp. 81-123 in *A Critique of Pure Tolerance*. Boston: Beacon Press.

———. 1978. *The Aesthetic Dimension: Toward a Critique of Marxist Aesthetics*. Boston: Beacon Press.

———. 1993. "Some Remarks on Aragon: Art and Politics in the Totalitarian Era." *Theory, Culture, and Society* 10:181-95.

Marx, Karl. 1964. *Selected Writings in Sociology and Social Philosophy*. London: McGraw Hill.

———. 1967. "Economic and Philosophical Manuscripts." Pp. 283-357 in Lloyd D. Easton and Kurt H. Guddat, eds., *Writings of the Young Marx on Philosophy and Society*. New York: Doubleday.

Matthews, Mervyn. 1978. *Privilege in the Soviet Union: A Study of Elite Life-Styles under Communism*. London and Boston: George Allen and Unwin.

Merriam, Alan. 1964. *The Anthropology of Music*. Evanston, IL.: Northwestern University Press.

Mestrovic, Stjepan. 1991. "Why East Europe's Upheavals Caught Social Scientists Off Guard." *The Chronicle of Higher Education* September 21:A56.

———. 1993a. *The Road from Paradise: Prospects for Democracy in Eastern Europe*. Lexington: University Press of Kentucky.

———. 1993b. *Habits of the Balkan Heart: Social Character and the Fall of Communism*. College Station: Texas A&M University Press.

Mills, C. Wright. 1959. *The Sociological Imagination*. New York: Oxford University Press.

———. [1940] 1963. "Situated Activities and Vocabularies of Motive." Pp. 439-52 in Irving Lewis Horowitz, ed., *Power, Politics, and People*. London and New York: Oxford University Press.

Milner, Murray. 1980. *Unequal Care: A Case Study of Interorganizational Relations in Health Care*. New York: Columbia University Press.

———. 1993. *Status and Sacredness: A General Theory of Status Relations and an Analysis of Indian Culture*. New York: Oxford University Press.

Mitchell, Richard G. 1991. "Secrecy and Disclosure in Fieldwork." Pp. 97-108 in William B. Shaffir and Robert A. Stebbins, eds. *Experiencing Fieldwork: An Inside View of Qualitative Research*. Newbury Park, CA and London: Sage.

Moore, Barrington, Jr. 1954. *Terror and Progress USSR: Some Sources of Change and Stability in the Soviet Dictatorship*. Cambridge, MA: Harvard University Press.

Motyl, Alexander J. 1990. *Sovietology, Rationality, Nationality*. New York: Columbia University Press.

———. 1992. "Building Bridges and Changing Landmarks: Theory and Concept in the Study of Soviet Nationalities." Pp. 255-70 in Alexander J. Motyl, ed., *Thinking Theoretically About Soviet Nationalities: History and Comparison in the Study of the U.S.S.R.* New York: Columbia University Press.

Nader, Laura. 1993. "Paradigm Busting and Vertical Linkage." (Review of *Ethnography Unbound: Power and Resistance in the Modern Metropolis* by Michael Burawoy, Alice Burton, Ann Arnett Ferguson, Kathryn J. Fox, Joshua Gamson, Nadine Gartrell, Leslie Hurst, Charles Kurzman, Leslie Salzinger, Josepha Schiffman, and Shiori Ui.) *Contemporary Sociology* 22:6-7.

Nelson, Lynn D., Lilia V. Babaeva, and Rufat O. Babaev. 1992. "Perspectives on Entrepeneurship and Privatization in Russia: Policy and Public Opinion." *Slavic Review* 51:271-86.

Nettl, J. P., and Roland Robertson. 1966. "Industrialization, Development, or Modernization." *British Journal of Sociology* 17:274-91.

Nove, Alec. 1989. *Glasnost in Action: Cultural Renaissance in Russia*. Boston: Unwin Hyman.

O'Sullivan, Tim, John Hartley, Danny Saunders, and John Fiske. 1983. "Subculture." Pp. 102-104 in *Key Concepts in Mass Communication*. London and New York: Methuen.

Orland, Leonard. 1989. "Insulting the Soviet President and Other Political Crimes in Mikhail Gorbachev's 'Rule of Law' State." *Connecticut Journal of International Law* 5:237-70.

Owen, David. 1991. "Autonomy and Inner Distance: A Trace of Nietzsche in Weber." *History of the Human Sciences* 4:79-91.

Panovsky, Ervin. 1957. *Gothic Architecture and Scholasticism*. New York: Meridian Books.

Park, Robert Ezra. 1967. In Ralph Turner, ed., *On Social Control and Collective Behavior: Selected Papers*. Chicago: University of Chicago Press.

Pattison, Robert. 1987. *The Triumph of Vulgarity: Rock Music in the Mirror of Romanticism*. New York: Oxford University Press.

Peacock, James L. 1990. "Ethnographic Notes on Sacred and Profane Performance." Pp. 208-20 in Richard Schechner and Willa Appel, eds., *By Means of Performance: Intercultural Studies of Theatre and Ritual*. Cambridge, U.K., and New York: Cambridge University Press.

Peck, Merton J., and Thomas J. Richardson. 1991. *What Is to Be Done? Proposals for the Soviet Transition to the Market*. New Haven: Yale University Press.

Poole, Ross. 1991. *Morality and Modernity*. London: Routledge.

Przeworski, Adam. 1991. *Democracy and the Market: Political and Economic Reforms in Eastern Europe and Latin America*. Cambridge and New York: Cambridge University Press.

Ramet, Pedro, and Sergei Zamascikov. 1990. "The Soviet Rock Scene." *Journal of Popular Culture* 24:149.

Riordan, James, ed. 1988. "Soviet Youth: Pioneers of Change." *Soviet Studies* 4:556-72.

Ritzer, George. 1993. *The McDonaldization of Society*. Newbury Park, CA: Pine Forge Press.

Roksi Ekspress. N.A. 1990. Vol. 1. Leningrad.

Rorty, Richard. 1985. "Habermas and Lyotard on Post-Modernity." Pp. 161-75 in Richard J. Bernstein, ed., *Habermas and Modernity*. Cambridge, MA: MIT Press.

Roszak, Theodore. 1969. *The Making of a Counterculture: Reflections on the Technocratic Society and Its Youthful Opposition*. Garden City, NY: Anchor Books.

Ryan, John. 1985. *The Production of Culture in the Music Industry: The ASCAP-BMI Controversy*. Lanham, MD: University Press of America.

Ryback, Timothy. 1990. *Rock around the Bloc: A History of Rock Music in Eastern Europe and the Soviet Union*. New York: Oxford University Press.

Sachs, Jeffrey. 1990. "The Economic Transformation of Eastern Europe: The Case of Poland." *The American Economist* 36:3-11.

Saroyan, Mark. 1988. "Beyond the Nation-State: Culture and Ethnic Politics in Soviet Transcaucasia." *Soviet Union/Union Sovietique* 15:219-44.

Sayer, Derek. 1991. *Capitalism and Modernity: An Excursus on Marx and Weber*. New York and London: Routledge.

Schumpeter, Joseph. 1950. *Capitalism, Socialism, and Democracy*. 3d. ed. New York: Harper and Row.

Schutz, Alfred. 1951. "Making Music Together: A Study in Social Relationships." *Social Research* 18:76-97.

———. 1970. *On Phenomenology and Social Relations: Selected Writings*. Edited by Helmut R. Wagner. Chicago and London: University of Chicago Press.

Shaffir, William B. 1991. "Managing a Convincing Self-Presentation: Some Personal Reflections on Entering the Field." Pp. 72-81 in William B. Shaffir and Robert A. Stebbins, eds., *Experiencing Fieldwork: An Inside View of Qualitative Research*. Newbury Park, CA and London: Sage.

Shalin, Dmitri. 1990. "Sociology for the Glasnost Era: Institutional and Substantive Changes in Recent Soviet Sociology. *Social Forces* 68:1019-40.

Shavel', S. A. 1988. *Sotsial'naia sfera obshchestva i lichnost'*. Minsk: Nauka i Tekhnika.

Shlapentokh, Vladimir. 1984. *Love, Marriage, and Friendship in the Soviet Union: Ideals and Practices*. New York: Praeger.

————. 1987. *The Politics of Sociology in the Soviet Union*. Boulder and London: Westview Press.

————. 1989. *Public and Private Life of the Soviet People: Changing Values in Post-Stalin Russia*. New York: Oxford University Press.

Siklova, Jirina. 1990. "The 'Grey Zone' and the Future of Dissent in Czechoslovakia." *Social Research* 57:347-64.

Silver, Allan. 1990. "Friendship in Commerical Society: Eighteenth-Century Social Theory and Modern Sociology." *American Journal of Sociology* 95:1474-1504.

Simmel, Georg. 1971. In Donald N. Levine, ed., *On Individuality and Social Forms: Selected Writings*. Chicago: University of Chicago Press.

————. 1986. *Schopenhauer and Nietzsche*. Amherst, MA: University of Massachusetts Press.

————. [1907] 1990. In David Frisby, ed., *The Philosophy of Money*. New York: Routledge.

Sironneau, Jean-Pierre. 1982. *Secularisation et religions politiques*. La Haye: Mouton editeur.

Smith, Gerald Stanton. 1984. *Songs to Seven Strings: Russian Guitar Poetry and Soviet "Mass Song."* Bloomington: Indiana University Press.

Soja, Edward. 1989. *Postmodern Geographies: The Reassertion of Space in Critical Social Theory*. London and New York: Verso.

Solomon, Maynard, ed. 1979. "Bertolt Brecht." Pp. 355-69 in *Marxism and Art: Essays Classic and Contemporary*. Detroit: Wayne State University Press.

Staniszkis, Jadwiga. 1984. *Poland's Self-Limiting Revolution*. Princeton, NJ.: Princeton University Press.

Starr, S. Frederick. 1983. *Red and Hot: The Fate of Jazz in the Soviet Union, 1917-1980*. New York: Oxford University Press.

Stites, Richard. 1985. "Iconoclastic Currents in the Russian Revolution: Destroying and Preserving the Past." Pp. 1-24 in Abbott Gleason, Peter Kenez, and Richard Stites, eds., *Bolshevik Culture: Experiment and Order in the Russian Revolution*. Bloomington: Indiana University Press.

————. 1992. *Russian Popular Culture: Entertainment and Society Since 1900*. Cambridge, U.K. and New York: Cambridge University Press.

Strutinskii, V. S. 1987. *Kommunisticheskaia lichnost': stanovlenie i vospitanie*. Kiev: Vyshcha Shkola.

Supicic, Ivo. 1987. *Music in Society: A Guide to the Sociology of Music*. Stuyvesant, NY: Pendragon Press.

Tambiah, Stanley J. 1985. *Culture, Thought, and Social Action: An Anthropological Perspective*. Cambridge: Harvard University Press.

Taussig, Michael. 1992. *The Nervous System*. New York and London: Routledge.

Thomas, William Isaac. 1966. In Morris Janowitz, ed., *W. I. Thomas on Social Organization and Social Personality: Selected Papers*. Chicago: University of Chicago Press.

Thompson, John B. 1993. "The Theory of the Public Sphere." (Review of *The Structural Transformation of the Public Sphere: An Inquiry into a Category of Bourgeois Society*, by Jürgen Habermas. Cambridge, MA: MIT Press; Cambridge, U.K.: Polity Press, 1989.) *Theory, Culture, and Society* 10:173-89.

Tiryakian, Edward. 1992. "Dialectics of Modernity: Re-enchantment and De-differentiation as Counterprocesses." Pp. 78-94 in Hans Haferkamp and Neil J. Smelser, eds., *Social Change and Modernity*. Berkeley: University of California Press.

Tolstoy, Leo. [1896] 1960. *What Is Art?* New York: Macmillan.

Tocqueville, Alexis de. 1969. In J. P. Mayer, ed., *Democracy in America*. Garden City, NY: Doubleday and Co.

Troitsky, Artemy. 1990*a*. "Neformaln'ye gruppy molodezhi i rok-muzyka." Pp. 244-45 in *Rok Muzyka v SSSR*, compiled by Artemy Troitsky. Moskva: Kniga.

———. 1990*b*. "Pops." P. 271 in *Rok Muzyka v SSSR*, compiled by Artemy Troitsky. Moskva: Kniga.

———. 1990*c*. "Rok praktika." Pp. 287-92 in *Rok Muzyka v SSSR*, compiled by Artemy Troitsky. Moskva: Kniga.

Tsoy, Marianna, and Aleksandr Zhitinskii, eds. 1991. *Viktor Tsoy: Stikhi, Dokumenty, Vospominaniia*. Sankt Peterburg: Novyi Gelikon.

Tucker, Robert C. 1987. *Political Culture and Leadership in Soviet Russia: From Lenin to Gorbachev*. New York: Norton.

Turner, Bryan S. 1984. *The Body and Society: Explorations in Social Theory*. Oxford, U.K., and New York: Basil Blackwell.

Turner, Victor. 1969. *The Ritual Process: Structure and Anti-Structure*. Chicago: Aldine.

Vaksberg, Arkadii. 1991. *The Soviet Mafia*. London: Weidenfeld and Nicolson.

Veblen, Thorstein. 1934. *The Theory of the Leisure Class: An Economic Study of Institutions.* New York: The Modern Library.

Verdery, Katherine. 1991. "Theorizing Socialism: A Prologue to the 'Transition.'" *American Ethnologist* 18:419-39.

Wagner, Peter. 1993. *A Sociology of Modernity: Liberty and Discipline.* London and New York: Routledge.

Walker, John A. 1987. *Cross-Overs: Art into Pop/Pop into Art.* New York and London: Methuen.

Warner, W. Lloyd. 1963. *Yankee City.* New Haven: Yale University Press.

Watson, Ian. 1983. *Song and Democratic Culture in Britain: An Approach to Popular Culture in Social Movements.* London: Croom Helm.

Weber, Max. 1930. *The Protestant Ethic and the Spirit of Capitalism.* Translated by Talcott Parsons. London: G. Allen and Unwin.

———. 1946a. "Politics as a Vocation." Pp. 77-128 in H. H. Gerth and C. Wright Mills, eds., *From Max Weber: Essays in Sociology.* New York: Oxford University Press.

———. 1946b. "Science as a Vocation." Pp. 129-156 in H. H. Gerth and C. Wright Mills, eds., *From Max Weber: Essays in Sociology.* New York: Oxford University Press.

———. 1978. In Guenther Roth and Claus Wittich, eds., *Economy and Society* (2 vols.). Berkeley: University of California Press.

White, Stephen A. 1979. *Political Culture and Soviet Politics.* New York: St. Martin's Press.

Wicke, Peter. 1991. *Rock Music: Culture, Aesthetics, and Sociology.* Cambridge, U.K. and New York: Cambridge University Press.

Williams, Raymond. 1981. "The Analysis of Culture." Pp. 43-52 in Tony Bennett, Grahamn Martin, Colin Mercer, and Janet Woollacott, eds., *Culture, Ideology, and Social Process: A Reader.* London: Open University Press.

Willis, Paul E. 1977. "The Cultural Meaning of Drug Use." Pp. 106-25 in Stuart Hall and Tony Jefferson, eds., *Resistance through Rituals: Youth Subcultures in Post-War Britain.* London: Hutchinson.

———. 1979. *Learning to Labor: How Working-Class Kids Get Working-Class Jobs.* Farnborough, U.K.: Saxon House.

———. 1990. *Common Culture: Symbolic Work at Play in the Everyday Culture of the Young.* Boulder, CO: Westview Press.

Wills, Geoff, and Gary L. Cooper. 1988. *Pressure Sensitive: Popular Musicians under Stress.* London and Newbury Park, CA: Sage Publications.

Wolff, Janet. 1983. "Aesthetics." Pp. 6-8 in Tom Bottomore, ed., *A Dictionary of Marxist Thought.* Cambridge, MA: Harvard University Press.

Wolff, Kurt. 1976. *Surrender and Catch: Experience and Inquiry Today.* Dordrecht, Holland and Boston, MA: D. Reidel Publishing Co.

Yelin, Lev. 1990. "Demoted to the Rank of People's Deputy." Summary: Interview with Oleg Kalugin. *RCDA: Religion in Communist Dominated Areas* 29:86-89.

Yinger, J. Milton. 1982. *Countercultures: The Promise and the Peril of a World Turned Upside Down.* New York: Free Press.

Zapesotskii, Aleksandr, and Aleksandr Fain. 1990. *Eta neponyatnaya molodezh': problemy neformal'nykh obedinenii.* Moskva: Profizdat.

Zassoursky, Yassen N. 1991. "Mass Culture as Market Culture." *Journal of Communication* 41:13-15.

Index